Canadian
Modern
Architecture

Canadian Modern Architecture

1967 to the present

**Edited by Elsa Lam
and Graham Livesey**

Princeton Architectural Press
New York

Canadian Architect
Toronto

2019

Foreword

Kenneth Frampton

This survey of Canadian architecture covering half a century of development, from Expo 67 in Montreal to works from the first decades of the twentieth century, may be seen as a delayed recognition of the wide-ranging scope of Canadian architecture over the past fifty years. Unlike the earlier half-century of creativity in the United States, lasting from 1945 to the millennium—that is to say from the swan song of the New Deal to the postwar euphoria of the Pax Americana—the first indications of a similar fertile moment in Canada began with Ron Thom's Massey College, patently derived from the Oxbridge model but nonetheless a subtle *répétition différente* realized for the University of Toronto in 1963.

Four years later at Expo 67, the world's attention was drawn to Canada by an exceptionally audacious work: namely Moshe Safdie's Habitat 67, an eight-to-twelve-story assembly of garden apartments, ranging from single-story units to duplexes, ingeniously poised on top of a giant reinforced concrete superstructure in such a manner that the top of one apartment served as the roof terrace for the next. This updated Babylonian image had the effect of putting Canada on the world map as far as architecture was concerned. Moreover, Habitat 67 was more than a match (symbolically and otherwise) for the overbearing geodesic sphere of Buckminster Fuller's US Pavilion. Safdie's avant-gardist audacity in Montreal was answered by the University of Toronto's Scarborough College, completed one year before as a serpentine "city-in-miniature" to the designs of the then-émigré Australian architect John Andrews.

Around the same time in Montreal, there was another significant but self-effacing achievement—namely Ray Affleck's Place Bonaventure—executed in the same bush-hammered "corduroy" concrete as Paul Rudolph's Art and Architecture Building in New Haven of 1963. Accompanying the ingenious hotel atop a six-story merchandise mart was a secret paradise garden by Sasaki Associates.

Equally inventive, however much it may have been inspired by Shadrach Woods's Free University in Berlin of 1963, was Eberhard Zeidler's McMaster Health Sciences Centre, completed in Hamilton, Ontario, in 1972. This unique hospital would be matched by the same architect's equally brilliant Eaton Centre of 1977, which remains, even now, a seminal if insufficiently valued contribution to the received repertoire of urban design.

Something similar may surely be claimed for Arthur Erickson's Simon Fraser University, designed with Geoffrey Massey in 1963, and built just outside of Vancouver over the following decade. Equally prescient was his Robson Square development, built twenty years later in downtown Vancouver, which was not in fact a square at all, but a multilevel megastructure that, by virtue of its mixed-use programming, served as a catalyst for the revitalization of a decaying downtown. This idea of inserting a linear "space of public appearance" as a cultural catalyst in an otherwise all but totally privatized environment had, in fact, been broached a decade earlier on the Canadian scene, and indubitably rationalized in part as a reasonable response to an exceptionally harsh climate. This was accomplished by the remarkable student dormitories designed in 1971 for the University of Alberta by the émigré American architect Barton Myers: the one-off piece known as the HUB building was, in effect, an elevated, top-lit galleria flanked on both sides by five-story student residential accommodations.

The more overtly regional aspects of this anthology come to the fore in chapters such as one devoted to the work of those Canadian architects who have dedicated themselves to serving First Nations of the country, particularly as part of a nationwide, government-backed cultural endeavor that has yet to find its parallel in the United States; such is the tragic scale of the initial American genocide and the systematic maltreatment of the native population ever since. This chapter focuses on works designed specifically for the aboriginal population of Canada, with a more heightened sensitivity perhaps in British Columbia than in any other province. One thinks in this regard of the Seabird Island School, designed by Patkau Architects and completed in Agassiz, British Columbia, in 1991. It was built by a First Nations community after a meticulous scale model in wood (which was designed and fabricated by the architects themselves); this device allowed the community to realize the school without needing to have recourse to drawings. This heroic work testifies to a particularly civilized moment in Canadian history, when an enlightened bureaucracy could momentarily back a federal policy of allowing native peoples to build subsidized schools directly for their own occupation.

Elsewhere in Canada, a sensitive approach to the culture of the country's rural landscapes is demonstrated by contemporary practitioners, including Brian MacKay-Lyons, whose work at Shobac is particularly notable, comprising a collection of neo-vernacular structures grouped together in Upper Kingsburg, Nova Scotia, and erected in the space of a decade. Equally seminal has been the work of Brigitte Shim and Howard Sutcliffe, whose realizations in Toronto include the Residence for the Sisters of Saint Joseph of 2013, a commission that demonstrates their propensity for typological invention. The late Dan Hanganu's housing and urban buildings combine an industrial aesthetic with sensitivity to sites' layered historical contexts, particularly evident in his Musée Pointe-à-Callière in Old Montreal of 1992.

This anthology, edited by Elsa Lam, editor of *Canadian Architect*, and by professor Graham Livesey of the University of Calgary, amounts to a major achievement of collective scholarship. It comprises the contributions of seventeen scholars representing successive generations of Canadian intellectuals in the field, ranging from academics to critics and to architects and, in many instances, individuals who are all three. By any standards, this is an encyclopedic *tour de force* documenting fifty years of Canadian architectural production across the expanse of what is still a sparsely populated continent. The result is a selection of several hundred notable buildings of widely varying provenance. The work featured in these pages is surely what it takes, over time, to arrive at a national culture of architecture worthy of the name. It is a privilege for me, as an *aficionado* of Canadian architecture, to contribute to this anthology in the form of this foreword.

Introduction

Elsa Lam and Graham Livesey

In his magisterial *A History of Canadian Architecture*,[1] Harold Kalman devotes only one of fifteen chapters to modern architecture. And yet it can be argued that distinctively Canadian architecture only emerged midcentury and fully blossomed after 1967, Canada's centennial year. As a result of the country's long colonial history, earlier architecture tended to be derivative of styles from the United States and Europe.

The first truly modern Canadian works of architecture appeared in the 1940s and 1950s in and around Vancouver. The West Coast Style, apparent in houses such as the 1942 residence in West Vancouver designed by modernist artist B. C. Binning (1909–1976) for himself, was influenced by trends in California and in the Pacific Northwest, but was adapted to the area's particular climate and plethora of sites perched between forested mountains and expansive ocean.[2] Meanwhile, pioneering Vancouver firms such as Semmens + Simpson Architects, and Sharp and Thompson, Berwick, Pratt turned their efforts to the design of institutional projects, applying strategies gleaned from residential projects to work in various ways with the land [see chapter 9].[3]

In the 1950s, the International Style arrived in Toronto, Montreal, and Winnipeg.[4] In Toronto, the formation of the first large national firm, John B. Parkin Associates, would have a dramatic impact [see chapter 14].[5] British expat Peter Dickinson (1925–1961) would also contribute significantly to modern architecture in Toronto. The following decade brought influential work by foreign architects to the city, notably Viljo Revell's Toronto City Hall (1965) and Mies van der Rohe's scheme for the Toronto-Dominion Centre (1969).

Similarly, I. M. Pei and Luigi Moretti would transform the Montreal skyline with spectacular skyscrapers.[6] In Quebec, francophone architects, such as Roger D'Astous (1926–1998) and Jean-Marie Roy (1925–2011), pioneered in developing a modern Quebec architecture; meanwhile, Montreal's multicultural firm ARCOP Associates was establishing a national and international reputation [see chapters 1 and 13]. Winnipeg would also emerge as a hotbed of modern design, influenced by the faculty of architecture at the University of Manitoba—itself housed in the Mies van der Rohe–inspired John A. Russell Building (Smith Carter Katelnikoff Associates, 1959) [see chapter 10].[7] Noteworthy projects from the period can also be found in Calgary and Edmonton, and in the nation's capital, Ottawa.

Canada's centennial year would prove to be a national watershed. Politically and culturally, Canada came into its own in the 1960s, as signaled by the international reception of figures such as Lester B. Pearson (1897–1972), Marshall McLuhan (1911–1980), Jean-Paul Riopelle (1923–2002), Oscar Peterson (1925–2007), Glenn Gould (1932–1982), and Buffy Sainte-Marie (1941–). Canada's flamboyant Pierre Elliott Trudeau (1919–2000), first elected as prime minister in 1968, exuded a new image of Canada as young, hip, and innovative. These were also qualities showcased at the landmark Expo 67, held in Montreal. In their pavilions for the fair—and in projects across the country commemorating the Centennial—Canadian architects demonstrated increasing confidence as they negotiated between international trends and regional factors.

In order to tell the story of Canadian architecture since 1967, this book is divided into four sections: National Movements, International Influences, Regional Responses, and Centers of Influence.

National Movements

Starting with the commissions for Canada's centennial year, a host of architectural projects have contributed to defining Canadian institutions and infrastructure. Government-sponsored buildings, such as museums, embassies, and airports, explicitly represent the nation. Provincially funded university campuses expanded tremendously in the 1960s and have been leading the way in architectural experimentation. Recent decades have seen an emerging focus on projects for Indigenous First Nations communities that respond appropriately to the specific needs of their numerous cultures across the country.

The opening chapter documents the architecture created for Canada's centennial year. Marco Polo and Colin Ripley describe the Centennial Grants Program and Confederation Memorial Fund, developed by the federal government to celebrate the country's one-hundredth year, which resulted in 2,301 projects across the country—including cultural institutions of national importance. The crowning event of the centennial year was Expo 67. One of the most successful international expositions ever, it showcased the work of a number of important Canadian architects, as well as international figures such as Buckminster Fuller and Frei Otto.

Authored by George Thomas Kapelos, the next chapter examines the architecture of key Canadian public institutions. Kapelos looks at the evolving architectural expression of Canadian buildings commissioned by federal, provincial, and municipal governments since 1967. The examples include national museums, city halls, and Canadian embassies. Kapelos also evaluates the architectural legacy of the three Olympic Games hosted in Canada since 1967, and finally turns his eye to that most important building type for a wide-spanning country—the airport terminal.

Lisa Landrum's essay studies the history of university architecture in Canada since the early 1960s through four celebrated campus designs: Massey College at the University of Toronto; Trent University in Peterborough, Ontario; University of Toronto Scarborough; and Simon Fraser University in Vancouver. These seminal projects provide a jumping-off point for discussing developments in Canadian campus design and architecture during subsequent decades of university expansion.

In the final chapter on national trends, Odile Hénault presents the transformative changes that have occurred in architecture for First Nations communities in Canada since the 1980s. In British Columbia and in northern Quebec, a number of architecture firms have worked closely with Indigenous clients to produce culturally sensitive designs. A new generation of First Nations designers is now emerging, following in the footsteps of Alberta-born Douglas Cardinal (1934–), the pioneering architect of the Canadian Museum of History (formerly the Canadian Museum of Civilization) near Ottawa and the National Museum of the American Indian in Washington, DC. A recently established school of architecture at Laurentian University in Ontario places further emphasis on design for First Nations and northern communities.

International Influences

In the fifty years since 1967, there have been many global changes in architecture. Canada has not been immune to these influences, and in a number of cases, Canadian architects have played a crucial role in the development of international trends. In his essay, George Baird explains how the concept of the "megastructure" building was widely embraced in Canada during the 1960s and 1970s. These large, adaptable buildings were used in designs for university campuses, including the University of Lethbridge in Alberta; urban projects, such as Place Bonaventure in Montreal; the influential Health Sciences Centre at McMaster University in Ontario; and Robson Square in downtown Vancouver. Some Canadian firms also embraced the high-tech architectural style inspired by British practices.

Larry Wayne Richards studies the impact of postmodernism on Canadian architecture, derived mainly from the work of American proponents such as Robert Venturi, Denise Scott Brown, and Charles Moore. Toronto-based architects Jack Diamond (1932–) and Barton Myers (1934–) were early promoters of a refined postmodernism. Eventually the style's influence would spread across the country through the work of architects such as Richard

Henriquez (1941–) in Vancouver, Barry Johns (1947–) in Edmonton, Peter Rose (1943–) in Montreal, and Brian MacKay-Lyons (1954–) in Halifax. Two of the most internationally celebrated postmodern projects are in Canada: Mississauga City Hall near Toronto, and the Canadian Centre for Architecture in Montreal.

In the 1960s, following the failures of post–Second World War "urban renewal" efforts, a focus on the revitalization of cities became an international phenomenon. Ian Chodikoff looks at a number of important projects in Canadian cities. Vancouver has a history of urban reinvention, and in its 1970s revitalization of Granville Island, it created a vibrant hub for its central waterfront district. Montreal's waterfront underwent a significant rejuvenation in the 1980s following the relocation of the port facilities during previous decades. In Toronto, a number of urban industrial sites in key downtown locations have undergone transformation. More recently, the Woodward's redevelopment in downtown Vancouver addresses complex social and commercial interests.

In the last essay on international influences, Steven Mannell details the history of green building legislation in Canada, demonstrating how Canadian architects have responded to evolving demands for sustainable construction. It may seem paradoxical for a resource- and energy-rich economy, but Canada has produced significant developments in sustainable design. In the 1970s, early experiments in the self-sustaining single-family home eventually led to designs for larger buildings across the country. As the world moves toward low-carbon design, Canadian architects are becoming increasingly proficient.

Regional Responses

As the country with the second-largest landmass in the world, Canada is defined by its distinctive regions. This section addresses the regional architecture of the West Coast (British Columbia), the three Prairie Provinces (Alberta, Saskatchewan, and Manitoba), the Atlantic Provinces (New Brunswick, Prince Edward Island, Nova Scotia, and Newfoundland and Labrador), and the North (Yukon, Northwest Territories, and Nunavut). "Critical Regionalism," as described by Alexander Tzonis, Liane Lefaivre, and Kenneth Frampton, is a particularly pertinent concept for Canadian architects, who have found a variety of ways to respond to local geographies, climates, and cultures.[8]

Sherry McKay starts off this section with an essay on the Pacific seaboard. The iconic West Coast house was essential to the emergence of modern architecture in Canada in the 1940s and 1950s, including early houses by Arthur Erickson (1924–2009). A similar approach to the West Coast style of working with landforms and vistas was used to design larger buildings in Vancouver, such as Erickson's MacMillan Bloedel Building and his Museum of Anthropology at the University of British Columbia. The latter demonstrated an increasing sensitivity to the cultures of West Coast First Nations. Other contributors to Vancouver's developing architecture scene included Peter Cardew (1939–), Richard Henriquez (1941–), and the emerging duo of John and Patricia Patkau (1947–; 1950–).

Graham Livesey lays out the evolution of Prairie architecture in four phases. Architects Étienne Gaboury (1930–), Clifford Wiens (1926–), and Douglas Cardinal pioneered in the development of modern work in the region in the 1960s. A second phase was shaped by environmentalism and a willingness to design buildings so that they engaged with the Prairie landscape; this was followed by a postmodern period during which architects drew inspiration from colonial and farming settlements. In the current period, young architects in the Prairie Provinces are producing work that is both local and global in its inspirations.

Brian Carter looks at the recent architecture of the four Atlantic Provinces. The school of architecture at Dalhousie University has been an important influence for many architects, including Nova Scotia–based Brian MacKay-Lyons—an architect internationally recognized for his critical regionalist designs. Younger firms are now also building on the unique traditions of the region. This is reflected most strikingly in a series of projects by Todd Saunders (1969–) on Fogo Island, off the coast of Newfoundland.

Heading north, Lola Sheppard and Mason White review the architecture of Canada's Arctic since the 1960s. They examine efforts to develop standardized housing for First Nations communities, experiments in developing new towns for the North, and technological solutions that have informed the approaches to building in the region. They discuss a number of projects that have used a consensus-based process to more sensitively address the particular challenges faced by remote northern communities.

Centers of Influence

Canadian culture is defined in large part by its three largest cities: Montreal, Toronto, and Vancouver. During the last fifty years, each of these cities has spawned a range of important architectural practices. David Theodore's essay explores distinctive aspects of Quebec architecture since 1967. Theodore shows how Quebec's cultural revolution of the 1960s impacted subsequent developments, including the emergence of key French-speaking architectural studios. The design competition system adopted by the Quebec government built on this legacy, resulting in many cultural sector projects by younger firms. Montreal continues to be a center of urban innovation, as demonstrated by projects across a range of scales, from civic to residential.

As Canada's financial capital, Toronto is home to many significant commercial buildings, several of which were built in the wake of the 1956 international competition to design a new city hall. Elsa Lam describes how Toronto has drawn on the talent of prominent foreign, émigré, and local architects as opportunities to develop educational and cultural institutions have proliferated. Geographical features of the city, including its lakeshore and ravines, have been the subject of ongoing design thinking. Typological development continues to occur in dense inner-city neighborhoods as well as in Toronto's expanding suburban periphery.

Lastly, Adele Weder looks at recent architecture on the West Coast. Since Expo 86, Vancouver's downtown has developed as a forest of glass condo towers. Scattered throughout this environment are well-considered works of architecture by some of Canada's most influential firms, including Busby & Associates (now Perkins+Will), James K. M. Cheng Architects, Patkau Architects, Bing Thom Architects (now Revery Architecture), Henriquez Partners Architects, HCMA, and Acton Ostry Architects. The very high cost of housing in Vancouver has resulted in a range of experiments in alternative housing forms. In the suburbs, significant civic projects provide urban amenities in lower-density environments. Vancouver has also become a hotbed of development in mass-timber structures, in synergy with the region's timber industry.

Future Legacy

What is the legacy of modern architecture in Canada? For historians Rhodri Windsor Liscombe and Michelangelo Sabatino, Canada's contribution to modern architecture reflects a "distinct Canadian design attitude: a liberal, experimental, hybrid, and pragmatic praxis, intent less upon the sources or dogma of architectural convention than the realization of inclusive spaces and places of community."[9] Since 1967, this can-do attitude has resulted in a pluralistic architecture that has had profound local impacts, and that has occasionally enjoyed international recognition. The brutalist cultural buildings marking the country's centennial, Safdie's experimental Habitat 67, and the megastructures of ARCOP and Zeidler Roberts were much admired in the 1960s and 1970s. In today's era of accelerating globalization and climate change, Canadian architecture offers powerful lessons in other domains: reconciling regional identities with contemporary practice, adapting environmentally sensitive design to a diversity of climates (particularly the extreme temperatures of the Arctic), and increasing the density of residential fabric in Canada's urban centers. In other areas, such as building for First Nations, Canadian architects are in the midst of an ongoing learning process that includes nurturing long-term relationships with local communities, as well as educating new architects from within them.

Contemporary Canadian architecture defies the quick-consumption age of digital media—it is not reducible to a single style or iconic image. But this very diversity and complexity is its strength. Often working with modest budgets, Canadian architects have been resourceful in finding ways to adapt contemporary architecture to a large variety of climates and contexts, and to one of the world's most multicultural societies. The result is work that is often unpretentious, but houses rich stories beneath the surface. Our hope is that the following pages highlight the exceptional quality of recent Canadian architecture and of the design thinking behind it.

National
Movements

1

The Centennial Projects: Building the New

Marco Polo and Colin Ripley

Opening Act: *Kraanerg*

On the evening of June 2, 1969, a crowd of Ottawa dignitaries, including Prime Minister Pierre Trudeau (1919–2000) and Governor General Roland Michener (1900–1991), arrived at the brand new National Arts Centre, one of the last of the Centennial Projects commissioned by the government to celebrate the one-hundredth anniversary of Canadian Confederation. A festive atmosphere settled over the gala for the official opening of the building, coming almost two years after the actual 1967 Centennial. Sitting in stark contrast to nearby buildings, the message of the National Arts Centre—with its brutalist exteriors, its orientation away from the fabric of the city, and its hexagonal plan—was clear, if not entirely comfortable for Ottawa residents: Canada and Canadian culture would be about the future, about new forms and new ideas.

The performance that awaited the sold-out audience in Southam Hall, the largest stage in the facility, pushed the boundaries of newness further still. The main work on the program was a full-length ballet, *Kraanerg*, commissioned for the opening and choreographed by National Ballet director Roland Petit (1924–2011). Written by the avant-garde composer (and architect) Iannis Xenakis (1922–2001), *Kraanerg* was, as historian Jim Harley puts it, an aggressively modern, highly abstract "dialogue" on the "ideological disorders" facing

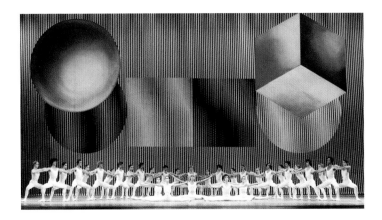

the world—a work based in the upheavals of the time of its writing in 1968 and 1969.[1] The set design, by Victor Vasarely (1906–1997), was equally abstract and stridently modern. **FIG 1** The whole production was a work of ambitious, avant-garde art, connected to contemporary politics on the highest international level.

Looking back on that evening across fifty years of intervening history, we could well ask: *How had Canada become so modern?*

Building a New Canada

The 1950s and 1960s were a time of celebrating the new in Canada, as in much of the world. In the aftermath of World War II, there was a desire to concentrate on ways of moving forward rather than dwelling on the past. In Canada, thousands of servicemen returned home to start families and careers, eager to get on with their lives, giving rise to the baby boom and a culture of youth. It was also, of course, the Atomic Age, with all its promise and threat. In 1952, the first Canadian television stations started broadcasting; Toronto opened its first subway in 1954; and the planned suburbs arrived with the Don Mills neighborhood in 1953. Canadian artists played a central role in the development of this "culture of the new" throughout the 1950s, with the formation of Painters Eleven in 1953, the emergence of Paul-Émile Borduas (1905–1960) and Jean-Paul Riopelle (1923–2002) in Quebec, and Jack Shadbolt (1909–1998) and B. C. Binning (1909–1976) in Vancouver, among others. Canadians understood their country to be a country of the future.

The Massey Report

By the late 1940s, it had become clear that new infrastructure would be needed to continue the development of the arts in Canada. This led to the establishment of the 1949 Royal Commission on National Development in the Arts, Letters, and Sciences—commonly known as the Massey Commission or, more recently, the Massey-Lévesque Commission, after its chairman Vincent Massey (1887–1967) and its representative for French Canada,

1 opposite
Karen Bowes, Vanessa Harwood, Veronica Tennant, Garry Semeniuk, Timothy Spain, and artists of the ballet *Kraanerg*. Stage design by Victor Vasarely, 1969.

2 right
Festival Theatre, Stratford, Ontario. Rounthwaite and Fairfield, 1957.

Georges Henri Lévesque (1903–2000). After two years of meetings, the Commission published its report, which recommended that the federal government participate in, and fund, development of the arts and sciences in Canada. As a result, in 1957, the Canada Council for the Encouragement of the Arts, Letters, Humanities, and Social Sciences (later renamed the Canada Council for the Arts) was founded, while expanded roles were assigned to the National Film Board and the National Gallery and funding to universities was increased significantly.

The Massey Report devoted a scant six of its roughly five hundred pages explicitly to architecture and town planning. Within those pages, the report suggested that "all important buildings should be designed in open competition."[2] More importantly, the Commission accepted the observation presented to it by its panel of architectural experts that architecture was at best poorly understood by the general public, stating that:

> There was general agreement…between non-professional groups, professional architects and government agencies, that it is of the first importance to arouse public interest and develop public understanding on a matter of such universal consequence.[3]

On the heels of the Massey Report, the 1950s saw the construction of a significant number of cultural facilities both in Canada and representing Canada abroad. The Canadian Pavilion at the Venice Biennale, designed by Ernesto Rogers (1909–1969) of the Italian firm BBPR, was commissioned by the National Gallery in direct response to a recommendation of the Massey Report and opened in 1958.[4] A highly idiosyncratic building best described as a stylized steel-and-glass wigwam, the Pavilion was among the first attempts to define a Canadian identity through modern architecture.[5]

In Canada, the list of important cultural facilities included the Festival Theatre in Stratford, Ontario (Rounthwaite and Fairfield, 1957), which opened a year before the Biennale pavilion and was awarded a Massey Medal in Architecture in 1958. **FIG 2** In 1961, the O'Keefe Centre for the Performing Arts (Earle C. Morgan and Page + Steele Architects, with Peter Dickinson, 1925–1961, as lead designer) opened in Toronto. **FIG 3** Two years earlier, the Queen Elizabeth Theatre had opened in Vancouver, the result of a design

competition won by a group of young architects from Montreal: Affleck, Desbarats, Dimakopoulos, Lebensold, Michaud, and Sise (later known as ARCOP). **FIG 4** As a result of this project, the firm established a reputation for the design of theaters and was awarded the contract to design Place des Arts in Montreal, which opened in 1963.

The Centennial as an Opportunity

As Canada became conscious of itself as a country of the new, the fast-approaching Centennial of Confederation became an opportunity to push several agendas forward. To this end, two Canadian prime ministers—John Diefenbaker (1895–1979) in 1960 and Lester Pearson (1897–1972) in 1964—addressed the Royal Architectural Institute of Canada's (RAIC) annual meeting. **FIG 5** Both prime ministers spoke about the prospects that would be made available to architects in relation to the upcoming centennial, although Diefenbaker's announcement was less specific than Pearson's, since in 1960 no concrete programs had yet been developed.

More crucially, though, the prime ministers elaborated on how the Centennial related to nation-building, and on the vital role that architecture had to play. Diefenbaker discussed the similarity between building buildings and building nations, asking for a poetic response from the architects involved in the Centennial:

> …something to touch the hearts of Canadians, something to represent the unity of our country, something to embody the paradox of two great national stocks which joined together to make Confederation possible, something that will well represent the tremendous contributions of persons from all races and creeds who have come to Canada from all parts of the world.[6]

Pearson spoke along similar lines, although he was even more explicit in his view that architecture had the job of making Canada the country of the future, and that the unity of English and French Canadians was at stake. Without "equal opportunities for all our people and provinces…there can be no other foundation for national unity," he told the

3 opposite, left
O'Keefe Centre, Toronto,
Ontario. Earle C. Morgan
and Page + Steele, 1961.

4 opposite, right
Queen Elizabeth Theatre,
Vancouver, British Columbia.
Affleck, Desbarats,
Dimakopoulos, Lebensold,
Michaud, Sise, 1959.

5 right
Sir Robert Matthew, PRIBA,
and Prime Minister Lester B.
Pearson, on the occasion of the
prime minister's address to the
57th Annual Assembly of the
the Royal Architectural Institute
of Canada, St. Andrew's, New
Brunswick, 1964.

audience of gathered architects.[7] The message was clear: the Centennial would be used to create a new and united Canada, and architecture would be a key tool in achieving this goal.

The Centennial Commission

Beginning in the late 1950s, grassroots and local initiatives to celebrate Canada's upcoming Centennial of Confederation had started to form. Preparations for the Centennial officially began with the passing of the National Centennial Act on September 29, 1961. With the appointment of John Fisher as commissioner in 1963, planning began in earnest. In addition to the two main funding programs—the Centennial Grants Program and the Confederation Memorial Program—many programs and events of national significance were overseen and funded by the Centennial Commission. Most of these were traveling exhibitions, such as the Centennial Train and Caravans (the Commission's largest single expenditure, which received $11.4 million), but other programs included performances, publications, films, the minting of Centennial medals, the promotion of youth travel, pageants, sporting events, and so on.

Several construction projects were undertaken in the National Capital Region, including the creation of the Centennial Flame on Parliament Hill, the replacement of stained glass windows in the Houses of Parliament, and the erection of a new National Library and Archives building. In terms of architecture, the most significant of these was the creation of the National Arts Centre (1969), designed by Fred Lebensold (1917–1985) of Affleck, Desbarats, Dimakopoulos, Lebensold, and Sise (Jean-Charles-Édouard Michaud had left the partnership in 1959), which received $2.1 million in grants from the Centennial Commission. Including buildings and cultural programming, the Centennial Commission was responsible for total expenditures of approximately $85 million (roughly $600 million in 2018 dollars).[8]

Taken as a whole, the programs overseen by the Centennial Commission and their resulting projects clearly manifest a drive toward creating a new Canada. They make good on Prime Minister Pearson's call to create a modern and united nation, looking ahead rather than memorializing.

The Centennial Projects

The Centennial Commission's architectural undertakings were largely organized under two major building programs: the Centennial Grants Program and the Confederation Memorial Program (funding for the National Arts Centre fell outside of the mandate of these two programs). Expo 67—one of the largest efforts and one that is still closely identified with the Centennial—was organized outside the purview of the Commission and will be discussed later in this chapter.

The Centennial Grants Program provided matching funds to municipalities to support projects of a lasting nature, preferably those related to culture or recreation. The program provided one dollar for every resident of every community in Canada, matched by a second dollar from the province and a third from the community itself, for a total amount of three dollars per capita (approximately $21 in 2018 dollars). This relatively small amount of money funded 2,301 projects across the country, including some 860 buildings (including renovations and restorations) and an additional 520 recreational structures.[9]

The scope of these projects varied considerably from community to community, but the simple fact remains that hardly a place in Canada was untouched, and many of the resulting buildings have become crucial parts of the nation's urban cultural infrastructure. Consider, for example, the number of libraries constructed as part of this program—in Ontario alone, new libraries were built in eighteen municipalities.

Other projects have contributed significantly to Canada's cultural education, such as the Cape Breton Miners' Museum in Glace Bay, Nova Scotia (C.A. Fowler & Associates, 1967); the St. Lawrence Centre for the Arts in Toronto (Gordon S. Adamson and Associates, 1970); and the Théâtre Maisonneuve at Place des Arts in Montreal (David, Barott et Boulva, 1967). Still others, such as the Centennial Planetarium in Calgary (McMillan Long and Associates, 1967), remain significant for their architectural merits.

The Confederation Memorial Program provided funds to each province to support a single project of a lasting nature in each provincial or territorial capital. Unlike the Centennial Grants Program, the impetus for which came from within the Centennial Commission (in particular from its director of special projects, Peter Aykroyd), the Confederation

Memorial Program arose in response to existing local initiatives. Fundamental to the program's development was work being undertaken in Charlottetown, Prince Edward Island, where Frank MacKinnon, principal of Prince of Wales College (precursor to the University of Prince Edward Island), had for a decade been promoting the construction of a memorial of national scale to mark the centenary of the first Confederation Conference, held in Charlottetown's Province House in 1864.[10] MacKinnon assembled a national board to assist him in this effort, and in May 1961, the Fathers of Confederation Memorial Citizens' Foundation was incorporated, the mandate of which included seeking funding from the federal government.[11]

According to Aykroyd, the award of a grant to the Prince Edward Island project prompted Quebec to request funding for Le Grand Théâtre de Québec, in recognition of the second Confederation Conference, held in Quebec City, also in 1864. A design competition was held in 1964, supported by a Centennial Commission grant awarded the previous year. In February 1964, these two grants were incorporated into the Confederation Memorial Program, which was open to all provinces. In total, $20.7 million in federal funds was disbursed as part of the program.[12] With the exceptions of Nova Scotia, which constructed the Sir Charles Tupper Medical Building at Dalhousie University, and New Brunswick,

8
Fathers of Confederation
Memorial Buildings,
interior of Memorial Hall,
Charlottetown, Prince
Edward Island. Affleck,
Desbarats, Dimakopoulos,
Lebensold, Sise, 1964.

which built a provincial government administration building, all provinces built projects of a cultural nature: six performing arts spaces or cultural centers, two museums and archives, and the Centennial Centre for Science and Technology (later renamed the Ontario Science Centre).

In addition to the projects that fell under the funding programs of the Centennial Commission, many other buildings were built in honor of the Centennial, funded either by other levels of government or privately. Some of these buildings, such as Coronation Pool in Edmonton (Hemingway and Laubenthal Architects, 1970), continue to be recognized as significant works of architecture.

The Centennial Buildings

A first glance at the Centennial buildings suggests that they were less about memorializing and recognizing Canada's first hundred years than about imagining and building its foundation for the next hundred. Although a few projects explicitly celebrated Canada's history—such as the renovation of Toronto's historic St. Lawrence Hall—the vast majority of Centennial buildings emphasized modernity. Since the Massey Report, and following the clear message of Diefenbaker's and Pearson's addresses to the RAIC, this orientation to the future had been central to all discussions about building a national identity. If the Centennial was about recognizing the diverse contributions of the various peoples that came together to form Canada, it was equally—and perhaps even more importantly—about forging out of those diverse experiences a common vision and identity.

The Fathers of Confederation Memorial Buildings in Charlottetown (1964), the first Centennial project to be completed, created an important precedent for those that would follow—particularly with respect to the formal and expressive qualities of the ensemble, but also in terms of its commitment to the new. Initiated through a national design competition, the project envisioned a significant cultural facility, including a theater, gallery, and public library, on a key downtown site adjacent to the historic Province House. The forty-seven submissions clearly showed an appetite for modern approaches to memorialization. While

all the shortlisted proposals were unabashedly modern, the most strikingly so were an extraordinary monumental scheme by a young Raymond Moriyama and a fantastic, futuristic proposal by John B. Parkin Associates; the latter received a mention. Third prize was shared by a spiraling tower-based design by Gordon L. Cheney and a striking Miesian pavilion by Bland, LeMoyne & Edwards, while second prize went to a more straightforward and pragmatic scheme by Mandel Sprachman. The winning scheme, by Dimitri Dimakopoulos (1929–1995) of Affleck, Desbarats, Dimakopoulos, Lebensold, and Sise, was announced in Ottawa in January 1962.[13] **FIG 6**

The programmatic elements of Dimakopoulos's project are expressed as discrete buildings rising from a podium elevated above street level and surrounding, on three sides, the dominant void of Memorial Hall, a multipurpose gathering space on the concourse below. Its fourth side is bounded by Province House. **FIGS 7–8** The new buildings are clad in Wallace sandstone from the same Nova Scotia quarry that supplied the stone for Province House. While this material treatment as well as the height of the new complex defer to the historic Province House and the intimate scale of Charlottetown, the complex as a whole suggests a more aloof attitude to its small-town setting. The massing does not address the surrounding streets, instead defining a fortress that protectively envelops its activities. This sense of separation is further emphasized by the podium, which isolates the Memorial Buildings in their constructed landscape, as well as by their uncompromisingly abstract formal composition.

On the heels of their success with the Fathers of Confederation Memorial Buildings, Affleck, Desbarats, Dimakopoulos, Lebensold, and Sise received the commission for a building that would serve as the flagship of the Centennial Projects, and the nation's premier cultural performance venue. For the National Arts Centre project, led by partner Fred Lebensold, the architects elaborated on themes already developed in the Charlottetown project, creating a series of discrete performance spaces that were clearly expressed as distinct buildings emerging from a series of terraces. However, where the Fathers of Confederation Memorial Buildings' modernity is tempered by their nod to context through scale and material treatment, the National Arts Centre unabashedly turns its back on the

built context of Ottawa to instead engage the Rideau Canal. **FIG 9** In addition, its embrace of the rugged language of textured concrete in various forms places it squarely in the brutalist tradition, expressing a break in historic continuity. The entry sequence eschews the formal, frontal approach typical of performance spaces in favor of a distributed, interconnected system of multileveled lobbies, expressing the project more as a constructed landscape than a conventional building form. **FIG 10**

The new was also evident in art installations associated with the National Arts Centre. The building and its grounds were filled with contemporary Canadian art, including Micheline Beauchemin's (1929–2009) magnificent stage curtain in Southam Hall, enormous cast-aluminum doors by Jordi Bonet (1932–1979) leading into the salon, William Martin's (1923–2012) crystal DNA chandeliers in each of the building's hexagonal stairways, and a massive bronze sculpture on the roof terrace by Charles Daudelin (1920–2001). **FIGS 11–12** The National Arts Centre was one of several Centennial Projects that commissioned significant artworks to articulate national and regional narratives.

The Fathers of Confederation Memorial Buildings and National Arts Centre demonstrate two primary modes in which the Centennial Projects approached and expressed the new. First, both projects manifest in their programs what could be called a *constructive*

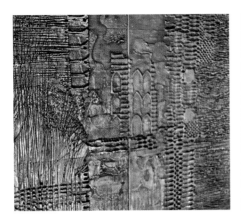

11 left
**Detail, cast aluminum
doors to the Salon,
National Arts Centre,
Ottawa, Ontario. Jordi
Bonet, 1969.**

12 right
**Crystal DNA chandelier,
National Arts Centre,
Ottawa, Ontario. William
Martin, 1969.**

13 opposite, top
**Fathers of Confederation
Memorial Buildings,
exterior view,
Charlottetown, Prince
Edward Island. Affleck,
Desbarats, Dimakopoulos,
Lebensold, Sise, 1964.**

14 opposite, bottom
**National Arts Centre,
exterior view from
northwest, Ottawa,
Ontario. Affleck, Desbarats,
Dimakopoulos, Lebensold,
Sise, 1969.**

futurity. This mode is in keeping with the aims of Diefenbaker and Pearson to encourage the development of a unique and mature Canadian culture through the construction of important institutional buildings. The provision of performance spaces, galleries, and libraries was a critical component of this cultural infrastructure. Second, both projects embraced an *architectural futurity*: that is, rather than looking back to precedents or working from the position of memorialization, the projects engaged with current and even futuristic modes of architectural thinking. This includes brutalism, as can be seen in the form and materiality of the projects, and systems thinking, as can be seen in their organization. **FIGS 13–14** Furthermore, both projects considered how these architectural tropes could be usefully applied to the Canadian context, creating a specifically Canadian architectural modernity.

These two forward-looking modes can be recognized in many of the projects funded by the Centennial Grants Program and built in honor of the occasion. The Centennial buildings' orientation toward the present and future can also be read in the programs chosen for many of them. There were art galleries, theaters, and libraries, reflecting the desire to build a national culture; sports facilities like Centennial Pool in Halifax and Coronation Pool in Edmonton, offering recreation for a new leisure society; and places of scientific education, such as Vancouver's and Calgary's planetariums and the Ontario Science Centre, celebrating

the space age. Meanwhile, many of these projects were architecturally ambitious and situated clearly within a modern paradigm. Two examples from Edmonton—the Centennial Library and Coronation Pool—are, while very different buildings, emblematic of this position.

Coronation Pool (1970, since renamed, in honor of its architect, the Peter Hemingway Fitness & Leisure Centre) is a fine example of Prairie expressionism, typified by idiosyncratic curvilinear forms and an expressive use of structure, such as is found in Douglas Cardinal's St. Mary's Church in Red Deer, Alberta (1968), and in Étienne Gaboury's Église du Précieux Sang in St. Boniface, Manitoba (1968) [see pages 302–306]. Also, the use of tensile cables for the roof structure refers to iconic clear-span athletic facilities such as Kenzo Tange's buildings for the Tokyo Olympics (1964) and Eero Saarinen's David S. Ingalls Rink at Yale University (1958), situating the project in both regional and international architectural culture. **FIG 15** Coronation Pool's sinuous forms embed it in the surrounding landscape, as do the muscular concrete piers to which the cable structures are anchored. Extensive glazing provides a high degree of transparency between the pool's interior and the surrounding park, enhancing the relationship between building and landscape.

Edmonton's Centennial Library (renamed Stanley A. Milner Library; Rensea, Minsos, and Holland, 1967) provided a new central library on Churchill Square in the heart of the city's downtown. The library's construction contributed to the radical modernization of Edmonton's core, where the library sat alongside City Hall (Dewar, Stevenson and Stanley, 1957; demolished 1989), the CN Tower (Abugov and Sunderland, 1966), and the Edmonton Art Gallery (Bittorf and Wensley Architects, 1969; radically altered by Randall Stout into the Art Gallery of Alberta in 2010). While glazing at the ground floor provides a degree of transparency, the stories above have very few openings, expressing the library as a fortress within the city. The library itself is housed in a two-story podium, out of which rises a four-story office block. Natural light is introduced into the stacks by means of large circular skylights, creating nodes of activity where the light falls on the grid of large floor plates. **FIG 16** A rigorous program of public art and furniture design once complemented the library's uncompromising modernity; much of this character has been lost as a result of subsequent alterations.

THE WORLD'S FIRST FLYING SAUCER LANDING PAD
St. Paul, Alberta. A Centennial project of Car-Ouells Construction Co. Ltd.

Other Centennial Grants projects took on the theme of the future in a more literal way. The most extreme of these projects was the world's first UFO landing pad built by the town of St. Paul, Alberta, to the design of engineer Alex Mair. **FIG 17** St. Paul established its reputation as "Centennial Town, Canada" by pursuing over one hundred Centennial Projects of various scales and types, from the renaming of streets after the Fathers of Confederation to the production of six thousand Centennial toques (close-fitting knitted caps) for distribution worldwide. The construction of the UFO Landing Pad, an official Centennial Project opened on June 3, 1967, by Minister of National Defence Paul Hellyer, complete with a flyover by Canadian Air Force jet fighters, was the quirkiest of the town's projects. **FIG 18** The landing pad includes a map of Canada composed of stones from each province and territory. Although the project was built in commemoration of Canada's Centennial, it had an international—even intergalactic—aim. A plaque at the site reads:

> The area under the World's First UFO Landing Pad was designated international by the Town of St. Paul as a symbol of our faith that mankind will maintain the outer universe free from national wars and strife. That future travel in space will be safe for all intergalactic beings, all visitors from earth or otherwise are welcome to this territory and to the Town of St. Paul.

A direct interest in futurity can also be seen in a set of more mainstream projects that embraced the space age: Gerald Hamilton's Centennial Planetarium and Museum in Vancouver (1967); McMillan Long and Associates' Calgary Centennial Planetarium (1967); and Raymond Moriyama's Ontario Science Centre (1969).

Vancouver's Centennial Planetarium and Museum is housed in three rectilinear blocks, but its main identity resides in the conical roof of the planetarium theater. **FIG 19** This form refers to the iconic woven hats of the Haida First Nation as well as the roof of Clifford Wiens' John Nugent Studio in Lumsden, Saskatchewan (1960). **FIG 20** The monolithic quality of the museum is tempered by delicately patterned precast concrete panels and by glazed colonnaded bases that create the illusion of weightlessness, in keeping with the lighter, filigreed language of West Coast Modernism. Addressing both the local culture and trends

in contemporary architecture, the project is simultaneously of the place and of the moment. George Norris's stainless steel crab sculpture adds an additional note of regional flavor. **FIG 21**

The Calgary Centennial Planetarium was the result of a design competition. The winning scheme by McMillan Long and Associates was praised by the jury for its functional efficiency and aesthetic response. The original design called for an observation deck raised 80 feet (24.4 meters) above the ground to shield the telescopes from light pollution, but this was abandoned due to the high cost of stabilizing the telescopes at this height. **FIG 22** Jack Long (1925–2001) noted that the design "emerged from the ideas of earth forms—the sloping walls relate to river chasms, the freer forms (curved concrete walls) were influenced by Le Corbusier and…Erich Mendelsohn."[14] The planetarium adopts the rough concrete expression typical of brutalism, and its irregular forms situate it within the tradition of Prairie expressionism and refer to the craggy forms of the Rocky Mountains. **FIG 23** Converted in 1987 to the Calgary Science Centre, the building has sat empty since 2011 when its programming was relocated to a new facility. At the time of writing, it is being repurposed as a multiuse culture and arts space.

Of all the architectural projects completed under the auspices of the Centennial Commission, Raymond Moriyama's (1929–) Centennial Centre for Science and

21 above
Stainless steel crab sculpture, Centennial Museum and Planetarium, Vancouver, British Columbia. George Norris, 1967.

22 opposite top
Calgary Centennial Planetarium, section drawing, Calgary, Alberta. McMillan Long and Associates, 1967.

23 opposite bottom
Calgary Centennial Planetarium, exterior view.

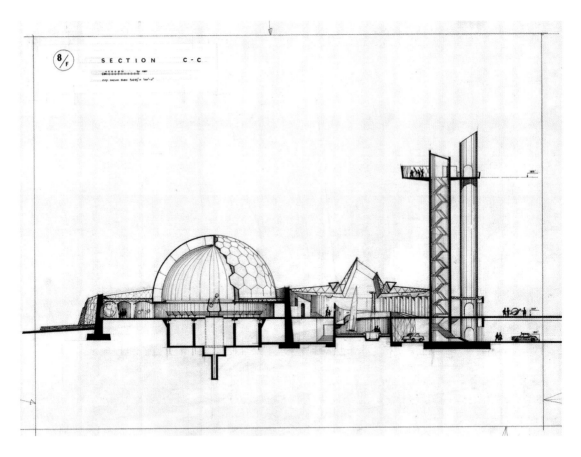

Technology—better known as the Ontario Science Centre—best represents what critic Peter Buchanan described as "the 'heroic period' of Canadian architecture."[15] This term refers to major works of the 1960s and 1970s, such as Erickson Massey's Simon Fraser University and John Andrews's Scarborough College [see pages 108–113 and 157–160], which, by virtue of their large scale and tough character, Buchanan argued, "confront the landscape as an equal."[16] The Ontario Science Centre takes full advantage of its ravine site to engage with the landscape, presenting a low, one-story building at the entry level that spills down the slope to nestle in a dense forest. The building expression is unflinchingly brutalist (a character compromised by ensuing additions and alterations), employing rough, board-formed concrete throughout to describe a series of large, rugged masses that simultaneously express the building as a bastion and as an extension of the terrain. **FIG 24** Moriyama's building reflects the wonder of an optimistic future. The architectural drawings communicate the utter novelty of this project: its cast-in-place concrete cylinders and tube-shaped passageways, complete with HVAC and plumbing systems, nestled into and flying over the forested valley below, were unlike any other architectural experience in southern Ontario. **FIGS 25–26**

Expo 67

As already mentioned, the orientation to modernity and the future represented by the Centennial buildings were central to discussions about the establishment of a national identity in the wake of the 1951 publication of the Massey Report. While this remarkable building program was primarily directed at a domestic audience, the drive to build "the new" was also an unmistakable purpose of the most ambitious of the projects completed in Canada for the Centennial, an undertaking that addressed the world stage: Expo 67, a World's Fair.

Administered as a special project outside the purview of the Centennial Commission, Expo 67 was Canada's most significant event of the year. This is reflected in both its budget and attendance record: the fair cost over $430 million and attracted over 50 million visitors, generating revenues of about $220 million (but leaving a deficit of $210 million).[17]

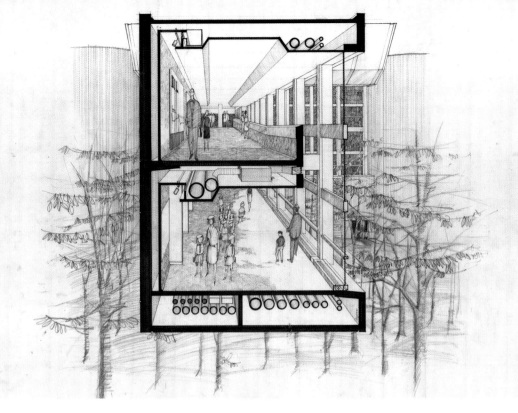

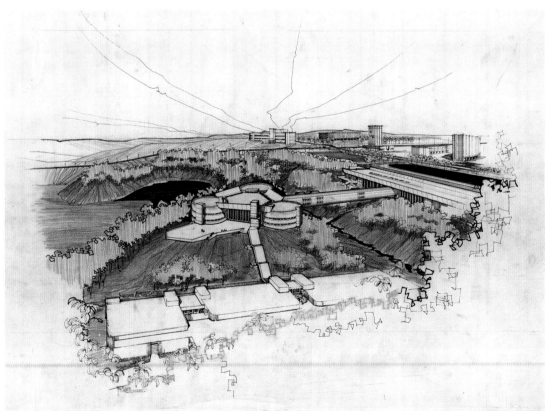

27 left
Pulp and Paper Pavilion, Expo 67, Montreal, Quebec. William Kissiloff, 1967.

28 right
Polymer Pavilion, Expo 67, Montreal, Quebec. Ron Thom, 1967.

29 opposite, top
US Pavilion, Expo 67, Montreal, Quebec. Richard Buckminster Fuller, 1967.

30 opposite, bottom
Habitat 67, Montreal, Quebec. Moshe Safdie, 1967.

It remains the first thing most Canadians think of in relation to 1967. It was, of course, a blockbuster. Peter C. Newman described it as follows:

> [T]he greatest thing we have ever done as a nation.... [T]he more you see of it, the more you're overwhelmed by a feeling that if this is possible, that if this little sub-arctic, self-obsessed country of twenty million people can put on this kind of show, then it can do almost anything.[18]

Given this kind of effusive delight and the nostalgic affection with which Expo 67 is still regarded, it's worth noting that the World's Fair almost didn't happen in Montreal. In 1960, by a vote of 16 to 14, the International Exhibitions Bureau (IEB) awarded the 1967 fair to Moscow over Montreal. However, when the USSR—whose expo would have commemorated the fiftieth anniversary of the 1917 October Revolution—withdrew in 1962 due to financial constraints, the IEB changed the venue to Montreal.[19]

The theme of Expo 67 was "Man and His World"—inspired by Antoine de Saint-Exupéry's 1939 memoir *Terre des Hommes*—and the fair aimed to embody a utopian world of the future. Its planning, graphic design, and public amenities presented a unified systems approach to building the new. This approach was also reflected in the architecture

31 above
West German Pavilion,
Expo 67, Montreal, Quebec.
Frei Otto and Rolf Gutbrod,
1967.

32 opposite, top
Canadian Pavilion, Expo
67, Montreal, Quebec,
Ashworth, Robbie, Vaughan
and Williams, 1967.

33 opposite, bottom
Man the Producer, Expo 67,
Montreal, Quebec. Affleck,
Desbarats, Dimakopoulos,
Lebensold, Sise, 1967.

34
National Arts Centre, site
plan, Ottawa, Ontario.
Affleck, Desbarats,
Dimakopoulos, Lebensold,
Sise, 1969.

of the pavilions, many of which "adopted an architectural language of primary geometric forms, an approach that was well suited to the creation of structures that would be easy to build"—and easy to dismantle.[20] Almost all of the pavilions at Expo 67 were temporary in nature, unfettered by the programmatic complexities and demands for durability and environmental performance faced by the permanent Centennial buildings.

While a spirit of experimentation permeated the architecture of Expo 67, including that of smaller industry pavilions such as William Kissiloff's Pulp and Paper Pavilion and Ron Thom's Polymer Pavilion, a handful of major structures emerged as emblematic icons of the World's Fair. FIGS 27–28 Among these are the familiar US Pavilion in the form of a giant geodesic dome designed by Richard Buckminster Fuller; Moshe Safdie's Habitat 67, a "village" of precast concrete modules, representing a bold experiment in prefabricated housing; the experimental tensile roof of Frei Otto and Rolf Gutbrod's West German Pavilion; the Canadian Pavilion by Ashworth, Robbie, Vaughan, and Williams; and the rigorous tetrahedral geometry of ARCOP's Man the Explorer and Man the Producer theme pavilions. FIGS 29–33

ARCOP's two theme pavilions at Expo 67, designed under the direction of Guy Desbarats (1925–2003), reflect some of the same geometric preoccupations that led to the hexagonal plan forms at Lebensold's National Arts Centre. FIG 34 The pavilions indulged fully in the architectural rhetoric of the tetrahedral structural frame [see chapter 5]. Reyner Banham's enthusiastic descriptions of Man the Producer include a comparison—meant as a compliment—to "a collapsed and rusting Eiffel Tower," while also calling it a prototype of "the multi-level city centres of the future."[21]

Another theme pavilion, Arthur Erickson's (1924–2009) Man in the Community, also experimented with the geometry of the hexagon. FIG 35 Constructed as a series of stacked rotating hexagons of enormous West Coast Douglas fir timber beams, the pavilion evoked the ancient forms of the pyramid and the ziggurat, while its gentle parabolic curvature situated it in a more contemporary context. The Canadian Pavilion also referenced a pyramid, albeit turned on its head, with its nine-story height supported by four columns. Named Katimavik—the Inuktitut word for "gathering space"—the structurally audacious inverted pyramid housed a theater and four exhibit halls, and was topped by an observation deck.

Each of these projects can be read within the tradition of World's Fair architecture: structurally experimental, formally provocative, and, with the notable exception of Habitat, programmatically flexible and forgiving. In addition, Expo 67 came along at a time when the new social phenomena of the postwar era, most notably an emphasis on leisure and play, had become the inspiration for vigorous architectural experimentation. As Reyner Banham has pointed out, the architecture of Expo 67 drew inspiration from Constant Nieuwenhuys's Situationist New Babylon project (1959–1974), Cedric Price's Fun Palace (1964), and the ludic experimentation of Archigram[22]—including an unbuilt proposal by Peter Cook for the Montreal Entertainments Tower at Expo 67.[23]

Today, only a few of Expo 67's structures remain. These include the US Pavilion, re-purposed as the Montreal Biosphere; the French and Quebec Pavilions, combined to house the Casino de Montréal; André Blouin's now largely abandoned Place des Nations, which accommodated public events and was one of the fair's few understated compositions; and Habitat 67, which remains a highly desirable residential address. But there's no doubt that the fair had a strong and lasting impact on the perception of Canada as a modern nation. The fair's architectural experimentation also yielded dividends in terms of influence on subsequent projects: Frei Otto, in collaboration with Günther Behnisch, would go on to design the Olympic complex for the 1972 summer games in Munich using similar tensile roof technology to that in his German Pavilion at Expo 67; Craig, Zeidler and Strong's Ontario Place, completed in Toronto in 1971, has clear antecedents in the architecture of the Montreal fair [see page 169]; and Expo 67's overall fascination with modular systems design found clear expression in the high-tech architecture of the 1970s and beyond, including Renzo Piano and Richard Rogers's Pompidou Centre in Paris, completed in 1977.

The most significant remaining structure from Expo 67 is the site itself. Île Ste.-Hélène, in the St. Lawrence River, was expanded, and an entirely new island, Île Notre-Dame, was constructed, both using material excavated in the construction of the city's new subway system. **FIG 36** A spit of land along the riverbank was also extended and serves as the site for Habitat 67. The fair not only *represented* the new: the very ground it sat on was new, a feat of modern construction techniques linked, both literally and conceptually, to the new metro. Here was a representation of Canada as a modern nation, built from the ground up.

Many of the speculative architectural projects from which Expo 67 drew inspiration participated in a discourse that questioned the traditional role of architecture as an endur-ing artifact. They proposed an alternative view in which the built environment created an infrastructure that supported temporary multimedia installations and events. Inside Expo 67's actual pavilions, each country showcased innovative technologies, often with an em-phasis on space exploration, transportation, and communications, and it has been noted that "critics were alternately frustrated and fascinated by the way in which the architectural

35
Man in the Community
Pavilion, Expo 67, view
of the entrance, Montreal,
Quebec. Erickson / Massey
Architects, 1967.

spaces had been eclipsed by the programming in them, and by how sound and image had been deployed in the creation of a new kind of 'total environment.'"[24]

This notion of the future of architecture as a media-saturated environment reflected the vision of Canadian media theorist Marshall McLuhan (1911–1980), who had published two essays in *The Canadian Architect* in 1961 and 1966.[25] In these prescient articles, McLuhan argued that the most important environments were, increasingly, not the physical spaces themselves, but rather the invisible information environments created by new electronic media. This emerged as a common theme at Expo 67, with numerous multimedia installations featuring immersive projection technologies, including multiscreen theaters and other advances in audiovisual media, as well as emerging computer technologies, such as an installation and demonstrations by IBM in the Canadian Pavilion.[26] On the whole, the fair prefigured the information revolution of subsequent decades.

Conclusion

In "The Invisible Environment," McLuhan argued that "the really total and saturating environments are invisible. The ones we notice are quite fragmentary and insignificant compared to the ones we don't see…in the case of environments that are created by new technologies, while they are quite invisible in themselves, they do make visible the old environments."[27] If we apply this logic to the architecture of Expo 67 and the Centennial Projects, then should we surmise that the utopian, modern vision expressed through the buildings of 1967 represented a version of the future whose time was already past?

As Canada embraced the idea of modernity as a defining national trait and expressed this in the forward-looking architecture of the Centennial buildings and Expo 67, modern architecture itself was coming under attack from a variety of forces, challenging the optimism that had characterized much of the postwar period. The exhortation from Prime Minister Diefenbaker to use the Centennial and its representations as expressions of national unity was undermined when, on July 24, 1967, French president Charles de Gaulle caused an international incident with his exclamation "Vive le Québec Libre!" from a balcony

at Montreal City Hall. By then, tensions between Quebec and English Canada were already high, with an increasingly militant Front de libération du Québec (FLQ, a separatist paramilitary group) emerging on the scene.

The youthful enthusiasm for the future that fueled the Centennial fever of 1967 and the Trudeaumania of 1968 had, by the early 1970s, been eroded by disappointment and cynicism. The celebratory atmosphere of the late 1960s was supplanted by the shock of the 1970 October Crisis and invocation of the War Measures Act, enacted following the FLQ kidnapping of the British trade commissioner James Cross and the assassination of senior Quebec cabinet minister Pierre Laporte. The economic instability of the mid-1970s, culminating in the highly unpopular imposition of wage and price controls, further eroded the optimistic anticipation of the future that characterized the Centennial year. The generous spending on cultural and educational initiatives that flourished in the 1960s gave way to an era of great austerity that, by the early 1980s, had led to significant reductions in the budgets of institutions like the National Arts Centre.[28] The emergence of a neoliberal political culture that swept through Western governments, accompanied by ideological antipathy for public investment in the cultural sector, saw the erosion of many of the initiatives that had emerged in the wake of the Massey Report.

Not only did these shifting concerns change the way new architecture was being conceived and produced, they also profoundly affected how the Centennial Projects were interpreted in the context of the changing cultural climate. Modernism fell into disfavor, the style of architecture was no longer valued, and, in some instances, the Centennial buildings were altered in ways at odds with the original architecture.

Today, the Centennial buildings can be read as relics of a time when architecture was understood to play an essential role in Canadian culture. The 1982 Report of the Federal Cultural Policy Review Committee noted that while the thirty years following the Massey Report of 1951 were characterized by "putting up buildings and establishing organizations"[29]—accomplishments dismissed as "relatively simple tasks…[that] add up to…more an industrial and employment policy than a cultural policy"[30]—Canada "must place a new emphasis on encouraging the best use of our concert halls, theatres, cinemas, galleries and airwaves for the presentation to Canadians of the finest works of Canada's own creative artists."[31]

This expresses a view that buildings themselves have little value as cultural objects, but serve only as vessels for other content. In recent years, however, the recognition of the heritage value of this generation of buildings has brought their significance (and their vulnerability) to the fore. The emergence of initiatives, such as the Modern Heritage Programme, established jointly by UNESCO, ICOMOS, and DoCoMoMo in 2001, has contributed to a new understanding and valuation of this era of architectural design and production. In the case of the Centennial buildings, this establishes the framework for a new appreciation of how architecture has given shape to the values, aspirations, and enthusiasms that drove the development of Canada as the country entered its second century.

2

The Architecture of Public Institutions

George Thomas Kapelos

This chapter examines the architecture of Canadian public institutions and the role of the state in architectural patronage in the fifty years after 1967. The attention paid to the design of national galleries, museums, city halls, embassies, international expositions, sports facilities, and national infrastructures—and the sheer number of buildings that were built to house these institutions—points to the importance of public buildings as an expression of Canada's architectural consciousness.

The impulse behind the construction of these buildings can be traced to the recommendations of the 1951 Massey Commission [see pages 20–22]. The broad mandate of the Commission was "in the national interest to give encouragement to institutions which express national feeling, promote common understanding and add to the variety of and richness of Canadian life."[1] For architecture, the message was clear: "In an age of increasing urbanization, it is more than ever essential for Canadians to become aware of the influence exercised by architecture on the lives of all citizens."[2] The Massey Commission recommended the use of architectural competitions as an essential component of a national strategy to enhance the quality of Canadian architectural works, with the state playing the vital role of patron and powerful client.[3]

The architecture of this period also sought to reference the Canadian landscape and the distinct character of place and setting. Canada's formation goes to the root of the human-nature dialectic. Following their first encounters with Indigenous populations, European invaders sought to protect themselves from the forbidding landscapes of the New World. Only through conquering this new territory could they reconcile themselves to it. Images of the fort-in-the-wilderness dominated early architectural and urban preoccupations; the siting of Canada's parliament in Ottawa typifies this stance. The 1867 Confederation created a nation—the Dominion of Canada—whose very title signified the domination of humans over their untamed wilderness.

The spread of settlement, through the replication of the surveyor's grid across the nation, sought to remake the image of Canada from an uncertain wilderness into a fixed and ordered landscape. Nature and the creation of urban spaces in this landscape are recurring themes in the narratives of national architecture. As the wilderness was conquered, a subtle shift in design took place. Nature was no longer a force to be grappled with; rather, it was to be emulated formally and spiritually. Soon the power of the landscape took hold in the Canadian architectural imagination. With the maturing of the nation, some architects endeavored to reconcile public spaces and built form with natural forces and context, often using materials and forms rooted in the environment. New architecture spoke of a nation mindful of its past, anchored to its place, and ambitious for the future.

Ottawa: Home of National Cultural Institutions

The 1950 Plan for the National Capital by French architect Jacques Gréber (1882–1962) set the framework for the location and construction of national cultural institutions in Ottawa and its environs, many of which were realized in the decades since 1967.[4] These buildings present a diverse range of architectural approaches to landscape, history, culture, and the city, and collectively form symbols of the vibrant and diverse country they represent.

The idea of open architectural competitions was immediately applied to the creation of a new National Gallery in 1952. However, it took thirty-five years and three competitions for the project to be completed. The first competition in 1954 led to the selection of a scheme by Green, Blankstein, Russell, and Associates of Winnipeg, but the project was shelved and the Gallery moved to a repurposed office building.[5] The 1967 Centennial reinvigorated interest in a competition for the National Gallery, and in 1975, the government announced a second competition. When a waterfront site west of Parliament Hill was selected, attention turned to the Ottawa River and the natural riverine spine that dominates the region's landscape. In 1977, a scheme by Parkin Architects and Planners of Toronto was chosen.[6] Parkin's design featured a strong diagonal axis across the site, linking the water to the city's orthogonal grid, and giving a rational order to the landscape that was subtle yet clear in its formal intent. The scheme was not built, but it established an imperative to engage with the river.

In 1983, Prime Minister Pierre Elliott Trudeau (1919–2000) announced plans to build the National Gallery along with a new museum, the Museum of Man (later renamed the Museum of Civilization in 1986 and subsequently the Museum of History in 2013). These institutions were sited on prominent locations, facing each other across the Ottawa River: the National Gallery in Ottawa (1988) adjacent to Nepean Point, and the Museum of Man (1989) at Parc Laurier in Hull, Quebec. This siting strategy, spearheaded by architect and planner Roger du Toit (1939–2015), created a visible link between the two communities. It signified a dialogue between history and art as well as a crossing of the physical boundary and political divide that separated the two central Canadian provinces that were founding members of the new Dominion of 1867. For the Gallery, an open competition was abandoned.[7] Instead, twelve short-listed firms were invited to make a booklet submission presenting "a measure of [each firm's] imagination."[8] This vagueness left the selection open to interpretation and in the hands of the Canadian government, who selected Moshe Safdie (1938–) as design architect, in collaboration with Parkin/Safdie Architects Planners.

Initially, Safdie had not expressed interest in designing the Gallery. Among the passed-over schemes was that of Barton Myers (1934–), whose submission displayed a capacity for reconciling historic, urban architectural forms with new cultural institutions in a sympathetic and creative manner. Safdie's scheme was eventually built. However, one commentator later described the competition's outcome as a reflection of a tendency in Canadian architecture of the "cult of personality" taking precedence over design quality and objectivity.[9]

While the saga of the National Gallery was playing out, the federal government was developing plans for a companion institution that would "enhance Canadians' knowledge, understanding and appreciation of events, experiences, people and objects that reflect and have shaped Canada's history and identity."[10] In 1983, the government named Douglas Cardinal (1934–) and Tétrault Parent Languedoc et Associés as architects for the new Museum of Man. It was clear that in the selection of the architects for both the National Gallery and the Museum of Man the hand of Prime Minister Trudeau was at work.

The two museums take distinct positions in relation to landscape. The National Gallery is laid out on a grid that responds to Ottawa's urban context. It includes public galleries on the main and upper levels, with the lower floor given over to the museum's administrative and support spaces. The L-shaped plan leads from an entrance pavilion along a glass-encased ramped colonnade to the Great Hall, then turns northward through a long concourse to an octagonal rotunda. This rotunda references the geometric chapter-house form of the Parliamentary Library, seen in the distance on the riverbank. FIG 1 In the architect's words, "I designed my building actually growing out of the Ottawa River."[11] The gallery design includes carefully proportioned gallery spaces with indirect lighting, paying homage, in part, to Safdie's early-career work in Louis Kahn's Philadelphia offices.

1 above
**The National Gallery,
view from the south,
Ottawa, Ontario. Moshe
Safdie (design architect)
in collaboration with
Parkin / Safdie Architects
Planners, 1988.**

2 opposite
**Canadian Museum of
History, Gatineau, Quebec.
Douglas Cardinal and
Tétrault Parent Languedoc
and Associés, 1989.**

3 opposite, top
Canadian War Museum, view from Victoria Island, Ottawa, Ontario. Moriyama & Teshima Architects in joint venture with Griffiths Rankin Cook Architects, 2005.

4 opposite, bottom
Canadian War Museum, entrance.

5 right
Canadian War Museum, interior view of Regeneration Hall.

Cardinal's organic and sinuous design for the Museum of Man is the antithesis of Safdie's highly ordered and crystalline Gallery. The undulations of the building form were in part driven by view cones delineated by the National Capital Commission. The building's *parti* is defined by two wings named after geologic forms: the Canadian Shield on the north, housing curatorial spaces, conservation laboratories, and administration offices; and the Glacier Wing to the south, housing public exhibition halls. **FIG 2** The project's centerpiece is the Grand Hall, where a recreated West Coast First Nations village stands opposite a glass wall framing the view of Parliament Hill. According to Cardinal, the buildings "speak of the emergence of this continent, its forms sculpted by the winds, the rivers, the glaciers."[12] The remarkable way in which the building descends to the shore of the Ottawa River, creating a public plaza and viewing place for the Parliament Buildings on the adjacent river bluffs, adds to its aura and power.

In the early 2000s, three new national museums were built—two in Ottawa and one, surprisingly, in Winnipeg. These heralded a new era of institutional architecture that responded to Canada's history and cultural aspirations. The Canadian War Museum and the Canadian Museum of Nature were developed on traditional models and evolved from existing museum collections. The third museum, the Canadian Museum for Human Rights,

signaled a new type of museum based on the national ideals of human rights and respect for others.

The Canadian War Museum (2005) was carefully sited along the necklace of the National Capital Commission's ceremonial routes, a looping circuit of roads linking Ottawa and Hull that would be taken by dignitaries on state visits to Canada, developed in 1983 by Du Toit and his firm. Following in the tradition of other national museums in responding to the landscape, the museum's placement reinforces the complex relationship of architecture to setting.

Moriyama & Teshima Architects in joint venture with Griffiths Rankin Cook Architects created a building that appeared to grow out of the landscape of LeBreton Flats, overlooking the river. **FIGS 3-7** The undulations of the surrounding grounds recall the scarred battlefields of World War I, which saw the overwhelming sacrifice of Canadians to the war effort and the concomitant birth of the Canadian nation. The building is designed to seemingly emerge from the earth like a geological formation, and elements of the building's form gesture to other symbols of the National Capital, including the nearby Peace Tower. The building's narrative balances abstract concept with artifact. The interior spaces of the building comprise four rich and evocative permanent exhibition spaces.[13] Messages of remembrance are inscribed in the museum's Regeneration Hall, while thirty-degree canted walls recollect subterranean war bunkers. The building serves a dual purpose: to remember the atrocities of past wars and to serve as a positive beacon of hope, reconciliation, and regeneration.[14]

Regeneration, in a different form, marks the renewal of the Canadian Museum of Nature, which reopened in 2011. **FIG 8** Located in the Victoria Memorial Museum Building, the museum inherited collections of the Geological Survey of Canada dating to 1842. The original building, completed in 1912, was designed by architect David Ewart (1841–1921) in a style that combined the neo-Gothic language of Ottawa's original parliament with Beaux Arts ideas and inspirations.[15] The original foundations, however, were built on unstable ground and were thus inadequate from the start, forcing the demolition of the museum's tower shortly after the building's completion.

7 opposite
Canadian War Museum,
view at entrance, Ottawa,
Ontario. Moriyama &
Teshima Architects in
joint venture with Griffiths
Rankin Cook Architects,
2005.

8 right
Canadian Museum of
Nature, the Queen's
Lantern above the entrance
pavilion, Ottawa, Ontario,
2010. Barry Padolsky
Associates Architects,
Kuwabara Payne McKenna
Blumberg Architects,
and Gagnon Letellier
Cyr Richard Mathieu
Architectes.

A complete overhaul of the structure, systems, and envelope, along with a renovation of interior spaces, took place from 2004 to 2010, led by a team consisting of Barry Padolsky Associates Architects (Ottawa), Kuwabara Payne McKenna Blumberg Architects (Toronto), and Gagnon Letellier Cyr Richard Mathieu Architectes (Quebec City). A new structural system was inserted into the building. A glass tower was constructed over the original entranceway, while a low-rise rear addition provided additional space for support facilities. The building represents a historical continuity, with the new glass tower replicating the original stone tower and creating, in the words of one reviewer, "a dialogue of subtle contrast with shared geometries and clear distinctions between old and new."[16]

Canada's newest national museum, the Canadian Museum for Human Rights, stands apart from its peers in both location and focus. Its private patronage signals a new approach to national museum formation, focusing on public-private partnerships to create institutions with specific messages and ideological mandates. Opened in 2014, the Winnipeg museum aims "to enhance the public's understanding of human rights, to promote respect for others and to encourage reflection and dialogue."[17]

In 2004, an international design competition selected US-based Antoine Predock (1936–) as the design architect, with Architecture 49 (formerly Smith Carter Architects

and Engineers) of Winnipeg as executive architect. The building's form expresses "a symbolic statement of both the rootedness and the upward struggle for human rights."[18] Sited prominently at the confluence of the Assiniboine and Red Rivers in Winnipeg, the building's mass appears as a tower thrusting skyward from an encircling glass sheath. **FIG 9** The museum follows a carefully constructed narrative bringing visitors on a journey "from darkness to light," beginning with a descent into the earth.[19] The main space of the museum—its Great Hall—is conceived as a place of reflection, leading to a series of themed galleries exploring stories of the struggles and accomplishments of human rights movements. It's a somber setting and offers a spatial experience with strong material qualities and evocative architectural spaces.[20]

City Halls and Civic Centers

Ottawa is not the only place where architecture has shaped the symbolism of public institutions. Canada's population continues to shift from rural to urban, with 80 percent of Canadians living in cities in 2006 compared to only 37 percent at the turn of the last century. With this shift, municipalities have sought to create city halls and civic centers

9 opposite
Canadian Museum for Human Rights, view from southeast, Winnipeg, Manitoba. Antoine Predock (design architect) with Architecture 49 (formerly Smith Carter Architects and Engineers), 2014.

10 right
Kitchener City Hall, view of civic square from competition entry, phase II, Kitchener, Ontario. Kuwabara Payne McKenna Blumberg Architects, 1989.

that represent the aspirations of urban Canada and the importance of civic government in everyday life.[21]

Toronto's 1958 open design competition for a city hall and civic square became a model for the procurement of new facilities [see pages 423–429]. Inherent in subsequent city halls was the search for a formal identity in civic government buildings, particularly as municipalities in new and expanding urban areas sought to showcase their ascent. A number of design competitions and commissions for public buildings were inspired by Toronto's competition, including Brantford City Hall (1967, Milutin Michael Kopsa), Boston City Hall (1968, Kalman McKinnel and Knowles), West Vancouver Municipal Hall (1964, Toby, Russell and Buckwell), and St. John's City Hall (1970, Parkin Architects with Horwood, Campbell, Guiham).

In Ontario, two competitions of the 1980s reaffirmed the value of open, anonymous competitions. In 1982, the City of Mississauga launched a competition for a city hall to be built on farmland in the heart of a growing suburban metropolis west of Toronto. The winning scheme, completed in 1987 by J. Michael Kirkland Architect in association with Edward Jones Architect, represented a thoughtful foray into postmodernism [see pages 199–203]. The 1989 competition for the new city hall in Kitchener likewise succeeded in both creating a symbolic monument and reinforcing the civic space of a historic main street. The winning scheme by Kuwabara Payne McKenna Blumberg Architects pointed to a proto-modernist direction for public architecture and to the value of symbolic civic space.[22] **FIGS 10–12**

Sited on Kitchener's main commercial street, Kitchener City Hall (1993) affirmed a commitment to the urban core while embodying the aspirations of a humanized modernism by providing a legible and accessible monument. The city hall has its primary level of address off a King Street–facing public square, an outdoor public room that accommodates large gatherings and public programming. The architects used a distinct material to express each of the main building components, establishing a clear reading of the city hall's parts. Two-story ocher Indian sandstone walls, which front the office space for elected officials and support staff, embrace the plaza and give an intimate scale to the building in its urban setting. Front and center, a ten-story office tower dominates the composition. Clad in

aluminum and partially wrapped by *brise soleils*, it is reminiscent of constructivist monuments of the 1920s. On the interior, a rotunda houses an internal public space, while the council chamber—located to the west and accessed on the second floor—plays a recessive role in the composition.[23]

On its opening, British historian Kenneth Frampton praised the design, writing: "There is not a single provincial town in the US that has built itself a city hall in the last two decades that is in any way comparable to the contextual responsiveness, tectonic depth and civic pride that is evident in Kitchener's City Hall."[24]

The Mississauga and Kitchener city hall competitions reflected a trend toward using city halls to support the creation and renewal of the urban fabric. This trend arose concurrently with a growing awareness of the importance of architectural history, preservation of community heritage resources, and stewardship of the built fabric. Similarly, in Ottawa's 1988 competition for a new city hall, the city's old modernist hall (Rother Bland Trudeau, 1958) was incorporated into the winning scheme by Moshe Safdie and Associates with Murray and Murray. In Safdie's design (completed in 1994), however, the old city hall is overpowered by the geometric forms of the new city hall.

Modernist visions of democratic civic and government spaces expressing openness and transparency—an idea originally promoted in the United Kingdom in the interwar period—inspired Canadian cities to create civic centers. The civic center was envisaged as a place combining administrative offices, community resources, and commercial uses, acting as a catalyst for urban growth and consolidation in established communities. Three striking projects reaffirm the continued emphasis on the civic center and public space as important elements of the urban landscape.

The Thompson-Nicola Regional District Civic Building (1998) in Kamloops, British Columbia, designed by Peter Cardew (1939–) with Nigel Baldwin Architects, houses regional government offices, a community library, and an art gallery. The building responds to the urban context of this rail-and-mill town and creates an interior town square. On a microscale, the square embodies the ongoing civic aspirations of Canadian municipal architecture. It presents public space, interiorized to address the harshness and extremes of the

13
Thompson-Nicola Regional
District Civic Building,
Victoria Street Entrance,
Kamloops, British
Columbia. Peter Cardew
Architects with Nigel
Baldwin Architects, 1998.

Canadian climate and assembled in a thoughtful way using a contemporary architectural vocabulary.[25] **FIG 13**

In the Lower Mainland of British Columbia, the Greater Vancouver Regional District (GVRD) introduced a plan in 2004 to decentralize work opportunities in the rapidly expanding region [see pages 493–497]. The plan focuses on the town of Surrey, anticipated to become the province's most populous municipality within the next twenty-five years. The proposal by Bing Thom Architects includes commercial towers, municipal services, and a new university.[26] Initial phases were completed in 2014 with the creation of Surrey City Hall, by Moriyama & Teshima Architects and Kasian Architecture, which anchors a new downtown transit-oriented precinct that includes a library, a site for a future performing arts center, and an impressive city hall plaza.

In 2006, Toronto's Nathan Phillips Square was revitalized by Shore Tilbe Irwin & Partners (now Perkins+Will) and PLANT Architect.[27] The square's renewal was effected through a series of interventions including new pavilions, a stage structure, and landscape redesign [see pages 462–464].[28]

Toronto's renewal of its magnificent square, Kitchener's remaking of a historic main street, Surrey's ambitions for a new public place, and the modest public space of Kamloops's administrative building continue the important tradition of public space as a corollary to civic building that has shaped the landscape of Canadian civic life since 1967.

Canada and the World:
Embassies and Expositions

Architecture has figured prominently in the projection of Canada's image abroad. New modes of expression, distinct architectural forms, and building materials reminiscent of the Canadian environment have been employed to portray an image of a progressive, open nation. Embassies, exhibitions and pavilions at world expositions, and stadiums for international sporting events are key to how Canada presents itself on the world stage.

Embassies and their chanceries offer glimpses of Canada to potential visitors, immigrants, investors, and curious citizens abroad. The construction of Canadian embassies has primarily been the responsibility of the Department of Foreign Affairs and International Trade (DFAIT).[29] The architecture and appearance of the buildings that house our foreign delegations have evolved, particularly in the postwar period, with the professionalization of the diplomatic core and the expansion of Canada's role on the international stage.

In the early 1970s, DFAIT developed a strategy to differentiate Canada from its continental neighbor to the south, and this strategy played out in the design of embassies. Beyond providing a place for the conduct of diplomatic affairs, new chanceries included exhibition rooms, auditoriums, and libraries, where aspects of the Canadian nation—its culture, arts, literature, social norms, and economic activities—could be displayed and promoted.[30]

For the most prestigious projects, DFAIT ensured that commissions were given to high-profile Canadian architects. The Canadian Embassy in Washington DC (1989), for instance, was designed by Arthur Erickson (1924–2009) and built on a prominent site on Pennsylvania Avenue [see page 186]. A hybrid of traditional and modern, the scheme acknowledges Washington's strong neoclassical traditions while asserting an essential Canadian-ness through the inclusion of a major public landscaped area at ground level, opening the building to the street and creating an urban park. **FIG 14** The embassy design emphasizes the street corner with a colonnaded rotunda, perched at the entrance. The strong horizontal and vertical forms characteristic of Erickson's restrained modernity still come through, as the embassy distinguishes itself along the streetscape.[31] The Washington embassy's architecture represented a new trend in Canadian chancery design, presenting an architecture that mediates between national values and those of the host country. The embassy reflects Canada's growing confidence about its national power and global presence while using symbolic forms to capture the essence of Canadian ideas.

Another striking example of this approach is the Canadian Embassy and Chancery (1991) in Tokyo, Japan, designed by Moriyama & Teshima Architects. The design is inspired by the three principle elements of ikebana, the Japanese art of flower arranging: the

14 above
**Canadian Chancery,
south elevation, view from
Pennsylvania Avenue NW,
Washington, DC. Arthur
Erickson, 1989.**

15 opposite, top
**Canadian Embassy and
Chancery, aerial view
from the northwest, Tokyo,
Japan. Moriyama &
Teshima Architects, 1991.**

16 opposite, bottom
**Canadian Embassy and
Chancery, view of garden.**

earth, represented in the rectilinear stone base; heaven, in the triangular roof; and, in the middle, the people, who meet each other in the entrance way. Practical reasons also dictated the building's form. The angle of the roof had to be designed so as not to cast a shadow on the neighboring Imperial Palace grounds for more than two hours a day. The building could have been higher and more densely built on the site; however, these options were not pursued both for security reasons and as a sign of *enryo*, or respect for the neighborhood, including the palace grounds, as Canadian deference to local customs superseded other values.[32] The building program comprises a two-story lobby, a 233-seat theater, an exhibition gallery, and a 13,000-volume library. Moriyama & Teshima's design stands as a symbol of the Canadian nation—distinct in the Tokyo cityscape, but intentionally showing respect for its host nation, quietly projecting Canadian values of accommodation and modesty. **FIGS 15–16**

Two projects convey their Canadian-ness through the use of natural materials and allusions to the Canadian wilderness. For Canada House, the Canadian Embassy in Berlin (1999), DFAIT selected Kuwabara Payne McKenna Blumberg (Toronto) with Gagnon Letellier Cyr (Montreal), Smith Carter (Winnipeg), and Vogel Architects (Toronto).[33] The architects chose to exemplify the essence of Canada through an elegant modern building

17 opposite, left
Canadian Embassy, aerial view, Berlin, Germany. Kuwabara Payne McKenna Blumberg with Gagnon Letellier Cyr, Smith Carter, and Vogel Architects, 1999.

18 opposite, right
Canadian Embassy, Timber Hall, Berlin, Germany.

19 right
Chancery and Canadian Diplomatic Complex, street view, Seoul, Korea. Zeidler Partnership Architects with Vogel Architect and Art International, 2007.

constructed of Canadian materials. The nine-story structure is clad in Manitoba Tyndall limestone, and its centerpiece conference facility, the Timber Hall, is lined with British Columbia Douglas fir overlooking a floor of Quebec maple.[34] **FIGS 17–18**

In a similar vein, in their design for Canada's new Chancery and Canadian Diplomatic Complex in Seoul, Korea (2007), Zeidler Partnership Architects with Vogel Architect and Art International chose to directly allude to recognized Canadian symbols. Taking inspiration from images of the Canadian landscape, the architects' design references paintings by the Group of Seven, a group of Canadian landscape painters formed in the 1920s. Building materials are specifically Canadian: a screen of slats made from Canadian western red cedar wraps portions of the curtain wall, allowing for privacy while providing natural light; and a cladding of Canadian gray granite pays homage to the Canadian Shield.[35] **FIG 19**

In the design of exhibition pavilions, Canadian architects have a relatively high degree of creative freedom in presenting a Canadian image to the world. Since 1967, Canada's architectural presence at international expositions has shifted from the symbolic to the literal.[36] This shift can be attributed to the changing nature of communications and information flows. Past fairs provided opportunities for gathering and knowledge exchange; in recent years, instantaneous communications have negated this necessity, and all that remains is

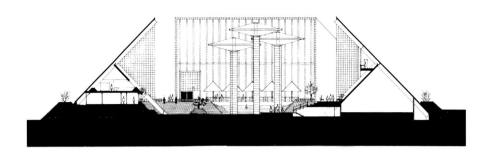

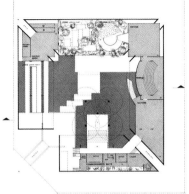

20 opposite, top
Expo 70 Canada Pavilion, exterior looking to interior court, Osaka, Japan. Erickson/Massey Architects, 1970.

21 opposite, bottom
Expo 70 Canada Pavilion, east-west section.

22 left
Expo 70 Canada Pavilion, colored architectural perspective.

23 right
Expo 70 Canada Pavilion, ground-floor plan.

spectacle and presence. A comparison of Canada's pavilions at Expo 70 (Osaka) and Expo 92 (Seville) demonstrates this transformation.

The wave of excitement of Expo 67 carried into ambitions for Canada's pavilion at Expo 70. In the competition-winning design scheme by Arthur Erickson and Geoffrey Massey (1924–), the pavilion is square in plan, enclosed by tall, mirror-sheathed walls that slope inward on a forty-five-degree angle over an open central courtyard. In the words of the architects, these "create an ambiguity of scale, distance, position and mass."[37] Once again, landscape inspires the architectural form, creating multiple readings of "sky or hills, solid or void, arctic ice, mountain masses, prairie sky or the glitter of Canadian water."[38] The architects presented a building open to above and revealing an ever-changing sky pattern through its revolving umbrella-structures, acknowledging one primary tenet of Eastern wisdom, that "change is the only constant of reality."[39] Paying homage to the host nation, the architects constructed a kinetic "room" over the central performance stage, where five multi-colored spinners reminiscent of Japanese paper umbrellas revolved slowly and noiselessly to create kaleidoscopic patterns high in the sky.[40] **FIGS 20–24**

By comparison, Canada's presence at subsequent fairs has been muted. For Expo 92 in Seville, a competition jury selected architect Bing Thom (1940–2016). Thom's pavilion—a

24 opposite
Expo 70 Canada Pavilion, Osaka, Japan. Erickson/ Massey Architects, 1970.

25 right
Expo 92 Canada Pavilion, exterior view, Seville, Spain. Bing Thom Architects, 1990.

rectangular box on a raised colonnade, wrapped in a decorative cladding of Canadian zinc and aluminum evocative of a Spanish tile theme—was criticized for its inhibited design, trite imagery, and absence of technical innovation. The pavilion is essentially a conventional warehouse building with applied symbols, or a "decorated shed" with an oversized government-issued logo dominating the exterior. The interior relies upon the romantic imagery of a waterfall cascading into a pool, providing respite to visitors from the hot summer sun. In the words of a visitor, the design did no more than convey "an old image of hewer of wood and drawer of water, rather than a sophisticated technically adept and socially concerned country."[41] **FIG 25**

The shift from architectural innovation to spectacle is evident at Vancouver's Expo 86. Taking to heart the lessons learned from Expo 67, where the site became redundant after the fair, planners conceived of Expo 86 as a catalyst for the redevelopment of industrial lands in Vancouver's False Creek district. The exhibition focal point was Expo Centre, a sphere containing an OMNIMAX theater set upon a faceted rotunda, along with exhibition space designed by Bruno Freschi (1937–), the chief architect-planner for the exhibition; it continues to be in use today as Vancouver's Science World.

The major constructions by the federal and provincial governments at Expo 86—a public plaza and a waterfront terminal—were planned to remain long after closing day, as were other buildings. Canada Place (1985), by a joint venture of Downs/Archambault Architects + Planners, Musson Cattell and Partners (later Musson Cattell Mackey Partnership), and Zeidler Roberts Partnership, was designed as a multiuse building on Burrard Inlet, over half a mile (one kilometre) from the main site. Housing a cruise ship terminal, hotel, convention center, and offices, the complex is a remarkable legacy. Inspired by a marine theme, the shape suggests a "prow thrusting into Burrard Inlet, a roofline of sails catching the wind and the superstructure of an ocean liner"[42] and remains a distinctive feature on the Vancouver skyline. **FIG 26**

While critics despaired that Expo 86 was nothing more than a "misconceived midway" and dismissed it for the lack of public spaces and celebratory gathering places within the Expo 86 grounds,[43] the CN (Canadian National) pavilion by Peter Cardew Architect, designed to showcase the Canadian National Railways, stands out. Reminiscent of the British

26 opposite
Canada Place, Expo 86,
bird's-eye view, Vancouver,
British Columbia. Joint
venture of Downs/
Archambault, Musson
Cattell and Partners,
and Zeidler Roberts
Partnership, 1985.

27 above
Canadian National (CN)
pavilion, Expo 86, model,
Vancouver, British
Columbia. Peter Cardew
Architect, 1986.

28 right
Canadian National (CN)
pavilion, Expo 86, bird's-
eye view of exhibition
plaza.

29
Model, Olympic Stadium
and velodrome for 1976
Olympic Games, Montreal,
Quebec. André Daoust
(chief architect) with Roger
Taillebert (consulting
architect), 1973.

architect Cedric Price's unrealized design for Fun Palace (1964), the pavilion is an experiment in socially interactive architecture.[44] A cylindrical building containing a theater sits on a large platform, roofed by an open metal space frame. The uncluttered stage created an austere but simple space amid the exhibition's hubbub and permitted a variety of public activities to occur.[45] **FIGS 27–28**

Canada and the World: Olympic Games

Since 1967, Canadian cities have sponsored international sporting events that reflect the ambitions of the host cities and send out messages of urbanity, sophistication, and global engagement. Hosting international sporting events is a matter of national pride, with governments at every level having a stake in the outcomes, as television screens feature views of the cities and sports venues between athletic competitions. The architecture created for these events often represents feats of engineering and logistics as much as architectural achievement, although sometimes this results in facilities with questionable long-term usefulness. Such is the case with Montreal's 1976 Summer Olympics facilities.[46] These considerations became a major factor in the planning for subsequent international sporting events.

When Montreal won the bid to host the 1976 Summer Olympic Games, the city's mayor turned to French architect Robert Taillibert (1926–), whose athletic facilities in France— the Chamonix Sports Centre, Deauville Swimming Pool, and the Parc des Princes in Paris —he admired. As consulting architect, Taillibert worked with chief architect, Quebecer André Daoust, to execute the main sports facilities for Montreal's games.[47] **FIG 29**

The Olympic Stadium is an impressive engineering accomplishment: a huge elliptical bowl married to a triangular-base, from which rises a fifty-story tower leaning almost 175 feet (53.5 meters) over the stadium field. It contains halls for sporting competitions, a swimming pool, and a diving hall. The rear leg of the tower was anchored deep into bedrock to offset the cantilever forces; guide cables strung from the top of the mast hold 180,000

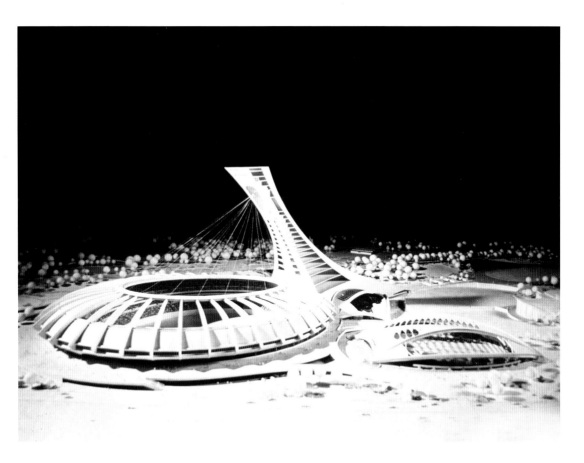

square feet (16,730 square meters) of retractable fabric designed to cover the stadium's elliptical opening. Adjacent, the velodrome's form is reminiscent of a "giant Paleozoic trilobite coming to rest at the bottom of the sea."[48] The roof of prefabricated concrete arches was assembled in a manner similar to that used in constructing Gothic cathedrals: the arches were lifted off temporary scaffolding and simultaneously lowered onto four supporting concrete abutments, providing a 400-foot-span (122 meters) over the cycling track. **FIG 30**

The spectacular architecture of Montreal's 1976 Olympic facilities received mixed reviews. The stadium was barely ready in time for the games. The retractable roof never functioned properly, and a fixed roof finally replaced it in 1998.[49] Montreal's debt of $1.6 billion took thirty years to retire. In 1989, the velodrome was converted to the Biôdome, a museum of ecology, which continues to be a major attraction today. The lessons from Montreal's 1976 Olympics—heroic architecture, massive cost overruns, huge debts, and facilities for which the city struggled to find new uses—were not lost on other Canadian cities hosting international sporting events in the decades that followed.

For the Winter Olympic Games in Calgary (1988) and Vancouver (2010), organizers planned smaller-scale facilities that would find extensive after-game use. New infrastructures were folded into large-scale, longer-term urban development strategies. Both games also

30 opposite
Velodrome, interior, 1976
Olympic Games, Montreal,
Quebec. André Daoust
(chief architect) with Roger
Taillebert (consulting
architect), 1973.

31 above
Richmond Olympic Oval,
2010 Olympic Games,
interior, Richmond, British
Columbia. Cannon Design,
2008.

developed partnerships with local institutions, dovetailing Olympic facilities with needed new developments. Calgary constructed a new arena, the Saddledome (Graham-McCourt Architects), to accommodate hockey and figure skating. Its Olympic Oval for indoor speed skating, by the same architects, was constructed to also house the University of Calgary's expanded athletics program.

Vancouver's 2010 Winter Olympics continued this modest-is-better theme. The organizers used Public Private Partnerships (P3s) for financing and constructing its facilities, and leveraged the games to support development in new urban areas and the revitalization of obsolete industrial zones. One purpose-built facility—the Richmond Olympic Oval (Cannon Design) for speed skating—stands out as a significant legacy of Vancouver's games. The soaring space of the Oval is roofed by a gull-wing-shaped form, whose gentle and undulating curvature is supported by steel and glulam composite arches and breaks the monotony of the structure. The use of pine for the underside of the roof is distinctive and symbolic of this timber-rich province. **FIG 31**

Infrastructures: Shaping the Future, Valorizing the Past

The vastness of Canada is daunting. Comprehending the space of the nation and coming to terms with its extent—both in space and time—has been a driving force in shaping Canadian identity. Architecture has played a role, physically and notionally, in bringing the nation together. Infrastructure buildings are significant points on the Canadian landscape and represent Canada at the national level, providing vital services and a continuity only assured by a federal system of government.

Canada's Centennial mixed nostalgic reminiscences with utopian aspirations, as the 1967 Confederation Train—a diesel locomotive with specially designed coach cars loaned by the Canadian National Railway, and which were filled with exhibits showcasing Canadian history and culture[50]—crossed the country, reminding Canadians of the vital role played by the railway in settlement and unification.[51] As the Centennial year unfolded,

Ottawa's new train station, by John B. Parkin Associates (1966), symbolized this important instrument of national unity.

The symbolism of the portal is central to Union Station's architectural idea. With a clear functional order and strong structural statement, Ottawa's modern station marked a gateway into a new urban world. The cruciform plan is dominated by a hovering 33-foot-high roof, spanning an area 150 by 300 feet (10 meters high, 46 by 91.5 meters). The roof is composed of an exposed two-way steel truss and supported by pin connections on eight massive concrete columns. A sumptuous circular ramp descends to connect the concourse to station platforms. The overscaled volume of space and the monumental presence of the object speak to the past grandeur of railway stations in a clearly modern language. **FIGS 32–33**

The new train station was the last of its kind, soon to be eclipsed by the air terminal. Canada's major airports include international gateways at Toronto and Montreal. Building airports has been a major focus of Canada's national infrastructure, and both metropolitan airports and those in the resource-rich hinterlands have undergone significant renewal in the past fifty years.

The form and program of the modern Canadian airport has evolved. Toronto's Aero-quay One (John B. Parkin, 1964, demolished 2004) was described as the "apogee of a

particular model of airport design."[52] Aeroquay One, like Ottawa's Union Station, was envisaged as a singular object in the landscape: sculptural and monumental, with its mechanical workings buried below grade. **FIG 34** The model idealizes the terminal as a beacon and gateway. However, the design, which funneled passengers through a single portal, became unworkable as increased passenger traffic demanded greater building porosity to effect efficient flows.

Additional terminals designed for Toronto (YYZ) and for Montreal's Mirabel airport (YMX)[53] adopted the new model of a linear structure with multiple entry points. To address the congestion at Toronto's Aeroquay One, Terminal 2 was opened in 1972 and, as traffic grew, Trillium Terminal Three (Scott Associates Architects with Bregman + Hamann Architects) opened in 1991.[54] **FIG 35** Soon, Aeroquay One was deemed obsolete and demolished. A new Terminal One opened in 2004 (Skidmore, Owings and Merrill, Arup, Adamson Associates, and Moshe Safdie and Associates). In a carefully designed sequence of light-filled spaces, the new Terminal One presents passengers with the soaring space of a check-in lobby, dominated by a massive set of clear-span trusses, allowing the ceiling to soar unimpeded above the room. The extensive expenditure for Terminal One ($3.2 billion for the first phase) was promoted as a "cultural investment," heralding Toronto's continuing ambitions to be Canada's premier gateway.[55]

In Montreal, different events unfolded. A new airport, Montréal–Mirabel International Airport (YMX), designed by Papineau, Gérin-Lajoie, LeBlanc, Edwards, later PGL Architects, was built 34 miles (55 kilometers) north of the city. The terminal—a sleek 330-foot-deep by 1,160-foot-long (100.5-meter-deep by 353.5-meter-long) glazed box of understated elegance—opened in 1975 (demolished 2016). **FIG 36** As an object building, Mirabel, like the terminal at Dulles International Airport outside Washington, DC, relied upon mobile lounges to move passengers between terminal and airplane. Mirabel functioned as a passenger terminal for twenty-two years, but in 1997, all Montreal-destined passenger flights returned to Montréal–Pierre Elliott Trudeau International Airport or Montréal–Trudeau, formerly known as Montréal–Dorval International Airport (YUL), much closer to Montreal's core, facilitating efficient transfers between international and domestic flights.

As Toronto and Montreal competed to build more efficient terminals, regional centers created new gateways—particularly in the north, as the expansion of air travel followed the growth of Canadian resource exploitation. One new airport in British Columbia is exemplary, responding to local community and landscape conditions as well as participating in the global network of air travel. The expansion of Prince George Airport (YXS) (McFarlane Green Biggar Architecture + Design Inc., 2005) was prompted by a national program to upgrade Canadian airports. The design integrates the existing airport building into a new facility through the use of its material palette, constructing a narrative that enfolds past and present. Wood is the dominant structural material, reflective of the town's history in logging and the community's vision for its future. The overall composition of materials and the transparent character of the building's enclosure, linking interior with exterior, seeks to enhance the experience of air travel and connection to place.[56] **FIG 37**

Conclusion

The range of institutional architecture presented is indicative of the search to symbolize the contemporary ambitions of a modern nation. Place, context, and landscape have shaped

36
Mirabel Airport, Rendering of
Departures Hall, Mirabel, Quebec.
Papineau, Gérin-Lajoie, LeBlanc,
Edwards, later PGL Architects, 1975.

AEROGARE DU NOUVEL AEROPO

NEW MONTREAL INTERNATIONA

PAPINEAU GERIN-LAJOIE LEBLANC EDWARDS ARCHITECTES

INTERNATIONAL DE MONTREAL
AIRPORT TERMINAL BUILDING

37
Prince George Airport,
exterior view, Prince
George, British Columbia.
McFarlane Green Biggar
Architecture + Design,
2003.

the architectural imagination. New urban places have been created. Materials evoking local histories, traditions, and industries evoke the *genius loci*. Government patronage has commissioned these new buildings, often turning to architectural competitions to engage the profession and achieve progressive design outcomes. Museums and libraries in the national capital, city halls across Canada, embassies and pavilions representing Canada on the world stage, sport facilities for international competitions, and terminal gateways across the country all share in the legacy of valorizing place, creating monuments and spaces that respond to the Canadian environment. These buildings speak to a culture of openness, optimism, and progressive ambition. Through these many projects, architecture has reshaped the ways Canadians view themselves, their heritage, and their identity.

The evolution of architectural procurement has shifted the role played by the architect in the conception and development of projects. The impetus behind the Massey Commission's admonition that all public buildings be commissioned by competition was rooted in a belief in the intrinsic value of good design and its ability to foster a heightened awareness of architecture as central to a national culture. But with the rise of the P3 process, this belief has been overtaken by explicit measures of project cost and performance. Fears of cost overruns, over-budget projects, and late project delivery have led to shifts in the role of the architect from designer to project manager. In some instances, mediocrity upstages excellence, challenging the imperative of design excellence above all else. Nonetheless, it is heartening to see recent public institutions of architectural delight and design innovation being built by enlightened patrons at all levels of government across Canada.

3

Campus Architecture: The Radical Medium of Learning

Lisa Landrum

In 1957, Canadian media theorist and University of Toronto English professor Marshall McLuhan (1911–80) predicted mass media would radically transform learning environments, having already "cracked the very walls of the classroom."[1] In a related 1967 article on the future of education, McLuhan foresaw "free-roving students" interacting within media-rich settings, reveling in the realization that "our place of learning is the world itself, the entire planet we live on."[2]

However prescient of twenty-first-century global connectivity, McLuhan's prediction of "classrooms without walls" did not come to fruition. In the decade spanning his predictions, McLuhan's own institution, the University of Toronto, expanded its downtown campus by 33 acres (13.35 hectares); constructed a plethora of new classrooms, labs, and dorms; and initiated construction of a mammoth fourteen-story library nicknamed Fort Book. **FIG 1** It also spawned two suburban satellite campuses (Scarborough and Mississauga) and a new autonomous university (York). Meanwhile, the province of Ontario established additional universities to serve the region. Throughout the 1960s, post-secondary institutions across Canada—from Moncton to Victoria—were created, expanded, and amalgamated to accommodate an influx of baby boomers eager to participate in government-supported higher education. The trend was global.[3]

In an address to architects at the 1964 Banff Session dedicated to campus architecture, Thomas Howarth (1914–2000), then director of the University of Toronto's School of Architecture and architect-planner of Laurentian's new campus in Sudbury, offered this appraisal of the boom: "Almost overnight the Canadian university has become a major patron of the architectural profession....It is doubtful whether any field of architectural endeavor in Canada has had or will have such a profound effect upon our profession."[4]

Much as the 1960s' enthusiasm for "classrooms without walls" ironically precipitated a surge in campus architecture, fifty years later the craze for online education coincides with a barrage of university building initiatives. Bolstered by billions in provincial and federal stimulus programs, Canadian universities from coast to coast are implementing ambitious master plans, building specialized research facilities, and devising interdisciplinary innovation hubs to keep pace with technological changes and market demands.

Such ambitions are fraught with paradox, today as in the 1960s. On the one hand, campus architecture is entangled with politics, profit, and projections of progress. On the other hand, campus architecture remains desirably intertwined with the perennial role of universities as havens of research and repose, places of "leisure"—the original meaning of the Greek word *scholé*, the root of *school*—where humanity's greatest potential is liberated, cultivated, and sustained. At their best, university settings are productive laboratories of peace and democracy, providing dignified and inspiring places to freely exercise the individual and collective capabilities of imagination, experimentation, interpretation, and dissent. More concretely, campuses are living paradigms for cities, exemplifying our best urban ecologies by planning for dense cultural diversity; by integrating mixed-use development with thriving natural landscapes; by responsibly adapting buildings that have accrued over time; by implementing sustainable technologies; and by creating transit-accessible and pedestrian-friendly environments conducive to lingering, meandering, and face-to-face contact. Because of all this, universities are, as Michael Sorkin asserts, "the closest we come to quotidian utopia."[5]

This chapter centers on four exemplary campus designs of the 1960s that have remained influential touchstones throughout the decades to follow: Ron Thom's Massey College

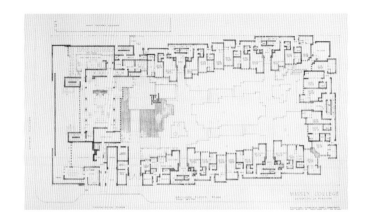

2 left
Massey College, University of Toronto. First-floor plan, 1961. Thompson, Berwick & Pratt, architects, with Ron Thom, designer.

3 opposite
Massey College, University of Toronto, view of courtyard looking south toward clock tower and dining hall.

(1960–1963) and Trent University (1963–1969); John Andrew's Scarborough College (1963–1965); and Arthur Erickson and Geoffrey Massey's Simon Fraser University (1963–1965). These projects catapulted Canadian campus architecture onto the international stage. More importantly, they realized academic ideals, offering instructive hypotheses on how built environments can foster not simply the production of knowledge, but also the more foundational skills of learning and living, reasoning and wondering. Learning at these universities was recognized as taking place not only in traditional classrooms, but also in settings beyond and between them. Such open and interstitial spaces served as informal forums for interdisciplinary discourse, serendipitous encounter, unscripted speculation, political activism, and edifying play.

In spite of their somewhat sequestered or suburban conditions, Massey, Trent, Scarborough, and Simon Fraser (SFU) each embody a radical urbanity, enabling a full spectrum of social exchange while being simultaneously apart from and involved in society. This double orientation, as Northrop Frye (1912–1991) argued, is not a retreat from reality, but a more intense encounter with reality—"the reality that lies behind the mirage of social trends."[6] Interpreting recent university architecture in relation to these exemplary 1960s campuses reveals that well-designed academic environments remain the education industry's most constructive social media.

Sanctuary in Community:
Ron Thom's Massey College

Massey College was the first graduate student residence in Canada. It was founded by the Massey Foundation at the instigation of the Right Honourable Vincent Massey (1887–1967), a Canadian-born Oxford-educated diplomat and patron of the arts, who served as chair of the influential Royal Commission on National Development in the Arts, Letters, and Sciences (1949–1951) and as governor general of Canada (1952–1959) [see pages 20–22]. In 1960, Massey invited four Canadian architects to participate in a limited design competition: John C. Parkin (1922–1988), Ron Thom (1923–1986), Arthur Erickson (1924–2009),

and Carmen Corneil (1933–). Massey himself formulated the evocative brief addressing the desired architecture for Massey College: "It should, in its form, reflect the life which will go on inside it, and should possess certain qualities—dignity, grace, beauty and warmth.... [It should become] a home for a community of scholars whose life will have intimacy but at the same time, academic dignity."[7]

Ron Thom, then lead designer with Vancouver's Thompson Berwick & Pratt, won the commission. As stipulated, Thom designed a closed quadrangle after the Oxford-Cambridge model. He created a nearly windowless surround of staggered brick walls facing busy streets and lanes, while arranging rooms for sixty-eight graduate students and fifteen senior fellows around a leafy garden, reflecting pool, and bell tower. He capped the quad's southern end with an impressive upper dining hall, commons lounge, library, master's house, porter's lodge, and ornate gate. **FIGS 2–5**

Embodying monastic order, Thom enlivened the scheme with what he called "studied diversity."[8] Uniquely configured rooms are stacked in three-story groupings, united by a shared stairway and direct entry from the quad. These groupings, or "houses," eliminate the need for continuous internal corridors while cultivating smaller social units within the larger community. Individual rooms step slightly in and out in plan, and up and

down in elevation, modulating privacy and light for sleep and study while generating syncopated harmonies in the garden-facing facades. Corresponding rhythms appear on the street.

Thom's "studied diversity" also develops through materials: wood, copper, limestone, and iron-spot brick each possess unique qualities and the propensity to change with age. Materials are also attuned to domestic and ceremonial activities: brick envelops private spaces; limestone—embellished with geometric finials and bas-reliefs—adorns social thresholds and the formal dining hall clerestory. Robertson Davies (1913–1995), Canadian novelist and first master of Massey College, worked with Thom to adjust details to the intimacy and dignity of college life, balancing academic formalities with domestic comforts and inspiring charm. Davies, like Massey, sought an edifying reciprocity of decor and decorum. As he explained, "A building is unquestionably an influence on the life we live in it, and never more so than when we are young."[9]

For Thom, diversity in the academic context was as much about freedom as enculturation. Architectural diversity within the unity of the campus reflected varied individual ambitions, balanced by common purpose and the mutual support of collegial living and learning. In the architect's words: "It represents, to the student within, a condensed piece of the world that must accommodate all his changing moods and attitudes…[T]he diversity of academic relationships undertaken within this building must be complemented by a corresponding diversity of space and interior paraphernalia." In the same text announcing his winning design, Thom further promised Massey College would be "capable of unfolding itself by degrees—probably never completely."[10] This openness to endless elaboration is characteristic of scholarly topics, inquisitive students, and any insatiably curious individual.

Thom himself had no direct experience of college life. He did not attend university, but became an architect by apprenticeship and self-challenging initiatives involving dialogue, music, and painting. Having designed more than forty houses prior to Massey College, Thom was also an astute listener.[11] Capable of interpreting client desires and responding to criticisms, he developed a nuanced sensitivity for the collegiate life Massey advocated while

inflecting his design with an eclecticism that students of diverse inclinations find engaging to this day.

Thom's design had its critics. Hardened modernists were hostile to its medieval model, neo-Gothic motifs, and stylistic quotations of Frank Lloyd Wright. Yet, as Brigitte Shim argues, "Massey College is now part of a broader definition of modernism that encompasses not only new materials and structural innovation but their correlative values: sensitivity to its urban context, exemplary craftsmanship and architectural invention."[12] Invention within tradition has remained the guiding principle in a series of sensitive alterations by Shim-Sutcliffe Architects, who, since the 1990s, have been stewards of the facility and the life it fosters.

Student housing continues to rise on Canadian campuses. While design briefs today can read more like generic real estate brochures than eloquent manifestos for the careful integration of learning and life, many projects have adapted Massey College's traditional collegial forms. On a larger scale, Macy DuBois (1929–2007), of Fairfield & DuBois, employed a sinuous courtyard within a perimeter block for the University of Toronto's New College (1969). The University of Toronto's Graduate House (2000), by Thom Mayne of Morphosis and Stephen Teeple, is configured, like Massey College, as a traditional quadrangle. **FIG 6** However, its enormous cantilevered cornice and deconstructive cladding emphasize the building's role as an iconic gateway more than an intimate incubator of collegial life.

Erindale Hall, designed by Baird Sampson Neuert Architects for the University of Toronto's Mississauga campus (2003), creates a more organically linear configuration of collegiality, with clusters of housing forming a "social spine" set in relation to the undulating landscape. The University of Toronto's recent housing initiative takes a more diversified approach by proposing to integrate fifty laneway houses and infill residences for students, faculty, and community into the Huron-Sussex neighborhood northwest of the Robarts Library. Instead of clearing city blocks, as in the 1960s, this infill scheme will interweave low- to mid-rise housing, community yards, and green pedestrian lanes within the existing urban fabric. This approach takes the connective intricacy of an urban village more than the cloistered intimacy of a collegial quadrangle as its model for academic community. Though the forms differ, the architectural and pedagogical aims are consistent: both cultivate diversified social units by accommodating individuality within a complex community; and both balance openness with concentration, outward engagement with inner calm.

Organic Urbanity:
Ron Thom's Trent University

Fresh with his success at the University of Toronto, Ron Thom was appointed master planner of Trent University in June 1963 by founding president Thomas Symons (1929–). Former dean at Toronto's Devonshire House, Symons knew Massey College well. Like Vincent Massey, Symons endorsed collegiate models of university architecture: forming smaller communities within the larger institution; fusing living and learning; fostering interdisciplinary exchange; and facilitating close-knit relationships and interaction between teachers and students, both formally and informally. Symons valued community but argued that "education is, inescapably, an individual experience—individual to each student, to each teacher, and to every scholar who may come to it."[13] He understood how physical

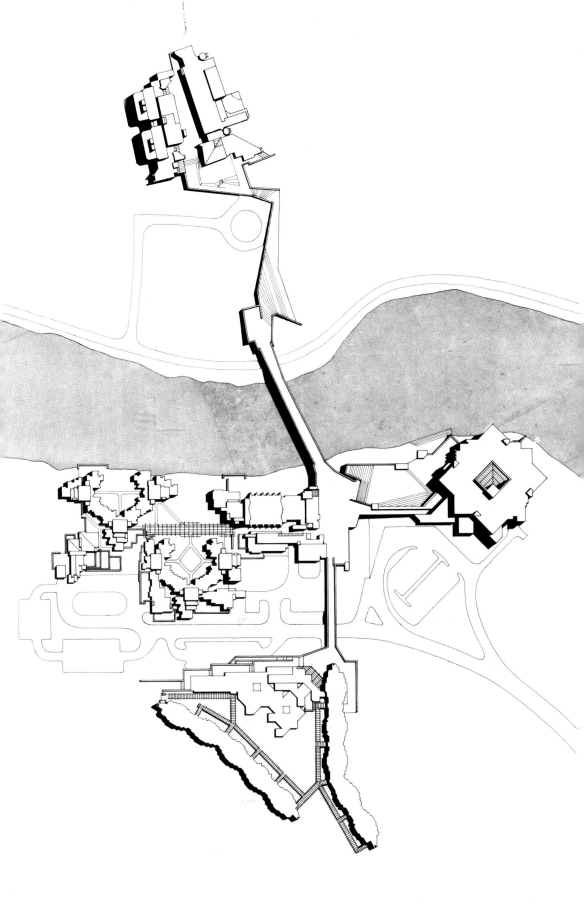

7 opposite
Trent master plan.
R. J. Thom & Associates /
Thompson, Berwick &
Pratt, 1967.

8 above
Champlain College,
Trent University, view
from the Otonabee River,
Peterborough, Ontario.
R. J. Thom & Associates /
Thompson, Berwick &
Pratt, 1967.

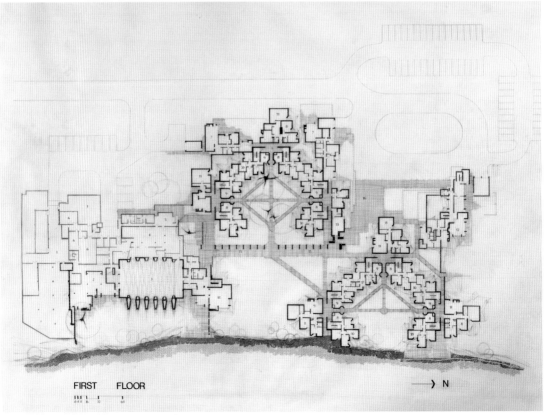

FIRST FLOOR

⟶ N

environments could encourage individual aspirations while reinforcing a common ground of shared pursuits. As the 1964 design brief stated: "We are not committed to any particular style of buildings, but only to a certain spirit.… It is a spirit of appropriateness and beauty, which gives the kind of aesthetic stimulation and sense of repose which encourages scholarly application." Together with diversity, this "unity of the university's purpose should be stated in its architecture."[14]

In contrast to the downtown site of Massey College, Trent occupies over 1,500 acres (607 hectares) of lush land on either side of the Otonabee River just outside of Peterborough, 80 miles (130 kilometers) northeast of Toronto. To achieve a mood of academic intensity, Thom proposed a relatively dense concentration of academic spaces, placing compact urban clusters within the expansive landscape: a constellation of fourteen colleges circumscribing the river, linked by two pedestrian bridges. Three social hubs—a library with adjoining square, a science complex, and a commercial village with theater and field house—were to provide triangulated order while meandering laneways, covered walks, grassy yards, paved courts, and stairs connected all.

Thom realized only a small yet distinctive part of this master plan, constructing two colleges (Champlain College and Lady Eaton College), the Chemistry Building, Reginald Faryon Bridge, and the Bata Library. **FIG 7** The composed irregularity of Champlain College exemplifies Thom's vision for Trent as a whole. **FIGS 8–11** Mixing natural, social, and academic life, the college accommodates two hundred private rooms, grouped (like at Massey) around stairways and courtyards. It also includes offices doubling as tutorial spaces, seminar rooms, lounges, a squash court, and a clock tower, and is anchored by a geometrically exuberant dining hall. The configuration interweaves artifice with nature, stimulation with repose, regimen with recreation. Faceted forms frame tranquil yards opening onto riverside diversions. Limestone, concrete, cedar, and copper meet in meticulous details but remain unfinished, to be embellished by weathering. Rubble aggregate walls emulate the irregular, glacier-carved terrain of the surrounding landscape; Thom designed them with interpretive precision, working with engineer Roland Bergmann of Morden Yolles to adapt a technique used by Eero Saarinen at Yale University's Morse and Ezra Stiles Colleges (1961).[15] Inside,

12 above
**Environmental Sciences
Centre, Trent University,
view from the Otonabee
River with the Reginald
Fayon Bridge in the
foreground, Peterborough,
Ontario. Henriquez &
Partners with Laszlo
Nemeth Associates, 1991.**

13 opposite
**Chemical Sciences
Building, Trent University,
Peterborough, Ontario.
Teeple Architects with
Shore Tilbe Irwin &
Partners, 2004.**

curvilinear furnishings (by Bruno Mathsson, Eero Saarinen, Alvar Aalto, Arne Jacobsen, and others) personalize the carefully carefree atmosphere.

Thom's 1964 design statement pledged: "Ultimately, the planning should produce harmony without rigidity."[16] Upon completion of phase one in 1969, Arthur Erickson commended "the harmony of the whole composition."[17] In truth, harmony proved difficult to achieve. In 1967, Trent hastily erected a temporary biology building, which remained for twenty years. The following year, an incongruous air-supported bubble was erected over the tennis courts. In 1973, Macy Dubois's Otonabee College more permanently disrupted the spirit of the place with its rigid linearity, industrial materials, and compartmentalized building programs. Gzowski College (2005) was labeled a "yellow misfit."[18]

Intervening additions were more sympathetic. The Environmental Sciences Centre by Richard Henriquez (1941–) with Laszlo Nemeth Associates (1991), and the Chemical Sciences Building by Teeple Architects with Shore Tilbe Irwin & Partners (2004) reflected the existing dense organic planning and continued the social web of interconnected paths, courts, and lawns. **FIGS 12–13** These science complexes echo Thom's compositional gestures and earthy materials while introducing narrative and topographical peculiarities that reinterpret the lore and allure of the site. More recent additions include the peripheral Community Sport and Recreation Centre by Perkins+Will (2010), and the Childcare Centre (1993) and Student Centre (2017), both by Teeple. Exemplary for craftsmanship and environmental stewardship, these projects eschew the peripatetic intertwining of learning and living for more segregated functions and easy vehicular access. The Trent Research and Innovation Park, currently in development beyond the limits of campus, somewhat abandons the ethos of close teacher-student contact. Yet if developed along the lines of Waterloo's Perimeter Institute for Theoretical Physics (2004), by Saucier + Perrotte architectes [see pages 385–388], such expansion may still have the potential to maintain the quantum urbanity necessary for critically advancing meaningful research.

While Trent and Peterborough struggle with sprawl, urban campuses are embracing holistic densification. Ryerson University, landlocked near Toronto's thriving Dundas Square, is a case in point. Pursuing intensification, pedestrianization, and design excellence, Ryerson

14 opposite
Student Learning Centre, Ryerson University, aerial view, Toronto, Ontario. Snøhetta with Zeidler Partnership Architects, 2015.

15 right
Image Centre and School of Image Arts, Ryerson University, Toronto, Ontario. Diamond Schmitt Architects, 2012

has become an ideal city builder, manifesting several award-winning infill and adaptive reuse projects. The 2015 Student Learning Centre by Snøhetta and Zeidler Partnership Architects provides an animated gateway and spectacular retreat for concentrated yet gregarious study. **FIG 14** The 2012 rejuvenation of Maple Leaf Gardens has won favor with heritage groups, students, and locals alike. Turner Fleischer, BBB, and ERA Architects preserved the 1931 exterior while transforming its cavernous hockey arena into the multi-purpose Mattamy Athletic Centre, and making room for a generous urban grocery in partnership with Loblaw Companies. Ryerson's initiatives to pedestrianize laneways (2016) and the student-led closure of Gould Street to traffic (2012) are further enlivening interstitial environments, as are the animated facades and edges of Diamond Schmitt's Ryerson Image Centre and School of Image Arts (2012). **FIG 15** Even the green roof/urban farm atop Moriyama & Teshima's George Vari Engineering and Computing Centre (2004) is feeding civic imagination.

The University of Ottawa, at the heart of the nation's capital for over 150 years, is similarly pursuing a compact, car-free core with sustainably integrated urban and natural edges. Its award-winning 2015 master plan articulates comprehensively what IKOY's 2002 School of Information Technology and Engineering has demonstrated on a compact segment of the campus. **FIG 16** Deftly configured on a tight triangle, IKOY's building negotiates a dedicated bus roadway and traffic intersection while optimizing canal-side views and pedestrian links. Architect Ron Keenberg employed passive-solar features and colorfully exposed structural, mechanical, and electrical systems, making the building itself a heuristic device. Such strategies were previously employed by IKOY in designs for the University of Waterloo's William Davis Computer Research Centre (1988) and the University of Manitoba's Earth Science Building (1986).

Montreal's urban situation is also spurring campus densification. Concordia University has become an interconnected vertical campus promoting cross-disciplinary scholarship while cultivating vibrant urban exchange at grade. Le Quartier Concordia is notably comprised of KPMB's Engineering, Computer Science and Visual Arts Integrated Complex (2005) and the John Molson School of Business (2009). At McGill University, the Schulich

16 left
School of Information
Technology and Engineering,
University of Ottawa, canal-
side view, Ottawa, Ontario.
IKOY Architects, 2002.

17 right
Schulich School of Music /
Elizabeth Wirth Music
Building, McGill University,
view from Sherbrooke Street,
Montreal, Quebec. Saucier +
Perrotte architectes, 2005.

18 opposite
Pavillon de Design,
Université du Québec à
Montréal, Montreal,
Quebec. Dan Hanganu
architectes, 1995.

School of Music (2005), by Saucier + Perrotte architectes with Menkès Shooner Dagenais, interprets its urban geography with strong vertical massing and subtle lateral shifts. **FIG 17**

At the Université du Québec à Montréal (UQÀM), Dan Hanganu's 1995 Pavillon de Design invigorates an edgy L-shaped lot with a quiet park-side gallery and bold facades doubling as projection venues. **FIG 18** Nearby, the Pierre Dansereau Science Complex (2005) interweaves new and refurbished buildings, green courts, and crisscrossing paths across two city blocks. These projects continue the urban integration of UQÀM's original Judith-Jasmin Pavilion (1979) by Dimitri Dimakopoulos (1929–1995) of ARCOP with Jodoin Lamarre Pratte et associés. Residing above the juncture of metro lines, at the nexus of commercial strips, and around the neo-Gothic steeple and transept of St. Jacques Church, this richly anachronistic pavilion, with its interior agora and intimate south garden, combines stimulation and repose in a spirit akin to Trent. Though larger in scale and contextually different, these urban campuses pursue a hybrid propinquity of civic immersion and collegial retreat.

Streetscapes and Landscapes:
University of Toronto's Scarborough College

The massive science and humanities wings of the University of Toronto's Scarborough campus initially appear as the antitheses of collegiate intimacy and traditional expectations for university environments. As Witold Rybczynski reflected, "This was clearly no ivory tower; the iconic vertical feature was not a spire or a belfry but the chimney of the heating plant....My chief impression of this building was of a no-nonsense work of engineering, like a dam or a highway overpass: scaleless, implacable, mute."[19] Some critics applauded these "concrete cliffs" as progressive manifestations of new brutalism and megastructure [see pages 157–160]. Students were skeptical. But they were less concerned with stylistic tags than with the alienating effects of the proposed closed-circuit televised lectures. When the inaugural 1965 ceremonies featured four university administrators addressing the student body as talking heads on screens, the quick-witted editor of the student newspaper,

Varsity, compared their ruse to the dehumanizing tactics used in George Orwell's *Nineteen Eighty-Four*.[20] TV teaching was ultimately abandoned.

In retrospect, Scarborough's futuristic hype and shock-and-awe first impressions obscured the designers' subtler ecological and urbanistic aims. Decades before *sustainability* became a buzzword, the University of Toronto enabled a sustainable approach to its first satellite campus by involving an interdisciplinary team: landscape architect Michael Hough (1928–2013), planner Michael Hugo-Brunt, architect John Andrews (1933–), and geographer-climatologist F. B. Watts. In just six summer weeks in 1963, these professor-practitioners produced a master plan for Scarborough's 202-acre (82-hectare) site. It was not sudden inspiration, as Andrews recalled, but "a common sense synthesis to a number of extreme and conventional conditions."[21] **FIGS 19–20** The single structure provided a climate-controlled environment for 1,500 students, with interior streets and bunker-like classrooms mitigating harsh winter winds and drifting snow. Its meandering form followed the irregular north ridge of the wooded Highland Creek ravine, dodging century-old beech trees while strategically stabilizing a vulnerable landscape. Topographic difficulties were turned to advantage: an area of weak soil unsuitable for building became a level garden; grade changes necessitating multilevel entrances became social junctures.

As the building design developed, Andrews attuned south-facing windows to solar angles and scholarly life, generating some of the most dramatic building sections in the canon of Canadian architecture. He stepped back the science labs to create skylights and integrated mechanical systems, and stepped out the humanities offices and seminar rooms to permit summer shading and penetrating winter warmth. Inside, tiered open halls and galleries formed a soaring yet snug atrium over the humanities wing, which intersected the science wing in a spacious skylit hall conceived as an interdisciplinary meeting place and "dignified, formal hub of college activity."[22] Thus, the forbidding exterior yields to socially animated interiors, filled with what Kenneth Frampton called "felicitous light."[23] Oscar Newman similarly commended Andrews's sensitive consideration of human scale and "almost Gothic concern with the mystique of light."[24] Scarborough's many-leveled, multifunctional meander was not a stylized gesture; it was a subtle ecological response and bold experiment in interior urbanism.

Interior streets remained key tropes in Andrews's later projects. For the University of Guelph's vast Housing Complex B (1968), he accommodated 1,800 students by conceiving of the dormitory as a city: clustering individual rooms around shared facilities, then distributing six-story clusters like houses along a network of internal streets and social yards. Andrews redeployed the concept of interior streets in Brock University's DeCew Residence (1969) and others in Australia. The street-like exhibition hall of Gund Hall (1972) for Harvard's Graduate School of Design was a compact translation of Scarborough's pedestrian spine.

By the 1970s, interior streets were revolutionizing Canadian campuses. Beyond responding to the cold climate, interior streets democratized university corridors, accommodating the informal lifestyle of a new generation of youths. The colorful supergraphics of the University of Winnipeg's Centennial Hall (1972) captured the popular vibe. Generous interior streets encouraged participation and interaction, enabling casual encounters, spontaneous public debates, performances, parades, and protests [see pages 175–177]. They also recreated within suburban campuses some of the vibrant urban complexity that was sadly being purged from downtown cores. For instance, while pedestrian life at Winnipeg's central Portage and Main intersection was being driven underground, Number 10 Architectural Group constructed the University of Manitoba's University Centre as an indoor town square, with daylit streets meeting in a multifunctional, multilevel "campo" (1969). Similarly, A. J. Diamond and Barton Myers created the Housing Union Building (HUB) for the University of Alberta's North Campus in Edmonton as a 985-foot-long (300-meter) mixed-use interior street with continuous skylight (1971). An amalgamation of a Parisian arcade and suburban shopping mall, this hybrid street links upper-level flats for one thousand students with dozens of lower-level amenities while providing protected passage to academic buildings [see pages 172–175]. Meanwhile, in Ottawa, Carmen and Elin Corneil (with Jeffrey Stinson) conceived Carleton University's School of Architecture (1972) as an intersection of interior and exterior streets. The design aimed to inaugurate a more urban alternative to campus development, creating city-like density within a site bounded by a pretty perimeter parkway, river, and canal.

Interior streets interconnected with landscaped promenades remain a versatile strategy of integrating academic environments within continuous urban fabrics. At the University of Toronto's downtown campus, the laneway-like atrium of KPMB's Telus Centre for Performance and Learning (2009) links busy Bloor Street to a meandering path called Philosopher's Walk. Trafficked by musicians, audiences, students, and tourists en route to rehearsal and performance venues, this skylit detour between new and old buildings also serves the flaneur with diverting galleries, a café, informal study spaces, and impromptu stages with projecting balconies for soloists and elevated walkways for strolling spectators.

Nearby, KPMB brings the public realm into the Joseph L. Rotman School of Management (2012) via a generous plaza, entry lounge, café, sunken court, sinewy central stair, and creative links with adjacent buildings. KPMB, together with Michael Van Valkenburgh Associates and Urban Strategies, is also re-pedestrianizing and re-landscaping Toronto's King's College Circle as a result of a 2015 design competition. By removing cars and adding webs of landscaped paths, the scheme assimilates the university's ceremonial lawn with daily academic and civic life.

The University of British Columbia has similarly reclaimed its historic core, previously colonized by vehicular access and surface parking. Following its 2009 Public Realm Plan, UBC transformed its Main and East Malls into broad tree-lined promenades with grassy lawns, generous seating, cycling infrastructure, fountains, public art, a well-placed basketball court, and the Indian Residential School History and Dialogue Centre by Formline Architecture (2017) [see pages 150–151]. New buildings along these promenades, including Patkau Architects' Beaty Biodiversity Centre (2009) and Perkins+Will's Earth Sciences Building (2012), have entrance, gallery, and laboratory spaces that are arranged to address the pedestrian pathways, continuing the public landscape in and through academic interiors.

Continuously interconnected public spaces within and between buildings have become defining features of universities. However, the signature interior streets and garden of Scarborough's Science and Humanities complex remain discrete oases on the campus, in spite of several noteworthy additions in recent years. Responding to this relative isolation, and building on its 2011 master plan, the University of Toronto at Scarborough is currently investing in an extended network of exterior streets, walkways, bicycle paths, green spaces, and rapid transit links, to be implemented over the next twenty-five to fifty years. The plan may well help this suburban satellite campus finally break free from the tyranny of automobiles—and further its designers' original vision of ecological urbanism.

Radically Rooted:
Simon Fraser University

Arthur Erickson was convinced that only part of learning takes place in the classroom. Drawing on McLuhan's *Gutenberg Galaxy* (1962), he emphasized the "mosaic of impressions" affecting one's apprehension of the world.[25] Erickson's own education was enhanced by a kaleidoscope of experience: extensive world travel, eclectic reading, and artistic ventures shaped his career as much as dedicated architectural studies at McGill University did. Global outlook, cross-cultural encounter, and interdisciplinary exchange became animating ambitions in his 1963 design for Simon Fraser University (SFU), sited atop Burnaby Mountain, just east of downtown Vancouver. **FIGS 21–23** Prepared as a competition entry with Geoffrey Massey (1924–), SFU is arguably Erickson's most consequential work, elevating his practice from the domestic to the civic sphere [see pages 157–160]. A timely critique and richly anachronistic vision, the design did not compartmentalize learning, but rather expressed what Erickson called the "universality of knowledge" while celebrating "the vital role of the university as both challenger and conserver of human culture."[26]

21
Simon Fraser University,
competition rendering,
Burnaby, British Columbia.
Erickson / Massey
Architects, 1963.

Like Andrews and Thom, Erickson and Massey opposed the epistemological fragmentation and academic specialization implicit in conventional campus architecture, with its piecemeal additions of isolated buildings for autonomous departments. Instead, they proposed four fluidly interconnected settings: an academic quadrangle for teaching and research wrapping a generous garden; a central covered mall for social exchange, flanked by a library, theater, and elevated arcade; a multipurpose student center for sporting and lounging; and student housing with shared courts and gardens for collegial living. A continuous pedestrian concourse—plazas, paths, bridges, and stairs—unified these settings and linked them to a discreet transit hub and parking garage beneath the mall.

Selected for its striking clarity and potential to be built quickly, the winning design was thrust into rapid production, earning the tag "instant university." Erickson and Massey became overall planners and architects of the concourse and mall, while runners-up realized major buildings under their direction: William R. Rhone and Randle Iredale (science complex); Zoltan Kiss (academic quadrangle); Robert Harrison (library); and Duncan McNab and Associates (theater, gym, and pool). Collaborating with engineer Jeffrey Lindsay (1924–84), a former associate of Buckminster Fuller, Erickson designed the mall's iconic tensegrity canopy—a 295-by-131-foot (90-by-40-meter) translucent space frame of

22 opposite
Simon Fraser University,
academic quadrangle,
Burnaby, British Columbia.
Zoltan Kiss, 1965.

23 right
Simon Fraser University,
central mall perspective
rendering, Burnaby, British
Columbia. Erickson /
Massey Architects, 1963.

pressure-treated fir trusses and stainless steel tension rods. Otherwise, rough unfinished concrete was used throughout: economical and expedient, it was also, according to Erickson, "as noble a material as any limestone."[27]

SFU opened to 2,500 students in September 1965. Not since Ernest Cormier's (1885–1980) Université de Montréal (1924–1943) had a Canadian institution of higher learning been realized on such a powerful site. Yet whereas Cormier's iconic tower soared upward from Mont Royal's steep slope, SFU's open spaces spread out horizontally along Burnaby Mountain's east-west ridge. Recalling Frank Lloyd Wright's dictum that a building should be *of* a hill, not *on* it, SFU sought a close rapport between building and setting. Large lecture halls and labs, with terraced roofscapes and sunken gardens, step down with the topography north and south of the quadrangle, receding into the mountain slope. Smaller seminar rooms and offices are gathered into monumental form, only to hover deferentially above and around the generous garden atop the mountain's crest. The configuration creates a calming cadence in the quad's garden, permitting views to higher peaks beyond and binding the intimate campus with its immense terrain.

Such contextual reciprocity is consistent with Erickson and Massey's earlier house designs [see pages 267–270], but the responsive siting of SFU has special significance for a public university. Its low-slung structures framing far-ranging vistas posit learning as a summit, simultaneously rooted and reaching. In Erickson's words, written as Burnaby Mountain was being prepared for construction, "The act of siting betrays to us the tenor of human aspirations."[28] In 1966, Erickson elaborated on the image, casting the mountaintop campus as "an appropriate Acropolis for our time."[29]

Erickson's design intentions were reaching and rooted not only spatially, but also temporally and philosophically: "I wanted to realize at Simon Fraser University what was at the same time most new and most ancient."[30] The Acropolis was one archetype in the "mosaic" of impressions influencing SFU. Among others: the university-mosque of Al-Azhar; the abandoned Mughal city of Fatehpur Sikri; and the terraced rice fields of Japan and Bali (all of which Erickson had visited). SFU's mall and quadrangle were further rooted in transhistorical practices of social assembly and quiet perambulation. The agora-like mall

provides the busy crossroads where individuals meet by happenstance and gather for festivals and rites (such as commencement and convocation). It was the site of mass student meetings and rambunctious rallies in the 1960s.[31] By contrast, the academic quad offers a tranquil space conducive to lingering in contemplative thought. As Erickson explained: "We considered that walking, in the palaestras of classical Greece, the gardens of Buddhist temples, or the cloisters of Christian monasteries, provided both aesthetic pleasure and intellectual stimulation." Indeed, he continued, all open and interstitial space where students stroll, gather, and talk "became the device for creating a meaningful environment for the formative mind."[32]

Erickson and Massey's 1963 design still informs SFU's master plan. A sympathetic highlight is Perkins+Will's 2008 Arts and Social Sciences Complex. Yet dozens of additions, some vehemently opposed by Erickson, have caused a drift from the intended synthesis of effect: most significantly, the 2002 mixed-use real estate development dubbed UniverCity, with a projected population of ten thousand. Commendable for its sustainable urbanism, UniverCity's array of twelve-story condominiums (with twenty-story towers to come) eschews Erickson's premise of low-profile architecture in deferential rapport with its natural setting. By building housing on the highest ground, the new development also inverts the

24
Simon Fraser University,
Central City Campus,
Surrey, British Columbia.
Bing Thom Architects,
2004.

intended eastward ascent: from the dormitories, through athletic and political settings, to the contemplative academic quad as the highest climactic setting. Since Erickson and Massey's housing scheme at the lower west end of Burnaby's ridge was never fully realized, SFU's challenge from the start was the summit's desolation on evenings and weekends. UniverCity addresses this but at the expense of SFU's unique character. A similar loss has been avoided at Erickson and Massey's Lethbridge University (1971), the sublime clarity of which is protected by its proximity to the Oldman River.

Aside from UniverCity, SFU's urbanizing developments include a downtown campus. Begun in the 1980s as a continuing education storefront, SFU at Vancouver's Harbor Centre now occupies a cluster of former department stores, including a portion of Woodward's [see pages 225–229]. In 2001, SFU partnered with UBC, the British Columbia Institute of Technology (BCIT), and Emily Carr University to found the Great Northern Way Campus Trust (GNWCT). This conglomerate is transforming the postindustrial site of False Creek Flats, just east of Vancouver's 2012 Olympic Village, into a vibrant arts and culture district. The 2017 Emily Carr University of Art and Design building by Diamond Schmitt Architects participates in the revitalization of False Creek just as the 1995 Emily Carr building by John and Patricia Patkau did for Granville Island.

Since 2002, SFU has also served students at its Central City location in nearby Surrey. **FIG 24** Accommodated in stunning daylit facilities straddling a once-declining shopping mall, this unconventional campus, designed by Bing Thom (1940–2016) and developed in partnership with the provincial government and an insurance company, is part of a massive rejuvenation of downtown Surrey [see pages 493–497]. This greater civic campus entails a new library, also by Bing Thom, a city hall and public plaza, plus corporate, commercial, and residential towers, all in easy reach of the SkyTrain.

Such initiatives treat university architecture as a catalyst for urban densification and renewal. In many ways, SFU's urbanized campuses, like OCAD's Creative City Campus in Toronto and others, seem to fulfill the postwar architect's vision of the university as a city. Taken too far, however, the total integration of campuses with civic and commercial fabric risks not only the loss of distinction between academic and urban environments, but also the dissolution of relative autonomy and critical distance from fiscal and political forces driving city development. There are, after all, significant differences between going to school and going to work at the office; between the discourse in a seminar room and a boardroom; between the aspirations of an academic quadrangle and an industrial park; between the mandate of a university and the prerogatives of a corporation.

Conclusion

To some extent, Marshall McLuhan was right. Ron Thom, John Andrews, Arthur Erickson, and virtually every architect designing for universities since the 1960s have understood that learning happens outside as much as inside the classroom. Twenty-first-century media has further intensified (and problematized) this fact. This does not mean that academic walls are obsolete, however. As McLuhan himself clarified in a 1977 interview: if learning has moved outside, questioning remains inside.[33] It is through questioning—maintaining a critical distance from the reality of the status quo in order to see behind and beyond it—that genuine learning is experienced.

As an intellectual disposition, the habit of questioning does not necessitate a particular physical environment. Indeed, learning has traditionally needed little by way of architecture: philosophizing with Socrates required only a convenient place in the shade; the first medieval universities were constituted by societies of wandering scholars (clusters of permanent buildings followed); and recuperating Indigenous knowledge depends more on protecting lands and cultural practices than on construction alone. In other words, campuses are fundamentally peripatetic, hosting "free-roving students" reveling in the realization that the world is a place of learning. Still, architecture matters: to ground, gather, and guard the social practice of learning.

Massey College, Scarborough, Trent, and Simon Fraser University are, in some ways, inimitable. Few universities today have the benefit of such intimate scales, dramatic sites, generous budgets, and enlightened leadership. Yet, at the same time, every university today is striving to continue the architectural and pedagogical project initiated by these exemplary works and their architects. This ongoing project pursues academic environments that are equally quotidian and utopian, hospitable to learning and open to dissent.

4

First Nations Architecture: A Long Journey Forward

Odile Hénault

Until the late 1960s, most Canadians had never thought about contemporary architecture in relation to First Nations communities. Fifty years later, things have changed considerably. On the one hand, there is increased awareness of noteworthy projects built over the last five decades. On the other hand, much groundwork has been laid institutionally, creating a solid base for recognition and for action. As we approach the year 2020, there are only a handful of registered architects of First Nations background in Canada, but there is no doubt that their numbers will grow in the years ahead.

Information on noteworthy projects built in Canadian First Nations communities over the past fifty years is fragmentary. Little has been written, except for one major publication authored by American scholars Joy Monice Malnar and Frank Vodvarka,[1] who included a number of mostly western Canadian works in their North American survey. This chapter offers a general introduction to the topic, from a Canadian perspective, and points to projects of interest built for First Nations, whether in their communities or in urban settings. It also aims to describe the general context—now evolving at an accelerated rate—in which architects have been able to intervene.

1 left
Museum of Northern
British Columbia,
Monument Gallery, Prince
Rupert, British Columbia.
Larry McFarland Architect,
1988.

2 opposite
First Nations Longhouse,
University of British
Columbia, Vancouver,
British Columbia. Larry
McFarland Architect, 1993.

1960–1980

The emergence of contemporary First Nations architecture can be traced back to a trio of projects built in western Canada in the sixties and seventies [see pages 301–313]. In 1967, a small parish church designed by Étienne Gaboury (1930–) of Gaboury, Lussier, Sigurdson Architects opened in St. Boniface, Manitoba. The Paroisse du Précieux Sang Church, which is still considered one of the province's most significant architectural works, was inspired by the Prairie tepee, transposed out of its familiar context and turned into an architectural element of universal appeal.

That same year, in Red Deer, Alberta, another church was built, shining the spotlight on a young Douglas Cardinal (1934–). Although the architectural vocabulary of St. Mary's Church was not specifically evocative of First Nations' traditions, it was the first major work by an emerging architect of great talent who came from mixed Blackfoot, Métis, and European ancestry.

Finally, in 1976, the Museum of Anthropology was inaugurated at the University of British Columbia (UBC) in Vancouver. It was to have a strong impact, partly due to the reputation of its architect, Arthur Erickson (1924–2009), but also because of his striking reinterpretation of the Northwest Coast's Indigenous post-and-beam construction system, as found in the traditional cedar longhouses of British Columbia [see pages 286–289]. Using concrete instead of wood, Erickson built a showcase for an important collection of aboriginal artifacts that had been housed by UBC for three decades.

While today works such as Gaboury's St. Boniface Church and Erickson's Museum of Anthropology might be questioned as acts of cultural appropriation, at the time, inspiration derived from Indigenous precedents was a sign that those cultures were being at last acknowledged and appreciated. Attitudes were beginning to evolve, especially in British Columbia, where a number of individuals were working independently toward proper recognition of West Coast First Nations traditions and artifacts. Worthy of mention, for instance, are anthropologists Harry and Audrey Hawthorn, both of whom were major players in creating UBC's Museum of Anthropology. Their son, architect Henry Hawthorn (1939–), was at the vanguard of those working for First Nations communities. One of his

contributions was an unpretentious museum, opened in 1976, which celebrated the culture of the Haida Gwaii on the Queen Charlotte Islands, as the territory was then called (it has since been changed back to Haida Gwaii) [see pages 289–293]. Hawthorn recalls that the original commission was for a local history museum that would describe the first white settlements, but, "happily, the native culture was so much more compelling, and the first curators/directors after the museum was built were anthropologists rather than historians, so the shift to a Haida-featured museum was inevitable." He continues, "In the design I was trying to capture the spirit of the place rather than mimicking historic Haida architecture."[2]

A few years later, Hawthorn would become involved with the highly symbolic U'mista ("the return of something important") Cultural Centre in Alert Bay, British Columbia, built to accommodate repatriated potlatch masks and ceremonial objects confiscated by the Royal Canadian Mounted Police in 1921 and subsequently dispersed around the world. Opened in 1980, the Centre's most striking feature is an inward-looking rectangular room, where artifacts from the Kwakwaka'wakw tradition have been displayed following their return from certain museums and private collections.

Prior to his work in Haida Gwaii, Hawthorn and his partners had designed the Nicola Valley Recreational Centre in central British Columbia, which was to host the Native

Canadian Games. The Centre was never built, but the architects received an award for the project in 1973 from *The Canadian Architect* magazine. While the building may have been meant for First Nations, the design did not reflect this cultural connection.

1980–2000

Until the 1980s, little work of architectural significance was built in First Nations communities outside British Columbia. Among the first projects to attract national interest was Gordon Atkins's Stoney Tribal Administration Building in Morley, Alberta. Completed in 1980, it received a Governor General's Award in 1982.

The situation would change quite dramatically in the following decade. In 1983, two architectural competitions were launched across Canada in order to select the architects of two major museums for Canada's capital area. After a highly controversial process, Prime Minister Pierre Elliot Trudeau's government surprised the nation by entrusting Douglas Cardinal with one of the country's most prestigious architectural commissions. The Canadian Museum of Man (1989, now the Canadian Museum of History) was to have a major impact on Cardinal's career, who until that point had mostly practiced in the Prairies. It

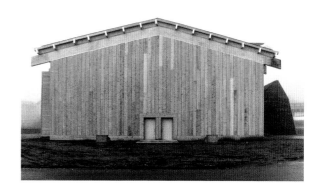

also made him, at age fifty, the quasi-official figure of Canadian First Nations architecture [see page 313].

While Cardinal was focusing on his museum mandate in the National Capital Region, Vancouver-based Larry McFarland (originally a sole practitioner, now of McFarland Marceau Architects) was quietly working with First Nations leaders in British Columbia. In 1989, a major project started to take form in Vancouver as prominent businessman Jack Bell donated $1 million to the University of British Columbia to support a building "for First Nations."[3] McFarland was then chosen by a selection committee mostly because of the Museum of Northern British Columbia, which he had just built in Prince Rupert, British Columbia (1988). **FIG 1** The architect's mandate included assisting in defining the program, assessing potential sites on the UBC campus, and securing additional financing. The resulting First Nations Longhouse (1993) was inspired by an archetype—that of the traditional West Coast longhouse—and awarded a Governor General's Medal in 1994. **FIG 2** It created a much-needed new building type, a home away from home for First Nations students in Canadian universities. With its gently swooping roof made of oversize cedar logs, the building still stands as one of the country's most poetic structures.

In the mid-1980s, a groundbreaking school-design program in British Columbia ushered in a new era of building with—and for—First Nations. Established by the federal government, this modestly funded initiative might have gone unnoticed had it not been for the presence of architect Marie-Odile Marceau, who was at the time regional architect for the Department of Indian Affairs and Northern Development. Acting as both client and community advocate, she developed a design process for school buildings that emphasized community involvement and high-caliber architecture—ingredients missing from an education system commonly administered in makeshift facilities.

Marceau's impact was first noticed with the Lalme' Iwesawtexw (Seabird Island) Elementary School (1991), built for a community near Agassiz, east of Vancouver. **FIG 3** Considered at the time to be one of Canada's most innovative education projects, the school brought attention to its architects, John and Patricia Patkau, and to Marceau's methods. During the period of a few years, 10 of British Columbia's 196 First Nations bands built new

5 opposite, top
Stone Band School, Chilcotin, British Columbia. Peter Cardew Architect, 1992.

6 opposite, bottom
Chief Matthews Primary School, Old Massett, British Columbia. Acton Ostry Architects, 1995.

7 right
Haisla Village School, Kitamaat, British Columbia. Hughes Baldwin Architects, 1994.

schools within the framework of this federal program. The architects were some of British Columbia's most talented firms: Richard Henriquez designed the Bella Bella Community School (1996); Peter Cardew built a shop for the Lach Klan School's industrial arts program (1988) and a school for the Chilcotin region's Stone Band (1992); Hughes Baldwin Architects was responsible for the Haisla Village School in Kitamaat (1994); and the emerging office of Acton Johnson Ostry Architects (later Acton Ostry Architects) designed the Chief Matthews Primary School in Old Massett, Haida Gwaii (1995). **FIGS 4–7** In Alert Bay, Henry Hawthorn worked with Roberto Pacheco on the design of T'lisalagi'lakw Elementary School (1996).

The new schools explored a wide spectrum of cultural and geographic references. The Seabird Island Elementary School's volume echoes the silhouette of the surrounding mountains, while its expressive southern facade alludes to traditional Salish boardwalks and salmon-drying racks. Richard Henriquez built a rather stern facade reminiscent of Northwest Coast longhouses, while Hughes Baldwin Architects chose a more contemporary approach using metal cladding and assertive curved volumes. What was particularly interesting, in the case of the Bella Bella and Old Massett schools, was the search for symbols perceived as meaningful by the individual communities. This exploration led to striking drawings, as did the study of sections that would allow natural light to penetrate into the heart of the buildings.

The architects responded to what community leaders considered vital for the education of their youth. For example, natural light was introduced everywhere in the buildings through the use of sloped roofs and clerestory lights that give life to central corridors. These corridors were often enlarged to double as gathering spaces. Storytelling areas were introduced to encourage encounters between elders and children. A close connection between classrooms and the outdoors was also considered essential. Wood was widely used as a building material, partly because of its traditional local importance and natural warmth, but also because it could be harvested and processed on-site. This meant greater involvement on the part of locals in the procurement of materials and in the construction process, a consideration particularly important to Marceau.

8 left
Nikanik Secondary School, Wemotaci, Quebec. Côté Chabot Morel architectes, 1996.

9 opposite, top
Hesquiaht Place of Learning, Hot Springs Cove, British Columbia. McFarland Marceau Architects, 2009.

10 opposite, bottom
Dänojà Zho Cultural Centre, Yukon. Florian Maurer Architect, 1998.

The ideas introduced in these British Columbia schools became widely attractive to other native communities across the country. One school that followed similar principles was the Nikanik Secondary School in the community of Wemotaci, near La Tuque, Quebec (1996). **FIG 8** It earned its Quebec City architects of Côté Chabot Morel (now CCM2) an award of excellence from the Ordre des architectes du Québec in 1997. The importance given to natural light in native schools eventually spread to numerous education buildings for nonnative communities as well.

Despite its success, the school-design initiative was discontinued in the late 1990s. Marceau went into private practice, where she has continued working with First Nations. Her ongoing commitment to the collaborative process is evidenced in projects such as her firm's Hesquiaht First Nation Place of Learning, built on the west coast of Vancouver Island (2009). **FIG 9** Illustrating Marceau's environmental concerns, it includes a rainwater detention pond used as a thermal sink for heating the building.[4]

During the 1990s, new buildings of other types—including cultural and interpretive centers—were also starting to appear in First Nations communities. In Saskatchewan, the Wanuskewin Heritage Park, designed by the Saskatoon firm aodbt, opened in 1992. Awarded the Premier's Design Award of Excellence, it is well integrated in its context, blending Prairie architecture traditions with Indigenous references. A few years later, as the one-hundredth anniversary of the Klondike Gold Rush (1896–1898) was being commemorated in Dawson City, Yukon, a small but striking structure, the Dänojà Zho Cultural Centre (1998), opened its doors. **FIG 10** Designed by Whitehorse-based architects Florian Maurer and Jack Kobayashi, the center tells the story of the gold rush from the perspective of the Tr'ondëk Hwëch'in First Nation. Its exquisite form draws inspiration from fishing gear traditionally used to catch spawning river salmon.

During the last decade of the twentieth century, a landmark project on a major scale was undertaken in northern Quebec: the creation of a new community for the Oujé-Bougoumou Cree First Nation on Eeyou Istchee territory. In September 1989, after years of negotiations, the Quebec provincial government had concluded a major financial agreement with the Cree Nation, and the federal government had followed suit three years later.

The agreements compensated the Cree for being forced to relocate several times over the years due to mining, forestry, and hydroelectric activities. A unique "experiment" ensued: using their new resources, the Cree decided to establish a model community, the planning of which was entrusted to Douglas Cardinal. The founding gesture, however, was the erection in 1989 of a symbolically charged open pavilion—inspired by the traditional *shaputuan*—at the center of the future settlement. **FIG 11** It was designed by Quebec architect Alain Fournier then working with architect Dana Kephart. Fournier's firm Fournier Gersovitz Moss Drolet architects (now EVOQ Architecture) has since worked with Inuit and First Nations communities throughout Quebec and Northern Canada.

Cardinal's office organized the village around a circular core, which was to include the main administrative and cultural buildings, in a design taking after the central pavilion. **FIG 12** During the planning process, it was decided that wood chips from nearby sawmills would be used to provide biomass-fueled district heating to Oujé-Bougoumou's public buildings and to more than one hundred homes. Inaugurated in the early '90s, the village received several national and international awards, including the 1995 Best Practices for Human Settlements designation by the Together Foundation and the UN Centre for Human Settlements.

Around the same period, in Gesgapegiag, Quebec, Fournier Gersovitz Moss Drolet architectes was commissioned to build the Walgwan Youth Rehabilitation and Treatment Centre (1996), one of five healing compounds to help Inuit and First Nations youth deal with substance abuse problems.[5] **FIG 13** The center's design is based on traditional Algonquin shelters. The architects write: "By evoking aboriginal culture, the building creates the setting to reconnect with cultural identity, reconstruct self-esteem, develop pride and empowerment."[6]

2000–2017

Starting in 2000, First Nations architecture began to shift toward larger projects and a wider range of building types. British Columbia was once more at the heart of this change.

This can be seen in the Nicola Valley Institute of Technology (NVIT), by Busby + Associates Architects with Alfred Waugh as design architect. **FIG 14** Waugh, whose mother was of First Nations descent,[7] had started his career as a student working in Larry McFarland's office while the UBC Longhouse was under construction. Although he had no direct involvement with the design itself, he was one of several guests, or "witnesses," called upon to speak at the opening ceremony.[8]

Located two and a half hours from Vancouver, the NVIT (2001) offers programs tailored to the needs of Indigenous students and communities.[9] Architecturally, its main building creates a dialogue between formal elements identified with First Nations traditions and current sustainability practices. As architectural writer Jim Taggart explains, NVIT "reveals its cultural context not as an assemblage of symbols and metaphors, but through the embodiment of intrinsic cultural values. Equally important, it reinterprets traditional architectural archetypes not simply as formal elements but as functional systems."[10] The concept evolved from Waugh's personal involvement with local representatives. Describing the project, Waugh writes that multiple site visits with local elders led to "the semi-circular shape…a meaningful and recurring native theme."[11] He adds that the "internal siting of functional spaces has been with the intention of eliminating any sense of

13 left
Walgwan Centre Youth Rehabilitation and Treatment Centre, Gesgapegiag, Quebec. Fournier Gersovitz Moss Drolet architects, 1996.

14 right
Nicola Valley Institute of Technology, Merritt, British Columbia. Busby Perkins + Will, Alfred Waugh, design architect, 2001.

15 opposite
Squamish Lil'wat Centre, Whistler, British Columbia. FormLine Architecture, 2008.

hierarchy."[12] Solutions that had first appeared in previous British Columbia schools were now being applied on a larger scale.

Alfred Waugh's next large commission was the Squamish Lil'wat Cultural Centre in the ski resort town of Whistler, British Columbia. **FIG 15** Completed in 2008, it allowed him to further explore environmental principles and forms inspired by tradition. Located near the resort's tourist center, the three-story building on a treed site features a curved glass facade and a spectacular exhibition room above the entrance. An upper-level mezzanine offers visitors views to the mountains beyond; from this space, one can appreciate the exhibit area's delicate proportions.

Two years earlier, an ambitious tourist-oriented project three decades in the making had been inaugurated in Alberta. Calgary architect Ron Goodfellow designed the 62,000-square-foot (5,760-square-meter) Blackfoot Crossing Interpretative Centre on the Siksika Nation reserve, describing it as "a literal metaphor of traditional Blackfoot iconography."[13] The center, which also integrates contemporary architectural ideas, features a major exhibition of Blackfoot artifacts along with a one-hundred-seat theater.

Among other facilities aiming to attract tourists to First Nations lands is the striking Nk'Mip Desert Cultural Centre (2006), situated in the Okanagan Valley on the unusually

16 above
Nk'Mip Desert Cultural
Centre, Osoyoos, British
Columbia. Hotson Bakker
Boniface Haden Architects
+ Urbanistes, 2006.

17 opposite
Hotel-Museum First
Nations, Wendake, Quebec.
Lemay Michaud, 2008.

arid lands of the Osoyoos First Nation. **FIG 16** Hotson Bakker Boniface Haden Architects designed the award-winning center, which features a reinforced rammed-earth wall inspired by traditional adobe construction. The project provided the architects with "an opportunity to evolve an authentically South Okanagan building technique."[14]

On a larger scale, near Quebec City, Lemay Michaud was commissioned by the leaders of Wendake's tiny Wendat Nation to design a hotel-museum hybrid, which would offer visitors a unique, first-class experience. The swift Akiawenrahk (St. Charles) River site was chosen for its beauty, reminiscent of the untamed waterways that were once the primary means of navigating the continent. The building, opened in 2008, meshes contemporary elements with traditional references. This is particularly true of its carefully crafted interiors. **FIG 17** As cultural tourism develops across the country, the Wendake Hotel-Museum is probably one of the most appealing examples of a successful touristic venture on First Nations lands.

Another venue worth mentioning is the Deer Clan Longhouse (2014) built by Brook McIlroy in the Crawford Lake Conservation Area, Ontario. **FIG 18** Traditional-looking from the outside and located within a reconstructed fifteenth-century Iroquoian village, the new "longhouse" was built as a series of contemporary interpretive learning spaces.

18 opposite, top
Deer Clan Longhouse, Crawford Lake Conservation Area, Ontario. Brook McIlroy, 2014.

19 opposite, bottom
Tseshaht Tribal Multiplex & Health Centre, Port Alberni, British Columbia. Lubor Trubka Associates Architects, 2007.

Designed through a consultation process with Indigenous representatives, elders, and community stakeholders, this rather exquisite project won the 2014 Ontario Wood Works Jury's Choice Award.

Better conceived health centers also began emerging in First Nations communities, inspired to an extent by the BC school program's approach.[15] Of particular interest is Port Alberni's Tseshaht Tribal Multiplex & Health Centre (2007), a 1,500-square-foot (140-square-meter) facility designed by Vancouver-based architect Lubor Trubka. **FIG 19** The site is a granite bluff over the Somass River. The wood-and-glass building follows the contours of the site, at times cantilevering over the tidal river rather than disturbing it with excavations and blasting.[16]

In northern Nova Scotia, a remarkable facility was built for the Pictou Landing Mi'kmaq Nation in 2007. It was designed by Richard Kroeker, who was at the time teaching at Dalhousie University in Halifax and had been interested in Mi'kmaq traditions for years. His closeness with local elders earned him their trust, and he was invited to plan, design, and build the health clinic in collaboration with Brian Lilley and Halifax architect Peter Henry [see pages 336–340]. The building provides the community with medical and dental facilities as well as a gathering hall. Particularly striking is its curvilinear plan and elevation, along with a unique roof structure created from paired, boomerang-shaped trusses. Green saplings—immersed in water to maintain pliability—were used for the curved chords.[17] Overlapping wood planks, which look like giant shingles from a distance, follow the undulating lines of the roof.

Since the 1990s, a number of architects across the country have built schools, recreation centers, and cultural centers for First Nations. Among them is the Edmonton-based office of Manasc Isaac Architects, which was one of the first firms to work extensively with Indigenous communities. Similarly, architect Richard Evans, who practiced for a number of years in Vancouver with Marie-Odile Marceau, became closely involved with small communities in northern British Columbia, providing them with modest but essential facilities, including schools, clinics, and band offices. The office of David Nairne + Associates also built numerous projects across British Columbia and in the Yukon.

20
Aanischaaukamikw Cree
Cultural Institute, Oujé-
Bougoumou, Quebec. Rubin
& Rotman Architects in
collaboration with Douglas
Cardinal, 2011.

21 above
**Aanischaaukamikw Cree
Cultural Institute, Oujé-
Bougoumou, Quebec. Rubin
& Rotman Architects in
collaboration with Douglas
Cardinal, 2011.**

22 opposite, left
**Indigenous Sharing
and Learning Centre,
Laurentian University
Parker Building, Sudbury,
Ontario. DSAI, 2017.**

23 opposite, right
**The Centre for Native
Child & Family Well Being,
Toronto, Ontario. LGA
Architectural Partners,
2010.**

The Montreal office of Rubin & Rotman Architects has established strong links with the Cree Nation over the years. It is responsible, among other projects, for the Nemaska Recreation Centre (2005) and the Rainbow Elementary School (2007), both in northern Quebec. Their most significant contribution is the Aanischaaukamikw Cree Cultural Institute (2011) in Oujé-Bougoumou, which they designed in collaboration with Douglas Cardinal. **FIGS 20–21** The building was the missing piece in the village's central core, as planned by Cardinal's office in the 1990s. Intended as a museum and gathering place, the institute showcases Cree artifacts—some reclaimed from institutions around the world—and hosts musical and storytelling events. It is also home to various associations dedicated to the preservation and transmission of Cree culture. The main space is open and elongated, reproducing the form of a *shaputuan*; in place of wood branches, its arched ceiling is made of locally produced glue-laminated curved wood beams.

Other notable works outside of British Columbia and Quebec include the Victoria Linklater Memorial School (2011), built for the North Spirit Lake First Nation in northern Ontario by Architecture 49, a work that takes inspiration from the nearby cliffs. In 2002, Ontario's Trent University commissioned Brian Porter of Two Row Architect in a joint venture with Dunlop Associates (now Stantec), to design the Enweying/Peter Gzowski College and First Peoples House of Learning at Trent University.[18] The building's Corten-clad lower entrance is somewhat reminiscent of a tent structure. In 2017, Two Row Architect, one of very few First Nations–owned firms in Canada was selected by OCAD University, along with Morphosis and Teeple Architects, to work on the Creative City Campus and its Indigenous Visual Culture and Student Centre in downtown Toronto.

Student centers for First Nations students were first built in British Columbia and are now included more and more frequently on university campuses, often added to existing buildings. An interesting example is located in Sudbury, Ontario, where Toronto-based Diamond Schmitt Architects (DSAI) have completed a major modernization project involving seven Laurentian University buildings (2017). The Indigenous Sharing and Learning Centre, with its circular interiors, was subtly added to the Parker Building, confirming the institution's commitment to the surrounding Northern Ontario First Nations population. **FIG 22**

Over many years, a growing number of people of First Nations descent have moved to Canadian urban centers. This phenomenon has spawned projects dating back to the 1970s, such as the Indian Friendship Centre by Gordon Atkins (1980) in downtown Calgary.[19] More recently, LGA Architectural Partners' Janna Levitt and Dean Goodman have designed a series of structures for urban First Nations groups, including the downtown Toronto Centre for Native Child and Family Well Being (2010). **FIG 23–24** They turned a rather nondescript four-story office building from the 1980s into a family-oriented center offering drop-in childcare alongside other family and social services. The most evocative part of the project is a room that aims to be "a contemporary iteration of a longhouse and healing lodge,"[20] adorned with simple wood elements that create a subtly intricate pattern. The rooftop features a traditional sweat lodge and a small garden; it is reached through flights of stairs open to a skylight above to symbolize direct communication between the earth and the sky. The desire for this connection was expressed by elders involved in the project.[21]

In Vancouver, architect Joe Wai's Skwachàys Lodge and Residence (2012) on the edge of Chinatown is another example of a distinctly urban project. **FIG 25** Initiated and run by the Vancouver Native Housing Society, it was designed to provide apartments for First Nations people awaiting medical treatment in the city. To generate income, it also includes a small

24 opposite
The Centre for Native
Child & Family Well Being,
Toronto, Ontario. LGA
Architectural Partners,
2010.

25 right
Skwachàys Healing
Lodge, Vancouver,
British Columbia. JYW
Architecture, 2012.

hotel with an exhibition space in the lobby where First Nations artists can show their work. As with the center in Toronto, the rooftop includes a sweat lodge. The facade also features a large mural and a totem pole. It was intended to be, according to Wai, "a home with a First Nations identity and a place for healing, physically and spiritually."[22]

At the University of Victoria, BC, the increasing enrollment of First Nations students led to the creation of a First Peoples House (2011). **FIGS 26–28** Architect Alfred Waugh created a luminous and elegant structure set on a small plot with indigenous plants and a pond. Carefully detailed, the simple, elongated building was designed with environmental performance in mind, inspired by traditional techniques that enabled native communities to persist through harsh climatic conditions over centuries. It features a remarkable central gathering space with woven cedar interiors.

Winnipeg has the largest First Nations population of any Canadian city.[23] Local firm Prairie Architects has built numerous projects over the years, working closely with indigenous community members.[24] Their portfolio includes the Indigenous Student Centre on the University of Manitoba's Fort Garry Campus (2008), which uses local Tyndall limestone and an architectural vocabulary somewhat reminiscent of Douglas Cardinal's work. One of the firm's most significant projects is the Aboriginal Peoples Television Network

26 opposite, top
**First Peoples House,
University of Victoria,
Victoria, British Columbia.
FormLine Architecture,
2010.**

27 opposite, bottom
**First Peoples House,
University of Victoria,
entrance view.**

28 above
**First Peoples House,
University of Victoria,
elevational view.**

29 left
APTN Corporate Office and
Studio, Winnipeg, Manitoba.
Prairie Architects, 2015.

30 opposite, top
Native Youth Centre,
Commercial Drive elevation,
Vancouver, British Columbia
[unbuilt]. McFarland Marceau
Architects, 2005.

31 opposite, bottom
Gathering Circle, Spirit
Garden, Thunder Bay, Ontario.
Brook McIlroy, Ryan Gorrie,
designer, 2011.

(APTN) corporate office and studio on Winnipeg's Portage Street (2015). **FIG 29** As with downtown Toronto's Centre for Native Child and Family Well Being project, the architects recuperated two existing buildings and adapted them to the needs of Canada's First Nations television network. Two elements strongly reflect the program: a dramatic copper "ribbon of life," which runs from one facade to the other and acts as a signpost for the organization; and a two-level, wood-clad, drum-like studio space. Anishinabekwe architect Eladia Smoke, now principal of Smoke Architecture, worked on the initial concept. She describes it as follows: "Reaching out from the building to connect with the street, the recording studio is in the shape of a drum, which represents the shared heartbeat of life. APTN captures stories important to us, and the drum represents the resonance of communication between our nations, and between people and the land. A copper ribbon unravels from the drum to link both facades; it rises and takes flight like the aurora borealis, broadcasting to the entire nation, connecting our hearts together."[25] Although the adaptively reused buildings impose their intrinsic logic on the project, of particular interest is how a strong Indigenous voice emerges through the medium of contemporary architectural materials.

Worth mentioning is an as yet unbuilt project intended to address the new urban conditions of Indigenous youth. The Native Youth Centre, designed in 2005 by McFarland Marceau Architects for a location in Vancouver's Downtown Eastside, was intended to support First Nations youth through social, educational, counseling, health, athletic, and cultural programs.[26] **FIG 30** The ambitious proposal would have tackled pressing issues faced by Indigenous youth, offering spaces such as a gymnasium, community kitchen, childcare center, alternative school, drop-in center, sweat lodge, and other amenities. The project has not been completely abandoned and may be developed in a very different form.

In 2006, the architectural firm Brook McIlroy was commissioned by the City of Thunder Bay to work on a revitalization project for Prince Arthur's Landing on the Lake Superior waterfront. Through their research, the architects became aware of the cultural and historic roots linking First Nations to the shoreline.[27] They proposed to erect an outdoor pavilion called the Gathering Circle located within a landscaped Spirit Garden (2013). **FIG 31** The design, by Anishinaabe architect Ryan Gorrie, then still a student, evolved from a series of workshops

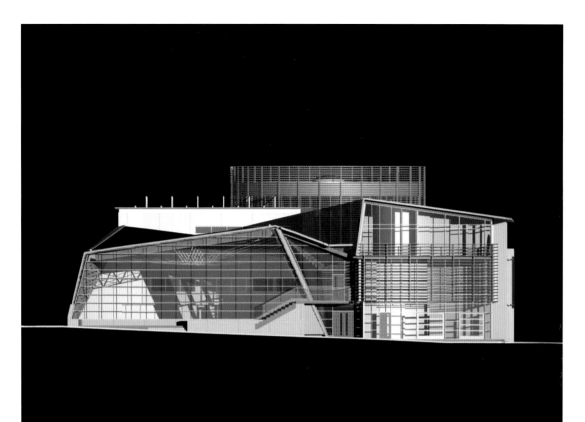

with representatives from the nearby Fort William First Nation, Robinson Superior Treaty Communities, and the Red Sky Métis. According to the architects, the award-winning pavilion reflects "aboriginal concepts of the inclusive circle, peaceful coexistence and respect for nature."[28] Gorrie now heads Brook McIlroy's Indigenous Place Making practice.

Another commemorative project, this time in Batoche, Saskatchewan, was completed in 2016 by Halifax-based firms Form:Media and Ekistics Planning and Design, already known for their thoughtful work in comparable Eastern Canada contexts. Their project for Batoche National Historic Site, the site of a decisive battle in the North-West Rebellion, is a poetic display of graphics and interpretive architecture. **FIG 32** Three Corten-clad elements are positioned on the land as viewing platforms to recall the Indigenous and Métis community that once inhabited the area. Form:Media's John deWolf explains: "Our goal was to portray a culture, once thriving in Batoche."[29]

In a much more remote context, a multipurpose hall of note was recently completed in 2017 in the northern village of Kuujjuaraapik, in the southernmost part of Hudson Bay. Although initiated by and for the Inuit community, Katittavik (meaning a "place of gathering" in Inuktitut, 2017) is intended to respond to the needs of the local Cree community of Whapmagoostui as well. **FIG 33** The slightly lopsided shape of this 7,300-square-foot

32 opposite
**Storyboard on the
Landscape, Batoche
National Historic Site,
Batoche, Saskatchewan.
Form:Media and Ekistics
Plan + Design, 2016.**

33 above
**Katittavik, Kuujjuaraapik,
Nunavik. Blouin Orzes
architectes, 2017.**

(678-square-meters) building alludes to the form of an iceberg. Built to include a professional stage, it provides a venue for traditional festivals and the popular Inuit Games, as well as for performances by contemporary artists. The challenge for Montreal-based Blouin Orzes architectes was to create an inspiring meeting place while coping with the formidable cost and transportation issues linked to working in isolated northern communities.

Extreme climate conditions and remoteness were also faced by the Whitehorse office of Kobayashi + Zedda Architects as they built the John Tizya Centre in the Vuntut Gwitch'in village of Old Crow, Yukon (2010). **FIG 34** Like numerous small First Nations communities, the village can only be reached by plane most of the year [see pages 377–379]. This created a major technical constraint for the architects, who had to ensure all building materials could fit through the one-meter-wide door of a small aircraft. Sustainability, a prime objective, meant integrating solar panels into the design. This led to the project's receipt of a 2011 AIBC Special Jury Award for Ingenuity. Kobayashi + Zedda later also built the Old Crow Arctic Research Facility, which includes the largest photovoltaic array in the Yukon, a significant asset for a community reliant on diesel-powered generators for its electrical needs.[30]

Although the pace of construction is accelerating, housing continues to be a major unresolved issue for most First Nations communities. Several initiatives have attempted to

34 left
John Tizya Centre, Old
Crow, Yukon. Kobayashi +
Zedda Architects, 2010.

35 opposite
Indian Residential
School History and
Dialogue Centre,
University of British
Columbia, Vancouver,
British Columbia.
FormLine Architecture,
2017.

address this ongoing crisis over the years, but they have generally been limited in scope. One particularly inspiring example is the work of architect Guillaume Lévesque in collaboration with Emergency Architects of Canada and the Frontiers Foundation. From 2009 to 2014, the group renovated seventy houses in the impoverished village of Kitcisakik, Québec. One essential component of the project was the on-site training of several native workers, who were subsequently able to use their newly acquired skills to earn a living. In 2012, Lévesque, along with involved community members, received a Governor General's Award in Architecture for this work.

Conclusion: "What does reconciliation look like when transformed into form?"[31]

Major changes are finally, if gradually, taking place in Canadian society with respect to recognizing the needs and aspirations of the numerous First Nations across the land. Unjustifiable damages caused by the residential schools program are slowly being acknowledged, thanks to the work of the Truth and Reconciliation Commission of Canada. Its report, issued in 2015, has gone a long way in raising nationwide awareness. In the aftermath of the commission's work, Vancouver architect Alfred Waugh was asked to design the Indian Residential School History and Dialogue Centre (2017) on the UBC campus. **FIG 35** Waugh describes how he perceived this emotionally charged project as he started working on it: "The building was meant to evoke Indigenous culture but it could not refer to any specific First Nation. As the son of a mother who went through the residential school system, it was extremely important for me to design a building that would be a symbol of resilience and pride for all First Nations People."[32]

In 2016, the Royal Architectural Institute of Canada (RAIC) launched an Indigenous Task Force. Among its members are several architects, designers, academics, intern architects, and architecture students, either of Indigenous background or who work with First Nations. The task force's initial chairman was the well-known Nisga'a Nation activist-architect Patrick Luugigyoo Stewart, the first Indigenous architect to have been registered

in British Columbia and the first to have been elected chair of his provincial association, the Architectural Institute of British Columbia. Under his leadership, an International Indigenous Architecture and Design Symposium was held in Ottawa in 2017. The event included First Nations delegates from the United States, New Zealand, and Australia, working in private practice or academia. The first-of-its-kind symposium is notable as a milestone in terms of institutional recognition and empowerment.

Another important step in bringing First Nations into Canada's architectural landscape came with the 2013 launch of a new school, the McEwen School of Architecture, at Laurentian University in Sudbury, Ontario. The vision of founding director Terrance Galvin involved incorporating Bauhaus teachings as well as First Nations' traditional know-how and philosophy. **FIG 36** From the start, several teachers and guest lecturers have been recruited from among First Nations academics and professionals. Succeeding Galvin, David Fortin is the first Métis director of a Canadian school of architecture. He writes:

> As the train rattles by, students hover around laptops to discuss community-led projects in places like Chapleau, Powassan, Sault Ste. Marie, or Wahnapitae First Nation…Occasionally, Elders lead small ceremonies to offer a prayer and smudge to our students, faculty and

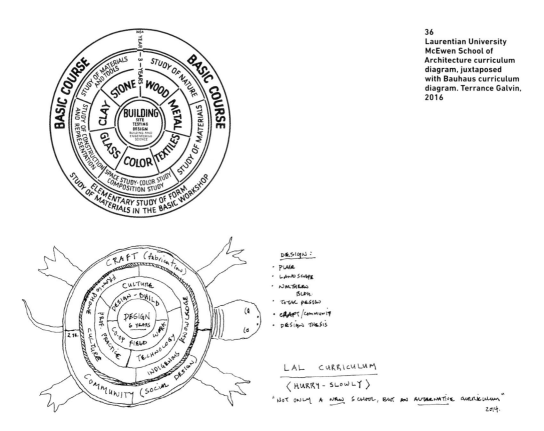

36
Laurentian University
McEwen School of
Architecture curriculum
diagram, juxtaposed
with Bauhaus curriculum
diagram. Terrance Galvin,
2016

community members, in hopes of positive progress…This is already a school of architecture like no other, and it's just getting started.[33]

One might say the same of First Nations architecture in Canada more broadly. Over the past fifty years, the landscape has gradually evolved toward improved communication, sensitivity, and, ultimately, participatory inclusion of First Nations in designing the places they live, learn, work, and play in. The work itself has shifted from being imitative of traditional structures to incorporating contemporary building solutions adapted to First Nations' ways. Gradually, we are arriving at a point in time when it seems that a genuine two-way dialogue may be possible between Indigenous and non-Indigenous architecture. It has been a long journey forward—one that promises much for the road ahead.

International
Influences

5

Megastructures
and High-Tech

George Baird

From the mid-1960s until the late 1970s, one of the most remarkable episodes occurred in the history of architecture in Canada. From Montreal to Vancouver, some dozen buildings designed and erected during this period commanded admiration from around the world. Indeed, no series of Canadian buildings has since elicited such widespread interest and praise. Most of these buildings can be described as "megastructures"; some can be described as "high-tech"; and a small number exhibit features associated with both of these two important international design tendencies.

The concept of the "megastructure" was conceived concurrently in Europe and Japan. In the early 1960s, Dutch architect Jacob Bakema (1914–1981), a founding member of the group of urban thinkers known as Team 10, became fascinated by the form of the ancient city of Split, Croatia. The city originated as a summer palace constructed by the Roman emperor Diocletian; after falling into ruins, it later reemerged as a significant medieval urban settlement on account of its easily navigable harbor. **FIG 1**

Bakema noticed that as medieval Split developed, it gradually integrated the earlier ruins. One can still clearly read the form of Diocletian's palace in the plan of modern-day Split, with some of the palace's former corridors now serving as streets, and some of its major interior spaces transformed into public squares. This led Bakema to

see a provocative analogy between the building (the original palace) and the city (downtown Split).[1]

This concept of a building that can also be a city became one of the leitmotifs of Team 10's subsequent work and a defining feature of the "megastructure." The best-known example of this megastructure approach is the Free University of Berlin, designed by Candilis Josic Woods with Manfred Shiedhelm, and constructed in the western Berlin suburb of Dahlem in 1964. **FIG 2** In this extraordinary project, the entire university campus is designed as a single building, organized around a two-way grid of corridors. The relatively large plan is infilled by a series of classrooms, seminar rooms, faculty offices, and outdoor courtyards.

While the concept of the megastructure was unfolding in Europe, a group of Japanese architects led by Kenzō Tange (1913–2005) formed a group known as the "Metabolists." One of the early manifestations of Metabolist thinking was a utopian proposal for erecting a series of very large triangulated structures on platforms above Tokyo Bay, which would accommodate housing and other urban functions. The plan was never implemented, but it piqued the curiosity of architects around the world, including in Canada.[2]

Soon after, a number of still younger architects, mostly based in London, England, launched a campaign to reinvigorate a stream of modernist design thinking that focused

on images of technological virtuosity. The collective known as Archigram produced a series of influential pamphlets illustrating their provocative ideas for concepts such as a gridded, "plug-in" city.

Before very long, a trio of more practical visionaries—Norman Foster (1935–), Renzo Piano (1937–), and Richard Rogers (1933–)—picked up ideas from Archigram. Their careers commenced with building designs that were not only technologically sophisticated, but which also made the technology of their building assemblies the main focus of their architectural iconography. Their approach was soon named "high-tech."

Two of this group—Piano and Rogers—collaborated on a competition submission for a new modern art gallery in Paris commissioned by the government of Georges Pompidou. When the Centre Pompidou opened in 1977, it was the world's first prominent built example of this new high-tech tendency in architecture. **FIG 3**

The Explosive Arrival of the Megastructure and of High-Tech in Canada

Architects in Canada in the mid-1960s were following these international developments with great curiosity. In 1963 and 1964 respectively, construction commenced on two revolutionary projects in Canadian architecture: Scarborough College in suburban Toronto, and Simon Fraser University on the fringe of Vancouver [see pages 108–113].

John Andrews (1933–), a young architect from Australia, had immigrated to Canada after placing as a finalist in the 1958 competition for the new Toronto City Hall. At the time, he had recently been appointed as a faculty member in the School of Architecture at the University of Toronto. Having been taught by José Luis Sert (1902–1983) at the Harvard Graduate School of Design, Andrews would certainly have been aware of Team 10's fascination with architectural megastructures. Despite his relatively young age, Andrews was successful in persuading the University of Toronto's administration to entrust him with the preparation of a master plan for a new suburban campus in the eastern suburb of Scarborough, and with the design of its first academic building. **FIG 4**

4 opposite
**Scarborough College,
University of Toronto,
aerial view, Toronto,
Ontario. John Andrews
with Page and Steele
Architects, 1966.**

5 above
**Roofed concourse at
Simon Fraser University,
Burnaby, British Columbia.
Erickson / Massey
Architects, 1965.**

Andrews's megastructural design for Scarborough College (1966) is astonishing. It disposes its program—lecture halls, seminar rooms, faculty offices, science laboratories, and common spaces—within a pair of closely interconnected buildings along the edge of the dramatic Highland Creek ravine. A science wing stretches westward, with a stepped-back cross-section of vertically stacked laboratories and faculty offices. These spaces are accessed by a double-height, single-loaded pedestrian promenade that opens onto a landscaped plateau to the north. At each "knuckle" where the wing bends to respond to the winding ravine edge, the splay in the plan provides spaces for tiered lecture halls.

A humanities wing, arrayed in the opposite direction, has a similarly complex cross-section but steps outward to the south as it rises. Faculty offices and seminar rooms face the ravine, accessed from a spectacular multistory interior loggia, which separates these facilities from a series of lecture halls ranged along the north side. At the mid-point of the complex, where the science wing meets the humanities wing, the "meeting place," a large, skylighted atrium with a monumental staircase, interconnects the two principal public levels of the building's overall sectional order.

The building is entirely constructed of cast-in-place concrete, and this makes it not only an extraordinary megastructure, but also a child of the "brutalist" concrete architecture pioneered by Le Corbusier (1887–1965) during the previous decade. So knowing is Andrews's architectural vocabulary, he is even able, in the chimney stacks for the building's mechanical equipment, to reprise the smokestacks from Antonio Sant'Elia's (1888–1916) dramatic illustrations of a possible futurist architecture, drawn just before the First World War.[3]

The same year that construction commenced on Scarborough College, another megastructural campus began to materialize on the West Coast. Arthur Erickson (1924–2009) and his partner Geoffrey Massey (1924–) won the competition to create a master plan for a new university named for the early British explorer of Canada's west coast, Simon Fraser. Equally as bold as Andrews's Scarborough College—of which Erickson was a keen admirer—the design located Simon Fraser University's campus (1965) atop a hill in the eastern Vancouver suburb of Burnaby.

The design is organized around a long, east-west spine, which steps down to the west, even as its north and south sides also slope down adjacent hillsides. At the highest point of the plateau is the academic quadrangle. A landscaped courtyard with reflecting pools is framed by a large, rectangular, linear building raised up on pilotis, which houses faculty offices and seminar rooms. A monumental exterior staircase leads down to the main public outdoor space of the campus, bordered by the library and a grouping of science laboratories. This large space is protected from the rainy West Coast climate by a flat, space-frame glazed roof that makes it the largest public outdoor loggia in all of Canada. The university holds its convocations (or commencements) there—even the funeral of Arthur Erickson himself eventually took place there.[4] **FIG 5**

In 1969, another dramatic megastructure was conceived for the rolling hills of Southern Alberta. Arthur Erickson followed up his Simon Fraser University triumph with a powerful proposal for a new university in Lethbridge. Like the first phase of Scarborough College, the design combined all the functions of the university in a single building. It is possible that Erickson was influenced by the surreal photographic montage *Aircraft Carrier City*, published in 1964 by Austrian architect Hans Hollein (1934–2014), which shows a large aircraft carrier nestled in a rolling rural landscape.[5] **FIG 6** This is almost exactly the image of his proposal for the University of Lethbridge (1971), especially the view of it from the adjacent river valley. **FIG 7**

Erickson's original proposal included two long, linear, multistory buildings housing academic offices and classrooms. The buildings are offset from one another, with a large, glazed atrium linking them. To be sure, Lethbridge is not a "mat building" on the model of Berlin Free University, but on account of its radical concentration of programs in a single structure, it still qualifies as a megastructure. Regrettably, neither the linear building nor the atrium was ever constructed.[6]

Megastructural Montreal

In 1967, the focus of Canadian megastructure development shifted to Montreal, where, as part of the Expo celebration of that year, Moshe Safdie's Habitat opened its doors [see pages 43–46]. Safdie (1938–) had studied architecture at McGill University, where his thesis advisor was Sandy van Ginkel (1920–2009) (a member of Team 10 who immigrated to Canada in the 1960s with his wife and design partner, Blanche Lemco van Ginkel [1923–]). The young Safdie turned to the work of Team 10, and to Tokyo Bay in particular, for inspiration for his thesis design. The lead-up to Expo 67 created conditions propitious for the entertaining of radical new ideas, and, as a result, Safdie persuaded Expo authorities to implement a Kenzō Tange–like structure for housing in the neighborhood of Cité du Havre, just inside the Expo site.

It quickly became apparent that to build Safdie's thesis—a large superstructure supporting prefabricated housing units high in the air—was too costly a construction proposition. **FIG 8** Accordingly, Safdie, with the assistance of noted structural engineer August Komendant (1906–1992), modified his design to eliminate the superstructure altogether, instead designing housing units that were stacked, each one on top of the one beneath it. This still produced an extraordinarily dramatic volumetric effect, with L-shaped housing units interspersed with large open voids beneath and around them, and with terraces serving many of the units.

The result merges two iconic images from the architectural imagery of the period: on the one hand, that of the vernacular Mediterranean village on a hill, popularized by Bernard Rudofsky (1905–1988) in his influential book *Architecture Without Architects* (published in 1964), and, on the other hand, the image of an entire "other" city floating above an existing city, as in the drawings of Situationist architect Yona Friedman (1923–). Habitat came to be one of the most iconic projects of the entire 1967 World's Fair.[7] **FIG 9**

Meanwhile, in downtown Montreal, the firm Affleck, Desbarats, Dimakopoulos, Lebensold, and Sise was at work on another megastructure. Well-known in Montreal, the firm had already had great success in a series of competitions across Canada to erect cultural centers in the run-up to the long-planned Canadian centennial of 1967 [see chapter 1], constructing

9
**Habitat 67, final version
under construction,
Montreal, Quebec. Moshe
Safdie and David, Barott,
Boulva (Associated
Architects), 1967.**

the Queen Elizabeth Theatre in Vancouver (1959), Place des Arts in Montreal (1963), and the Confederation Centre of the Arts in Charlottetown (1964).

In 1964, partner Ray Affleck (1922–1989) decided to depart from the firm's relatively traditional modernist architectural language for a large, new project on a block over the main passenger rail corridor, immediately south of Montreal's Central Station. The complex was to contain a convention center, shopping concourse, commercial office space, and even a hotel. But instead of expressing each of these disparate program elements separately, as a traditional modernist parti would have done, Place Bonaventure—as the project built between 1964 and 1967 was called—welded these diverse programs into a single architectural volume, with the hotel taking the form of a sort of penthouse with courtyards on its roof. Place Bonaventure is a megastructure by virtue of the volumetric unification of disparate programs into a single, monolithic architectural form—one that is nonetheless closely linked to the rest of Montreal's downtown by means of its connections to the city's underground pedestrian walkway and subway systems. **FIG 10**

Craig, Zeidler & Strong's
Megastructure Trio

From the late 1960s through the early 1970s, the focus of these radical new design approaches shifted back to Toronto, where three remarkable projects commenced, all designed by the firm Craig, Zeidler & Strong (later to become Zeidler Partnership, then Zeidler Roberts Partnership). Eberhard Zeidler (1926–), a talented and energetic German immigrant to Canada, gradually became the firm's design leader. Much as Ray Affleck had done in Montreal, Zeidler—with a cadre of talented associates—consciously shifted the design focus of the firm away from the traditional modernist principles that it had been following and toward megastructure and high-tech ideas.[8]

The first of this trio of projects was the new Health Sciences Centre (1972) for McMaster University in Hamilton, Ontario. In 1965, McMaster appointed noted cardiologist and medical researcher John Evans as the founding dean of its medical faculty. Zeidler

12 left
McMaster Health Sciences Centre, main floor plan, Hamilton, Ontario. Craig, Zeidler & Strong, 1972.

13 opposite
Ontario Place, Toronto, Ontario. Craig, Zeidler & Strong, 1971.

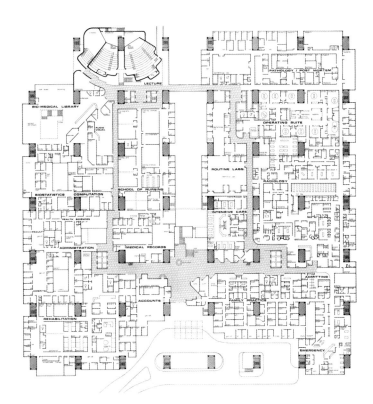

and Evans were acquainted with one another and shared an interest in innovative design; Zeidler's firm was thus approached to create a nontraditional facility for McMaster. The resulting design combined a number of current ideas about megastructure. The Health Sciences Centre is a "mat building"—a gridded matrix not unlike Berlin Free University.[9] But while Berlin Free University is only two stories high, the McMaster Building includes three occupied stories. **FIG 11**

Particularly notable are the new ideas Zeidler proposed for future flexibility and changeability, particularly through the device of the interstitial floor. Between each occupied story of the medical facility was located an entire separate story of space devoted to the specialized mechanical and electrical systems that form part of contemporary health-care design, and which could be modified or replaced without the building having to be evacuated. American architect Louis Kahn (1901–1974) had introduced the idea of interstitial spaces in buildings in the early 1960s, and the European members of Team 10 as well as the Japanese Metabolists were admirers of his. The resulting McMaster Health Sciences Centre is a megastructure comprising a very large three-dimensional matrix of habitable and service spaces. As one would expect, it makes this feature of its design its primary architectural iconography.[10] **FIG 12**

Zeidler and his colleagues continued their explorations on the megastructure theme with Ontario Place (1971), a recreational complex comprising a series of exhibition pavilions and entertainment venues erected partly on man-made extensions of the Lake Ontario shoreline, and partly over the lake itself. The scheme emerged from the provincial government's desire to emulate the great public success of Expo 67 in Montreal. Archigram's celebratory technological imagery is powerfully reprised in Ontario Place, and Yona Friedman's idea of an altogether new city hovering above the old one is equally visible in it. Zeidler also brought a sure sense of architectural detailing to this dramatic new iconography, which has made Ontario Place an unforgettable Canadian architectural icon of the 1970s—one which is both a megastructure and a triumphant display of high-tech virtuosity—even if the province of Ontario has not found suitable programming for the site in recent years.[11] **FIG 13**

Shortly after commencing work on the McMaster Health Sciences Centre and Ontario Place, the Zeidler firm found itself facing an even more complex design challenge. For a decade, Eaton's, once one of Toronto's (indeed Canada's) legacy department store companies, had been engaged in a project to launch an urban redevelopment project in downtown Toronto that would comprise a new retail store as well as a series of other uses, including a substantial quantity of office space. Early designs for a new "Eaton Centre" involved the

demolition of a number of historic buildings on the site—among them Toronto's 1899 Old City Hall, which had been rendered functionally redundant with the completion of Viljo Revell's (1910–1964) New City Hall (1965) [see pages 423–424]. To the company's dismay, Toronto residents rose up in opposition to the demolition. Between 1968 and 1972, the political situation in Toronto grew even more contentious with the arrival of an energetic new "reform" faction within the city council following the 1968 municipal election, and with that faction's takeover of political power following the 1972 election of reform mayor David Crombie (1936–).

These political developments worsened the prospects for city approval of Eaton Centre, so the company decided to bring in a major developer: the Cadillac-Fairview Corporation. Cadillac-Fairview had already enjoyed political success with its Toronto-Dominion Centre (1969) designed by Mies van der Rohe (1886–1969), the first phase of which was already complete and occupied. Phyllis Lambert (1927–), a member of the wealthy Bronfman family that controlled the Fairview portion of Cadillac-Fairview—and by this time also a militant advocate of heritage preservation—stepped in, suggesting that new architects be considered for the projects. She recommended making Zeidler Roberts part of the design team for Eaton Centre, which already included Bregman and Hamman. The new involvement, it was hoped, would improve the design and facilitate its passage through approvals in Toronto's changed political climate.

The choice of the Zeidler firm to rescue the Eaton Centre project proved to be brilliant. The newly expanded design team decided to accept the retention of not only the entire Old City Hall, but also the venerable Church of the Holy Trinity, another important building on the project's superblock site. Locating the new Eaton's store at the edge of the site at Dundas Street allowed them to keep the existing store, south of Queen Street, open until the new one was ready for occupancy. The plan included other urban innovations as well. The completed project (1977, phase one) would extend all the way from Queen Street to Dundas Street on a site that sloped very gradually to the north, with existing subway stations at each end. It therefore became possible to create a unique architectural cross-section for the project: the shopping concourse had four different levels, each directly connected

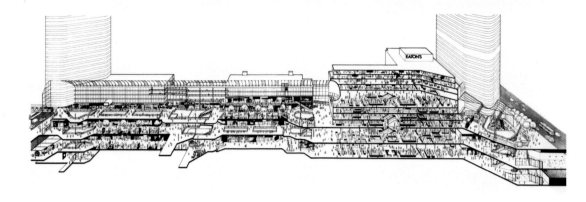

15 above
Eaton Centre, cut-away north-south cross-section, Toronto, Ontario. Bregman and Hamann Architects and Zeidler Partnership, 1977.

16 opposite, top
Eaton Centre, aerial view.

17 opposite, bottom
Eaton Centre, original Yonge Street facade, now demolished.

with ground level, a below-grade transit concourse, or an over-street pedestrian bridge. This multilateral connectivity surpassed that of any other shopping facility in Canada. In a design tour-de-force, Zeidler proposed that the multilevel shopping concourse be modeled on the great Victor Emmanuel Galleria in Milan (1877). Finally, the design team developed a vocabulary of architectural detail for the project that began with a glistening white super-structure and was fleshed out with a brilliantly detailed metallic interior. For example, free-standing cylindrical aluminum heat diffusers at the entrances are modeled directly on the ones in Otto Wagner's Post Office Savings Bank in Vienna (1906).

Toronto thus came to possess the most dramatic shopping mall in all of Canada. In its bold, if historically sensitive, design concept and its superlative technical detailing, it married the twin ideas of the megastructure and high-tech, with success unsurpassed anywhere else in the world.[12] **FIGS 14–17**

Prairie Megastructures

After the University of Lethbridge, megastructure ideas were also introduced to other cities on the Canadian Prairies. In 1969, Toronto firm Diamond and Myers and Edmonton

18
HUB (Housing Union
Building), view of mall,
University of Alberta,
Edmonton, Alberta.
Diamond and Myers
Architects and Rick Wilkin
Architect, Barton Myers,
partner-in-charge,
1971.

architect Rick Wilkin were appointed architects for a new student residence at the University of Alberta. Jack Diamond (1932–) and Barton Myers (1934–) were both relative newcomers to Canada, having immigrated in the mid-1960s and established a partnership in Toronto. The concept of the HUB building (1971) is utterly simple—similar, in fact, to that of Zeidler's Eaton Centre. A long, skylighted galleria forms an elevated, indoor pedestrian street. Retail and student service facilities are located along its length, while student housing is located on the stories above. Some of the student rooms open onto the upper void space of the galleria, while others face out toward the rest of the campus. **FIG 18** In 1970, further south in Alberta, a distinctive urban idea was launched by planners working for the City of Calgary under the guidance of architect Harold Hanen (1935–2000).[13]

Hanen and his colleagues imported a European idea that had been developed by members of Team 10—that of an urban pedestrian walkway system elevated one story above grade—and proposed that it be extended throughout the built fabric of downtown Calgary. Eventually named the +15 system (on account of its approximate height, fifteen feet above street level), Hanen's idea gradually gained acceptance. From the early 1970s onward, it continued to expand throughout Calgary's downtown, making the elevated pedestrian system the most extensive of its type in the world.

Also in 1970, the Winnipeg office of Moody, Moore, Duncan, Rattray, Peters, Searle, and Christie brought yet another of Team 10's ideas to their city. Like their counterparts in Montreal and Toronto, the firm was known for its mastery of the traditional vocabulary of international modernism, but it chose a new direction for the design of the University of Winnipeg's Centennial Hall (1972). Rather than demolishing an existing building on the site, it proposed constructing a new building partly over the top of it, using an independent structural system to carry the new construction above. Predictably enough, the visual expression of the project centers on the bold vertical and horizontal trusses that pass over the existing building below. **FIG 19**

The last project in Winnipeg is, in a number of respects, an outlier in this commentary, for it is not a megastructure—it is not a large building, nor is it mixed-use, nor does it attempt to emulate a "city" in its architectural form. However, the Winnipeg office building

19 opposite, top
Centennial Hall, University of Winnipeg, Winnipeg, Manitoba. Moody, Moore, Duncan, Rattray, Peters, Searle, Christie, 1972.

20 opposite, bottom
IKOY office, interior view, Winnipeg, Alberta. IKOY Architects, 1978.

that the IKOY Architects built for itself in 1978 is arguably the period's most sophisticated example of "high-tech" architecture in Canada. Two tilt-up cast-in-place concrete walls are the building's primary means of vertical structural support. Open-web steel joists span the space between these side walls, and the two end walls are entirely glazed—one of them looking out over a tributary of Winnipeg's Red River. Within this double-height, clear-span space, a freestanding pavilion accommodates meeting rooms and service areas, with an open mezzanine overhead.

Not only does IKOY's office building (1978) display elegant and minimalist interior detailing, it does so in an extraordinarily cost-effective way. Principal Ron Keenberg's (1941–) and his colleagues' ability to come up with economical yet visually compelling architectural solutions is aptly captured in this small building. **FIG 20**

Robson Square, Vancouver

For the last building complex in this sequence, we return to Vancouver and to the remarkable project for Robson Square (1983) designed by Arthur Erickson [see pages 177–179]. Vancouver's Provincial Courthouse had for many years been in need of expansion or replacement. The last Social Credit government of British Columbia, headed by Premier W.A.C. Bennett (1900–1979), had commissioned a design for a high-rise tower to accommodate courthouse functions on the block south of the existing courthouse. But in 1972, a general election led to the victory of the provincial New Democratic Party (NDP). One of the new government's first moves was to cancel the scheme for the high-rise tower and to hire Arthur Erickson to prepare an alternative design. Erickson responded to this challenge with a radically different approach, creating in the process the extraordinarily distinctive project for downtown Vancouver that Kenneth Frampton has called a "megaform" building. Eschewing altogether the high-rise format of the previous scheme, Erickson proposed instead a three-block-long linear megastructure. It weaves over and under the existing ground plane of downtown Vancouver, creating a recreational space that is extensively landscaped with the assistance of long-time collaborator Cornelia Oberlander (1921–). **FIG 21–22**

21
Robson Square, site
model, Vancouver, British
Columbia. Arthur Erickson
Architects, 1983.

On the northernmost block sits the original courthouse building, designed by noted British Columbia–based architect Francis Rattenbury (1867–1935), refurbished as a facility for the Vancouver Art Gallery. A new south entrance for the gallery opens onto a sunken plaza that passes under Robson Street, before starting to gradually rise up toward an elevated public platform that passes over Smithe Street. A further ascent leads to the public entrance to the spectacular concourse of the new Law Courts building, which occupies the southernmost block of the site. Indisputably a megastructure as well as a landform, Robson Square radically transforms the sectional character of downtown Vancouver while not in any way interrupting the continuity of public open space at grade. Both Robson Street and Symthe Street remain continuous at grade, and the great public landscape that passes under the first street and over the second street includes extensive plantings, reflecting pools, and even waterfalls. Oberlander's landscape scheme, now fully mature, provides downtown Vancouver with one of its most lush swaths of verdant green shrubbery and trees.

The courts themselves are organized in a stepped-back section facing northwest onto a large, skylighted entrance concourse. Public balconies accessing the various levels of the courts look down over the concourse within a vast and serene public room. The roof overhead is a sloping space frame, which produces a light condition even more luminous than that under the space frame at Simon Fraser University. Adding to the feeling of lightness, the roof is supported on delicate diagonal metal connectors that rest on top of the dramatic cast-in-place concrete "knees" that are the building's primary structure.[14] **FIG 23**

Conclusion and Epilogue:
The Eventual Demise of the Megastructure,
and the Assimilation of High-Tech into
Normative Practice

It is notable that none in this series of remarkable buildings was designed by a "starchitect" from abroad. Ray Affleck, Arthur Erickson, and Ron Keenberg of IKOY were born and bred Canadians who spent their entire careers working primarily on Canadian projects for sites in Canada. Moshe Safdie immigrated to Canada as a teenager and was trained and began his career in Montreal before moving to the United States later on. John Andrews, Eberhard Zeidler, A. J. Diamond, and Barton Myers all immigrated to Canada as adult professionals and established their practices here. Zeidler and Diamond elected to remain based in Toronto, and even Andrews and Myers, who eventually returned to their home countries, nevertheless had long, successful, deeply rooted practices in Canada. Yet despite their collective Canadian rootedness, this group was largely responsible for the creation of a set of projects that put architecture in Canada on the world stage in a way that has not been surpassed either before or since.

What has become of the megastructure project now? The best-known chronicler of the megastructure, historian and critic Reyner Banham (1922–1988), titled his 1976 history of

the typology *Megastructure: Urban Futures of the Recent Past*—an unexpectedly elegiac phrase for a usually passionate advocate of the "new" in architecture. In his book, Banham notes that after the 1970s, the megastructure simply ceased to be a force in architecture.[15] And that is certainly the case in Canada.

A few key factors may have played a role in this disappointing turn of events. For a start, a number of the Canadian megastructures discussed here turned out to be quite expensive to construct. For example, despite its glamorous allure, not until very recently has anyone attempted to reprise Habitat 67—even without the originally proposed Tange-like super-structure. Moreover, one might recall James A. Murray's observation made not long after Habitat was completed—that despite its precocious architectural form, it does not generate a residential density much higher than normal suburban single-family housing.[16] Erickson's building for the University of Lethbridge also proved to be costly, and this is probably one of the reasons that the original design was never entirely completed.

Then there is the promise of future flexibility that a number of these buildings purport-ed to offer. In the case of Zeidler's Eaton Centre, the "glistening white superstructure" that produced its dramatic, original exterior appearance was designed to support different future facade elements over time. And sure enough, some years later, Cadillac-Fairview did, in fact, re-skin the entire Yonge Street frontage of the complex. But alas, the re-skinning com-pletely traduced the original Zeidler facade concept. The glistening white superstructure was obliterated, and the new facade was utterly shallow—physically shallow in its failure to embody any of the volumetric plasticity of the original scheme, and formally shallow in its embarrassingly inept pastiche of the historical shop fronts that had once existed on the site.

In the case of the McMaster Health Sciences Centre, few of the opportunities for change offered by the interstitial space have been acted upon in the intervening years. It seems as well that the design reprised three of the problematic issues that were inherent in the Berlin Free University model. First, the building perimeter is daunting to approach as a pedestrian—the putative "urbanity" of the interior matrix does not transition well to the surroundings. Second, both buildings have a problematic relationship to ground level. With their main floors raised above the surrounding grade, they are somewhat socially severed from pedestrian routes around them. Finally, at McMaster, as at Berlin, many of the interior circulation routes do not quite succeed at feeling like public streets.[17]

Then there is the problem of the elevated urban pedestrian walkway system. Although Calgary has continued to expand the +15 system—the real-estate industry has become attached to it—it is not without its critics. Many see it as having sapped the life out of pedestrian activity at grade. At a planning conference in Calgary a few years back, a member of the city planning staff remarked that having the +15 system in the city was a bit like having an elderly and crazy aunt living in your attic: you never knew whether or not to acknowledge her presence to visitors to your home. Diamond and Myers, in their design for the HUB building, also located its public concourse one level above grade, a move which has constrained its full integration into the overall campus network of pedestrian routes.

The high-tech aspiration has fared better. Rather than having been abandoned, it has simply been absorbed into mainstream architectural practice. One sees it, for example, in Barton Myers's Wolf House in Toronto (1974), as well as in more recent projects by firms such as architectsAlliance in Toronto and Marc Boutin Architectural Collaborative in Calgary.

Contemporary reconsideration is perhaps most owed to the final project in my sequence, Erickson's Robson Square. Along with Eaton Centre in Toronto, it is the project from the megastructure era that has had the greatest impact in Canada, particularly on the form and the character of Vancouver's downtown. It is, in short, Erickson's masterpiece. Only a few years after it was completed, Erickson was awarded the Gold Medal of the American Institute of Architects, one of only three Canadian architects to be so honored. Yet since 2000, it has been seriously neglected by its owner, the government of British Columbia, which has been responsible for a series of maladroit modifications to its details that compromise the project's integrity. Moreover, the Vancouver Art Gallery has commissioned a design for a new facility, which, if built, will entail the departure of the gallery from its Robson Square quarters. There is some risk that the necessary funding will not be found, in which case it will probably prove necessary for the gallery to expand its facilities on the Robson Square site instead.

Let us hope that in either of these two eventualities, the government of British Columbia will step up to the plate, and provide the economic means and enlightened leadership both to respond to the needs of the Vancouver Art Gallery and to restore Robson Square as a whole—reflecting pools, waterfalls, and all—to its original Ericksonian glory.

6

Postmodernism: Reconnecting with History, Memory, and Place

Larry Wayne Richards

Heterarchy and the International Context

In the 1960s, a reaction to modern architecture and its limitations emerged in Canada, Europe, and the United States. Modernism's post–World War II emphasis on abstraction, technologically driven rationality, avoidance of ornament, and disregard for history became suspect. Architects began to consider how deeper connections might be made with specific histories and contexts to create distinctive, human-centered places. Embracing relativism, pluralism, hybridity, and popular culture, a bold critique of modernism gained momentum, reflecting the heterarchical nature of a radically changed world. This rupture generated a postmodern architecture in Canada that appeared from coast to coast and as far north as Yellowknife, capital of the Northwest Territories.

As a cultural phenomenon, postmodernism is elusive. It operates under the broader geopolitical umbrella of global postmodernity, wherein modern notions of time and space became radically compressed following World War II. Among prominent philosophers and writers, there are divergent positions about how postmodernity and postmodernism evolved and how they operate within globalized late-capitalism.[1] A central question remains unanswered: is postmodernism a radical departure from modernism or a critical

1 left
Mississauga City Hall, view from southeast, Mississauga, Ontario. Jones & Kirkland Architects, 1987.

2 opposite, left
Vanna Venturi House, front facade, Chestnut Hill, Pennsylvania. Robert Venturi Architect, 1964.

3 opposite, right
Kresge College, view of piazzetta, University of California Santa Cruz. Moore and Turnbull / MLTW Architects, 1974.

rewriting of modernity? Regardless of definitions, notions of time-space simultaneity and fluidity have accelerated in recent decades with the development of the internet, social media, and digital convergence—phenomena that characterize the early twenty-first century Information Age and that underscore anxieties around the loss of meaning in architecture.[2] Postmodernism in architecture must be considered within this complicated historical trajectory.

In Canada, hints of an emerging postmodern architecture appeared in the 1960s, and full-fledged postmodern buildings were realized a decade later. The core group of early postmodernists—including George Baird, Melvin Charney, Jack Diamond, Richard Henriquez, Roger Kemble, Brian MacKay-Lyons, Barton Myers, and Peter Rose—were measured and reserved in their deployment of the style. They sought architectural expression reflecting deep relationships with history and the city, and they established subtle linkages to vernacular buildings and local landscapes. Canadian postmodernism reached its zenith in the 1980s with internationally acclaimed examples such as the Mississauga City Hall (1987) and the Canadian Centre for Architecture (1989). **FIGS 1 & 22–26** Similar to other eruptions in the march of modernism, the postmodern style only lasted a few decades, effectively subsiding in the 1990s.

To understand Canadian postmodernism, it is useful to examine the origins of the style. Postmodernism's arrival on the world stage was signaled by the seminal research of the American architect Robert Venturi (1925–2018), a member of the Philadelphia School.[3] His 1966 book, *Complexity and Contradiction in Architecture*, was broadly influential. While writing it, Venturi designed the first building in the United States displaying the pure tenets of postmodernism—a house for his mother, Vanna Venturi, completed in a Philadelphia suburb in 1964. Imaginatively manipulating scale and incorporating nonmodern elements, such as a gabled roof and applied ornament, the Vanna Venturi house was confrontational and provoked an "aha" moment that sparked a new direction for architecture. **FIG 2**

Around the same time, Charles Moore (1925–1993) designed the first phase of the Sea Ranch development on the coast of California.[4] Completed in 1965, the rugged "shed style" recalled barns in the region and western mine shafts, rebuking the placelessness of the International Style. Moore became a leader in the American postmodern movement, gaining acclaim for his 1974 Kresge College on the Santa Cruz campus of the University of California. **FIG 3** Conceived like an Italian village winding up the hillside, the residential college was colorful and playful, underscoring postmodernism's irreverent breach with pious modernism.

Postmodernism ignited internationally in the 1970s. Agents for change included Hans Hollein in Austria; James Gowan, James Stirling, and Terry Farrell in England; Christian de Portzamparc in France; Ricardo Bofill in France and Spain; Alessandro Mendini, Paolo Portoghesi, and Aldo Rossi in Italy; Arata Isozaki, Hiroshi Hara, Kazuhiro Ishii, and Minoru Takeyama in Japan; and Léon Krier in Luxembourg. Gowan said about his work: "We were reacting against the older generation, setting up a critique of what might be done—a reaction against boredom, plainness and the mechanical nature of contemporary rationalism, of social rationalism and dainty well-produced things."[5]

The architecturally tumultuous decade of the 1970s was capped by the first Venice Architecture Biennale, directed by Paolo Portoghesi in 1980 and titled "The Presence of the Past." The most prominent and debated component of the Biennale was *La Strada Novissima*, a hypothetical postmodern street constructed in the Corderie dell'Arsenale and consisting

4 left
Municipal Services
Building, Portland, Oregon.
Michael Graves Architect,
1982.

5 opposite
York Square, view from
southeast, Toronto,
Ontario. Diamond & Myers
Architects, 1968.

of twenty full-scale theatrical facades by prominent architects. The selection zeroed in on the historicist wing of postmodernism, which, for the most part, meant installations by architects committed to postmodern classicism or freestyle classicism.

The broad desire to reconnect with history, memory, and place that manifested in architecture from the 1960s through the 1980s was complicated and controversial. Canadian-Israeli architect Moshe Safdie (1938–) penned a critique of postmodernism, "Private Jokes in Public Places," published in 1981.[6] He attacked the likes of American postmodernists Michael Graves (1934–2015), Charles Moore, and Stanley Tigerman (1930–), seeing their work as narcissistic and obsessed with image. But, ironically, just a few years after his dismissal of postmodernism, Safdie designed the striking National Gallery of Canada in Ottawa using a heavily Gothicized architectural language inspired by the nearby Notre-Dame Basilica and the Parliament Hill Buildings across the Ottawa River.[7] Similarly, highly respected Canadian architect Arthur Erickson (1924–2009) decried postmodernism while giving more than a nod to it in his 1989 Canadian Embassy in Washington, DC—an elegant but stylistically ambiguous work of architecture that translates aspects of Washington's classicism.[8]

The postmodern movement led to extremes, such as the cartoonish classicism of Michael Graves (Municipal Services Building, Portland, 1982), Philip Johnson and John Burgee

(AT&T Building, New York, 1984), and Robert A. M. Stern (Roy O. Disney Animation Building, Burbank, 1994). **FIG 4** In contrast, and to their credit, Canadian postmodernists were largely more subdued and less image conscious than their American counterparts. Driven by interest in local traditions, a desire for specificity, and a deep commitment to city building and the public realm, the most thoughtful postmodern expressions in Canada offered a welcome counterpoint to the placeless, dehumanizing side of modernity.

Early Postmodernism
in Canada, 1963–1983

In Canada, perhaps the earliest sign of postmodern thought was the opening of Massey College by Ron Thom (1923–1986), with Thompson, Berwick & Pratt, in 1963 [see pages 94–98]. The University of Toronto residential college resulted from a 1960 national design competition. Inspired by the colleges of Oxford and Cambridge and incorporating cut-stone ornament, the building was considered by many modernists to be too traditional —and for many traditionalists, too modern. Although not postmodern in the current definition of the term, Massey College confronted orthodox modernists.

Five years later, in 1968, Jack Diamond (1932–) and Barton Myers (1934–) completed Toronto's York Square in the then hippy village of Yorkville. It was an innovative urban infill project, incorporating Victorian houses around a courtyard. York Square's public face included an imposing brick wall with huge circular windows and bold supergraphics by Barrie Briscoe. York Square was certainly proto-postmodern—if not brazenly postmodern. **FIG 5**

The first thoroughly postmodern project in Canada was a church near Toronto by architect and theorist George Baird (1939–), completed in 1974. Four years earlier, Baird and Charles Jencks had coedited *Meaning in Architecture*, a postmodern exploration of architecture and semiology.[9] The late nineteenth-century Dunbarton-Fairport United Church was gutted by fire in 1973; the following year, Baird and his young design team generated a solution that symbolically incorporated the memory of the fire through a dense layering of old and new elements. **FIG 6** The rebuilt sanctuary paid homage to Venturi's call for complexity and contradiction, whereas the concrete block annex—in Baird's words, "a rather deadpan addition"[10]—reflected Baird's notion that a "thoughtful ordinary" attitude is often appropriate. The church reconstruction was one of a family of modest but inventive postmodern projects that Baird completed in the early 1970s, displaying contextual specificity and multivalence.[11]

While Baird's church reconstruction was underway in Ontario, Peter Rose (1943–) was making waves in Quebec. Rose, a native of Montreal, graduated from the Yale School of Architecture, where he studied under two leading proponents of postmodernism, Charles Moore and Vincent Scully (1920–2017), and attended lectures by visiting professor Robert Venturi. As Rose puts it: "The late-1960s…it was a tumultuous time. Woodstock, campus riots at Columbia University, the Black Panthers in New Haven. The Yale School of Architecture was at the center of things. Postmodernism was, in part, a product of this great cultural upheaval."[12] From 1973 to 1975, Rose designed the Gothic-inspired Bradley House in Quebec's Eastern Townships. Completed in 1979, the inventive house related to the vernacular buildings of the region. **FIGS 7–8** Numerous projects in Rose's distinctive "organic postmodern" style were realized, including the picturesque Pavilion Soixante-Dix at Saint-Sauveur, Quebec (1977).[13] The ski lodge was the only Canadian project included in

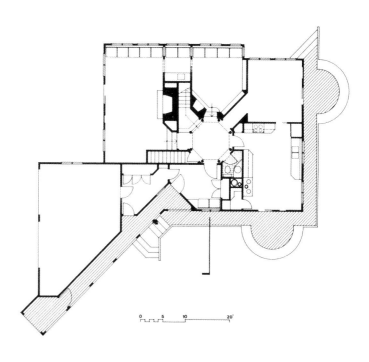

Charles Jencks's 1980 publication *Post-Modern Classicism: The New Synthesis.* Rose's highest achievement came a decade later: the Canadian Centre for Architecture (CCA) in Montreal, designed with consulting architect Phyllis Lambert (1927–) and associate architect Erol Argun.

Another Quebecer, Melvin Charney (1935–2012), was also launching postmodern provocations in the 1970s. His densely layered drawings, collages, and site-specific installations spanned art, architecture, and urbanism; often taking the form of public art, his work embraced a critical outlook and inspired civic action. Charney's ambitious Montreal construction *Les maisons de la rue Sherbrooke* (1976) consisted of two full-sized facades made of rough plywood mounted on pipe scaffolding. **FIG 9** The facades looked like stage sets and were built to mirror two greystone townhouses on the opposite side of the intersection. Charney explained that:

> The material disposition of the facades recalls the articulation of elaborate cut-stone facades supported by ordinary brick side walls found elsewhere in the street; it also echoes the essential scenographic structure of the street. In contrast to nearby buildings, however, the hollow openings and exposed underpinnings of the installation represent either the

9 opposite
Les maisons de la rue Sherbrooke, installation on Sherbrooke Street, Montreal, Quebec, for the exhibition *Corridart*. Melvin Charney Architect, 1976.

10 right
Melvin Charney, *Fragments [1]: La Maison de la Rivière-des-Prairies*, 1975–1978. Reprographic copy with colored pencil.

ruins of a building or the pieces of a building under construction. In either case, the installation describes something more physical than a drawing and less material than a finished building.[14]

Charney's narrative presented a sophisticated critique of Montreal's sometimes mindless, modern "urban renewal," with its general disregard for the city's history. Intended to accompany the city's Olympic Games, the project was perceived as highly confrontational, and one week after the installation, municipal authorities ordered its destruction. In a similar vein, photographic projects by Charney presented neglected, deteriorating vernacular buildings in marginal areas of the province's industrial towns and cities. **FIG 10**

Charney's haunting images of disembodied building faces presaged the early postmodern work of Vancouver architect Richard Henriquez (1941–), whose Firehall No. 22 (1979) features a detached facade. **FIG 11** There is a symmetrical, billboard-like front that frames the entry and hides a pair of exterior, steel exit stairs. Inspired by the screen-wall facades of Robert Venturi and Romaldo Giurgola (1920–2016), Henriquez had played with "masks" in earlier urban projects, such as the Lee Building and Gaslight Square (with Robert Todd). Masks imply multiple identities: the real person hides behind a fictional character. This double-coding was integral to postmodern thinking.

Architects Bruno Freschi (1937–) and Roger Kemble (1929–) were also prominent in Vancouver's postmodern movement. Freschi's 1980 Ping Pong Gelateria on Vancouver's Robson Street—a fanciful essay in color, light, and form—included a neon-lined barrel vault supported on classical Corinthian columns, recalling Italian Renaissance architecture. The columns served as handles for the oversized apricot-orange hoops above, together implying ping-pong paddles. **FIG 12** Kemble, an *enfant terrible* in the Vancouver architecture community, realized his beguiling Smith Villa on a waterfront site in 1982. It fused aspects of Art Deco and suburban spec-builder vernacular with energy-conserving strategies.

In Canada's Prairies, Daniel Jenkins, Barry Johns, David Lieberman, Leslie Stechesen, Jeremy Sturgess, Fred Valentine, and Rick Wilkin produced spirited postmodern work in the 1970s and 1980s [see pages 324–325]. One of the most delightful buildings from this era is the house Stechesen (1934–) designed for his family. The home spans a ravine on the banks of the Red River in Winnipeg. Completed in 1975, the barnlike structure is clad in rough-sawn cedar and has long, horizontal bands of windows with traditional, small panes that contrast with the quirky diamond-shaped windows dotting the gabled ends of the house like staccato notes. **FIG 13** The rustic form of the Stechesen House, along with details such as the dining room's saddle-bag bay window, recall Charles Moore's Sea Ranch of 1965.

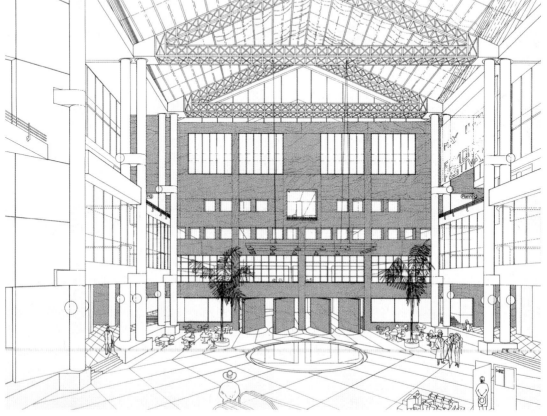

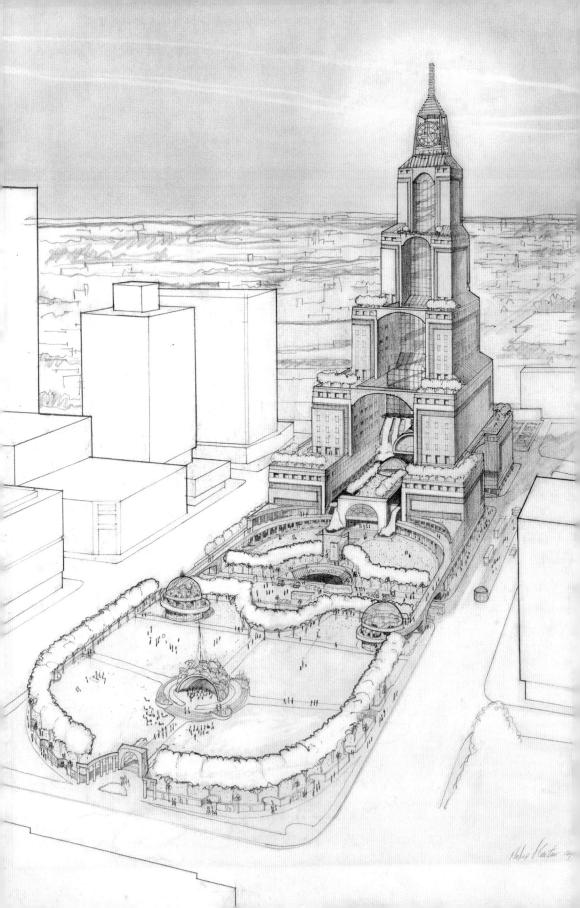

15 opposite
Perspective view, Edmonton City Hall competition submission by Phillip J. Carter Architect, 1980.

16 above, left
Lyons Tower, Five Island Lake, Nova Scotia. Networks, 1980.

17 above, right
Axonometric drawing of MacKay-Lyons farmhouse, Upper Kingsburg, Nova Scotia. Brian MacKay-Lyons Architect, 1986.

The 1980 Edmonton City Hall Competition, which received ninety-nine entries from across Canada, produced an outpouring of postmodern designs.[15] The winning project by Gene Dub (1943–), completed in 1992, presents an extruded scheme that is stylistically mute on the outside but packed with postmodern elements inside, such as its building-within-a-building council chamber. Michael Kirkland's (1943–) highly symmetrical design, which received a merit award, was among the more compelling postmodern submissions. Aspects of Kirkland's proposal foreshadowed his winning project with Edward Jones (1939–) two years later in the Mississauga City Hall Competition—particularly the imposing City Room that appears in both projects. **FIG 14** The competition also produced grandiose visions, such as Phillip Carter's monumental city hall, reminiscent of the art deco skyscrapers of the 1920s and '30s. **FIG 15** Carter would become one of Canada's definitive postmodernists, as exemplified by his Lillian Smith Public Library in Toronto (1995).

On the east coast, Brian MacKay-Lyons (1954–) conducted a series of postmodern experiments between 1978 and 1980 with the Halifax-based group Networks, including a residential tower addition at Five Island Lake, Nova Scotia.[16] **FIG 16** Later, MacKay-Lyons studied and worked in California—first with Charles Moore and then with Barton Myers.

18 left
Joe Tobie Building, front
entry facade, Yellowknife,
Northwest Territories.
Michael D. Hilchey
Architect, c. 1983.

19 opposite, top
Unionville Library, exterior.
Markham, Ontario. Barton
Myers Associates Architect,
1984.

20 opposite, bottom
Unionville Library, interior.

Soon after returning to Nova Scotia in 1983, he completed a project on the Atlantic coast for his family that inserted a new lighthouse-inspired tower into a nineteenth-century farmhouse (1986). **FIG 17** The skillful postmodern synthesis of old and new was born out of MacKay-Lyons's deep attachment to the landscape and vernacular buildings of his native Nova Scotia, underpinned by his broader commitment to cultural continuity [see chapter 11]. Eventually his allegiance to the playful placemaking emphasized by his early mentor, Charles Moore, yielded to a stronger attraction to critical regionalism, defined by Kenneth Frampton in Hal Foster's 1983 book *Postmodern Culture*.[17]

Postmodern architecture also spread to the northern territories of Canada, where it can be seen in the classically symmetrical, colorfully patterned Joe Tobie Building in Yellowknife, Northwest Territories. Designed by Michael Hilchey and completed in 1983, the building's clownish exuberance is striking in downtown Yellowknife, particularly during the long, dark winter. **FIG 18** But is this a welcome frivolity or the imposition of a foreign style unsuitable for Yellowknife's history and climate? The Tobie Building represents the extent to which the postmodern aesthetic and its accompanying cultural controversies had, by 1983, reached all corners of Canada.

Pinnacles of Canadian Postmodernism, 1984–1989

Across the spectrum of Canadian postmodernism, three buildings resonate strongly—Unionville Library (1984), Mississauga City Hall (1987), and the Canadian Centre for Architecture (1989)—along with a set of Vancouver towers by Richard Henriquez. Realized within a five-year period, these projects represent high points in Canadian postmodernism.

Unionville Library, 1984

During the 1980s, then Toronto-based architect Barton Myers designed several buildings that successfully merged high-tech and postmodernism: the Portland Center for the Performing Arts in Portland, Oregon; the Seagram Museum in Waterloo, Ontario; and the

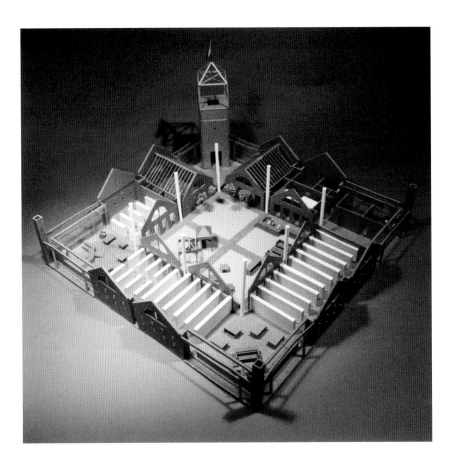

Unionville Library in Markham, Ontario. Of these, the 1984 Unionville Library is the most rigorous and refined. **FIGS 19–21**

The library's articulated red and yellow brick volume rises from a square plan that is divided into a grid of sixteen smaller squares. The four central squares constitute what Myers calls a "village square," graced above by a grid of sixteen canvas-lined skylights. Eight "houses" face the central square. An intentionally half-complete civic tower, set at forty-five degrees, announces the entry corner, while fireplaces, also set at forty-five degrees, anchor the other three corners of the building. This geometric rigor stems from Myers having studied and worked under architect Louis Kahn (1901–1974) in Philadelphia.

Contextually, the library fits comfortably with its surroundings. Myers says: "In response to the town's strict architectural guidelines, the library represents a playful reinterpretation of the Victorian tradition, creating a modern building completely at home within the sensitive historical context."[18] Some thirty years later, the Unionville Library continues to be a dignified oasis of calm: an astutely scaled, well-proportioned, humanizing environment. Moreover, its contextual fit—its sense of place—transcends matters of style.

21 opposite
Unionville Library,
architectural model,
Markham, Ontario.
Barton Myers Associates
Architect, 1984.

22 right
Mississauga City Hall,
view of the City Room,
Mississauga, Ontario.
Jones & Kirkland
Architects, 1987.

Mississauga City Hall
(now Mississauga Civic Centre), 1987

In 1982, the City of Mississauga invited Canadian architects to participate in a one-stage competition for the design of a new city hall and civic square. Located immediately west of metropolitan Toronto, Mississauga had a population of 327,000 and was rapidly growing. Guided by its ambitious mayor, Hazel McCallion, the city wanted a civic landmark and a building that would inaugurate a new pattern of denser urban form and pedestrianization. **FIGS 22–23**

From the 246 competition submissions, the international jury—comprising George Baird, Russell Edmunds, Douglas Kilner, Phyllis Lambert, Jerome Markson, and James Stirling—unanimously selected the Toronto firm of Jones & Kirkland as the winner, stating in their report that the submission was "superior by a significant margin to any other entry."[19] Barton Myers Associates, whose Unionville Library project was being concurrently designed, received second place.

Volumetrically and spatially complex, the completed building is an aggregation of five components: a long, pedimented south-facing block stretching across the center of the site; a low entry block to the north with a pyramidal skylight; a formal outdoor square focused

23
Mississauga City Hall,
view from southeast,
Mississauga, Ontario.
Jones & Kirkland
Architects, 1987.

on a reflecting pool and bordered on the east and west by freestanding arcades; an administrative tower block and clock tower to the northwest; and a cylindrical form accommodating the council chamber. The heart of the composition is the City Room, a flexible public gathering space clad in green marble and bathed in natural light from pyramidal skylights above. From the City Room, one reaches a monumental stair that flows westward, rising through the administrative tower block, and narrowing eccentrically at the top.

Jones and Kirkland explained their concept: "The idea of the City Hall representing the memory of the city in miniature came to mind—the explicitness of a Bastide town, geometrically finite within its own internal logic, indifferent to its [largely suburban] surroundings."[20] They developed an architectural language for the public elements "indebted to Gunnar Asplund's Court House of 1921 and Stockholm City Library of 1920,"[21] retrieving and translating Nordic classicism. Imagery for the city hall was also drawn from Ontario's nineteenth-century tradition of robust masonry civic buildings and from clusters of farm buildings, including barns, grain silos, and sheds. The scheme owes some debt, moreover, to Leon Krier's 1978 project for a school at Saint Quentin-en-Yvelines, France.

Rooted in European neoclassicism while avoiding overt historicism, the Mississauga Civic Centre simultaneously embraces Frampton's critical regionalism with its references

to Ontario's municipal and vernacular buildings. Jones and Kirkland fused various 1980s tendencies into a strong, original polemic, creating an enduring architecture.

Canadian Centre for Architecture and Gardens, 1989

The Canadian Centre for Architecture (CCA) was founded by Phyllis Lambert in Montreal in 1979 "as an independent study centre and museum to further the understanding of architecture and to help establish architecture as a public concern."[22] Lambert shaped a vision for the future building as "a place of discourse, a literate architecture that is part of the contradictions and realities of the city and of history."[23] In 1983, she engaged architect Peter Rose to work with her to realize the project. **FIGS 24–25**

For Rose and Lambert, Montreal was a subject of study, "a treatise on how buildings are put together and how they relate to each other." Lambert writes, "Although we had been trained very differently (he by Charles Moore, I by Mies van der Rohe), the architecture of Montreal was our common ground."[24] Construction commenced in 1985 on a building deeply related to the landscape, history, and culture of the city. Through a design

26 left
CCA Garden, Canadian
Centre for Architecture,
view looking north,
Montreal, Quebec. Melvin
Charney, Architect, 1990.

27 opposite
Vertical City proposal
for Vancouver, British
Columbia. Richard
Henriquez Architect,
various iterations, 1985-
2015. Digital model
collage, 2015.

competition, Melvin Charney received the commission for the adjacent sculpture garden (1990). **FIG 26**

The CCA's E-shaped composition includes the restored nineteenth-century greystone Shaughnessy House, which faces Boulevard René-Lévesque. Lambert bought the grand, bilaterally symmetrical mansion (actually two semidetached houses) in the early 1970s, saving it from demolition. Realized in the French Second Empire style, the house became a key generator of the essentially classical language of the CCA. The historic Shaughnessy house was surrounded by a new C-shaped building, courtyards, and a public garden and park.

Materially, the new building contrasts weighty, local Trenton limestone with light-reflecting aluminum fittings, the latter a system of abstract ornament inspired by Otto Wagner's work in Vienna. The disciplined interior spaces—galleries, library, study center, bookstore, and offices—are enlivened and warmed by carefully orchestrated natural light and exquisitely detailed birch paneling.

Across Boulevard René-Lévesque, the CCA sculpture garden is nestled between two expressway ramps and traffic tunnels. The marginal site presented huge challenges, but architect-artist Melvin Charney saw opportunity in the "layers of memory" that "cut deep, transcend place and time, and summon forth typologies of an ideal city and models of rural idylls and Arcadian forest edge."[25] He created a scenographic garden—simultaneously urban garden, museum garden, and neighborhood garden—populated by a mirror-image ruin of the Shaughnessy House and a series of totem-like columns that present a narrative of Montreal's architectural history.

A classical ordering system permeates the CCA. The hierarchical composition of the site plan, building, and gardens, down to every detail, is pervasive. But this is an imaginatively transformed classicism—architecture that is critical in questioning, testing, and commenting on itself.[26] The CCA's architectural language takes us beyond classicism's constraints and into the realm of critical classicism, setting the building apart from the overwrought American postmodern classicism generally associated with the era. Moreover, the CCA can be thought of as a constructed idea—a call for restored architectural consciousness.

Towers by Richard Henriquez, 1984–1989

Richard Henriquez realized numerous postmodern buildings in Vancouver. These built works are bracketed by a series of elaborate constructions, collages, drawings, and stories—speculating on the past, present, and future—that give us insight to Henriquez's imagination and highly conceptual approach. His work epitomizes postmodern preoccupations with history, memory, and continuity through time. **FIGS 27–30**

The three residential towers in Vancouver's West End—the Sylvia Tower (1984), Eugenia Place (1987), and the Presidio Tower (1989)—had their conceptual roots in elaborate narratives.[27] The site of the first, the Sylvia Hotel Condominium Tower, is sandwiched between the 1912 red brick Sylvia Hotel and the 1958 Miami modern–style Ocean Towers apartment building. Henriquez redeployed history and fantasized a scenario wherein the new seventeen-story tower would appear to have been built in 1912 and then renovated in the 1980s to conform to contemporary standards. The elevations of the new tower are traditional, clad in brick and incorporating double-hung windows similar to those of the original Sylvia hotel. But at the corner facing English Bay, the geometry is cranked thirty degrees with a fully glazed, modern-looking protrusion capped with a prismatic glass turret positioned to take advantage of the spectacular views.

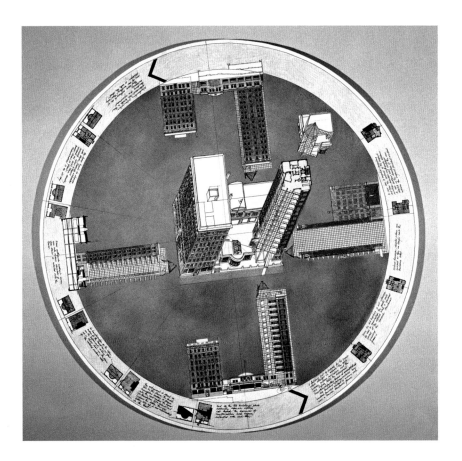

28 above
Sylvia Hotel Condominium Tower, concept drawing, Vancouver, British Columbia. Richard Henriquez Architect, 1984.

29 left
Sylvia Hotel Condominium Tower, view from English Bay.

30 opposite
Eugenia Place Tower, composite drawing showing overlays of site development, Vancouver, British Columbia. Richard Henriquez Architect, 1987.

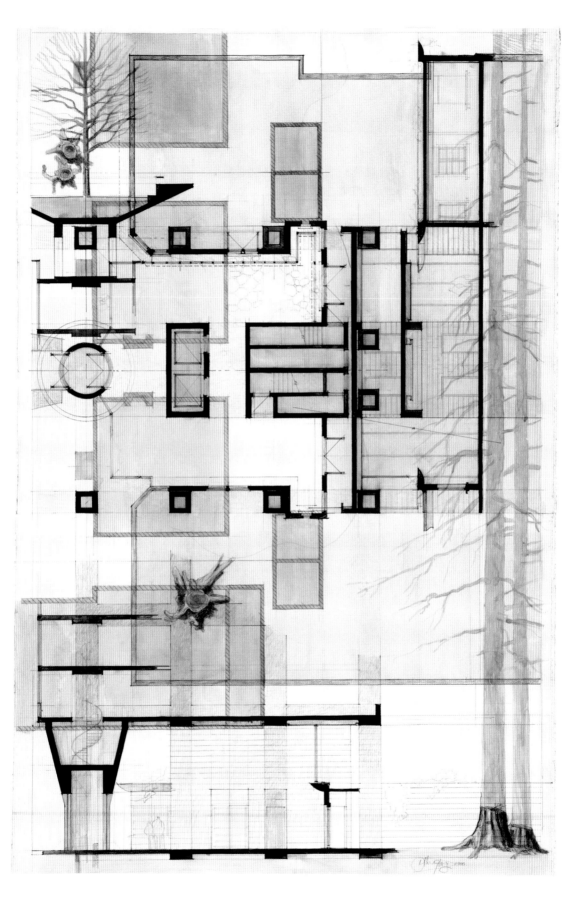

31
Jericho Circle House,
view of living room
under jacked-up 1937
bungalow, Vancouver,
British Columbia. Richard
Henriquez Architect,
1986.

The second tower, Eugenia Place, is derived from the memory of the tall cedar and fir groves that stood on the site for centuries. Henriquez represents majestic trees as concrete stumps, designed as planters for indigenous ferns. For the retaining walls of the tower's gardens, he reconstructs the former foundations of four bungalows that occupied the site in the 1920s. During World War II, the bungalows were replaced with a Tudor-style apartment block, fragments of which Henriquez recreates in the tower's common room. On the main facade, a dramatic cylindrical, glass volume houses sunrooms for the condominiums, topped by a huge dish-like planter sporting a symbolic pin oak tree. At street level, the dish and cylinder are supported by a fat, tapering column that marks the building entrance. In Henriquez's imagination, this vertical architectural ensemble represents a giant, pop-scale screw—or, perhaps, the "screwing" of history.

The metanarrative of the twenty-two-story Presidio Tower is even more elaborate. Here, Henriquez creates a fictional history drawn from early European modernism and inflected by an additional, rather preposterous, urban narrative about a dyslexic surveyor. (In this story, the surveyor mistakenly drafts a mirror-image site and roadway plan. Some of the errors are then incorporated as elements in the constructed project.) Henriquez selected the 1906 Villa Karma by Adolf Loos (1870–1933) as the conceptual driver for the project, wherein he reproduced and stacked ten Villa Karmas to make the tower. Supersized drawing compasses support the entry canopy—traces of the absent surveyor.

The engaging narratives of the Sylvia Tower, Eugenia Place, and the Presidio Tower are part of Henriquez's densely layered, often surrealistic approach to the design of buildings and cities. For example, architectural historian Howard Schubert notes the architect's inspiration from Marcel Duchamp (1887–1968) for a theoretical skyscraper project: "Henriquez has employed the Surrealist artist's most famous work, *The Bride Stripped Bare by Her Bachelors, Even* (1915–23), also known as *The Large Glass*, as part of a theoretical skyscraper project, presented in the form of a physical and digital model."[28]

As well, the elaborate projects created by Henriquez flow in part from his strong political positions, such as his opposition to the Vancouver zoning laws that impose and protect view corridors from the city center to surrounding landscapes. His provocative responses include a scenario with a single, enormous skyscraper that would house the city's entire population, enabling wholesale democratization wherein *everyone* could see the landscapes and mountains beyond.

If most Canadian postmodern architects have been conservative, avoiding irony and fantasy, Henriquez swerved in the other direction, opening windows across space and time into wondrous scenes of what might be. His *Memory Theatre*—a circular wooden pavilion displayed at the Vancouver Art Gallery in 1994 and at the Canadian Centre for Architecture in 1995—displays artifacts revealing his personal history and cultural upbringing in Jamaica. It recalls seventeenth-century cabinets of curiosity as well as the work of artist Joseph Cornell (1903–1972). *Memory Theatre* is now incorporated into his family's Vancouver home (1986), a 1937 bungalow that he jacked up on six giant screws in order to create additional living space. **FIG 31** For Henriquez, the lines blur between personal histories (including his own), art, and architecture. He decries the erasure of history while reveling in its layered reconstruction, even if it is fictitious. Richard Henriquez simultaneously criticizes and celebrates the indeterminacy of the postmodern era.

Coda: The Vagaries and Future of Postmodernism

By 1988, the winds of closure were knocking at postmodernism's door: the New York Museum of Modern Art launched its polemical *Deconstructivist Architecture* exhibition, and German historian Heinrich Klotz's *The History of Postmodern Architecture* was published.[29] During the thirty years since its assumed demise, architectural historians, critics, and theoreticians have continued to debate aggressively the very definition of postmodernism, some maintaining that the movement is still alive, reinventing itself and morphing in multiple directions.[30]

Critic Colin Fournier asks how the postmodern city will evolve:

> The communication systems of late capitalism have embraced the pluralistic principles of Postmodernism much more effectively than its architecture has, and the question… will be how, under these hybrid conditions, part material, part immaterial, the Postmodernist city will evolve and reinvent itself.[31]

Thus, we might speculate that the greatest challenges lie ahead, in the realm of cyber-postmodernity, where, once again, history, memory, and place will need to be imaginatively reclaimed.

Six diverse Canadian projects, presented here as a coda, reveal the unpredictability, quirkiness, and longevity of postmodernism. Seen by some as progressive, by others as regressive, the postmodern experiment continues:

Europa Boulevard at the West Edmonton Mall, 1985 **FIG 32**

Themed fantasy experience is an exaggerated manifestation of postmodernism. The counterfeit European boulevard at the West Edmonton Mall, designed by Maurice Sunderland (1926–2002), is a prime example. Authentic urban experience is supplanted by a commerce-driven, make-believe stage set.

Lighthouse Theatre, Toronto, 1988 **FIG 33**

The celebrated Italian architect-theorist Aldo Rossi (1931–1997) completed his first North American project on the shore of Lake Ontario. Realized by Visual Arts Ontario for the 1988 exhibition titled WaterWorks, which took place at Toronto's R. C. Harris Water Filtration Plant, the structure consisted of an open, semicircular amphitheater punctuated by a boldly striped, 50-foot (15-meter) tower resembling a lighthouse. The temporary installation recalled Rossi's 1979 Teatro del Mondo, the floating theater he designed in Venice.

Rogers Building, Toronto, 1992 and 2004 **FIG 34**

The Rogers Building (originally Confederation Life Headquarters) is an extravagant postmodern concoction—a retrofuturistic structure that is simultaneously exhilarating and ponderous. Eberhard Zeidler (1926–) won a 1987 design competition for the building, and it was completed in 1992, with north and south wings added in 2004. The overt historicism recalls Confederation Life's earlier Romanesque Revival headquarters of 1892 and relates to the immediate context of nineteenth-century Victorian houses.

Abbey Church of Saint-Benoît-du-Lac (Quebec), 1994 **FIG 35**

Quebec architect Dan Hanganu (1939–2017) realized the postmodern Abbey Church of Saint-Benoît-du-Lac in 1994 [see pages 411–412]. Hanganu's Romanian upbringing, understanding of classicism, engagement with vernacular construction, and deep respect for

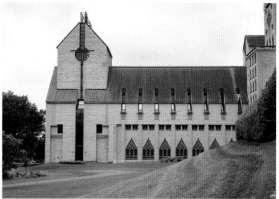

the abbey's original architect, Dom Paul Bellot, led him to a highly personal vision for the church that is alluringly suspended in history, seeming at once both old and new.

One Saint Thomas Residences, Toronto, 2008 **FIG 36**

In 2008, New York–based Robert Stern (1939–), who by then had abandoned his earlier cartoonish approach for a "new classicism," completed the One Saint Thomas Residences in Toronto's tony Yorkville. The limestone-clad twenty-nine-story luxury tower was inspired by the grand era of New York City apartment buildings in the 1920s and 1930s. The solidity, urbanity, and beauty of One Saint Thomas separate the building from the hundreds of generally undistinguished modern glass condominium towers that have flooded Toronto in the early twenty-first century.

Mirvish + Gehry Toronto, Toronto, begun 2013 **FIG 37**

By 2020, two extraordinary condominium towers—eighty-two and ninety-two stories— are expected to rise on the west side of downtown Toronto as part of a large mixed-use

36 left
**One Saint Thomas
Residences, view from
southeast, Toronto,
Ontario. Robert A. M. Stern
Architect, 2008.**

37 right
**Mirvish + Gehry Condo-
minium Towers, south
elevation of model, Toronto.
Ontario. Frank Gehry
Architect, ongoing.**

development. These sculptural landmark "totems" by Canadian-American architect Frank Gehry (1929–) will incorporate industrial fabrication using computer-driven manufacturing, enabling extreme heterogeneity of the architectural components. Appearing like giant, twisting metallic robots in friendly conversation, the pair of towers signals a new techno-postmodernity.

7

Urban Revitalization

Ian Chodikoff

Architects' voices are among the many associated with efforts to revitalize our cities. Architects are often facilitators of change, collaborating with politicians, planners, real estate developers, and citizen groups. They contribute to the evolution of our contemporary cities and the many threads that comprise the urban fabric, including affordable housing, animated public spaces, and progressive environmental sustainability initiatives. Architects bring these threads together to form complex, yet vibrant examples of placemaking.

It would be naive to imagine any urban-scaled revitalization effort that excluded these elements. But what are the urban design themes that distinguish the evolution of Canadian cities? Examining the role of the architect in a series of key Canadian projects illustrates that the overarching sociopolitical culture found in Canadian society is one where differences are debated but largely tolerated, and where inclusive communities are desired, if not always achieved.

Canadian contexts for urban revitalization often include the transformation of industrial lands, the development of new models for housing, and the leveraging of historic and cultural assets. These contexts are useful rallying points for identifying urban visions that manifest through architecture, even if architects fill only one of the many significant roles required to ignite change.

1 left
Granville Island, view from its early industrial context, Vancouver, British Columbia. Hotson Bakker Architects, 1986.

2 opposite, left
Granville Island, street view.

3 opposite, right
Project 56, sketch, Vancouver, British Columbia. Arthur Erickson, unrealized concept, 1955.

Interdependencies with Our Industrial Past

Cities are founded upon industry and commerce. From one generation to the next, however, factors such as technology, environmental awareness, and the global economy impact where within our cities we build spaces of production. The industrial lands that factories once occupied are difficult to transform, requiring significant efforts to adapt them for contemporary use. Under these circumstances, an architect inevitably faces numerous challenges: convoluted land ownership, ineffective government policy, shifting environmental concerns, and varying sensitivity to heritage issues.

One notable example can be seen along Vancouver's shorelines. Visitors to Granville Island are immediately struck by its pedestrian-focused streets, where automobiles circulate but do not dominate. Here, an industrial past merges with a host of active contemporary structures and a mix of retail, industrial, recreational, and commercial uses. **FIGS 1–2**

Granville Island began as two sandbars in False Creek. By 1916, the federally administered Vancouver Harbour Commission had created 41 acres (16.5 hectares) of landfill, leasing it to tenants who eventually built factories and mills in post-and-beam structures clad in corrugated tin. By the 1960s, industry began to fade while the surrounding False

Creek grew increasingly polluted—just as the world began paying more attention to environmental issues.

In 1973, the federal government transferred the management and redevelopment of the island to the Central (now Canada) Mortgage and Housing Corporation (CMHC). At the time, the CMHC was also redeveloping the nearby south shore of False Creek for multiunit housing plans initiated in 1968 by University of British Columbia geography professors Walter Hardwick and Peter Oberlander. While the False Creek project targeted a mix of equal parts housing, park, and institutional uses, Granville Island was to exist as a place primarily of the public realm. Its transformation defined the careers of architects Norman Hotson (1947–) and Joost Bakker (1948–), of Hotson Bakker Architects (now DIALOG), who described their initial plan as "a space for creative artists, artisans, performers, and entrepreneurs; and active art and recreation."[1] Since Granville Island is owned by the federal government, city zoning doesn't apply, which ultimately helped in the strategy to focus its activities on retail, arts and crafts, maritime products, and the popular public market.

Granville Island's redevelopment began in 1975 with various infrastructure-related improvements. Norman Hotson led the coordinating efforts with the CMHC to bring about an active street life.[2] With the opening of the public market in 1979, the island was well on its way to enjoying a dynamic urban future. Over time, buildings for notable tenants, such as the Emily Carr University of Art and Design (Patkau Architects / Toby Russell Buckwell and Partners, 1994), the False Creek Community Centre (Henriquez Partners Architects, 1991), and nonprofit groups like Arts Umbrella, as well as several private-sector developments ranging from restaurants to a small boutique hotel, contributed to its mix. An industrial presence continues on Granville Island; most notably, an active concrete manufacturing facility serves the city's ubiquitous construction sites.

Vancouver's shoreline today is not only influenced by its industrial legacy, but by the spectacular and inescapable backdrop of mountain and ocean views. These natural features had a heavy influence on many urban-scaled projects in the city. Arthur Erickson's speculative and unrealized Project 56, sited along the shoreline of English Bay and just across from

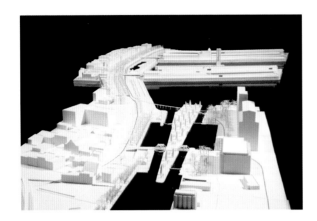

4 left
Old Port master plan, model view (detail), Montreal, Quebec. Peter Rose + Partners with Cardinal Hardy et Associés, Chan Krieger & Associates, and Jodoin Lamarre Pratt architectes, 1992.

5 opposite
Evergreen Brick Works, exterior of Centre for Green Cities connecting to rehabilitated industrial buildings, Toronto, Ontario. Diamond Schmitt Architects, 2010.

Granville Island, proposed two vast "landform" towers on higher ground and was shaped by the city's relationship to its landscapes. **FIG 3** This preoccupation also guided many high-rise developments in the city's postwar history, such as C.B.K. Van Norman's three-towered Beach Towers scheme (1965), which was constructed where Erickson's scheme might have existed. Presaging Vancouver's point towers, the narrow floor plates of Van Norman's towers were designed to preserve mountain views for residents of adjacent towers by creating a sufficiently gap-toothed skyline. This approach evolved into an effective tool for redevelopment that can be readily observed in other former industrial lands of the city—particularly Coal Harbour and the north shore of False Creek—from the 1990s onward.

The point-tower-and-podium high-rise model has since come to define an approach to urban development known as Vancouverism, one that has been practiced by architects such as James K. M. Cheng (1947–), who perfected its use through the many towers he designed in False Creek and Coal Harbour [see pages 465–468]. Meanwhile, Hotson and Bakker's vision for Granville Island stands as a reminder of the city's industrial legacy while continuing to defer to its vista-rich setting. The vision of the architects and the CMHC to leverage and preserve an aspect of Vancouver's maritime industrial past resulted in one of Canada's most successful urban revitalization projects.

By comparison, the revitalization of Montreal's former waterfront industrial lands, beginning at roughly the same time as Granville Island, yielded a much different result that helped stitch together adjacent downtown districts [see page 419]. The industrial use of Montreal's Old Port began to shift in 1959 when the Saint Lawrence Seaway opened and ocean-going vessels were able to reach the Great Lakes without having to stop in Montreal to unload. Montreal's port facilities moved eastward, and by 1978 the Port of Montreal finally ceded the Old Port to a city-run development corporation. A linear park along Rue de la Commune, along with the removal of obsolete rail lines and infrastructural elements, were the first indications of change. Old Montreal was initially declared a heritage district in 1964 but it wasn't until 1980 when the process of transforming the Old Port and surrounding area began in earnest after a series of agreements were established between the City of Montreal and the provincial government. The subsequent establishment of the

Montreal Urban Community (MUC) continued to help lay the ground work for the development of open spaces along with a more thorough inventory of existing historic buildings. The momentum of the 1980s triggered a series of public consultations in 1985–1986, which created the basis for a 1990 master plan led by architect Peter Rose (1943–). His thoughtful plan drew upon the area's historic qualities by employing a quasi-archaeological approach that served as a point of departure for future development.[3] **FIG 4**

The restoration of Bonsecours Basin at the mouth of the Lachine Canal, in addition to upgrades for King Edward Pier, marked the first major phase of the Old Port's restoration, completed in 1992. In the 2000s, a major initiative supported by the private sector and the Quebec government for a high-tech cluster known as Cité Multimédia—an area located along the Old Port between Old Montreal, Griffintown, and Downtown Montreal—transformed a number of industrial buildings into residential units and began to infill vacant lots in the area with new projects. The Montreal firm Groupe Cardinal Hardy et associés was involved with a number of these projects, in addition to the multiphase planning of the area. Economic cycles and market demand are insurmountable obstacles if the timing is not right for redevelopment, but the richness of Montreal's urban fabric has proven that over time these urban development efforts can succeed.

6
Evergreen Brick Works,
overview of site, Toronto,
Ontario. Joe Lobko
and du Toit Architects
with DTAH and Claude
Cormier + Associés
(landscape architects),
architectsAlliance (master
plan), and ERA Architects
(heritage), 2010.

Nature as a Driver for Change

While Vancouver enjoys the presence of the ocean and the glorious snowcapped mountains beyond, one of Toronto's defining natural features is its system of ravines [see pages 435–439]. As Robert Fulford described in *Accidental City*, "The ravines are to Toronto what canals are to Venice and hills are to San Francisco. They are the heart of the city's emotional geography, and understanding Toronto requires an understanding of the ravines."[4] The recent creation of Evergreen Brick Works showcases the ravines as one of Toronto's invaluable assets; the park shapes the culture of urban life while acknowledging its industrial past. **FIGS 5–6**

Evergreen Brick Works is a significant marker in the history of Canadian cities: a former industrial site transformed into an exemplary urban park. It leverages the city's natural history while providing a venue for outdoor and indoor public events focused on environmental stewardship and education. Strategically located in close proximity to the downtown core, the site is divided into two components: an industrial heritage site and a larger park. The complex has become a year-round destination for its office and meeting spaces, event spaces, skating rink, restaurants, garden center, and a variety of farmers' and public markets.

7
Evergreen Brick Works, site plan, Toronto, Ontario. Joe Lobko and du Toit Architects with DTAH and Claude Cormier + Associés (landscape architects), architectsAlliance (master plan), and ERA Architects (heritage), 2010.

From 1889 to 1984, the Don Valley Brick Works, an operation that once produced over forty million bricks annually, occupied the site. After the site was expropriated in the mid-1980s by the Toronto and Region Conservation Authority, it was leased to Brampton Brick, which operated a retail site on the property until 1989, when it was finally rezoned as parkland.[5] A dozen years later, the sixteen existing buildings were collectively designated a heritage site, but the site remained relatively inactive until 2007, when the right combination of public and private funding enabled change. Geoff Cape—the founder of Evergreen, a nonprofit organization dedicated to green space and community building—led the site's transformation. Although several architects were involved in the design process, Cape's vision and direction succeeded in raising public interest (and capital) through strategic partnerships with socially conscious organizations. This enabled the further rehabilitation of the landscape and industrial buildings.

An initial comprehensive master plan, completed in 2006 by architectsAlliance, was useful in garnering interest from several levels of government that would eventually help fund the site's redevelopment. But to Cape, this plan wasn't enough to secure a strong identity and build the necessary momentum for redevelopment. By the fall of 2006, Evergreen assembled a joint venture collaboration: Toronto-based Joe Lobko Architect and the Toronto firm du Toit Allsopp Hillier (DTAH) were to lead the process of redeveloping the Brick Works. The integrated design team also included Montreal landscape architect Claude Cormier, Toronto's Diamond + Schmitt Architects, and heritage specialists ERA Architects. Other consultants examined issues of stormwater management, flood and erosion controls, and other environmental protection measures, such as the elimination of invasive species. **FIG 7**

Completed in 2010, the Centre for Green Cities remains the only completely new building on the site to date. Certified as a LEED Platinum building when it opened, it incorporates a welcome center, retail and amenity space, administrative offices, and workspaces for various partners. In early 2017, a new center for sustainable cities in Canada was announced. When completed, it will be housed in a new facility integrated into one of the existing buildings and serve as a vibrant place to bring together academics, industry, and the community. Occupying one of the existing industrial sheds, it will serve as "ground zero for a number of current sustainability issues—flooding, heritage, and brownfield remediation,"[6] notes Janna Levitt of LGA Architectural Partners, who will lead the project. It remains to be seen how the Brick Works will continue to evolve. As it stands, this revitalization project demonstrates the successful collaboration of several architects and landscape architects under the leadership of a client and social entrepreneur. The resulting revitalization of the site's existing industrial buildings, and the addition of new buildings, continues to attract hundreds of thousands of visitors to the Brick Works every year, reacquainting them with the extraordinary context of the surrounding ravines, an important facet of Toronto's urban identity.

Community Stakeholders and Involvement

One measure of a city's success is how it manages the housing needs of individuals and families with modest incomes. Canada's urban history provides many examples of neighborhoods reinvigorated as a result of carefully considered planning and architectural initiatives. These examples demonstrate the value of the architect as arbiter or mediator: a professional who can synthesize the desires of community stakeholders with the needs of developers and politicians, informing socially and economically healthier communities.

At Montreal's Benny Farm, issues of environmental sustainability guided a neighborhood's regeneration. **FIG 8** In Vancouver, the redevelopment of the Woodward's building represents a singular—albeit programmatically complex—project that addresses issues of gentrification and inclusion in a neighborhood in social decline. Toronto's Regent Park and St. Lawrence developments both focus on healing disconnected neighborhoods. Whether it is a push for affordability or using sustainability to rally a unifying vision, the ultimate objectives for all these initiatives are similar: to create inclusive neighborhoods that empower their citizenry while improving the overall quality of urban life through better design.

Benny Farm is an 18-acre (7.3-hectare) residential site situated in the Notre-Dame-de-Grâce borough of Montreal. It incorporates community empowerment, locally produced energy, and other sustainability concepts to support rental housing. The site was initially designed as a 384-unit development in 1946–1947, intended primarily for Second World War veterans. After sixty years, new ideas about energy efficiency, along with changes to the neighborhood's social and urban context, meant the project required a major overhaul.

The first phase of Benny Farm's redevelopment was overseen by the CMHC and the Canada Lands Corporation (CLC) between 1997 and 2002. However, it was the second phase of development, led by Danny Pearl (1961–) and Mark Poddubiuk (1959–) of the Montreal-based architecture firm L'OEUF (l'Office de l'éclectisme urbain et fonctionnel) that set in motion a widespread and successful program for redevelopment. L'OEUF's efforts are notable for the firm's determination in leading hundreds of meetings, discussions, and consultations with the community in order to envision a project consistent with the

stakeholder participation

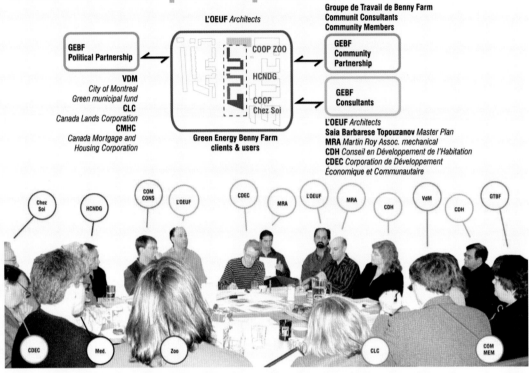

L'OEUF *Architects*

Groupe de Travail de Benny Farm
Communit Consultants
Community Members

**GEBF
Political Partnership**

COOP ZOO

HCNDG

COOP
Chez Soi

**GEBF
Community
Partnership**

**GEBF
Consultants**

VDM
City of Montreal
Green municipal fund
CLC
Canada Lands Corporation
CMHC
*Canada Mortgage and
Housing Corporation*

**Green Energy Benny Farm
clients & users**

L'OEUF *Architects*
Saia Barbarese Topouzanov *Master Plan*
MRA *Martin Roy Assoc. mechanical*
CDH *Conseil en Développement de l'Habitation*
CDEC *Corporation de Développement
Économique et Communautaire*

Chez Soi · HCNDG · COM CONS · L'OEUF · CDEC · MRA · L'OEUF · MRA · CDH · VdM · CDH · GTBF

CDEC · Med. · Zoo · CLC · COM MEM

9 above
**Benny Farm, diagram of
stakeholder participation,
Montreal, Quebec. L'OEUF,
2005.**

10 opposite, left
**Lore Krill Housing Co-op,
view through courtyard,
Vancouver, British
Columbia. Henriquez
Partners Architects, 2002.**

11 opposite, right
**Lore Krill Housing Co-op,
exterior view.**

site's historical, cultural, and political contexts. **FIG 9** This aligned well with the City of Montreal's objective to create a model affordable housing program.

Pearl and his design team were instrumental in helping establish the affectionately named Z.O.O. or Zone of Opportunity Non-Profit Housing Cooperative to manage the repair and upgrading of existing buildings while maintaining social diversity and rental affordability. Developing the site's sustainable energy systems, which involved some planning and financial considerations, was another impetus that led to the establishment of a nonprofit corporation, Green Energy Benny Farm. Under the leadership of L'OEUF, the nonprofit ensured the long-term financial viability of green infrastructure at Benny Farm, drawing on the human resources of residents, community representatives, and technical experts to manage various aspects of the system. Benny Farm was eventually acquired by the Office municipal d'Habitation de Montreal (OMHM), the city's housing corporation, in 2007. The legacy of the project is clear: the extensive commitment and leadership of its architects led to a strengthening of community.

Diplomacy, partnerships, and community relations were similarly necessary to the success of the Woodward's redevelopment in Vancouver's Downtown Eastside. Prior to its completion in 2010, project architect Gregory Henriquez (1963–) of Henriquez Partners Architects noted that architecture extends far beyond aesthetics, writing that architectural production itself exists amid a critical examination of the world around us.[7] This philosophy drove his determination for Woodward's: a public-private partnership where a community advisory council, the City of Vancouver, and enlightened developers shared common ground to make a better neighborhood.[8]

Henriquez's previous social housing projects included Bruce Eriksen Place and the Lore Krill Housing Co-op (2002), for which he received a Governor General's Medal in Architecture in 2004. **FIGS 10–11** Woodward's was by far his most complex commission to date, comprising one million square feet (92,940 square meters) of mixed-use redevelopment divided into four distinct components: a 43-story triangular condominium tower with 366 market-rate units; a 32-story building with retail space, offices, subsidized family housing, and condominiums; the Hastings Building, which includes retail space, the Goldcorp

13 left
Woodward's redevelopment,
view of tower from West
Cordova Street, Vancouver,
British Columbia. Henriquez
Partners Architects, 2010.

14 opposite
Woodward's redevelopment,
interior view of atrium.

Centre for the Arts, and subsidized singles' housing; and finally the Heritage Building—a restored department store that includes retail and office space. **FIGS 12–13**

The project's programmatic diversity helped reestablish Vancouver's Downtown Eastside, a once vibrant retail and commercial district that had been in decline since the 1970s, as a safe and viable part of the city. The project necessitated a complex financial partnership and local political wrangling that began when the British Columbia provincial government acquired the site in 2001. The following year, squatters took over the building, driving political awareness of the need for change. The City responded by negotiating to acquire the Woodward's building, which in turn initiated a process to select a team comprising local developer Westbank, the Peterson Investment Group, and Henriquez Partners Architects. Henriquez had previously worked with Ian Gillespie, founder of Westbank, and had his trust. By 2005, Simon Fraser University committed itself as an additional partner, contributing to the project's financial feasibility.

One of the significant challenges was to successfully integrate and balance the amount of low-income social housing with family and market housing. Henriquez contributed to the solution by engaging in a collaborative process that yielded an architecture that is contemporary but suitably urban. Character-defining urban design elements at the ground level

include a central atrium and an interior courtyard that operate as year-round public spaces. In severe weather conditions, the atrium can be used as a temporary shelter for the homeless.

Of significant cultural importance is a 30-by-50-foot (9.1-by-15.2-meter) photograph in the atrium by artist Stan Douglas, printed on a series of glass panels. **FIG 14** Complete with actors and props akin to a film set, the image is a meticulously choreographed, fictitious representation of the nearby 1971 Gastown riots, which Henriquez sees as representing the inherent social tensions in the neighborhood.[9] Perhaps the Douglas work also symbolizes how conflict is both inevitable and necessary when bringing together divergent voices and positions for the purpose of revitalizing a neighborhood.

Toronto's St. Lawrence and Regent Park neighborhoods demonstrate how balancing public and private interests and connecting new housing projects to the city's urban fabric remain important priorities on a larger scale—goals that are achievable even though the process is often fraught with conflict [see page 431].

The St. Lawrence neighborhood is considered one of Toronto's housing triumphs: a 1970s mixed-use, housing-dominated redevelopment, realized through a combination of political will, local activism, and the dedicated work of architects and urban planners. In 1974, architect and academic George Baird (1939–) was hired by the City of Toronto to

advise on the planning of 3,500 residential units, along with a school, library, community center, and retail space. Baird's team published an influential booklet titled *On Building Downtown*, which proposed a street-and-block framework that would extend the north-south streets from the historic Town of York into the revitalized St. Lawrence neighborhood. To complement this new grid, a 100-foot-wide (30.5-meter-wide) esplanade would act as a linear east-west open-space armature. Perhaps one of the most significant measures the City adopted, on Baird's recommendation, was an eight-story height limit throughout the nearly 45-acre (18.2-hectare) site, which contributed to a healthy mid-rise urban density. Finally, the support of Toronto mayor David Crombie (1936–), a major figure in the civic reform movement during the late 1960s, combined with the influence of Jane Jacobs (1916–2006), who had decamped to Toronto from New York and whose activist spirit put an end to the Spadina Expressway proposal, meant that St. Lawrence's future was assured. Today, the neighborhood's townhouses, front porches, and mid-rise buildings designed by Jerome Markson (1929–), Irving Grossman (1926–), Eberhard Zeidler (1926–), and Ron Thom (1923–1986), among others, thrive amid a rising Toronto skyline. St. Lawrence emerged from the combined efforts of architects, activists, and politicians to create a liveable downtown. Political will and social activism cannot be ignored, for it was this energy and commitment that underpinned the architectural and urban design vision for a neighborhood currently housing over thirty thousand residents.

Similarly to the Woodward's redevelopment, Toronto's Regent Park depended heavily on complex negotiations between the City, nonprofits, private developers, and community interests to ensure a profitable market and nonmarket mix of housing with sufficient community amenities while serving a diverse population. The inclusion of many voices in the large-scale, ongoing redevelopment has already yielded several discrete and well-received projects designed by a number of architecture firms.

Originally developed by the CMHC, Regent Park emerged from nearly 69 acres (28 hectares) of dilapidated Victorian-era row houses that were razed between 1948 and 1957. **FIGS 15–16** The goal was to eradicate what was widely viewed at the time as deplorable, overcrowded housing, where narrow streets and laneways created problems associated

15 opposite, left
Oak Street, before Regent Park urban renewal, Toronto, Ontario.

16 opposite, right
Street scene, before Regent Park urban renewal, Toronto, Ontario.

17 above
Maisonette Towers, Regent Park, north facade, Toronto, Ontario. Peter Dickinson with Page and Steele, 1958.

18 left
Block 22, Regent Park,
northeast view of town-
houses and residential
tower, Toronto, Ontario.
Giannone Petricone
Associates, 2015.

19 opposite
Daniels Spectrum, view
of east facade, Toronto,
Ontario. Diamond Schmitt
Architects, 2012.

with crime and public health—a vision colorfully articulated in the National Film Board's documentary *Farewell Oak Street* (1953).

The 1950s revamp of Regent Park took place in two distinct phases. In the first, completed in 1952, a series of three- to five-story brick-faced apartments designed by John E. Hoare Jr. yielded 260 residential units. The second phase, designed by Peter Dickinson (1925–1961) while he was still working at Page & Steele, presented a convincing mix of high-, mid-, and low-rise buildings inspired by the International Modern Style. **FIG 17** According to the assessment of historians Rhodri Windsor Liscombe and Michelangelo Sabatino, "Regent Park came to define the aesthetic success but societal deficiency of the majority of CMHC public housing projects from the period, not for the want of architectural and planning vision so much as the politics and funding of social housing."[10] While Dickinson was pivotal to the uptake of modernism in Canada, he worked with three urban planners—Eugene Faludi, Humphrey Carver, and Albert Rose—who possessed "a hackneyed and patronizing view of the people."[11]

Faludi (1897–1981) led the plan for Regent Park, where buildings would be arranged across a *tabula rasa* of superblocks devoid of streets. In their place, isolated and dangerous walkways were created, along with vast, unusable open spaces. The impact of the plan quickly became apparent in the alienated precinct, which comprised low-income tenants rapidly becoming economically marginalized from a burgeoning Toronto. Despite these challenges, a diverse population with a strong sense of community and identity emerged, as became readily apparent when the planning process for the contemporary revitalization project began in the 1990s.[12]

In 1995, residents began organizing meetings with the Metro Toronto Housing Authority and the provincial Ministry of Housing. Newsletters were printed in half a dozen languages, and open meetings ensued with architects and urban planners. With the newly amalgamated City of Toronto came the newly formed Toronto Community Housing Corporation (TCH), an organization that managed over 58,000 affordable units throughout the city, including over 2,000 units in Regent Park. An initial plan for Regent Park's transformation was completed by Markson Borooah Hodgson Architects and Greenberg

Consultants in 2002. The plan sought to integrate market and social housing with a ratio just under two-to-one (in favor of market housing) and to reestablish roadways through Regent Park and into the surrounding neighborhoods. The same basic strategies remained in subsequent plans: to strengthen physical and social links between Regent Park and the city around it; to pursue a rate of development that would maintain the social fabric of the existing community; and to allow social-housing residents to return to the area if they wished. With a new park, recreation facilities, and ground-oriented housing along secondary streets, it was believed that Regent Park could once again become a dynamic neighborhood connected to the city.

After several years of negotiations between the community, public sector players, and private interests, the Sackville-Dundas apartments (architectsAlliance, 2009) became the first new residential building completed. The two-tower complex comprises a twenty-two-story building with 224 TCH family-oriented apartments and an eight-story tower with 159 units for seniors. A daycare and the neighborhood's district energy plant occupy the ground floor. Other completed projects address the various needs of the community, including housing for the Toronto Christian Resource Centre (Hilditch Architects, 2010), a market-housing condominium tower (Diamond Schmitt Architects, 2009), a set

of townhouses (Graziani and Corazza, 2011), and a low-rise courtyard scheme (Giannone Petricone Associates, 2015). **FIG 18** Some of the more innovative projects include the Daniels Spectrum (Diamond Schmitt Architects, 2012)—a 60,000-square-foot (5,580-square-meter) arts-based community center named after the Daniels Corporation, one of the major developers of Regent Park. The Daniels Spectrum occupies the first three floors of a tower, with condominiums rising above it. **FIG 19** There is also the Regent Park Community Centre (CS&P Architects, 2015) and perhaps the most spectacular amenity completed to date: the Regent Park Aquatic Centre (MJMA, 2012). **FIG 20**

As the neighborhood develops, so too does the commitment of its residents. A film festival has begun, a grocery store has opened, and other community events continue to enliven this nascent community. Certainly, residents, community organizations, planners, architects, and developers can be proud of the work they have done to date.

Conclusion

No successful major urban development can be achieved without the input of diverse stakeholders. In Canada, the presence of various community interests may have ultimately quelled protomodernist planning visions in which a master plan espoused by a master architect attempted to dictate the shape of the city. In reality, diverse programmatic interests are critical for rich urban environments—the kind of complex mixes present in Toronto's Regent Park or Vancouver's Woodward's redevelopment. Effective planning principles remain critical, whether they are steeped in sustainable design practices, as at Montreal's Benny Farm, or whether they promote a neighborhood's connectivity to the rest of the city, as seen in Montreal's Old Port or Toronto's St. Lawrence neighborhood.

Much of what constitutes the Canadian city is dependent upon connections to the natural landscape, as witnessed on Vancouver's Granville Island or at Toronto's Brick Works. While these two projects differ in scale and programming complexity, they share common traits: both leverage their industrial past and natural geography, and both realize a desire to cultivate a public realm that contributes to the image of their city.

And where is the architect in all of these projects? The architect has the ability to sculpt a distinct approach to massing and detailing at the level of individual buildings. But revitalizing former industrial lands, rehabilitating neighborhoods in decline, or renewing the value of historic urban areas requires significant public, private, financial, community, and political resources far beyond an architect's scope. Nevertheless, it is precisely in these situations where the skills of an architect—as mediator and convener dedicated to synthesizing complex ideas into a coherent physical manifestation of change—are essential. One may even suggest that many of the strengths exhibited by Canada's best architects reflect aspects of Canadian society itself, wherein disparate voices are tolerated and often outright encouraged in order to foster community and promote the evolution of a richer, continuously urbanizing world.

8

Environmental Architecture

Steven Mannell

Environmental architecture arrived in Canada in the mid-1970s almost fully mature in the form of the Ark for Prince Edward Island, a "bioshelter" powered by sun and wind, designed to provide the food and energy needs of a family of four. The Ark was one result of substantial federal and provincial government efforts to encourage environmental design and renewable energy technologies, and by 1980 Canada was recognized internationally as a leader in the move toward a sustainable human environment. These environmental design approaches captured the popular imagination in Canada, and many important lessons were transferred from experimental projects to mainstream practices. Despite this precocious beginning, Canada's powerful resource-extraction industries, Canadian ambivalence about the country's own environmental leadership, and the innate conservatism of the building industry and design professions—not to mention economic stagnation—combined to push environmental approaches to the margins by the late-1980s.

In the 1990s, driven by the specter of anthropogenic climate change, a reawakening of the global environmental consciousness led the building industry to return its attention to the environmental impacts of its activities. Efforts to build technical capacity and policies to support sustainable design have been promoted by a mix of international agencies, governments, and industry groups. Exemplary individual buildings by forward-thinking

1 above
Ark for Prince Edward Island, view from the southwest in winter 1977, Spry Point, Prince Edward Island. Solsearch Architects with the New Alchemy Institute, 1976.

2 left
Ark for Prince Edward Island, section at barn, rock storage, and greenhouse.

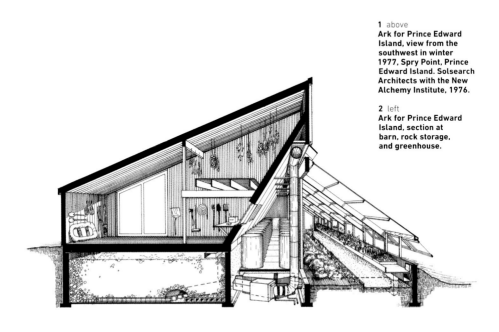

architects such as Peter Busby (1952–) have shown the feasibility of transforming contemporary design practice from within, while industry standards such as LEED (Leadership in Energy and Environmental Design) have provided tools for validating the sustainability of architecture to peers, clients, and the public. In the mid-2010s, LEED-defined sustainability has become a baseline expectation for many new commercial and institutional buildings, while the aspiration for all new buildings to achieve "net-zero" carbon emissions and energy use drives further innovation. The resulting improvements in the environmental impacts of Canadian buildings are an important contribution to addressing the climate challenge.

Explorations in Ecological Architecture, 1973–1978

The field of ecological design arose out of the optimistic pro-environmental mood surrounding the first Earth Day in 1970. It was spurred by the challenges identified by the 1972 United Nations Conference on the Human Environment in Stockholm, and built on the grassroots solutions proposed by the Appropriate Technology movement. When the 1973 oil crisis shook official confidence in the future of fossil-fueled growth, governments became interested and began to seek new sources of energy. In 1975, the federal and provincial governments invited the New Alchemy Institute, a US-based collective of scientists and humanists committed to environmentalism, to build a living demonstration of ecological architecture on a remote site in eastern Prince Edward Island. Funding and technical support came from federal agencies, while the Island provided the site at Spry Point and offered a hospitable policy environment with its commitment to alternative development pathways and a "small is beautiful" mindset.[1] David Bergmark and Ole Hammarlund of Solsearch Architects brought a synthesizing spatial vision to the assembly of techniques and ecosystems.

The official opening of the resulting Ark for Prince Edward Island in 1976 was incongruously heralded by a pair of helicopters bearing Canadian prime minister Pierre Elliott Trudeau (1919–2000) and Island premier Alex Campbell (1933–). The dignitaries were welcomed by a throng of alternative technology proponents, counterculture youth, and rural Islanders. An experimental demonstration of self-reliant ecological architecture, the Ark's mix of south-facing solar panels and greenhouse, and its earth-sheltered clapboard volumes to the north, evoked associations with various structures from space stations to old barns, aptly expressing the hybrid of advanced research and traditional common sense behind its vision of a self-sufficient, ecologically engaged family life. **FIGS 1–3** The stark contrast between the two sides of the building demonstrated the primary objectives: as much exposure as possible to the warmth and energy of the southern sun, and as much protection as possible from the cold north winds. There was no simple distinction between the architectural environment and the activities within: solar energy simultaneously drove photosynthesis in the food crops while providing heat and ventilation for the surrounding greenhouse;

3 left
Ark for Prince Edward
Island, view of the dining
room with the kitchen and
kitchen greenhouse beyond
in 1977, Spry Point, Prince
Edward Island. Solsearch
Architects with the New
Alchemy Institute, 1976.

4 opposite, top
Saskatchewan Conservation
House, winter view
from southwest, Regina,
Saskatchewan. Hendrik
Grolle Architect, 1976.

5 opposite, bottom
Saskatchewan Conservation
House, cross-section
showing systems.

the food-growing media of water and soil also stored heat for later exchange with the greenhouse space above; and waste from one system became feedstock for another—plant cuttings fed the fish, while nutrient-rich water from the fish tanks irrigated the planters. Human inhabitants of the Ark—a family of four lived there for a year and a half—managed the interplay of systems, enjoying the harvest of food while contributing their own wastes as compost to the nutrient cycle. Only gray water from the sinks and laundry escaped the Ark cycle, flowing into a dry well on site.

Though not much larger than a house, the Ark embodied ambitions to transform Canada's future away from consumerism and toward a "conserver society," enabling a new domestic lifestyle outside the materialist economy. Trudeau's remarks at the opening celebrated the Ark's "new commitment to living lightly on the earth," giving official sanction to the ideas of an emerging environmental counterculture. Over the next several years, thousands of people would visit the Ark, which functioned as both a research center and a demonstration project. Tourists and locals, architecture students, and appropriate technology advocates were drawn by the Ark's vision of a meaningful collaboration between humanity and nature. Later used as a fish hatchery, then as a community-run inn and restaurant, the Ark was demolished in 1999.[2]

Another noteworthy demonstration project from this period is the Saskatchewan Conservation House in Regina (1976) by Hendrik Grolle, Architect, which proposes a new kind of enclosure for a conventional domestic lifestyle in a typical suburban setting. **FIGS 4–5** The focus is on operating energy, with a mix of energy-reduction approaches, active solar panels, a water tank for heat storage, and a water-to-air heat exchanger. However, the effort to make this freestanding single-family house look like a "normal" house resulted in an awkward architectural expression, and the disconnect between the south-facing orientation needs of the solar energy system and the orientation requirements of subdivision plans has restricted easy reproduction of the design.[3]

Social sustainability is the primary goal at the Roseau First Nation Children's Centre in Manitoba by Dudley Thompson Architect (ca. 1978). Architects Thompson and Paul Moody explored building with appropriate technology as an enabling force for "a new

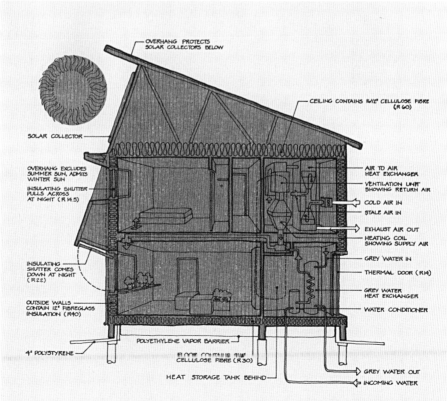

OVERHANG PROTECTS
SOLAR COLLECTORS BELOW

CEILING CONTAINS 16/12" CELLULOSE FIBRE
(R 60)

SOLAR COLLECTOR

OVERHANG EXCLUDES
SUMMER SUN, ADMITS
WINTER SUN

INSULATING SHUTTER
PULLS ACROSS
AT NIGHT (R 14.5)

AIR TO AIR
HEAT EXCHANGER

VENTILATION UNIT
SHOWING RETURN AIR

COLD AIR IN

STALE AIR IN

EXHAUST AIR OUT

HEATING COIL
SHOWING SUPPLY AIR

GREY WATER IN

THERMAL DOOR (R14)

GREY WATER
HEAT EXCHANGER

WATER CONDITIONER

INSULATING
SHUTTER COMES
DOWN AT NIGHT
(R22)

OUTSIDE WALLS
CONTAIN 12" FIBREGLASS
INSULATION (R40)

POLYETHYLENE VAPOR BARRIER

4" POLYSTYRENE

FLOOR CONTAINS 9/12"
CELLULOSE FIBRE (R30)

GREY WATER OUT

INCOMING WATER

HEAT STORAGE TANK BEHIND

world order." Their approach was to spend time "embedded" in the community as facil-itators of a self-build project deploying local materials and skills. The culturally relevant expressive form draws on the traditional Prairie earth lodge, organized around a central fire pit. **FIGS 6–7** Through this approach, the construction process became a tool for community self-actualization and for individuals' skill development. Major materials were selected for their low cash cost, despite being labor intensive. These included recycled utility poles for structure and the earth itself for walls and roof.

John Hix applies many of the tactics of the Ark and Conservation House in his 1976 Provident Solar House in Aurora, Ontario, including solar collectors with basement water storage, a small integral greenhouse, and a vertical-axis wind turbine. **FIG 8** Here, the par-adigm is the luxury country house, which provides an aspirational image of a sustainable "good life" but also deploys energy conservation as a form of "conspicuous consumption"—pointing to the ongoing paradox of high-design second homes making pro-environmental claims to offset a consumerist lifestyle.

Low-Energy Building,
1978–1987

John Hix played the role of early guide to low-energy architecture approaches as the guest editor of two special issues of *The Canadian Architect* magazine in 1977. A handful of so-cial sustainability case studies included the Ark for Prince Edward Island and a low-energy self-build housing prototype for Quebec First Nations. For the most part, the focus was on reduced energy consumption and renewable resources, aligning with federal government initiatives that sought potential energy technology spin-offs and aimed to create a Cana-dian export industry in renewable energy. To support this technology transfer effort, the federal department of Energy, Mines and Resources (EMR) sponsored the Low Energy Building Design Awards (LEBDA) program in 1980, including a design ideas competi-tion for low-energy buildings on sites in several Canadian cities, as well as awards for built projects.

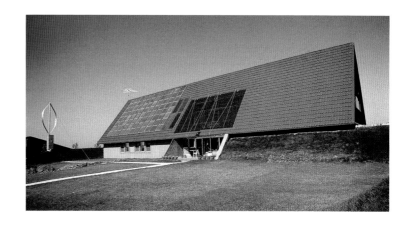

6 opposite, left
Roseau First Nation Children's Centre, exterior view, Roseau River Anishinaabe First Nation, Manitoba. Dudley Thompson Architect, 1978.

7 opposite, right
Roseau First Nation Children's Centre, interior view.

8 right
Provident House, exterior view from southeast, Aurora, Ontario. John Hix Architect, 1976.

Typical of LEBDA-awarded built projects is the Joseph E. Shepard Government of Canada Building in North York, Ontario (DuBois, Strong, Bindhardt Architects with Shore, Tilbe, Henschel, Irwin, 1977). A conscious counterpoint to the high-rise office tower, the complex articulates a set of mid-rise buildings that evoke traditional urban forms. The design reflects the influence of contemporary Dutch structuralist architects, such as Herman Hertzberger and Aldo Van Eyck, as seen in the frank interior exposure of raw structure and mechanical systems, partly screened by fine-grained surfaces and objects to create human-scale spaces for social interaction. **FIGS 9–10** A large interior atrium connects the volumes at lower levels, with multiple outdoor terraces throughout. The design achieves operating-energy savings of 90 percent compared to standard office buildings of the day. The exterior window area is minimized, all windows are non-operable insulated glass, floor plates are increased in depth to reduce the surface-area-to-volume ratio of the building, and systems are centrally controlled, all resulting in energy savings.

The energy efficiency aspects of the Shepard Building were widely emulated in commercial and institutional architecture in Canada during the 1980s, and architecture's environmental concerns were simplified to reducing building operating energy. Interest in incorporating renewable energy sources waned. The minimum-energy imperative led to increased insulation values, ever-deeper floor plates, lower lighting levels, hermetically sealed buildings, reduced mechanical fresh-air ventilation, and the virtual elimination of operating windows. With a plentiful supply of cheap fossil fuel available thanks to Reagan-era geopolitical changes, there was little incentive for further development of renewable energy systems, and solar water installations were often decommissioned when major maintenance was required. Architecture turned inward and, through the 1980s, grand interior atria joined the subterranean concourses and "plus-15" enclosed walkways of the 1960s, all elements of the ever-expanding continuous urban interior.[4]

By the 1990s, many unintended consequences of the "prophylactic" low-energy approach emerged in Canadian buildings large and small. Poor understanding of building physics, reduced ventilation rates, and deferred maintenance led to problems such as "sick building syndrome," wherein inadequate lighting levels, mold and virus growth (in air

handling systems and concealed spaces), and excess ozone, carbon dioxide, and volatile organic compounds (in interior air) contribute to chronic human health problems and hypersensitivities. Low-energy buildings also reduced productivity among alienated occupants with no agency in their work situation: no light switch, no thermostat, no operating window, little fresh air, and no view to the outside. Paradoxically, what began as "environmental building" had become increasingly "environment-excluding." Buildings had been conceived as absolutely controlled artificial environments: designers sought to avoid any ad-hoc exchanges of energy or matter between inside and outside, a profound shift from the more "osmotic" approaches of late 1970s environmental building, which welcomed two-way exchanges of energy, air, and biota.[5]

The Advent of "Sustainability," 1987–2003

"Sustainable development" entered public discourse in 1987 with the publication by the UN Brundtland Commission of *Our Common Future*. In the report, perceived conflicts between the environment and economic development were reframed based on the increasing recognition of inherent "limits to growth" on a finite planet.[6] Brundtland's approach was grounded in social and generational justice: according to the report, "sustainable development…meets the needs of the present without compromising the ability of future generations to meet their own needs."[7] These were resonant words, but they were abstract in their application to specific cases, and the next few years saw little direct effect on the built environment. Five years later, the Rio Earth Summit of 1992 mobilized public engagement, especially from youth and the developing world. Rio produced the UN Framework Convention on Climate Change, directing international attention to global threats to the biosphere, and reignited popular concern for Earth's environment, functioning as a kind of flashback to the first Earth Day of 1970.

As in the 1970s, this early 1990s environmental reawakening came to bear on the building industry through a mix of positive and negative stimuli. The optimism of the Earth Summit coincided with rising oil prices due to the Gulf War of 1990–1991, and anxiety about future supplies was expressed in media coverage of the "peak oil" hypothesis. Architecture began to revisit 1970s approaches to renewable energy, enhanced by now-viable wind-power technology and emerging low-cost photovoltaics. Energy-conserving design could now draw upon robust building science with research and academic backing, professional consultants, and tools to model and monitor building energy performance and climate response.

Rio's Earth Summit brought renewed attention to direct environmental engagement. Early post-Rio environmental buildings returned to the osmotic approaches of the mid-1970s, with natural ventilation and on-site renewable energy systems, while adding a new concern for "healthy" materials with low chemical off-gassing. For example, the Boyne River Ecology Centre in Shelburne, Ontario (Greg Allen, engineer, and Douglas Pollard, architect, 1993), is a self-sustaining classroom and activities building for an existing residential nature school, allowing thousands of Toronto schoolchildren to spend a week in a living example of ecological design.[8] **FIGS 11–12** Its octagonal mass evokes the Roseau Children's Centre, nestled into the slope with easy access to an outdoor classroom on the earth-sheltered roof. A central cupola facilitates natural ventilation, assisted by the fireplace in

the gathering space below; a surrounding ring of classrooms is finished with natural wood and linoleum. One sector of the octagon houses a "living machine"—a solar aquatic sewage treatment system.[9] On-site renewable-energy systems include solar panels, a wind turbine, and a microhydroelectric generator that charges a battery array.

Picking up the legacy of its 1970s predecessor, EMR, Natural Resources Canada (NRCan) sought to revive Canadian pro-environmental building policy under agency leaders Nils Larsson and Stephen Pope. Its C-2000 Program (1994) funded the costs associated with achieving 45- to 50-percent reductions in building energy. C-2000 required projects to follow an Integrated Design Process (IDP) in which the full design teams along with all key stakeholders take part in a kickoff concept workshop. This collaboration ensures full exploration of early design decisions, as these have the biggest impacts on ultimate building performance; it also gives clients and end users a shared responsibility for the key design choices.

Proof-of-concept for IDP came in 1993, when the University of British Columbia (UBC) undertook to build a "benchmark in sustainable design." The C. K. Choi Institute of Asian Research (Matsuzaki Wright Architects, 1996) is a modest 30,000 square feet (2,790 square meters) of offices, display gallery, and teaching spaces on three stories. **FIG 13** UBC

14 opposite, top
Toronto Healthy House, exterior view from laneway, Toronto, Ontario. Martin Liefhebber Architect, 1996.

15 opposite, bottom
Toronto Healthy House, cross section showing systems.

architecture professor Ray Cole helped set the project's sustainability ambitions, provided research supporting the design process, and disseminated lessons-learned to the architecture profession and building industry.

Preliminary IDP charrettes fostered deep collaboration among the consultant teams and stakeholders. The resulting design features careful siting within the campus ecology, allowing exchanges of air and energy across the building envelope conditioned by architecture and landscape. A procession of small towers, topped by curved metal roofs meant to evoke Asian built form, punctuates the brick facade. These serve as stack ventilation chimneys that draw in fresh air, as there is no conventional ducted air-handling system. Other innovative features include atria and shallow floor plates that ensure good daylighting; sensors that override user-operated light switches; "healthy" interior finishes; waterless toilets connected to a central composting system; and rainwater collection for landscape irrigation. Ambitiously, the building is more than 50 percent reclaimed building materials, including heavy timber structural elements from a nearby demolition and purple-red brick cladding from recovered Vancouver street pavers.[10] As intended, the Choi building is a benchmark of then-emergent trends in sustainable design.

Building on the Saskatchewan Conservation House legacy, Toronto's Healthy House (Martin Liefhebber Architect, 1996) won a 1991 national design competition sponsored by the federal Canada Mortgage and Housing Corporation (CMHC) that attracted over seven hundred submissions. CMHC's "Healthy Housing" agenda is blended with the architect's "notions on ecology and architecture" to create a two-unit party-wall duplex on a laneway site in the dense Riverdale district. **FIGS 14–15** Connecting environmentalism to context-sensitive urban revitalization builds on an important trend in Toronto architecture dating back to the 1960s. The "back to the land" counterculture had a "back to the city" counterpart, evidenced by Toronto's Yorkville scene and the parallel flowering of urban infill projects for downtown intensification [see pages 429–435].

Though the competition design's rooftop greenhouse was abandoned, the built version of the Healthy House goes beyond typical energy and water conservation to embrace technologies such as rainwater harvesting and on-site sewage treatment. Outside, the

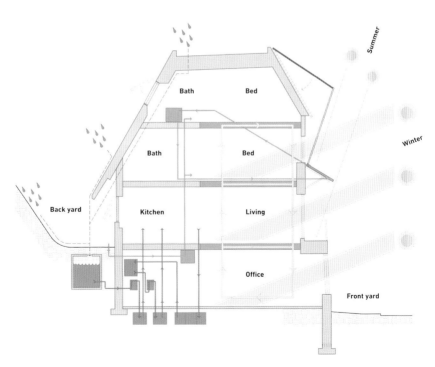

architecture leaves no doubt that this is not a typical urban Toronto house. Prominent exterior solar panels, including both photovoltaics and solar heating for domestic water, serve as sunshades and porch shelters. Each unit of the duplex presents a different approach to self-sufficiency, allowing for comparative study of urban sustainable design. The official CMHC Healthy House unit is entirely "off-grid." The second unit is grid-tied but still places much lower demand on city services compared to a conventional house, thereby expanding the ability of existing infrastructure to support urban intensification.[11] The Healthy House garnered positive public interest by bringing a lifestyle of minimized environmental impacts to the urban core.

Defining "Green" Building, 1997–2002

By the mid-1990s, architects could look to a growing body of pro-environmental "green buildings" in Canada and around the world. Ray Cole of UBC and Nils Larsson of NRCan initiated the Green Building Challenge (GBC) in 1995 to build knowledge and best practices by collecting green building case studies from multiple countries and regions. Each case study underwent a detailed, multiyear performance assessment. At the first conference held in Vancouver in 1998, the GBC examined issues such the comparability of performance assessment standards and the challenge of assessment across diverse regional climates and technical conditions.[12] Benchmark-related assessments comparing performance of a new design against the "typical practice," which varies by region, came to be preferred over absolute assessments. The legacy of the GBC program includes increased awareness and credibility of green building assessment systems among professionals, building owners, and the public, as well as a regionally diverse showcase of green building case studies.

During this period, "global warming" became a clear and present environmental danger linked specifically to carbon emissions. International focus on the threat and possible solutions was sharpest around the time of the signing of the 1997 Kyoto Protocol, with nations pledging to reduce emissions to significantly below 1990 levels. Climatologist Michael Mann's 1998 "hockey stick" graph, showing the sharp increase in global temperatures since 1900, also shine a spotlight on the issue. Though the Kyoto consensus soon unraveled, Canadian architects, engineers, and building policy makers maintained their commitment to building a sustainable, low-carbon future. The Canada Green Building Council (CaGBC), founded in July 2003 in Vancouver, adapted the US-developed LEED (Leadership in Energy and Environmental Design) standards, launched in 1996, to create LEED BC. A year later, LEED Canada was started.

The task of incentivizing green building shifted from the government to the private sector, and the incentive shifted from financial subsidy to reputational value in the marketplace. LEED evaluates the building design process, material decisions, and energy performance modeling to generate easily understood ratings. It has become an unofficial parallel

building code for high-profile commercial and institutional buildings, and each version of LEED (version 4 was implemented in 2014) raises the bar required to meet the rating levels. While LEED certification has been criticized for its focus on the building itself and its lack of attention to site, location, and social issues, it nevertheless is widely seen as offering an important contribution to a low-carbon built environment.

Mountain Equipment Co-op's Winnipeg store (Prairie Architects, 2002) was one of the first LEED-certified buildings constructed in Canada, built to C-2000 standards and certified Gold by the US Green Building Council (USGBC). **FIGS 16–17** The existing buildings on its prominent Portage Avenue site were dismantled to capture their embodied material energy and cultural value. Over 96 percent of this material by weight was reused in the new design, which employs bolted connections and a component approach to encourage future re-recycling. Exposed structural materials in the new store support passive energy storage and transfer, avoiding all fan-energy use. A green roof insulates the building, reduces heat island effect, and helps with rainwater collection; the toilets are all waterless and composting. IDP was essential to achieving such ambitious reuse of materials and integration of systems. The resulting collage of materials and systems provides a rich interior expression that is well-suited to the ethos of the client and customers while, on the outside, MEC plays a pioneering role in the revitalized Portage Avenue shopping district.

Peter Busby and the Advancement of Sustainable Design Practice

In contrast to the quirky specificity and recycled materials of the Mountain Equipment Co-op and Choi buildings, the Computer Science Building at York University in Toronto (Busby + Associates/architectsAlliance, 2001) tackles the challenges of designing a green building with a mainstream institutional expression for a building program with no inherent environmental agenda. The building contains a large floor plate at 100,000 square feet (9,295 square meters), including a 950-seat lecture hall and numerous large classrooms and labs. The plan is articulated by two atria, one a long, internal circulation hall and the other

an enclosed tree court. **FIGS 18–19** The low surface-area-to-volume ratio provides inherent energy efficiency, augmented by high insulation values in the walls and roof and by a green roof that provides evaporative cooling in summer. Computer labs are placed on the north side to take advantage of cooler summer temperatures while also utilizing waste heat in winter.

External shading devices manage unwanted solar gains, articulated to suit the different exposure conditions. These layers of louvers provide each face of the building with a distinct architectural character, resulting in an overall rhetoric of responsive technical systems. While these and other "green devices" mitigate the environmental impacts on the building, and some draw on the immediate environment as an energy source, they do not allow a direct engagement of inside and outside at the scale of the individual user. Essentially, the architectural envelope remains a "prophylactic" membrane. Natural ventilation and cooling strategies engage the surrounding conditions, but they are configured at the scale of the whole building and integrated into the central mechanical systems. Busby's design approach treats green devices as plug-in substitutes for conventional systems. The York building is a menu of practice-ready energy-conserving tactics and details, and effectively inaugurates mainstream "green" building in Canada.

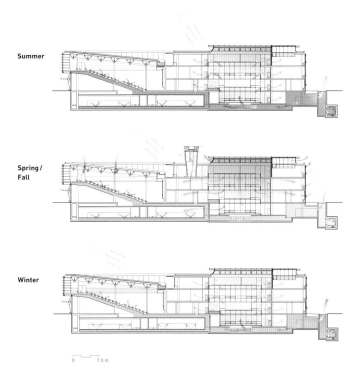

Summer

Spring/ Fall

Winter

0 7.5 m

Peter Busby's background in the British high-tech movement is evident in the design approach at York. Busby briefly worked for Norman Foster before returning to Vancouver in the early 1980s. He quickly established himself as an architect committed to advancing green building design. In Busby's approach, architecture is conceived as a matter of technical production, carried out by a diverse design team under the leadership of the architect, in response to the client's brief.[13] What and where to build, and questions around the social role of building, are largely understood as beyond the architect's scope. Within the design process, the focus is on those aspects of the design that can be quantified and predicted. Under the influence of his UBC professor Ray Cole, Busby expanded this scope to consider energy consumption and other impacts of the operating life of the building. The high quality of the form, composition, and detail of Busby's architecture demonstrates that green buildings can respond to the full range of contextual demands and cultural aspirations while at the same time delivering environmentally responsible outcomes in terms of energy consumption and material choices.

Busby's approach provides an effective "sustainability manual" for amending conventional architectural and engineering practice to improve environmental responsiveness and reduce environmental impacts. In contrast to the countercultural tendencies of earlier green

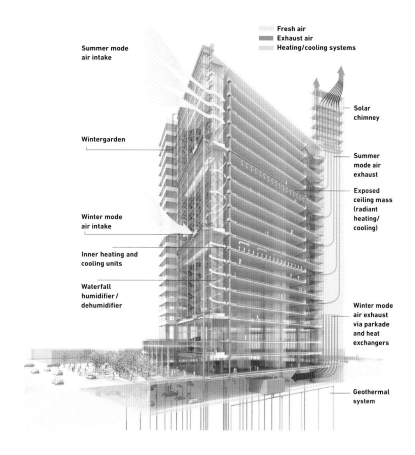

Summer mode
air intake

Wintergarden

Winter mode
air intake

Inner heating and
cooling units

Waterfall
humidifier /
dehumidifier

Fresh air
Exhaust air
Heating/cooling systems

Solar
chimney

Summer
mode air
exhaust

Exposed
ceiling mass
(radiant
heating/
cooling)

Winter mode
air exhaust
via parkade
and heat
exchangers

Geothermal
system

building, this is a method well-suited to the universalizing tendencies of globalization. And, indeed, Busby's corporate green-building approach was globalized through the 2004 amalgamation of his firm with US-based Perkins+Will, providing sustainability strategies to an existing multinational corporate practice. Its ecomodernist assumptions underpin the success of CaGBC and LEED Canada. The potential of this approach to mitigate the environmental impacts of building is substantial and important, and it is well suited to the corporate nature of most contemporary development and building procurement.[14]

Low Carbon Buildings, 2003–2017

The early millennium saw a number of efforts by the profession to mobilize architecture as a leader in the move towards sustainability. The 2006 Living Building Challenge (LBC) invokes the spirit of 1970s experiments in environmental architecture, seeking buildings that go beyond harm reduction to achieve a symbiosis with the surrounding environment. A "living building" "generates all of its own energy with renewable non-toxic resources, captures and treats all of its water, and operates efficiently and for maximum beauty."[15] Living buildings are judged on actual performance after a year of operation rather than on

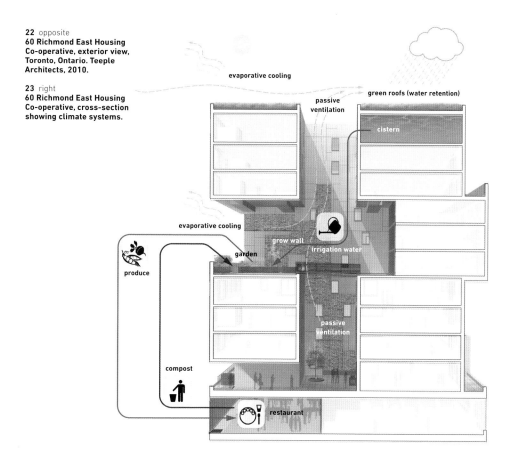

22 opposite
60 Richmond East Housing Co-operative, exterior view, Toronto, Ontario. Teeple Architects, 2010.

23 right
60 Richmond East Housing Co-operative, cross-section showing climate systems.

evaporative cooling

passive ventilation

green roofs (water retention)

cistern

evaporative cooling

grow wall

garden

irrigation water

produce

passive ventilation

compost

restaurant

the predictive models used by LEED. In 2007, the Royal Architectural Institute of Canada (RAIC) adopted the 2030 Challenge, an international call for all new buildings to be carbon neutral with no operating fossil fuel by 2030, and for the development of regional approaches to sustainable, carbon-neutral cities and buildings.[16] Following on 2015's COP 21 Paris Agreement, CaGBC's Zero Carbon Buildings Initiative (2016) calls for all new Canadian buildings to have a net-zero carbon footprint by 2030. The target accounts for regional differences in the carbon intensity of energy consumed, for carbon embodied and sequestered in the building fabric, and for renewable energy generated on-site.[17]

Manitoba Hydro Place in Winnipeg (KPMB Architects with Smith Carter Architects and Prairie Architects, 2009) is a benchmark high-rise for an extreme climate, and a flagship for the sustainability ambitions of mainstream architects and clients. **FIGS 20–21** German consultants Transsolar KlimaEngineering provided expertise for the double-skin glass facade, which connects a shallow south-facing atrium to an expressive solar chimney on the north, preconditioning fresh air that reaches occupants through operating inner windows. Flows in the system are seasonally responsive and supported by geothermal wells. Integrated solar shading permits maximum transparency and daylight penetration at the perimeter of the unusually shallow floor plates. Beyond its building energy accomplishments, Manitoba Hydro

24 left
Centre for Interactive
Research on Sustainability,
University of British
Columbia, exterior
view, Vancouver, British
Columbia. Perkins+Will,
2011.

25 opposite
Centre for Interactive
Research on Sustainability,
University of British
Columbia, cross-section
showing systems.

Place performs a significant role in social and transportation sustainability, bringing two thousand jobs from the suburbs to downtown Winnipeg, and inspiring a behavior-change program among employees to encourage downtown living and the use of public transport.

Urban social sustainability is the primary goal of the 60 Richmond East Housing Co-operative in Toronto (Teeple Architects, 2010). **FIGS 22–23** Stephen Teeple's green building exploits the internal energetics of occupant activities and equipment, harvesting and redistributing excess heat around the building as needed. Visual expression of technical sustainability systems is muted, while social sustainability elements are highlighted. Solid walls with punched windows clad the upper volume of eighty-five dwellings for hospitality workers, a commonsense approach to energy management that contrasts with the all-glass curtain walls typical of contemporary residential towers. Push-pull massing animates this solid zone to improve daylight access and create multiple terraces and sky gardens with varying microclimates, where food plantings and green roofs mitigate the urban heat island effect and symbolize the community's focus on food and livelihood. At the street level, a sweep of transparent wall gives views into a restaurant owned and operated by residents, supported by a training kitchen that enables residents (mostly in low-skill jobs) to apprentice as high-value restaurant staff. The menu draws on produce from the various

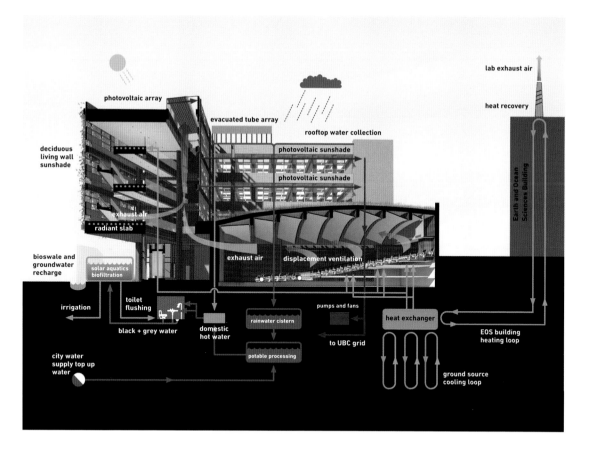

terrace gardens, irrigated by rainwater from the roofs and fertilized by kitchen compost. The building symbolizes an aspiration to "urban permaculture" while establishing nuanced relations between occupants and community, and between the building and surrounding environment.

Fifteen years after completing the Computer Science Building at York, Peter Busby made an intriguing evolution in his thinking: he now seeks to move green design beyond "harm reduction." His 2015 book *Architecture's New Edges* calls for a "regenerative sustainability" in which buildings help to "repair nature" through construction and operation. This goal reflects the research of John Robinson, founding director of UBC's Centre for Interactive Research on Sustainability (CIRS), and the continuing influence of Ray Cole. Busby, as director of Perkins+Will's Vancouver office, completed the CIRS building in 2011 following a decade-long collaboration with Robinson and Cole. Each of them describes the process as having gone much deeper than a conventional design process.

CIRS houses hundreds of sustainability researchers—from academia, industry, government, and NGOs—in a living laboratory designed to foster collaboration across disciplines and sectors. FIGS 24–25 A daylit auditorium and "locavore" café provide tangible experiences of a sustainable future, surrounded by public displays of the building's many features:

26
VanDusen Botanical Garden
Visitor Centre, exterior
view, Vancouver, British
Columbia. Perkins+Will,
2011.

rainwater harvesting, on-site biological wastewater treatment, 100 percent daylighting and natural ventilation, and building-integrated photovoltaics. Waste heat harvested from an adjacent building results in a net-positive energy system with negative carbon emissions, while the timber structure and extensive wood finishes (using Forest Stewardship Council–certified and beetle-killed sources) sequester carbon for the life of the building. An online building manual documents the overall intentions, design development and resolution, and lessons learned, along with reports of actual building systems performance over the first few years.[18] LEED Platinum–certified and winner of the 2015 RAIC Green Building Award, CIRS makes a first step beyond harm reduction toward an architecture that is net-positive in relation to its environment.

Building on the lessons of CIRS, the VanDusen Botanical Garden Visitor Centre in Vancouver (Perkins+Will, 2011) employs a unitary biomorphic form that expresses "sustainability" more poetically than Busby's usual hard-edged technomodernism. **FIG 26** Wood, and its tactility, provides the overall form and image. Public environmental education was a shared goal of the architect and client, and the resulting 50 percent increase in visitors to the garden shows the power of design to raise the profile of a site and to move popular imagination toward an optimistic vision of "regenerative sustainability." In addition to being certified LEED Platinum, the center is Busby's first living building, achieving LBC recognition for Site, Materials, Health, and Beauty.

Developing sustainable timber buildings is the focus of two dramatically different design-innovation practices. Piskwepaq Design's 2008 Pictou Landing First Nation Health Centre in Nova Scotia [see page 137] creates parametric trusses from malleable green spruce poles, expressing a dynamic longhouse form rising from an earth berm. Continuing in the spirit of the Roseau First Nation Children's Centre, which was built in late 1970s, the Pictou Landing center is also a tool for building community resilience through its use of locally harvested materials; through its associated program for youth to develop skills in forestry and green-timber building techniques; and through its construction approach in which the community built the structure while professional tradespeople handled the systems and finish work.

Standing in contrast to this low-tech, community-empowerment approach to sustainability is Michael Green's high-tech industrial timber development. In collaboration with the Canadian wood industry, Green is developing mass timber systems for widespread use in commercial and residential buildings. Columns, beams, and wall and floor panels are prefabricated with thick wood laminations, providing inherent fire resistance; combined with steel or concrete jointing elements, these mass timber components can be used to construct high-rise buildings. The Wood Innovation and Design Centre (WIDC) in Prince George, BC (MGA | Michael Green Architecture, 2015), is configured as an eight-story showcase of timber construction and functions as a hub for research, education, and commercialization of advanced wood building products and systems. **FIG 27** High-quality surface finishes of the mass timber elements are left exposed in the interiors, while the connections between elements are detailed to enable future disassembly and reuse; exterior cladding combines charred and weathered cedar panels with a custom wood-curtain wall system. WIDC serves as a proof-of-concept for Green and other designers now building a portfolio of mass timber high-rise projects in Canada and the United States [see pages 497–501].

New buildings such as Van Dusen and WIDC are the overwhelming preoccupation of organizations that promote green building ratings and standards. Yet in Canada renovations constitute ten times the volume of new builds, while building alterations and maintenance affect one hundred times the volume of new construction projects. Even modest improvements in the sustainability of the existing building stock will deliver far more benefit in the aggregate than all the new LEED certified buildings taken together.[19] Benny Farm in Montreal (L'OEUF, 2002–2012) [see pages 221–225] was recognized by the inaugural 2005 Holcim Foundation Sustainable Construction Awards for its community-led revitalization of 18 acres (7.3 hectares) of late 1940s veterans' housing, with high energy-performance retrofits and infill construction supported by green water infrastructure and on-site renewable energy production.[20] More than a decade of consultation and collaboration with residents ensured that social sustainability led the design agenda.

Scaling beyond a single site, the Mayor's Tower Renewal Project (ERA Architects and University of Toronto, 2008) produced a city-scale handbook for improving the sustainability of Toronto's hundreds of concrete apartment towers. **FIG 28** The approach admirably ignores the usual professional boundaries of architecture to set out a large-scale environmental and performance context to guide specific design projects at the level of individual buildings and complexes. Building-level decisions are understood at the scale of the district and city. The renewal approach reduces building energy consumption and emissions, avoids depopulating the city center, optimizes existing services and transit, and supports the existing social fabric of each tower community. CaGBC's 2017 report *A Roadmap for Retrofits in Canada* scales such site-specific and building-type-based renewal strategies to address Canada's entire stock of large, energy-inefficient buildings built between 1960 and 1979, promising national-scale carbon-saving potential.

27
Wood Innovation and
Design Centre, exterior
view, Prince George,
British Columbia.
MGA | Michael Green
Architecture, 2015.

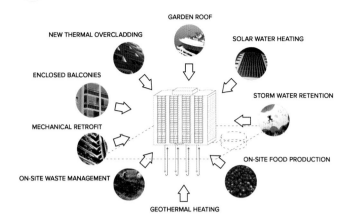

GARDEN ROOF

NEW THERMAL OVERCLADDING

SOLAR WATER HEATING

ENCLOSED BALCONIES

STORM WATER RETENTION

MECHANICAL RETROFIT

ON-SITE FOOD PRODUCTION

ON-SITE WASTE MANAGEMENT

GEOTHERMAL HEATING

28
Mayor's Tower Renewal,
renewal strategies
diagram, Toronto, Ontario.
ERA Architects and
University of Toronto,
2008.

Conclusion: Toward a Sustainable
Built Environment, 2017–2030

Canada today has begun to embrace an architecture that squarely faces the carbon crisis through energy savings and material choices. Busby's ideas of "regenerative sustainability" and the Living Building Challenge seek to move beyond this "harm reduction" paradigm to achieve net-positive effects in the environment while still functioning as individual buildings. KPMB's Manitoba Hydro Place represents the critical choice to build downtown, thereby reducing commuter impacts and helping revive an urban neighborhood, while Teeple's 60 Richmond Co-op links its residents to on-site food production and career skills development. Toronto's Tower Renewal seeks to capture existing material and community energy in a process of building-performance upgrades. Design and construction become enablers of social sustainability in Montreal's Benny Farm, and in the Pictou Landing Health Centre.

These are modest but important tactical steps in the face of the sustainability challenges posed by the contemporary Canadian built environment. For Canadian architects to engage meaningfully in building a truly sustainable future, they must collaborate with other professionals, as well as industries and governments, to craft sustainability strategies for the overall built environment and its built-in commuter transportation demands. New, net-zero buildings are an important signal of Canadian aspirations, but they are insufficient without substantial improvement to the sustainability of the vast stock of existing buildings and neighborhoods. While "nature" remains a powerful touchstone of Canadian identity, for most Canadians, cities and suburbs provide the setting for life. Not since the heady days of the 1960s have architects had such a potent opportunity to create buildings and neighborhoods to invoke radically new and liberating ways of being in the world.

Regional
Responses

9

West Coast Land Claims

Sherry McKay

Framed by the North Shore Mountains to the north, the oceanic Strait of Georgia to the west, and the narrow Fraser Valley to the east, Vancouver and its valley communities boast majestic views and vantage points that have long attracted people to the region. Traditionally, this geography supported Indigenous peoples in diverse settlements, which they occupied with impressive timber structures. It also shaped the region's modern building practices, which have often challenged conventional typologies. Starting from the late 1960s, West Coast architecture was additionally influenced by a growing awareness of Indigenous peoples' land claims and place within Canadian culture. This led to compelling commissions in Vancouver and throughout the province, as well as expanded visions of both modernity and landscape.[1]

The West Coast House

While the West Coast encompasses a broad territory, the majority of its architectural development has focused around Vancouver. In the years following World War II, inexpensive housing sites were created on seemingly inhospitable terrain along the coastline on the periphery of the city. The structures here deployed innovative post-and-beam construction

techniques and the abstract formal vocabulary of modern architecture, the latter derived in large part from American influences. Rapidly, a distinctive West Coast Modern Style emerged that responded to the unique qualities of the region. The style gained national recognition through such early modern residences as the Copp House (1951) by British Columbia architect Ron Thom (1923–1986) and the Porter Residence (1948) by New Brunswick–born architect John Porter (1915–1993), both of which received the Massey Medal, Canada's highest award in architecture. The residence that Vancouver architect Barry Downs (1930–) built for himself in 1959 complemented modern efficient planning principles and modular wood-framing techniques with carefully choreographed landscaping: Downs enveloped the dwelling with native plants arranged in a Japanese manner. **FIG 1** Arthur Erickson's Graham House (1962), designed with Geoffrey Massey, offered a complex concatenation of wood-frame structure and terraces, intimately poised within the irregular terrain of its West Vancouver site. **FIG 2**

While the 1950s produced a West Coast architecture that was modest in scale and deferential to the experiential aspects of the natural landscape, the mid-1960s and the subsequent decades saw a more expansive and complex relationship between building and site, as architects were forced to negotiate competing claims to the land. By that time, the city's development had been identified as a major issue: Vancouver's population had begun to scatter to the suburbs, city amenities were undermined by the singularity and uniformity of developer-driven high-rise apartments in the inner city, and its ability to attract enterprise was hindered by the lack of high-quality commercial space. The architectural community responded to these pressing urban issues in public debates and city proposals, as well as with building projects that remain eloquent declarations of the discipline's repositioned role in shaping urban land.

Many Vancouver architects who had honed their skills with iconic West Coast Modern post-and-beam homes were part of the group tackling these challenges. Perhaps the most prominent among them was Vancouver-born Arthur Erickson (1924–2009), who began a private practice in partnership with Geoffrey Massey (1924–) in 1953. The firm rose to prominence with its success in the design competition for Simon Fraser University in 1963

[see pages 113–119, 160–161]. Erickson, educated at McGill University, would eventually become Canada's most distinguished architect. While better known for their larger-scale works, the firm continued to develop low- and mid-rise buildings, such as the Point Grey Townhouses (1963). The design was a restrained version of Erickson's dynamically composed single-family houses. Five configurations of courts, bridges, and terraces descended with the fall of the land while remaining disciplined by the tight limitations set by party walls and inner-city lot sizes. **FIG 3**

Barry Downs also brought his established regional sensitivities to the city's new challenges, focusing in on questions of population mobility and the growing unaffordability of single-family homes. Downs created an expandable model house for the 1968 Vancouver Home Show, prefabricated in reconfigurable stand-alone modules. The project experimented with manufactured components, was innovative in its space-planning arrangements, and reconsidered the temporal dimension of housing.[2] **FIGS 4–5** Provocatively, it also tested existing zoning regulations and the design criteria used for mortgage approval. Downs's show house was designed for replication across neighborhoods, its small size made to appear larger with vistas borrowed across the courtyards and enclosed gardens and provided by the

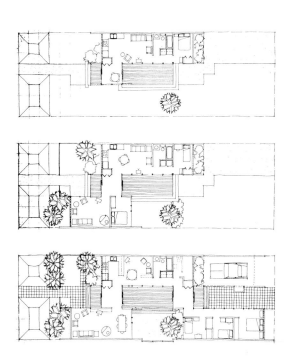

staggered configuration of its modules.[3] The issues of urban transformation and technologies of mass production were topical in the 1960s.[4] Downs's response was modest in scale,
circumspect about technology, accepting of common materials, and thoughtful toward
nature. As Downs commented: "I see this solution as a sort of interim housing, already
mobile, but not yet free of its traditional garb."[5]

West Coast Urban Response

A West Coast response to urban form developed in parallel with the domestic experiments
of Erickson, Downs, and others. On the vanguard of this response in 1957 was Thompson, Berwick & Pratt—one of the most established firms in the area—who designed the
regionally inflected, internationally noted, twenty-one-story BC Electric Building for the
provincial electric utility. **FIG 6** The building was strategically located on a slight elevation
just outside the downtown core, giving it visual prominence. As well, its economical footprint allowed for the opportunity to stretch a planted plaza across the building's southern
extent, while the grayed blues and greens of its cladding were deemed expressive of its
coastal environment.

By the mid-1960s, Vancouver's intensified commercial economy, which demanded
buildings to accommodate it, provided an opportunity to transform strategies for building
in the landscape into strategies for building in the city. Beyond the design of iconic houses
within Vancouver's restricted borders, sleek office towers commensurate with the scale of
the business and government activity of the era were introduced.

An alternative to the standard office block was presented in Erickson and Massey's Mac-
Millan Bloedel Building. **FIG 7** Upon its completion in 1968, this highrise was a discrimi-
nating anomaly among the masonry and curtain wall structures obligingly aligned along the
grand avenue of West Georgia Street. MacMillan Bloedel is pulled back from the sidewalk,
recessed below grade, and composed of over-scaled concrete members. The thickness of the
wall tapers dramatically over its twenty-seven-story rise, while the elevation is uniformly
dimensioned by 7-foot-square (2.1-meter-square) windows embedded within its depth. Its

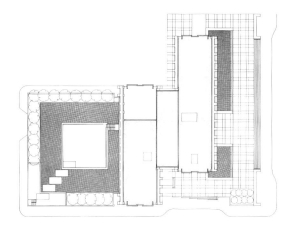

design occludes the engineering ingenuity of its vertical cantilever with a semblance of gravity-responding mass.

The MacMillan Bloedel Building is not a conventional single volume, but rather two parallel and subtly offset slabs, joined eccentrically by a service core. **FIG 8** Its efficacy results primarily from the designers' attentiveness to human use and to the building's interface with its site. The narrow floor plate provides natural light along an enlarged perimeter, and flexible office configurations are made possible by an interior unencumbered by structural elements. The layering of the building into its site facilitates the inclusion of the public realm: the westward slippage of the northern slab affords an independent entrance from the plaza to a shopping arcade. A concrete parking garage is recessed within the lower slope of the site and disguised as an ivy-clad embankment; its roof supports a terrace accessible from the mezzanine level. The building's walls and forecourt shape an urban precinct with monumental forms scaled to an extended geography and an artificial topography that differentiates it from the urban grid, uniting it with an enlarged landscape.

The building also marks a pivotal moment in the evolution of the MacMillan Bloedel Forestry enterprise, which had, by the mid-1960s, become the largest private corporation in British Columbia and was shifting its focus toward the global sphere.[6] Erickson and Massey's building transformed a natural resource into a national asset: built to house a forestry conglomerate, it also served the rhetoric of presenting Canada as a player on the international stage.

Beach Towers (1965) by Charles Burwell Kerrens Van Norman (1907–1975)—who was known in the 1930s and 1940s for his expertise in prefabricated wood-frame houses—responded to the need for affordable urban accommodation for a mobile demographic. Its studio and one-bedroom apartments are replicated across three identical cruciform concrete towers. **FIG 9** Set within a garden landscape and overlooking the water's edge, the generously glazed high-rises offered panoramic balcony views—and the novelty of urban density paired with suburban individuated spaciousness.[7]

A suburban sensibility would also influence large-scale mixed-use developments in the city, as exemplified in the post-industrial reconsideration of False Creek South. In 1974, a

LAURIER HOUSE MACDONALD HOUSE DOUGLAS HOUSE

comprehensive plan for the area by Thompson, Berwick, Pratt & Partners was an implicit critique of the downtown West End high-rise apartment model. The landfill and dock structures of the former industrial lands were transformed into a gradient from park-like open space at the water's edge to built-up form inland, the whole bordered by a public sea wall.[8]

The site was next partitioned into discrete architectural projects. Architect Richard Henriquez (1941–), recently relocated from Winnipeg, and local partner Robert Todd's False Creek Co-op Housing (1978) is an enclave of tan stucco townhouses topped by red-tiled shed roofs and accompanied by a similarly styled, award-winning elementary school. **FIG 10** Thomson, Berwick, Pratt & Partners' three-story townhouse complex possesses the scale and intimacy of a village (1977). The structures surrounding Leg-and-Boot Square, by various architects, continue the intimate scale of mixed housing, shops, and public space. British expat architect Peter Cardew (1939–), who then worked with Rhone & Iredale, designed the False Creek Townhouses (1980) to be suggestive of modern English terraces while avoiding direct historical allusions. **FIG 11** Rhone & Iredale also proposed the unrealized Lagoons—a residential complex set around artificial ponds to afford mountain views and a Southern California ambience.[9] During this transformative period, corporate

and housing forms had, if sparely, registered in urban form the West Coast interests in landscape of the previous decade. The developments in False Creek foreshadowed the development of Granville Island [see pages 214–216].

Public Landforms

In 1966, Arthur Erickson was interviewed about Vancouver urban design on national television.[10] The interview reveals much about the demands of building downtown. Erickson commented on the incursion of large-scale national and international real estate developers, the arrival of internationally oriented corporate clients, the increasing size of projects that now extended over large land assemblies, the growing discretionary power of city planners, and the representational and functional interests of civic and political institutions.[11]

In the 1970s, Erickson's proposal for Robson Square, occupying two city blocks in downtown Vancouver, navigated these challenges and brought his three-dimensional architectural thinking underground. The plan carved down into the earth to reveal underground malls and layers of vehicular traffic while also building upward over terraces and stairs and stretching laterally into plazas and overpasses [see pages 177–179]. Office towers,

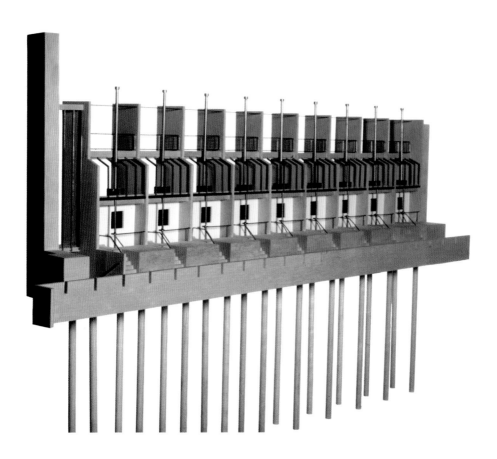

11 above
False Creek Townhouses, model view, Vancouver, British Columbia. Rhone & Iredale Architects, 1980.

12 opposite
Evergreen Building, view from northwest, Vancouver, British Columbia. Arthur Erickson Architects, 1980.

civic buildings, and a hotel rose above. Much in the manner of Victor Gruen's 1964 book *The Heart of Our Cities*,[12] Erickson focused on the city core; however, he sought to create a counterpoint to contemporary projects underway in the shopping and business center of Vancouver. He pointed to two in particular: Pacific Centre Phase 1, which included the Eaton's Building, Toronto-Dominion Bank, and the IBM Building (Victor Gruen & Associates, with Cesar Pelli and McCarter Nairne & Partners), and the CEMP Four Seasons Hotel in Vancouver (Webb, Zerafa, Menekes, Housden Partnership). Completed by the mid-1970s, both complexes were dominated by dark-glazed curtain-wall towers with perfunctory forecourts.[13] These echoed existing developments such as the two Bentall Center Towers (Musson & Cattell, 1967 and 1969) and the Guinness Tower (Charles Paine & Associates, 1969)—whose generic forms were a stark contrast to the subtleties of Robson Square.

Following Massey's departure from the partnership in 1972, Erickson designed the Evergreen Building in the downtown core (1980), a new interpretation of earlier urban landscape preoccupations. **FIG 12** Sited on a sloped, trapezoidal site, the structure was built for a local investor with exacting specifications regarding budgetary limits and amenities. Initially comprising prestige offices, a recreational health club, commercial space, and corporate

apartments, it also allowed for conversion to residential use. To that end, the ten-story concrete building follows the natural topography to maximize efficiency of land use, views, and exterior space. The whole of its southern facade is glazed to fit with the commercial nature of the street, while the western facade is rotated in a series of terraces that proffer vantage points to Coal Harbour and Stanley Park, and create a public view corridor to the North Shore Mountains. Heavily encased in plantings along balconies and terraces, the building in effect creates an artificial escarpment, recalling a past geology and lifting it from the transitory whims of real estate to the realm of a larger, archaic landscape.[14]

A similar concern with landscape is evident in Robson Square, particularly when the project expanded to include the Vancouver Art Gallery (Arthur Erickson Architects, 1983). A repurposing of the historic Law Courts, the gallery benefited from its reorientation from Georgia Street to turn toward the topographical cast of Robson Square. A new entrance pavilion and a generous cascade of stairs facing the square invites informal seating and views across the plaza to the new Law Courts and their civic park, the latter designed by Cornelia Oberlander (1921–). The new Law Courts were, in part, modern accommodations for an increased number of provincial courts and government services and also part urban-renewal initiative. **FIG 13**

Other projects responded to urban developments in the 1970s by manipulating plazas, towers, and sites in ways that exhibited a variety of preoccupations. Dramatically suspended 36 feet (11 meters) above West Georgia Street, the West Coast Transmission Building by Rhone & Iredale (1969) offered twelve floors of unencumbered office space for the BC-based natural gas pipeline company. **FIG 14** A technical tour-de-force, its steel floor plates are suspended from a concrete core by high-tensile-strength steel cables to provide earthquake resistance, and to allow for mountain views from a street-level plaza. The decision to eliminate what was, at the time, deemed an unprofitable ground-floor level warranted greater height overall, permitting the creation of distinctively designed offices with panoramic views for prominent business enterprises.[15]

Crown Life Plaza was commissioned by the Canadian-founded, Regina-based Crown Life Insurance Company (1978) and designed by Rhone & Iredale with project architect Peter Cardew. The tower marks the western edge of the business district at the junction where the city grid intersects with harbor-aligned streets. **FIG 15** In response, the two splayed, glass volumes of the tower float above just a portion of its prestigious West Georgia Street site. One volume faces the harbor to the north, rising fourteen stories from a series of thin and widely spaced columns. The other ascends twenty stories from its brick plinth

to face the gridded edge of the city to the west. A curvilinear three-story lobby joins them. They rise above a plaza that is as complexly composed as the vertical massing of the towers: its raised brick surface folds into a waterfall along the northern edge, pedestrian routes cut eccentrically across it, and a single-story retail pavilion marks its eastern edge. The twenty-story west facade is an intended grand entrance to downtown.[16]

A similar attentiveness to topography is also found across the harbor on the slope of the North Shore Mountains. For the North Vancouver Civic Centre (1975), Downs / Archambault & Partners composed a set of buildings and their interstices into an artificial terrain that celebrates daily life and its natural setting. **FIG 16** It is a prime example of what one of the lead architects, Barry Downs, has termed "building as landform."[17] Simple building forms are enriched by their layering into the site, their geometry nudged by landscape features and augmented by terraces, and their raw concrete surfaces enveloped by plant material trained on cedar sunscreens and trellises. **FIG 17** A pedestrian path cuts diagonally between the two main volumes, the library to one side and government offices and council chambers to the other. The sense of space expands with plazas and roof gardens, and becomes intimate in sequestered reading courts. Views open to distant mountains and focus in on nearby plantings. Water courses through cascades and is stilled in pools. Through

19 left
Museum of Anthropology, detail of entrance door, Vancouver, British Columbia. Arthur Erickson Architects, 1976.

20 opposite
Museum of Anthropology, site plan.

human-scaled spaces, a civic park is achieved on a modest-sized lot, recalling nature as a respite from the commercial and suburban surroundings.

The West Coast Transmission Building and Crown Life Plaza were designed in response to their sites as both natural land and valuable real estate. Technology and topography determined the form of the singular West Coast Transmission building, while site circumstances occasioned the massing of Crown Life Plaza and its enlarged topography. Although they responded to discretionary city-planning practices, these projects also gave expression to the local appetite for public amenity.[18] Arising as part of an artificial topography, Erickson's downtown projects allowed a federation of private enterprises and public institutions to exist with some degree of formal autonomy within the urban grid. For its part, the North Vancouver Civic Centre's "building as landform" strategy gestured to the distant coastal mountains and harbor; it was also generated from the existing topography and plant ecology. As one critic of the time noted, the complex was "refreshingly indigenous."[19] It was also indigenous in another way: commissioned for the mayor's office is a totem wall by Squamish First Nation artist Floyd Joseph, a reference to the traditional territory on which the city hall sits.[20]

Indigenous Landscapes

When the design for a new Museum of Anthropology at the University of British Columbia was initially revealed in 1972, Arthur Erickson expressed his hope that it "should vividly demonstrate to [First Nations] people of this province the enormous stature and vitality of their heritage. The magnificence of the artifacts that it will contain, and the setting in which they will be shown, will also command new respect from the [non-native] population for a culture that has largely disappeared [*sic*]."[21] **FIG 18** The museum—an exhibition and teaching venue for the university—began with certain requirements. It was to be unobtrusive from the street and to include easily accessible open storage—a large, environmentally controlled space to house fragile totem poles of great size, and another space for intimately scaled objects. The site was also to house an open-air museum for a village-like configuration of First Nations structures.[22] **FIG 19**

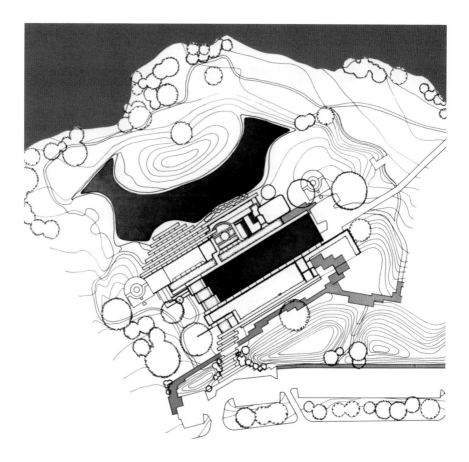

Opened in 1976, the museum stretches between a forest remnant on Marine Drive at the periphery of the campus and a cliff edge overlooking the Strait of Georgia. In plan, three lateral bars run parallel to the road and follow the slope of the land. **FIG 20** These clearly articulate the program and objectives of the museum, respectively housing academic facilities, visible storage, and public exhibition galleries and theaters. The whole museum sits on unceded Musqueam traditional territory.

The design is structured by immense concrete post-and-channel beams choreographed to the topography, and delights in the coastal light that falls on their surfaces. The beams are dimensioned for effect rather than structural necessity. In form and repetition, they evoke the Japanese *torii* gates that demarcate the passage between profane and sacred worlds. But visitors are also encouraged to see a kinship between the concrete beams that span beyond their supports, disguising their attachment points, and First Nations' timber house frames with their similarly concealed joinery [see page 122].[23]

Across the entrance threshold, the visitor's northward journey progresses down a ramped, low-ceilinged gallery of discrete exhibition bays. Passing under a set of First Nations house poles, the visitor arrives at the Great Hall, a lofty, skylit expanse, orchestrated by monumental structural frames rising from 16 to 45 feet (4.9 to 13.7 meters) and

21 left
Museum of Anthropology, interior great hall, Vancouver Britsh Columbia. Arthur Erickson Architects, 1976.

22 opposite
Queen Charlotte Islands Museum (now Haida Gwaii Museum), view from west, Skidegate, British Columbia. Henry Hawthorn and Robert Mansfield Associated Architects, 1976.

enveloped by light filtered through glazed vaults overhead. Within, immense totem poles—some rising 40 feet (12.2 meters)—are oriented outward to the forest and cliff, and beyond to the Strait of Georgia.[24] Unobstructed sky is visible through a glass wall rising the entire height and width of the north wall, while glimpses of forest are seen through glazed perimeter walls. **FIG 21** In its plan and structure, the museum responds to the existing landscape, but it also constructs a metaphorical one.

Within this framing of space and light, Erickson envisioned the artifacts of various First Nations displayed as if in their place of origin—along a coastline, at a forest edge, among spirits. Beyond the great glazed north wall is an outdoor museum of totem poles and communal houses of different First Nations, dispersed around an artificial lake—as if they were a fuller representation of what is displayed in fragments within the museum. The outdoor museum perhaps seeks to recover the past as captured in a much-referenced photograph of the abandoned traditional coastal village of SG̱ang Gwaay (formerly Anthony Island), Haida Gwaii.[25]

Erickson's archetypal forms, supported by landscape designed by Cornelia Oberlander, recreate a space where artifacts can be celebrated aesthetically but are also made available for future reinterpretation and use. Erickson strove to reference a past when "on this coast, there

was a noble and great response to this land that has never been equaled yet."[26] However, his architecture also captured the context of modern First Nations artists who sought to translate remembered stories for contemporary understanding as well as to maintain traditions.

The Museum of Anthropology in Vancouver is not this period's only architectural example of engagement with museum buildings focused on First Nations. When built in 1976, the Queen Charlotte Islands Museum in Skidegate (Henry Hawthorn and Robert Mansfield Associated Architects) was named after the northern archipelago's colonial moniker. **FIG 22–24** The islands have since been renamed Haida Gwaii, and the institution the Haida Gwaii Museum at Kay Llnagaay, reflecting Haida sovereignty.

Commissioned in 1973 by the recently formed Queen Charlotte Islands Museum Society, the creation of the center was a requirement in the terms agreed to for the return of regalia and artifacts confiscated or absconded with decades before—a redress of colonial occupation and a celebration of Indigenous culture. In speaking about the museum in 1976, architect Henry Hawthorn noted that his clients' "passion for the past" was historical but not dislocated from the contemporary world, including modern modes of construction.[27]

The architecture pays homage to the heritage of Haida timber construction by using a wood post-and-beam structure that could be built by local contractors with on-site milling.

Two parallel structures are lodged within a sloping outcrop—the entrance structure at grade, and gallery stucture raised on posts at its northern extremity, projecting toward a precipice and the ocean inlet view. The building is straightforward yet eloquent, offering maximum flexibility and opportunities for drama. The sloped boardwalk of the entrance affords a stage for ceremonies; the internal corridor with its elevated ceiling provides a place of significance for a totem pole; and the decks that continue the path of the corridor allow views to the land to which the totem refers.[28]

When the Haida Gwaii Museum opened in May 1976, one of ten repatriated poles was ceremonially raised. Prime Minister Pierre Elliott Trudeau (1919–2000) commented on the ability of the First Nations of the West Coast to adapt to their environment: "not to exploit it, but to live *with* it." They consequently were "able to develop a system of thinking, a society, a culture, which is equal in every way to the highest cultures of antiquity."[29] With this building and its program, the First Nations indicated that they were also equal among contemporary cultures. The museum marks the shifting significance of First Nations art and artifacts, which acquired new import as they represented Indigenous peoples on an enlarged cultural and political stage. The Haida Gwaii Museum has since been augmented with the adjacent Haida Heritage Center (David Nairne & Associates, 2008), with its

23 opposite
Queen Charlotte Islands Museum (now Haida Gwaii Museum), interior view, Skidegate, British Columbia. Henry Hawthorn and Robert Mansfield Associated Architects, 1976.

23 opposite
Queen Charlotte Islands Museum (now Haida Gwaii Museum), interior view, Skidegate, British Columbia. Henry Hawthorn and Robert Mansfield Associated Architects, 1976.

24 below
Queen Charlotte Islands Museum (now Haida Gwaii Museum), plan.

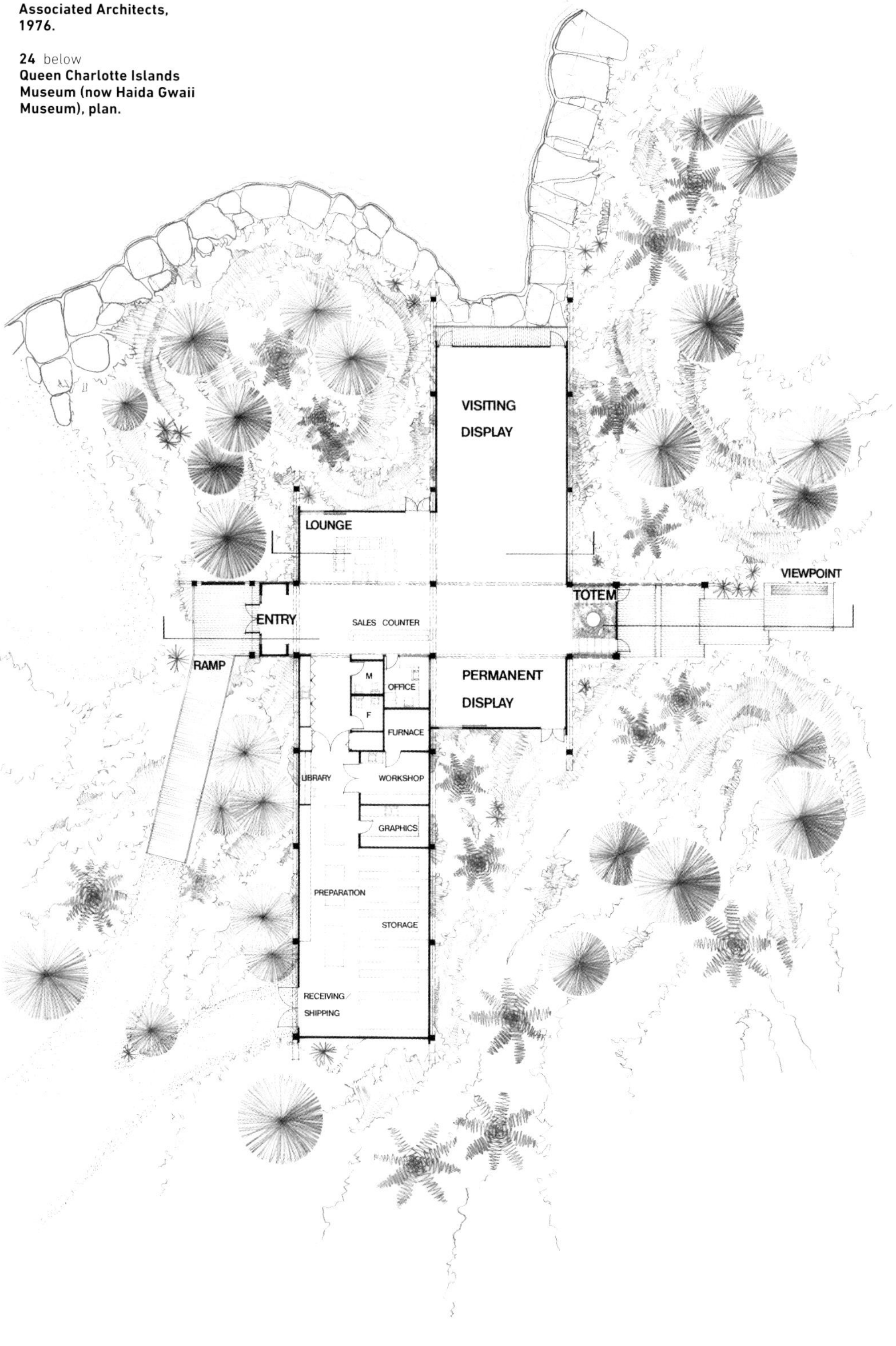

VISITING DISPLAY

LOUNGE

VIEWPOINT

ENTRY

SALES COUNTER

TOTEM

RAMP

M

OFFICE

PERMANENT DISPLAY

F

FURNACE

LIBRARY

WORKSHOP

GRAPHICS

PREPARATION

STORAGE

RECEIVING

SHIPPING

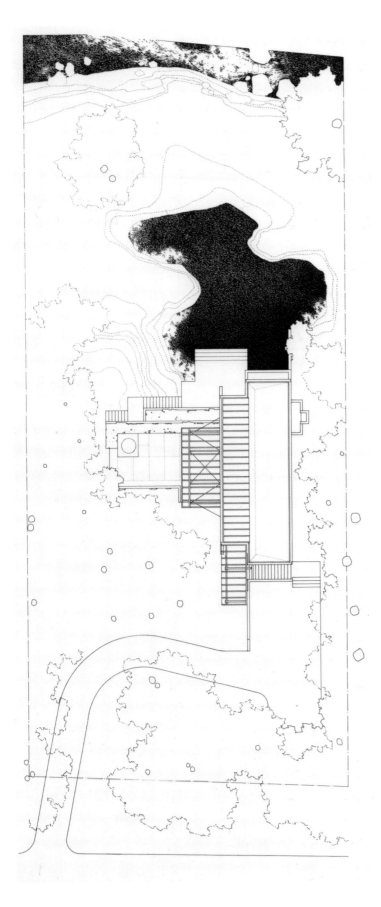

25 left
Patkau Residence, site plan, West Vancouver, Britsh Columbia. Patkau Architects, 1984.

26 opposite
Patkau Residence, elevation.

performing house, teaching center, and carving shed, spawning a new kind of institution. Art has become part of the First Nation's social process once again.[30]

Postmodern Alterations

The mid-1960s through the 1970s witnessed architecture on the West Coast that negotiated pressing financial, cultural, and political claims on the land. It was given a new cast in the 1980s, as postmodernism seeped into West Coast architecture in highly particularized ways.[31] Regional concerns were reoriented: topography was augmented with significant form; locality enlarged to encompass historical style; and concern with the sun and shadow of the Pacific Northwest climate translated into scientific analyses of solar paths and technological mediation.

Earlier concerns with shaping buildings in response to topography were reinvigorated with the arrival of John and Patricia Patkau (1947– and 1950–) of Patkau Architects on the West Coast from the Prairies in 1984. Their attentive reading of site and situation laid a claim to the land that was steeped in its material phenomena, the social etiquette of occupation, and the cultural attributes of form. Distinguishing themselves from earlier regionalist understandings of the West Coast, they have stated: "We believe we are working within both an international and a local context. These are the contexts of our architectural decisions."[32]

Local topography and landscape informed the section of the Patkaus' own house in West Vancouver (1984), which steps down a steep slope, opening at each level to the forest. **FIGS 25–26** At the Pyrch House in Victoria (1983), domestic space wraps around a rock outcrop, and the house arcs to frame distant vistas. **FIGS 27–28** The strategically placed, oversized column of the Appleton House, Victoria (1985), marks a significant volume while suggesting differentiated spaces. While local in the close mirroring of their respective sites, the work is also international in its allusions to the particularities of form and space, recalling work by Alvar Aalto and Charles Moore.

In the early 1980s, a postindustrial retrofit of the north-facing Fairview Slopes in Vancouver followed from the redevelopment of False Creek to the south. Brick warehouses and

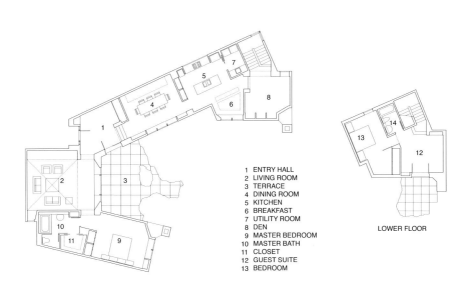

1 ENTRY HALL
2 LIVING ROOM
3 TERRACE
4 DINING ROOM
5 KITCHEN
6 BREAKFAST
7 UTILITY ROOM
8 DEN
9 MASTER BEDROOM
10 MASTER BATH
11 CLOSET
12 GUEST SUITE
13 BEDROOM

LOWER FLOOR

humble wooden houses were replaced with townhouses that are postmodern in sensibility: they allude to history, are iconic, and reintroduce tradition-evoking materials. James K. M. Cheng's three-story Willow Arbour Townhouses (1981) supplements a wood-frame structure with brick veneer, adding inner courtyard entrances and reorganizing the conventional plan to elevate living rooms to the third floor, where they enjoy water views. **FIG 29** The courtyard entrances fulfill expectations of the residential seclusion of suburban homes, while the units offer the novelty of canted roof decks and urban vistas. Roger Hughes's Fairview Terrace (1983) likewise exploits the north-facing slope to accommodate townhouses that step up the hill on the east, stretch along the northern edge of the street, and turn into the lane. The past is referenced in brick veneer, pronounced chimneys that demarcate separate "houses," and a planted courtyard that offers sanctuary. The courtyard and its semipublic walkway provided amenities that permitted greater density of both housing units and pedestrian traffic. It was a strategy that future developments in Vancouver would pursue.

Also explored in the 1980s were environmentalism and technological ingenuity [see chapter 8]. Peter Busby combined both in his energy self-sufficient "House for the 1980s" proposal (1980). **FIG 30** An assemblage of available hardware—including climatic sensors, solar collectors, and wind turbines—envelop a two-story, three-bedroom house complete

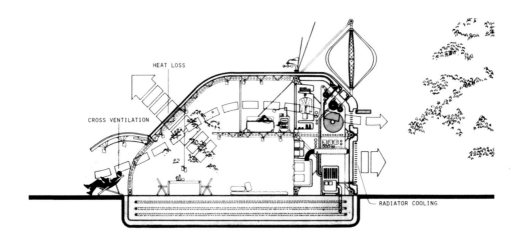

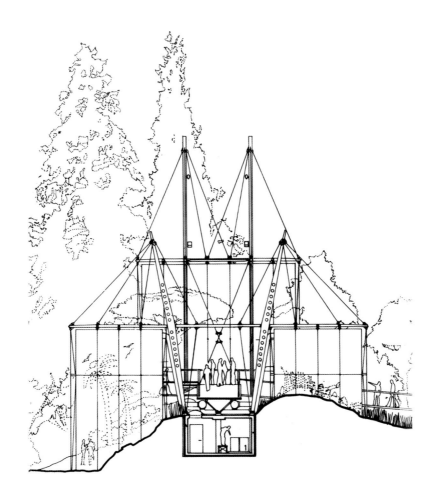

30 opposite, top
"House for the 1980s"
project, as published in *The Canadian Architect*. Peter Busby, 1980.

31 opposite, bottom
Stanley Park Tropical Centre, Vancouver, British Columbia. Busby Bridger Architects, 1986

32 above
Seabird Island School, Agassiz, British Columbia. Patkau Architects, 1991.

with solarium and carport. Busby, then working for Norman Foster, would return to Vancouver in 1984 to open his own office and, two years later, to form Busby Bridger Architects. The technologically sophisticated and topographically respectful Stanley Park Tropical Centre, Vancouver (1986), was the firm's first significant contribution to West Coast architecture. **FIG 31**

Peter Cardew's Canadian National Pavilion for Expo 86 offered dramatic vantage points from bridges and a terrace-topped cylindrical theater, all composed within and sheltered by a translucent canopy that was dramatically suspended from a 50-foot-high (15-meter-high) structure [see pages 77–80]. Perched on just three supports, the enormous space frame touched lightly on the unstable ground of the former industrial site at the southern rim of False Creek. In the aftermath of Expo 86, the surrounding landscape would continue to become both more global and more local, based on the exchange value of its real estate and mystique of the land.

Yet, nearby, in the Discovery BC Pavilion, carved First Nations "welcome figures" offered another vision of the land. Although romanticized within an artificial rainforest in the pavilion, they symbolized the existence of traditional lands and the contemporary presence of First Nations. This contemporary presence is heralded at Seabird Island School

(1991) by Patkau Architects, where an experiential reading of the phenomena of the site—orienting landscape features and materials—is augmented by an indigenous narrative of landscape. **FIG 32** Forms significant to First Nations' cultural practices, such as fish-drying racks and circular gathering spaces, are juxtaposed with western typologies, as exemplified in the enlarged south-facing porch [see pages 124–127]. The porch looks across to the small township of the island while the bulk of the building provides protection from the north winds. The spatial and formal articulation of the building encourages and enables culturally appropriate ways of learning. The Seabird Island School registers a land claim that is both confidently contemporary and fundamentally Coast Salish: it marks the distance traveled since the Museum of Anthropology and the Haida Gwaii Museum.

Conclusion

The mid-1960s to the mid-1980s on the West Coast witnessed compelling architectural responses to an intimate experience of the land, urban development on an increased scale combined with increased abstraction, and the introduction to modern architecture of narratives of the land as told by First Nations. Building on a legacy of postwar developments, architecture on the West Coast was continually refreshed by newly arrived practitioners, recent graduates, and global ideas—be they philosophical (phenomenology, postmodernism), technical (space frames, vertical cantilevers), or both (environmentalism). What perhaps distinguishes the West Coast in this time period is the augmenting of its regional cast with a more critically posed and open set of discourses on architecture's negotiation with the land.

10

Prairie Formations

Graham Livesey

The establishment of the three Prairie Provinces—Manitoba (1870), Saskatchewan (1905), and Alberta (1905)—was vital to the formation of Canada as a nation. Despite being labeled the "Prairies," the grassland landscape associated with that term covers a relatively small portion of the region, most of which is boreal forest, with the Rocky Mountains on the western edge. The traditional architecture of the area is that of First Nations peoples, including Blackfoot and Cree. In the nineteenth century, European colonial settlement followed in the footsteps of the fur trade, and Indigenous peoples were placed on reservations. The ensuing farms and settlements constructed throughout the Prairie Provinces used architectural styles derived primarily from Eastern Canada, the United States, and Europe.

A modern, internationalist architecture emerged in the Prairies in the 1940s through the 1960s. Early examples can be found across the region; however, it was in Winnipeg (the first major Prairie city, and the location of the University of Manitoba's architecture program, founded in 1913) that sophistication in modern architecture was first shown by a local professional community.[1] Noteworthy Winnipeg practices from this period include Green, Blankstein, Russell, and Associates; Smith, Carter, Searle, and Associates; Libling, Michener, and Associates; and the Number Ten Architectural Group.[2] In Saskatchewan, noteworthy modernist firms of the same era include Izumi, Arnott, and Sugiyama; Joseph

1 left
Wascana Centre Lookouts and Washrooms, view from south, Regina, Saskatchewan. Kerr, Cullingworth Riches and Associates, 1965.

2 opposite
Law Library, University of Saskatchewan, view from southwest, Saskatoon, Saskatchewan. Holliday-Scott and Paine Architects, 1967.

Pettick Architect; and Holliday-Scott and Paine Architects.[3] In Edmonton and Calgary, firms such as Rule Wynn and Rule Architects, W.G. Milne Architect, and Abugov and Sunderland Architects would pioneer the development of modernism in Alberta, often through institutional structures and office buildings for the emerging oil and gas industry.[4]

By the mid-1960s, a new, more culturally specific architecture began to develop across the region. This architecture responded more precisely to the area's indigenous and colonial history, its diverse landscapes, and its challenging climate of long, cold winters and hot summers. Projects that began to signal this shift include Kerr, Cullingworth, Riches and Associates' design for the Wascana Centre Lookouts and Washrooms, Regina, Saskatchewan (1965), which employs brutalist concrete in a manner that harmonizes with the lakeside site; and Holliday-Scott and Paine Architects' Law Library (1967) and Lutheran Theological Seminary (1968) at the University of Saskatchewan in Saskatoon, which are precisely organized and use concrete evocatively. **FIGS 1–2**

This chapter examines pioneering figures of the 1960s, architecture that responds immediately to the landscapes of the Prairie during the 1970s and 1980s, the postmodern period and its impact, and a re-emergent modernism that begins in the 1990s and continues to the present.

Three Pioneers

In 1979, *The Canadian Architect* magazine brought together a stellar group of Prairie-based architects and educators—R. Douglas Gillmor, Gustavo da Roza, Peter Hemingway, Clifford Wiens, Jack Long, and Dale M. Taylor—to debate whether "Prairie architecture" existed. The participants were pessimistic about the idea of a coherent regional architecture, although they made several references to Indigenous or First Nations architecture.[5] Since that time, it has become widely recognized in Canada that a distinctive Prairie architecture was forged by three architects who were born in and worked across the region, starting in the mid-1960s: Étienne Gaboury in Manitoba, Clifford Wiens in Saskatchewan, and Douglas Cardinal in Alberta.

Despite their diverse backgrounds, Gaboury, Wiens, and Cardinal each produced architecture that blended Indigenous and colonial traditions. The francophone Manitoban Étienne Gaboury (1930–) largely rejected orthodox international modernism in favor of a fusion of influences. Raised on a family farm, Gaboury graduated from the University of Manitoba in 1958 and then studied in Paris for a year. He returned to Winnipeg to join the firm of Libling, Michener, and Associates.[6] In 1963, Gaboury opened an office in partnership with Denis Lussier and Frank Sigurdson, working primarily in the Franco-Manitoban

4 opposite
**Église du Précieux-Sang,
view of ceiling, Saint
Boniface, Manitoba.
Gaboury, Lussier,
Sigurdson Architects,
1968.**

5 above
**Église du Précieux-Sang,
interior.**

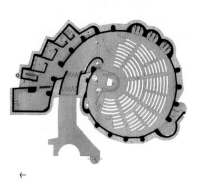

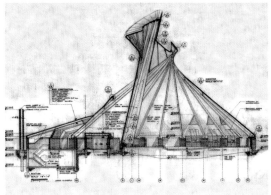

←

community of Saint Boniface, adjacent to anglophone Winnipeg. Much of Gaboury's early work shows the influence of Swiss modernist Le Corbusier (1887–1965). Noteworthy examples from this period include the civic center in Saint Boniface (1963) and the St. Anne's church and rectory in Regina, Saskatchewan (1967).

Gaboury established his national reputation with the Église du Précieux-Sang (Church of the Precious Blood) in Saint Boniface (1968). **FIGS 3–7** The design employs a spiraling shape and structure clearly derived from the tepee but adjusted to the new Catholic Church liturgical requirements following Vatican II. As Gaboury wrote in a detailed description of the evolution of the design, the spiral form achieves "dynamic movement of the congregation around the altar" while addressing functional and symbolic needs.[7] Although set in the middle of Saint Boniface, the building powerfully captures Prairie culture and landscapes.

In describing his work, Gaboury has detailed the environmental order of the iconic Canadian prairie farm, which has been a source of inspiration for Prairie architects over recent decades:

> I did not have to search long to unearth the mysteries of regional architecture; I needed to only rediscover the wisdom of our forebears. The family farm was imbued with this wisdom. Its layout, centred around the sun and the northwest winds and drawn from sections of land that seen from above look like a patchwork quilt, provided a basic lesson in regional urbanism. The north and west flanks of the farm were lined with rows of poplar, elm and spruce, forming windbreaks that were as effective as they were beautiful…The barn, granaries, house, garage and orchard were laid out according to their respective functions but were always dependent on direction, terrain and landscape.[8]

By the 1980s, Gaboury's office was embroiled in the postmodern debates of the period. He designed larger projects including the Royal Canadian Mint in Winnipeg (1975, with Number Ten Architectural Group) and the Canadian Chancery in Mexico City (1982). A more recent work is the pedestrian promenade Pont Provencher-Esplanade Riel, designed with Guy Préfontaine (2004), which links Saint Boniface to downtown Winnipeg and features a striking mid-bridge restaurant space. **FIG 8**

Clifford Wiens, born in 1926 in a Saskatchewan Mennonite farming community, created architecture with precise forms both on the prairie and nestled in valleys. Educated at the Rhode Island School of Design, he returned to Regina to develop a practice distinguished by its modest yet iconic structures. He strove to accentuate the horizon in his work by having his buildings float above it.[9] Wiens executed a number of buildings in the 1960s and 1970s that demonstrated his direct approach to constructing on the prairies. These buildings also demonstrated his interest in industrial design, materials, and construction methods. His Central Heating and Cooling Plant at the University of Regina (1967) is most indicative of his architecture in that it is seemingly straightforward, yet intricate in execution; its bold shape is reminiscent of both iconic Indigenous and agricultural forms. **FIG 9** Particularly poetic is his small summer chapel at Silton (1969), in the Qu'Appelle Valley north of Regina—a simple and elemental building for outdoor worship. **FIG 10** Other projects include churches, houses, offices, tourism structures, and eventually a number of institutional projects.

Douglas Cardinal was born in Calgary in 1934 and grew up in Red Deer, Alberta. His work draws extensively on his Indigenous (Blackfoot and Métis) and European heritage, based simultaneously on the soft prairie landscapes of Alberta and expressionist European

9 opposite, top
Central Heating and Cooling Plant, University of Regina, view from southeast, Regina, Saskatchewan. Clifford Wiens Architect, 1967.

10 opposite, bottom
Silton Chapel, view from east, Qu'Appelle Lakes, Saskatchewan. Clifford Wiens Architect, 1969.

11 above
Saint Mary's Church, view from north, Red Deer, Alberta. Douglas Cardinal Architect, 1968.

12 above
Grande Prairie Regional College, view from northeast, Grande Prairie, Alberta. Douglas Cardinal Architect, 1976.

13 opposite, left
Grande Prairie Regional College, courtyard.

14 opposite, right
Grande Prairie Regional College, atrium.

works. Cardinal studied architecture at the University of British Columbia and finished his education at the University of Texas at Austin. Returning to Alberta, he completed his internship in Red Deer before establishing his practice in 1964.

Cardinal's distinctive approach is remarkably captured in his first significant work, Saint Mary's church in Red Deer (1968), a building that has since achieved iconic status in Canada. Engaging in a comprehensive design process with the client, Father Werner Merx, Cardinal produced a complex curvilinear structure that recalls the landscapes of the prairies and forests, while referencing the work of Francesco Borromini, Antoni Gaudí, and Le Corbusier. **FIG 11** The project was also an early application of his pioneering use of computer-aided design and construction management, in this case used to make structural calculations for the roof.

After moving his office to Edmonton in the late 1960s, Cardinal became more engaged with his Indigenous heritage. He was also awarded a number of significant public commissions in Alberta, most notably the Grande Prairie Regional College (1976). **FIGS 12–15** In this project, he translated his distinctive language of curvilinear forms, which he had so convincingly presented in his Red Deer church, to a larger scale, aided by his comprehensive approach to program analysis and diagramming. The project also entailed designing a

range of both significant and subsidiary spaces. The college theater remains one of Cardinal's most striking interiors, showcasing his ability to create a space that is both sculptural and functional.[10] Other key projects from this period include the Ponoka Provincial Building (1977) and St. Albert Place (1984).

In 1983, Cardinal, who was by then the most recognized architect to have emerged from the Prairie Provinces, was awarded the commission to design the new Museum of Man (1989, subsequently called the Canadian Museum of Civilization, and currently the Canadian Museum of History) in Hull, Quebec, across the river from the Parliament of Canada in Ottawa. He subsequently moved his practice to Ottawa. The choice of Cardinal as the architect of the building was controversial; however, the project was completed in 1989 according to Cardinal's exacting requirements and has become a much-loved national institution [see pages 55–59]. In 1993, Cardinal was hired to design the National Museum of the American Indian in Washington, DC (2004). His uncompromising personality would eventually lead to his dismissal from the project; nevertheless, the museum was completed largely according to his design. Cardinal has continued to design projects in his distinctive manner across Canada for institutional clients and First Nations communities—notably the First Nations University in Regina, Saskatchewan (2003), and the Gordon Oakes Redbear Student Centre at the University of Saskatchewan (2016).

Landscape and Sheltering Forms

One of the themes that emerged for architects in the late 1960s was a consciousness about humankind's impact on the planet [see chapter 8]. As a result, many began experimenting with environmentally responsive designs. In some cases, in an effort to integrate with landscapes and reduce energy consumption, buildings were partially buried underground or employed earth berms. In the Prairies, these forms achieved a particular poignancy, and physical engagement with the earth became an established architectural approach in the 1970s and 1980s. While the nomadic Indigenous people of the Prairies tended to build lightweight structures, early colonial settlers, often desperately poor, would employ sod,

17 above
**Notre-Dame-des-Prairies
Cistercian Monastery,
view from southeast, near
Holland, Manitoba. Jacques
Collin with Smith Carter
Architects and Engineers,
1978.**

18 opposite
**Coronation Pool, view
from northeast, Edmonton,
Alberta. Hemingway and
Laubenthal Architects,
1970.**

earth, and logs to create their initial shelters. Echoing those structures, modern architects demonstrated a commitment to strong, sheltering architectural forms. It is also worth noting that recent immigrants and transplants from other parts of the world executed much of the best architecture during this period.

One of these works is the bold Winnipeg Art Gallery. The design for the gallery resulted from a national competition held in 1967, won by the émigré architect Gustavo da Roza (born in Hong Kong in 1933 of Chinese and Portuguese ancestry) with Number Ten Architectural Group. Completed in 1971, the building takes its formal cues from its triangular site. **FIG 16** The building is clad in the ubiquitous Tyndall stone (the Manitoba limestone that is Canada's national stone) and presents itself as something of an urban fortress with great expanses of solid wall, only intermittently punctured at strategic points. Inside, a dramatic stair rises to the third-level gallery but surprisingly does not connect directly with the spectacular roof-level sculpture garden, which affords views to the surrounding city.

The French-born architect Jacques Collin (1927–2000) studied in Paris and taught in the United States before joining the faculty of architecture at the University of Manitoba in 1964, where he taught until 1995. A demanding teacher, he also designed a small number of projects, including the Notre-Dame-des-Prairies Cistercian (Trappist) Monastery near

Holland, Manitoba (1978). **FIG 17** Located in a beautiful rural setting in southern Manitoba, the rigorously calculated design arranges the functional aspects of the monastery in a strong square form around a cloister. Hinting at the work of Le Corbusier, it features a distinctive church space that draws on vernacular barn construction methods.

The British-born architect Peter Hemingway (1929–1995) established himself in Edmonton (initially in partnership with Charles Laubenthal) and, over the course of his career, produced a number of precisely designed buildings in the city, including the Stanley Engineering Building (1967) and the Central Pentacostal Tabernacle (1972). His Coronation Pool (1970) was developed for Canada's Centennial [see page 34]; it employs a remarkable cable structural system and has a unique relationship to its park setting. **FIG 18** In the 1970s, Hemingway became enamored with pyramidal forms; his most striking example of this is his Muttart Conservatory project of 1976. **FIG 19** The building, which sits in Edmonton's North Saskatchewan River valley, features large glass pyramids, each covering a distinct ecosystem and floating on grass. Hemingway's architecture strikes a balance between the use of simple forms and a careful adjustment of those forms to the particularities of a site. The use of the pyramid was later taken up in the new Edmonton City Hall building, designed by Gene Dub and completed in 1992 [see page 195].

19 opposite
Muttart Conservatory, view from northwest, Edmonton, Alberta. Peter Hemingway Architect, 1976.

20 right
Shouldice Athletic Change Pavilion, view from southeast, Calgary, Alberta. Gordon Atkins and Associates Architects, 1982.

An exception to the phenomenon of the émigré architect is Calgary-born Gordon Atkins (1937–), who grew up in the largely Mormon community of Cardston in Southern Alberta and studied architecture at the University of Washington. Atkins established a practice in Calgary in 1963 with a focus on designing buildings responsive to the landscape of foothills in and around the city. Notable works include the Melchin Summer Homes (1966), for which he won a Massey Medal; the Drahanchuk Studio (1967); the Mayland Heights Elementary School (1969); and the Stoney Tribal Administration Building (1980), for which he won a Governor General's Award. In these works, he sought sheltering solutions and sometimes experimented with earth berms, as evident in the design for the Shouldice Athletic Change Pavilion (1982), an award-winning project that is integrated into its river-valley site as a landform. **FIG 20** Atkins favored dramatic forms and often carved spaces into the earth. He also achieved a rich tension between horizontal arrangements and sculptural vertical elements.

American Jack Long (1925–2001) settled in Calgary and established his practice in 1961. Four years later, he went into partnership with Hugh McMillan, and together they created the Calgary Centennial Planetarium (1967) [see page 36]. Under J. W. Long and Associates, he would design a host of public projects, including the Provincial Court and Remand

Centre (1974) and the Roger's Pass Visitor Centre (1978). The latter takes its cues from avalanche sheds, using a heavy wooden structure and a sod roof. Long, who was very active in the community and devoted to the concept of the "everyman as planner," was a well-loved public figure in Calgary and served a term as a city alderman.

Robert LeBlond, another Calgary-based architect, came to Alberta from Quebec in the late 1960s. His firm undertook a large range of work, from commercial buildings to renovations of iconic hotels in the Rocky Mountain national parks. His most ambitious project is the Head-Smashed-In Buffalo Jump Interpretive Centre (1987) near Fort Macleod in Southern Alberta. **FIG 21** Adjacent to the largest buffalo kill site in North America, the site was designated a world heritage site by UNESCO in 1981. Leblond's strategy was to effectively bury the building in the escarpment near the actual buffalo jump, and to organize the visitor experience around the archaeology of the site and the buffalo kill tradition itself. Overall, the scheme is a bold integration of architecture and the prairie landscape.[11]

University campuses throughout the Prairie provinces were active as sites of planning and construction during this period. Older campuses at the Universities of Manitoba, Saskatchewan, and Alberta struggled to balance existing campus plans with new buildings. Noteworthy examples of new work include Diamond and Myers's HUB Building

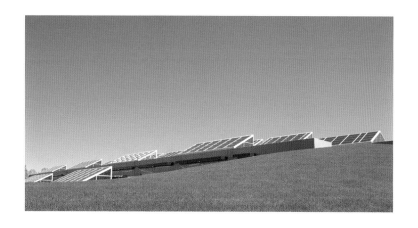

21 opposite
Head-Smashed-In Buffalo Jump Interpretative Centre, view from southeast, Fort Macleod, Alberta. The Leblond Partnership, 1987.

22 right
Advanced Technology Centre, view from west, Edmonton, Alberta. Barry Johns Architects, 1988.

(1971) at the University of Alberta [see pages 172–175] and a range of projects on the University of Saskatchewan campus. The latter, arguably the most attractive campus in western Canada, was established in 1907 in Saskatoon, adjacent to the South Saskatchewan River; its early buildings were designed in the collegiate Gothic manner. By the 1960s, as the campus continued to grow and evolve, architects strove to balance historical styles with the architecture of the period. Noteworthy projects include the massive Murray Memorial Library (1974) by BLM Architects and the carefully integrated Place Riel Student Centre (1980) by Ferguson, Folstad, Friggstad.

A Return to Colonial Influences

By the 1980s, architecture was transforming globally as postmodernism took hold. Inspired by American architects, such as Robert Venturi and Charles Moore, Prairie architects similarly aimed to reconnect with history [see chapter 6]. In a 1979 essay on this topic, Edmonton-based architect and critic Brian Allsopp wrote: "Thus the problem facing a post-modernist architect mired on the Canadian Prairies is the search for the image indigenous to the Prairies…This imagery seems to come from two sources: the local topography and the historical settlement pattern."[12] Allsopp noted that Prairie buildings such as grain elevators have strong silhouettes and forms that help shape a sense of place. Other sources of inspiration included false-fronted buildings on main streets, wood-frame construction techniques, and surviving colonial buildings associated with the railway and early settlement.

Early proponents of Prairie postmodernism include John and Patricia Patkau, who established their first office in Edmonton in 1978. Both were born in Winnipeg and educated at the University of Manitoba. Their early award-winning projects in Edmonton include the Galleria Condominium (1981), the McGregor Residence (1982), and the Blue Quill School (1982). Their subsequent move to Vancouver would establish a new direction for the work of the firm [see chapters 9 and 15]. In recent years, they have returned to the Prairies to produce a number of projects, including the striking ARTlab at the University of Manitoba (2012, with LM Architectural Group).

23 left
Duclos School, view from northeast, Bonnyville, Alberta. Barry Johns Architects, 1992.

24 opposite, top
Duclos School, view from north.

25 opposite, bottom
Duclos School, concept sketch.

Montreal-born Barry Johns (1947–) studied in Halifax and apprenticed with Arthur Erickson in Vancouver, establishing his architectural practice in Edmonton in 1981. Informed by the debates that shaped architectural postmodernism, Johns developed a body of work responsive to the prairies and to the social demands of his clients.[13] Projects include a series of schools, cultural buildings, and the design for the Grant MacEwan Community College campus in downtown Edmonton (1993). The Advanced Technology Centre in Edmonton (1988), a high-tech incubator facility, carves itself into a suburban site, creating a bold interplay with the earth. **FIG 22** Brian Allsopp, reviewing the building in 1989, noted how the building responds to the land and sky: "The beauty of the piece is in the subtle play of light between the skylights, and how through them one feels the sky's 'presence' at all hours of the day. More than the sculpting of the earth, this is why the building seems to be so much *of* the prairie."[14]

The Duclos School in Bonnyville, Alberta (1992), intelligently integrates references to the farmhouse, grain silo, and barn into an ensemble organized around an internal street. **FIG 23–25** The Duclos School design represents a successful attempt to adapt postmodernism to the local context. During this period, Johns wrote compellingly about his sense of a Prairie architecture:

> Living on the Canadian prairie, one comes to understand the uniqueness of the place, its vernacular origins and climatological prejudices. With its four seasons, hot summers and cold winters, the prairie urges us to work in harmony with the land, insisting that buildings should not be independent. Of these influences, it is the dramatic light of the prairie sky that is most inspiring. The harsh climate produces rose colored sunsets, violent spring storms, winter sun dogs and chinook arch. We think of this light as a building material, using the intense sun, cloud formations or the northern sky to make crisp or dappled shadow patterns deep inside our structures.[15]

Calgary-born architect L. Frederick Valentine (1939–) studied in Toronto and Boston, then worked for Parkin Associates in Toronto before returning to Alberta in 1978 to join the large Calgary firm J. H. Cook Architects and Engineers. The firm was known for a series

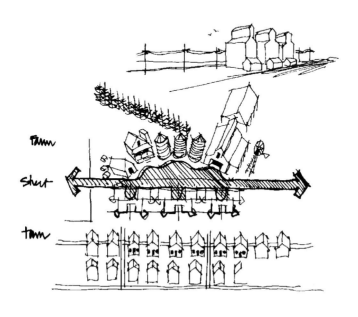

of highly ordered institutional and commercial buildings, including the tautly detailed Nova Corporate Head Office Building (now known as the Nexen Building) in Calgary (1982). By the 1980s, under Valentine's thoughtful guidance, the practice changed direction by embracing a "critical regionalist"[16] approach influenced by prairie landscapes and agricultural structures. The best example of this work is the firm's master plan and various buildings at Canada Olympic Park (1986), a set of colorful and carefully executed structures that remains one of the most significant architectural legacies of Calgary's 1988 Winter Olympics. **FIG 26**

Postmodernism had limited impact in Winnipeg, although the office of Stechesen and Katz Architects produced some work in the mode, particularly their striking addition to the Pantages Playhouse Theatre on Winnipeg's Main Street (1992). David Penner, who came onto the Winnipeg scene in the 1990s, briefly flirted with postmodernism with his own house (the Penner Residence, 1993). **FIG 27**

The notion of a Prairie architecture derived from colonial and agricultural precedents is also found in the Alberta pavilion, designed by Jeremy Sturgess for Vancouver's Expo 86, which referenced a range of vernacular building types. Sturgess, who grew up in Montreal, Toronto, and Calgary, began his practice in Calgary in 1977 after studying at the

University of Toronto. By the 1990s, his work had evolved into a distinctive regional modernism distinguished by strong forms, careful attention to site, and the use of bold colors. His work has focused on an evolving series of Calgary houses, including House on a Ridge (2002), Hilltop Terrace (2003), House on the Prairie (2004), and House on the Heights (2015). **FIG 28** Sturgess has also been actively involved in urban design, transit design for Calgary's LRT system, hotel design, and condominium design, and has worked on various institutional projects, including the award-winning Glacier Skywalk in Jasper National Park (2014). **FIG 29**

Prairie Architecture Since 2000

Since 2000, there has been a changing of the guard with respect to architects working in the three Prairie Provinces. Winnipeg in particular has reestablished itself as a center for architectural experimentation, with the emergence of a number of young firms. Many of these firms are involved in a revitalized modern architecture that is sensitive to existing urban contexts. Influences of contemporary European architects can often be found in their designs. The faculty of architecture at the University of Manitoba has been key

28 above
Hilltop Terrace, view from north, Calgary, Alberta. Sturgess Architecture, 2003.

29 opposite
Glacier Skywalk, view from southeast, Jasper National Park, Alberta. Sturgess Architecture, 2014.

30 opposite, top
Red River College Roblin Centre, view from southeast, Winnipeg, Manitoba. Corbett Cibinel Architects, 2003.

31 opposite, bottom
Buhler Centre, view from north, Winnipeg, Manitoba. DPA+PSA+DIN Collective, Architects and Designers, 2010.

32 right
Bloc_10 Condominiums, view from north, Winnipeg, Manitoba. 5468796 Architecture, 2011.
©James Brittain

in nurturing and maintaining a strong local architectural scene. Established firms, an important part of the mix, include Corbett Cibinel Architects, whose Red River College Roblin Centre (2003) revitalized a number of historic buildings in downtown Winnipeg, and Smith Carter Architects and Engineers, whose own workplace is a rigorously structured building adjacent to a busy highway (2004). **FIG 30** The younger generation of Winnipeg firms includes Peter Sampson, DIN Projects, 1x1 architecture, Syverson Monteyne, and 5468796 Architecture. Of the many evocative projects by these practices, the Buhler Centre in downtown Winnipeg (2010) by the collaboration of Penner, Sampson, and Neil Minuk of DIN Project, is very representative of the new generation. **FIG 31** Home to programs from the University of Winnipeg and the Plug-In Institute of Contemporary Art, the Buhler Centre is tailored to its triangular site and clad with white paneling derived from refrigeration systems to create a dynamic contemporary facility.

Led by Johanna Hurme and Sasa Radulovic, the Winnipeg firm 5468796 Architecture has won numerous awards and garnered much attention since its establishment in 2007. It is known for a series of well-considered condominium projects in Winnipeg, such as the typologically innovative Bloc_10 Condominiums (2011). **FIG 32** Their Parallelogram House in East Saint Paul, Manitoba (2014), is a striking take on the suburban house.

Recent work in Saskatchewan includes the Saskatchewan Provincial Court House in Prince Albert by aodbt architecture + interior design (2003) and the T.rex Discovery Centre in Eastend (2003) by McMillan Lehrer Ellard Croft Architects. **FIG 33** The Remai Modern art gallery project by KPMB Architects and Architecture49, completed in 2017, represents the ambitions of the city of Saskatoon in a global art scene with its sophisticated stacked forms and location on a dramatic riverside site. There are plans to establish a new school of architecture at the University of Saskatchewan in Saskatoon; if this comes to fruition, it will no doubt have important effects on design in the province.

Calgary has been a vital architectural design center since the 1960s, bolstered by the creation of an architecture program in 1971 at the University of Calgary in the newly established faculty of environmental design. The program's early faculty included its first

33 left
Saskatchewan Provincial
Court House, view from
east, Prince Albert,
Saskatchewan. aodbt
architecture + interior
design, 2003.

34 opposite, top
Poppy Plaza, view from
northwest, Calgary, Alberta.
Marc Boutin Architectural
Collaborative, 2013.

35 opposite, bottom
Ferrier Webb Residence,
view of courtyard, Calgary,
Alberta. Davignon Martin,
2010.

director, R. Douglas Gillmor, a well-recognized architect who had practiced in Winnipeg; architectural historian Dr. Michael McMordie, an active interpreter of Canadian architecture; and Alberta-born architect Dale M. Taylor. Since 2000, a new wave of Calgary-based architecture firms has emerged, many involving graduates of the program at the University of Calgary, including the Marc Boutin Architectural Collaborative, Nyhoff Architecture, McKinley Burkart, MoDA, Frank, Housebrand, Davignon Martin, and Spectacle. The Marc Boutin Architectural Collaborative has won many regional and national awards for its residential design and public space projects. Their Memorial Drive and Poppy Plaza project (2013) manages existing infrastructure, memorializes Calgary's war dead, uses weathering steel in evocative ways, and is representative of the firm's commitment to the public realm. **FIG 34** Davignon Martin's Ferrier Webb Residence in Calgary (2010) is a remarkable essay on the contemporary residence. **FIG 35** MoDA has garnered attention with a number of housing projects, including the award-winning Grow and Village projects designed in 2017. In recent years, there has also been a series of Calgary projects by international firms, such as Santiago Calatrava, Norman Foster, Allied Works, BIG, and Snøhetta.

The City of Edmonton, which in the 1970s and 1980s was a hotbed of architectural experimentation, saw a decline in the subsequent two decades. In 2005, former city mayor Stephen Mandel and city architect Carol Bélanger sparked an architectural renaissance with a procurement process based on short-listing firms that had been widely recognized for their design work. This has resulted in a spectacular series of public projects, mainly by out-of-province firms. Projects of note include the Commonwealth Community Recreation Centre (2012) by MJMA in collaboration with HIP Architects, and the Clareview Community Recreation Centre and Branch Library (2014) by Teeple Architects in collaboration with Architecture | Tkalcic Bengert. The Jasper Place Library (2012) and the Mill Woods Library, Seniors' Centre and Multicultural Facility (2014), both by HCMA with Dub Architects, are also vital new works. Gene Dub has been a leading force in the Edmonton architecture scene for many years and has become Canada's leading developer-architect. Manasc Isaac Architects, a well-established Edmonton practice known for their work with Indigenous communities and sustainable design, has recently produced the Mosaic Centre

for Conscious Community and Commerce (2015) in Edmonton, intended to be the first net-zero-energy commercial building in Alberta.

Conclusion

Between 1967 and 2017, the architecture of the three Canadian Prairie Provinces has seen many transformations as it has embraced both regional and international forces. Many accomplished firms have contributed to the shape of Canadian architecture during this period. The genuinely original regional work of Prairie architects of the 1960s and 1970s has given way to thoughtful work that is more strongly influenced by international trends. And the new generation of architects operating in Winnipeg and Calgary are among the most interesting young firms in the country. The best architecture of the region has been shaped by its climate, landscapes, and unique cultural histories while balancing influences from beyond.

11

Eastern Edge

Brian Carter

A threshold to North America, Atlantic Canada includes the traditional territories of the Mi'kmaq First Nations and Inuit of Nunatsiavut and what is now the provinces of New Brunswick, Prince Edward Island, Nova Scotia, and Newfoundland and Labrador. Viking explorers established a settlement at the northernmost tip of Newfoundland around 1000 AD, and Atlantic Canada was to be visited frequently and settled by many different people in the centuries that followed.

The landscapes of this maritime region vary from stony coastlines in the north to arable farmland in the south. **FIG 1** Indigenous populations built modest shelters in the region, and settlers constructed primitive huts to house people, animals, and tools. These structures varied in form and materials, yet all highlighted resilience, craft, and remarkable invention—qualities that continue to inspire the design of buildings in the area.

Atlantic Canada is not, however, merely a territory signaled by solitary buildings. It has also been shaped by cities that developed around natural harbors and trade routes. Although modest in size, Saint John's, Moncton, Fredericton, Saint John, and Charlottetown have long been influential hubs of government, business, and culture, while Halifax, a larger city and the provincial capital of Nova Scotia, provides important global connections and the setting for notable educational institutions.

1 left
View of harbor at Peggy's Cove, Nova Scotia.

2 opposite, top
Howard House, view from water's edge, West Pennant, Nova Scotia. Brian MacKay-Lyons Architecture + Urban Design, 1999.

3 opposite, bottom
Howard House, view framed by house.

A Distinctive School

A school of architecture and planning was established in Halifax in 1961. The only school in the region, it was first housed in the Nova Scotia Technical College, an institution that later became the Technical University of Nova Scotia (TUNS) before being amalgamated with Dalhousie University in 1997. Established as a cooperative education program, it had strong links with professional practice, and the appointment of architect Essy Baniassad as dean in 1981 helped to strengthen those connections. Baniassad encouraged the development of a program that highlighted the significance of vernacular buildings and architecture as a public service.

A series of pedagogic initiatives encouraged students to look and learn from their surroundings. Free Lab, a specially developed course, was first offered in 1991 and continues to be taught as an integral part of the school's pedagogy.[1] It has resulted in the construction of numerous small buildings and structures by teams of students and faculty working with communities throughout the region. Consequently, it also raises awareness of the potential of design while inspiring alternative models of architectural practice.

Brian MacKay-Lyons (1954–), a graduate of the undergraduate program in architecture at TUNS, joined the faculty there after completing graduate studies at UCLA under the direction of Charles Moore. He chose to advance his academic research through practice, and established an office in Halifax in 1985. An early project, a retreat for his family, was completed in 1986, and commissions to design other houses followed [see pages 195–196]. In 1989, MacKay-Lyons won an international competition to design an extension to the Faculty of Architecture and Planning in Halifax and has subsequently designed other significant civic buildings.

MacKay-Lyons's approach is evidenced in the Howard House (1999), designed in 1995 and constructed on a 4-acre (1.6-hectare) field at West Pennant, Nova Scotia, bounded on three sides by water. Created for a young family, the 2,000-square-foot (186-square-meter) house is a simple 12-by-110-foot (3.65-by-33.5-meter) rectangular box topped with a mono-pitched roof. The roof's high end allows for a large window that captures sunlight

and views out over the water. **FIGS 2–3** Clad in corrugated metal, it recalls the sheds of local boat builders.

House on the Nova Scotia Coast #12, commissioned a year later and completed in 1997, also takes advantage of its waterfront site. Located on Nova Scotia's South Shore, it developed similar design ideas but also reflects MacKay-Lyons's enthusiasm for the groupings of vernacular buildings on farms and along the coast. **FIGS 4–5** Consequently, this new house was organized as three linked buildings that define sheltered outdoor spaces and frame views of the ocean.

In 1994, MacKay-Lyons brought together students, faculty, and colleagues in a meadow in Upper Kingsburg, Nova Scotia, where they constructed a simple shelter over the foundations of a ruined house. The translucent fabric and rudimentary wooden frame referenced the location and dimensions of the original house and drew attention to the presence and tenacity of early settlers. At the same time, it recalled the archetypal house form. A particularly provocative image of that project, taken at dusk and with two figures silhouetted in a doorway by the light of a fire, suggests a strange apparition. **FIG 6** This project and the image marked the beginning of the Ghost Architectural Laboratory—an annual design-build event that was sustained over nearly two decades.[2] The program resulted in the design and construction of modest shelters and follies, sheds, houses, and a lookout tower. **FIGS 7–8** Subsequently, a nearby historic barn and a one-room school house were rescued and carefully reconstructed on the site. Together, the collection of buildings suggests a new village in the meadow overlooking the Atlantic. For the duration of the program, students, architects, tourists, and critics came from around the world annually to meet, play, work, and talk about architecture.

Other architects teaching in Halifax at the time also chose to advance their academic research through professional practice. Upon his arrival from Europe, architect Richard Kroeker was particularly inspired by buildings created by Nova Scotia's Indigenous communities. Their resourcefulness, thoughtful considerations of climate, and ingenious use of natural materials shaped Kroeker's teaching and influenced his work in collaborative design and construction with local First Nations groups [see page 137]. This collaborative

4 opposite, left
House on the Nova Scotia
Coast #12, overall view,
Nova Scotia. Brian MacKay-
Lyons Architecture + Urban
Design, 1997.

5 opposite, right
House on the Nova Scotia
Coast #12, view from
terrace.

6 above
Ghost 1, Upper Kingsburg,
Nova Scotia. Brian MacKay-
Lyons with collaborators,
1994.

7 opposite
**Enough House, Upper
Kingsburg, Nova Scotia.
MacKay-Lyons Sweetapple
Architects, 2015.**
©James Brittain

8 above
**Shobac, overall view of
collection of buildings,
Upper Kingsburg, Nova
Scotia. MacKay-Lyons
Sweetapple Architects,
ongoing.** ©James Brittain

9 left
**Pictou Landing Health
Centre, community room,
Pictou Landing, Nova
Scotia. Richard Kroeker
Design, 2008.**

10 opposite, top
**Pictou Landing Health
Centre, exterior view.**

11 opposite, bottom
**Black Gables, Louisdale,
Nova Scotia. Omar Gandhi
Architect, 2014.**

approach is seen at the Pictou Landing Health Centre, Nova Scotia, which provides clinics for doctors, dentists, and health-care workers. Developed together with the community, faculty colleague Brian Lilley, and Peter Henry Architects, the design uses local wood and construction techniques perfected by Indigenous people, who also helped to erect the building. Completed in 2008, the center consists of a series of timber arches that define a curved plan, which encloses a new medicine garden. **FIGS 9–10** The form and enclosure of the building were also designed to maximize thermal performance; on completion, energy consumption has proven to be 43 percent less than that of a conventional building. Beaverbank, a subsequent project, was designed and built by Kroeker with students from Dalhousie University and the Nova Scotia College of Art & Design (NASCAD). The modest shelter, used as an educational space, reused materials collected from the forest floor and employed construction systems derived from Indigenous lodges.

An Atlantic Canada School

The architecture program in Halifax, advanced by the work of faculty and students, has provided the foundation for a distinctive Atlantic Canada school of design. Works in this school can be characterized by their particular attention to siting and weather, and by inspiration taken from available materials and traditional construction techniques.

These considerations have also prompted the formation of other architectural offices. Omar Gandhi, a graduate of the University of Toronto, enrolled in the architecture program at Dalhousie University and worked with MacKay-Lyons Sweetapple after being inspired by maritime vernacular buildings. His practice focuses on the design of houses such as Black Gables (2014), which consists of two connected sheds. **FIG 11** One, a 1,200-square-foot (112-square-meter) single-story building, provides living space, while the other houses a 450-square-foot (42-square-meter) studio and darkroom. Each building is assertively colored and, together, the two all-black objects create a distinctive group on a rural site overlooking the ocean. Rabbit Snare Gorge Cabin, a retreat designed by Omar Gandhi in collaboration with DesignBase8, was completed in 2015. Planned with openings located to

track the sun, the form of the building recalls the archetypal house—albeit transformed to create a tall lookout tower that captures panoramic views over the Northumberland Strait and across Cape Breton Island. **FIG 12**

Susan Fitzgerald graduated from the architecture program at TUNS and worked with MacKay-Lyons before joining Fowler Bauld & Mitchell, a large Halifax practice. She subsequently joined the faculty at Dalhousie and began working with builder Brainard Fitzgerald, who is also her husband. Together, they designed a series of new buildings on urban sites and built several residential developments that advance new urban typologies and explore alternative ways of working. Their explorations of density, form, and use are best synthesized in Live/Work/Grow (2015), a project that consists of three separate units totaling 3,500 square feet (325 square meters). **FIG 13–14** Designed for a 25-by-100-foot (7.6-by-30.5-meter) site in the north end of the city, the project provides housing for a family of four, an office and studio, and an independent two-story live/work apartment. The buildings are integrated with landscaped courtyards, terraces, and planted roofs.

The fusion of teaching, research, and practice also characterizes the work of Niall Savage. Following the completion of a performance space for the Scotia Festival of Music (2002), Savage's firm collaborated with Grant Wanzel, an activist and former dean of the

Faculty of Architecture & Planning at Dalhousie University, whose research focuses on social equity and housing design. **FIG 15** Together, they promoted a series of new buildings that developed urban sites and expanded the range of affordable housing in the city. The completed project for the Creighton/Gerrish Affordable Housing Initiative (2011), which stitched together several small sites, provides 184 new units of housing with a mix of single apartments, detached residences, and condominiums. **FIG 16**

Expanding Networks

A close-knit network of small cities extends throughout the maritime region, fostering collaboration and the cultivation of ideas. Thanks to the strength of this network, the ideas of the Atlantic Canada school have been projected beyond Halifax. Dalhousie graduate Larry Jones was among the founders of BGHJ Architects, established in Charlottetown in 1976. The practice has designed significant new buildings in the region, including the Health Sciences Building at the University of Prince Edward Island (in collaboration with MacKay-Lyons Sweetapple, 2011). After graduating from Dalhousie in 1981, Jim Case established Sheppard Case Architects in Newfoundland and worked with Todd Saunders on

15 opposite
Scotia Music Room, interior of performance space, Halifax, Nova Scotia. Niall Savage Architecture, 2002.

16 right
Creighton / Gerrish Affordable Housing Initiative, Halifax, Nova Scotia. Savage Stewart Architecture and Niall Savage Architecture. Grant Wanzel Consultant, 2011.

the design of new buildings on Fogo Island. Chris Woodford, another Dalhousie graduate, partnered with NASCAD graduate Taryn Sheppard to found Woodford Sheppard in Newfoundland in 2013. New Brunswick's Acre Architects was established by Monica Adair and Stephen Kopp, two graduates from Toronto who have gone on to expand their practice and open a studio in New York City. In 2018, they were awarded the Professional Prix de Rome in Architecture.

The influence of the Atlantic Canada school and its focus on the vernacular also extends across the North American continent. Architects who trained at TUNS, NASCAD, and Dalhousie include founders of MOLO Todd MacAllen and Stephanie Forsythe, David Battersby and Heather Howat of BattersbyHowat, Mark Ostry of Acton Ostry Architects, and D'Arcy Jones, all of whom work in Vancouver. Other noteworthy graduates include Matthew Kennedy and Mark Erickson of Studio North in Calgary, Stephanie Davidson of Davidson Rafailidis in Buffalo, and Peter Yeadon in New York City. These practices are responsible for award-winning work that ranges from the design of houses and civic buildings to nanotechnology, paper walls, and high-rise timber towers.

Recognizing its role as a hub for architectural ideas, TUNS initiated a program of publications in 1994 that was designed to make books on architecture that would be readily accessible to students, professionals, and the public. A book on the work of John and Patricia Patkau inaugurated a series titled *Documents in Canadian Architecture*. The press currently continues operations under the name Dalhousie Architectural Press, with the support of school dean Christine Macy.

A publication was also responsible for bringing broad attention to a tiny fishing village on Fogo Island, eight miles off the northeast coast of Newfoundland.[3] Established by settlers from Ireland and England, the village of Tilting was the focus of research by architect and professor Robert Mellin, who traced the development of the place through the ingenious design and skillful construction of buildings by local residents. Mellin, who began documenting the settlement's buildings in the mid-1980s, subsequently worked with architecture students from McGill University to prepare measured drawings, sketches, photographs, and interviews with residents that form the basis for the book.

17
Long Studio, view from
the ocean, Fogo Island,
Newfoundland. Saunders
Architecture, 2009.

18
Tower Studio, view across
marsh, Fogo Island,
Newfoundland. Saunders
Architecture, 2011.

Publications highlighting both new work and vernacular buildings in Atlantic Canada —from the work of prominent firms such as MacKay-Lyons Sweetapple to the architecture of modest villages such as Tilting—continue to foster debate and cultivate interest in the new architecture of the region.

At the Edge of a Continent

The economy of Fogo Island was based on cod fishing, an activity that had provided the commercial basis and social foundation for livelihoods in Atlantic Canada for centuries. The Canadian government's declaration of a moratorium on cod fishing in 1992 had a devastating impact throughout the region. It was strikingly evident in Tilting. In 2001, Zita, Anthony, and Alan Cobb—members of a local family that had been successful in business elsewhere in Canada—returned to Fogo Island and established the Shorefast Foundation with the aim of regenerating one of Canada's oldest outports.

The Cobb family looked to the arts as a way of stimulating social entrepreneurship and rebuilding a strong, self-sufficient community. Their desire to bring artists from around the world to work on Fogo Island prompted a need for studios, and Newfoundland-born architect Todd Saunders (1969–) was commissioned. Saunders, who had studied in Halifax and Montreal before establishing a practice in Norway in 1998, designed a series of six tiny buildings. Each was about 300 square feet (28 square meters) and sited in the rugged landscapes of the island. Construction of the studios began in 2010 and was completed three years later. **FIGS 17–18**

The majority of these buildings have been lifted off the ground and supported on posts—an obvious strategy, considering the rocky sites, and one that recalls the local vernacular. The forms of these new buildings, however, with their twists, cuts, and folds, present a stark contrast to existing structures. They have assertively located Fogo Island on the international map and signal its regeneration.

The Shorefast Foundation went on to commission Saunders to design a twenty-nine-suite inn to provide accommodations for visitors. This substantially larger building, located on a prominent site overlooking the Atlantic, is a striking landmark. Like the studios, the Fogo Island Inn (2013) is radically different from its surroundings. **FIGS 19–20** It consists of a series of large, overlapping boxes that have been thoughtfully grouped to create a sheltered entrance court, offering exceptional views across land and water. Part of the building has also been lifted high above its rocky site and is supported at one end on a randomly arrayed collection of slender raking columns—a device that recalls fishing sheds at the nearby water's edge.

In addition to the predictable hotel amenities—spa, sauna, sundecks, bars, and a restaurant that offers menus based on local produce—this building also houses a library, cinema, and art gallery where work by visiting artists can be shown. The fitting out of these spaces has been developed by international designers who worked with local craftspeople to

19 above
Fogo Island Inn, evening view, Fogo Island, Newfoundland. Saunders Architecture with Sheppard Case Architects, 2013.

20 opposite
Fogo Island Inn, undercroft.

advance new ideas, foster new skills, and create workshops in the community. It has inspired the design and local fabrication of furniture, fabrics, wall coverings, and fixtures that ingeniously combine old and new.

Spectacular Vernacular

While the archetypal house and shed continue to inspire architects and clients across Atlantic Canada, the designers of larger civic buildings throughout the region have had to search harder for inspiration. The Rooms, a building designed to house the Art Gallery of Newfoundland and Labrador together with the Provincial Archives and Museum (2005), is a distinctive landmark situated on a hilltop above Saint John's. In designing it, architect Philip Pratt looked to the gable-roofed sheds called "fishing rooms" that are a familiar sight along the coast of Newfoundland. However, inevitable changes in scale generated by the need to accommodate different activities introduced radical transformations of the vernacular.

More recently, the design of a new public library in Halifax (2014) suggests another search for inspiration from the vernacular. Designed by Fowler Bauld & Mitchell in association with the Danish practice Schmidt Hammer Lassen, this is one of the most notable

21
Halifax Public Library,
main entrance, Halifax,
Nova Scotia. Schmidt
Hammer Lassen with
Fowler Bauld & Mitchell,
2014.

new civic buildings in the region. **FIG 21** Its ambition and scale highlight a remarkable level of commitment and insight from the client, local community, and provincial government. Located on a prominent site in the city, the library provides an impressive range of spaces that accomodate not only books, but an auditorium, restaurants, study areas, and community meeting rooms. These spaces are housed within a series of large, fully glazed boxes that have been stacked high and stepped to provide cantilevered lookouts and landscaped terraces at a busy urban corner. The building offers sweeping views over the Citadel and Halifax Harbor and across the water to Dartmouth and the seascapes and forested horizon beyond. It assertively recalls contemporary landscapes of stacked shipping containers on waterfronts. Although such images are familiar in Atlantic Canada, the expressive gesture of big boxes, casual stacking, and demonstrative cantilevers now also characterizes a new international style in contemporary architecture.

An enthusiasm for the vernacular, clearly demonstrated by architects in the region, together with the projection of design into local communities by students and teachers, has stimulated a widening awareness and interest in architecture throughout Atlantic Canada. People there have become enthusiastic patrons of and advocates for contemporary design. Simultaneously, increasing flows of international capital into the region have prompted those patrons to seek out and commission both emerging and internationally established architects to design new buildings in the region. In contrast to the modesty of earlier projects, many of those buildings are substantial in size and flushed with ambition. Consequently, clients and architects, searching widely for inspiration, are now creating new buildings in Atlantic Canada that, responding to a seemingly insatiable appetite for striking imagery, are radically transforming the vernacular into spectacle.

12

Arctic Architecture: Standards, Experiments, and Consensus

Lola Sheppard and Mason White

Architecture has played a subtle yet forceful role in transforming the Canadian Arctic, arguably becoming the most legible tool of "internal colonialism" during the region's dramatic modernization of the past century.[1] Prior to contact, movement and impermanence were ingrained in the culture and spatial practice of Indigenous people of the Arctic, producing architecture that was adapted to each season. This abruptly changed with the introduction of permanent structures, built using nonlocal materials and forms. But how did these imported buildings relate to the cultural, logistical, and environmental aspects of the North? And what are the possibilities for an authentic northern vernacular in terms of expression, siting, and programming?

From the 1890s to the 1940s, trading posts, mission buildings, and Royal Canadian Mounted Police military installations across the Arctic catalyzed rapid transformation.[2] These early structures served as colonial nodes of southern economic, cultural, and defense networks. The presence of trading, missionary, and military organizations spurred seasonal camps, which then gave rise to more permanent settlements. These developments imposed more permanent housing, which created shifts in domestic patterns on Indigenous people, profoundly changing the social life of inhabitants. Today, there remains considerable variety in urban form and architecture across the Arctic—from west to east, from coast to inland, from urban capitals to remote hamlets. Subtle distinctions exist between the various northern peoples' land claim agreements and responses to cultural preservation and modernity. Furthermore, resource and infrastructure development as well as urbanization have occurred unevenly. And limited access to these communities by air, road, and water generates disparities in the capacity for delivering goods and building supplies. However, these challenges remain common among small, dispersed Arctic communities and have sometimes yielded Arctic-specific architecture, urban design, and infrastructure responses.

The radical transformations that have occurred in Arctic Canada over the past fifty years is remarkable. The evolution of the three territorial capital cities provides a useful barometer. Whitehorse, capital of Yukon, was incorporated in 1950 with a population of 2,500. It has grown tenfold to over 25,000 residents today. Yellowknife, capital of the Northwest Territories since 1967, was incorporated as a city in 1970 with roughly 6,000 people; it has also grown rapidly, to 19,600 today. Iqaluit, capital of Nunavut, was only recognized as a settlement in 1970, with a population of approximately 2,000; today it has 7,800 residents.[3] The modest size of communities in Arctic Canada becomes evident when comparing them to Russia's or Alaska's larger polar municipalities. However, the rapid rate of growth in Canadian territories has defied conventional methods of providing social, cultural, and mobility infrastructure.

This chapter observes three key phases in the evolution of Canada's Arctic architecture over the past fifty years: (1) the search for design standards, (2) an era of design experiments, and (3) the introduction of consensus-building. These phases are not sequential but rather overlap and coexist. Subsequent to the settlement period, from the 1950s and 1960s onward, government agencies deployed housing prototypes that represented a search for standardized design solutions, often without regard for climatic and cultural nuances. These standards were of little architectural value, though their legacy of efficiency and expediency remains evident in design and construction approaches today. During the 1960s and 1970s, a series of experiments produced novel technological responses to Arctic building challenges. Urban design approaches specifically calibrated to the climate of the region also began to emerge during this time. More recently, since the 1990s, there has been a shift toward consensus-based design that is more sensitively informed by Indigenous culture.

The Search for Standards

Most housing prototypes introduced since the 1950s were grossly insensitive to the Arctic's unique social structures and harsh climate. They were poorly built and finished, without proper insulation, and were far too small to accommodate traditional extended families.[4] The earliest units, offered by the federal government, were prefabricated plywood dwellings under 300 square feet (28 square meters); they were nicknamed the "matchbox" because of their small size and simple shape. **FIG 1** Another unit type was named the "512" in reference

1
Matchbox House 370A,
Northwest Territories,
c. 1960.

to its square footage (47.6 square meters). Evidently, the intent was to provide only the minimum structure and space that might qualify as shelter. The matchbox and the 512 became a unit-by-unit colonial force that created significant social and cultural problems still evident today.

Despite the deployment of over twelve hundred units, only a few years after the loan program began, the houses were failing to fulfill the most basic promise of affordable home ownership for Inuit. They were "drafty, cramped, unsafe and totally unsuited" to life in the Arctic.[5] The 1960s saw a policy move toward rental housing, which started to address issues of affordability, although social and environmental needs remained neglected. As home ownership and rental availability increased within communities, planning tailored to context was overlooked, leaving urban form to be "designed on a pattern suited to southern Canadian suburbs."[6]

A turn toward more suitable housing came with the creation of the Northwest Territories Housing Corporation (NWTHC) in 1974, which also served the territory of Nunavut until its separation in 1999, and the Yukon Housing Corporation from the Housing Corporation Act of 1972. In its first six years, NWTHC constructed and deployed over thirteen hundred new rental units and implemented programs that encouraged families to build their own homes from local materials while offering assistance with such essentials as windows, doors, and hardware. One of these deployed units was the "Weber" house type, purchased from Weber Homes of Saskatchewan, which became the standard government-issued house by the late 1970s. **FIG 2** At 900 to 1,600 square feet (83.5 to 149 square meters), it was larger than the matchbox and began to address the needs of Inuit family structure. Another type, the "Woolfenden," developed specifically for the region by the Woolfenden Design Group in 1979, offered a multiunit configuration.

A few years later, NWTHC developed an improved Woolfenden model that sought to address "the pattern of extensive and long-term visiting between households, and storage requirements for bulk foods, storage and maintenance of hunting equipment, snowmobiles and the like."[7] Over the ensuing eight years, NWTHC worked iteratively through five types of units. In contrast with previous standardization efforts, there was an interest

in integrating technological innovations with social accommodations. In 1979, they introduced a two-bedroom duplex at 1,000 square feet (93 square meters), with an enclosed porch and an unheated storage room, observing that "a house must effectively represent the needs of the hunter."[8]

The practice of developing and deploying housing prototypes across the territory—often with little adaptation to context and shifts in culture—remains a legacy of government housing approaches in the Arctic. In the 2010s, the Nunavut Housing Corporation, established in the wake of Nunavut's 1999 separation from Northwest Territories, experimented with 10-, 24-, and 33-unit multiplex buildings. While they better addressed quantitative housing needs, these multiplexes revealed complex cultural issues as they pushed the limits of appropriate population density for a people for whom connection to the land is central to identity. Indigenous people tend to consider the land as home rather than a house as home, a concept evident in the greater continuity between inside and outside in traditional architecture—something the large multiplex with stacked units did not successfully provide.[9] Arguably, the five-plex house could be considered the most effective at balancing urgent housing shortages with cultural needs, land availability, and today's construction logistics.

Ongoing housing shortages in Nunavut, Nunatsiavut (northern Labrador), and Nunavik (northern Quebec) continue to create immense pressure to quickly supply cost-effective housing stock in large quantities. However, high transportation costs, tight construction timelines, and the risk of cost overruns render design experimentation challenging. This has resulted in a tendency to pursue standard, repeatable housing typologies.

Rethinking the Domestic

In the past two decades, there has been an ongoing effort to redesign housing prototypes to better accommodate contemporary life and energy requirements, and to facilitate a more inclusive design process. In 2006, the Canada Mortgage and Housing Corporation (CMHC) initiated a study led by researcher William Semple to develop the Northern

Sustainable House. Designs were produced through workshops with the Nunavut Housing Corporation in Arviat, the Tr'ondëk Hwëch'in First Nation in Dawson City, Yukon, and with the Northwest Territories Housing Corporation in Inuvik. Through this extensive community consultation, the project attempted to address technical challenges as well as cultural practices and comforts. Critical spatial elements—such as cold porches, sealift storage, large open rooms to hold family gatherings, and separate seasonal entrances—were all identified and incorporated. Cultural needs to host family feasts, prepare traditional country food, and sew skin clothing in a cool room (kept cooler than a living room or bedroom) were also integrated into the design.[10]

There have also been shifts in the design of multiunit housing in the North, notably in architect Gino Pin's housing in Behchoko for the Tlicho community, and in his McDonald Drive condominiums (2008) in Yellowknife's Old Town neighborhood. **FIG 3** The eight-unit McDonald complex uses the consistent thermal warmth of the site's rocky outcropping for energy benefits. In Whitehorse, Kobayashi Zedda Architects has been building small-scale condo units in the center of the city, such as the eight-unit Judy Condos (2009), offering an antisprawl alternative to the predominant oversized houses on large lots.[11]

Most houses in the territories are rentals that are financed, built, and maintained by the territorial housing corporations. The terms of rental housing limit spatial modifications by their occupants in response to cultural desires or entrepreneurial pursuits. Scholars such as Frank Tester have suggested that alternate ownership models, like cooperative housing, might provide greater flexibility in the housing continuum of Canada's northern territories.[12] Tester explains that one of the challenges of housing in the Arctic is "to develop a social housing policy that attempt[s] to treat housing as a social need and not a market commodity."[13] Housing must also be seen as a cultural need, reinforcing Indigenous community and family patterns, not resisting them. Although many recent initiatives by architects have considered these issues, there remains an unwillingness to fund this type of approach on a larger scale. The housing needs in the Arctic are dire, particularly in Nunavut, Nunavik, and Nunatsiavut—however, the solution cannot simply be more housing. Rather, what is needed is more culturally responsive housing and ownership models.

Experiments I: Arctic "New Towns"

Parallel to the search for standards, several designers and government organizations took risks in the search for new Arctic typologies. In particular, the rapid growth of Frobisher Bay (renamed Iqaluit in 1987) presented an ideal context for imagining an Arctic-specific urbanism. The area's population has increased sharply since the 1950s due to an influx of government and military administrators as well as subsequent Inuit migration. Frobisher Bay transitioned from a military base to an administrative headquarters for the construction of the Distant Early Warning (DEW) Line from 1955 to 1957[14]; following this intense activity, it remained an informal collection of temporary structures, shacks, and hangars.

3
McDonald Drive
condominiums, Yellowknife,
Northwest Territories.
Pin/Taylor Architects, 2008.

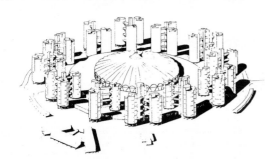

4 left
New Town I, overall sketch
and plan, Frobisher Bay
(now Iqaluit), Nunavut. E. A.
Gardner, Chief Architect
of the Department of
Northern Affairs, 1958.

5 opposite
New Town I, perspective.

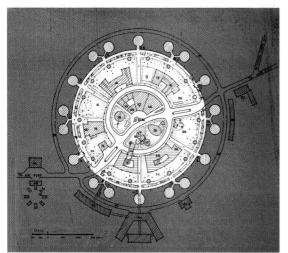

The Frobisher Development Group Committee was formed in 1958 to establish a civilian Arctic "New Town."

The first (unofficial) proposal for a town on Frobisher Bay was a futuristic plan by the federal chief architect's office to house one thousand people. **FIGS 4–5** New Town I was organized as a dozen clusters of twelve-story housing towers around a large central dome; the latter contained two schools, two churches, a community center, a fire hall, government offices, shops, restaurants, and a hotel, all within a massive atrium. In its ambition for total metabolic and programmatic self-sufficiency, New Town I included an atomic heating plant, a hydroponic vegetable garden, and a battery-powered internal monorail. The tower clusters were linked to the dome and to each other by a series of enclosed elevated walkways, providing an interior environment protected from the harsh climate.[15]

A second, more viable proposal was solicited in 1960 from Peter Dickinson Associates of Toronto, working with Rounthwaite & Fairfield. Three versions of the scheme tested high-, medium-, and low-rise apartment buildings. The low-rise scheme, composed of three slab buildings of six to eight stories, was deemed most feasible. It incorporated a cinema, hotel, nursery, and auditorium in an elevated plaza. The residences formed long wall-buildings that enclosed a courtyard, sheltering it from the strong Arctic winds.[16]

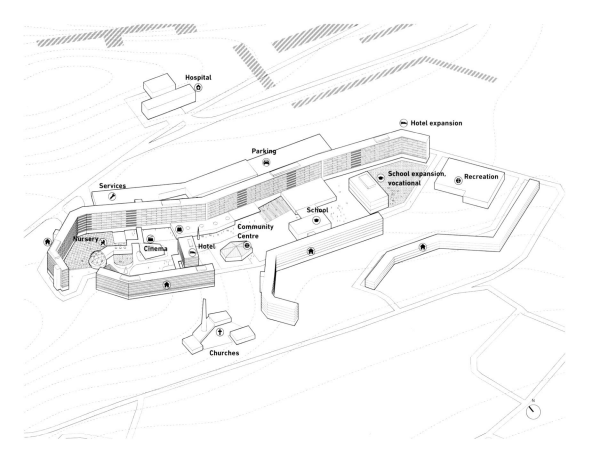

Dickinson's New Town II (1960), though not built, informed the eventual realization of the Astro Hill Complex (1976), a modest aggregation of four buildings, including two residential slab towers set on bedrock, overlooking the bay. Today, the complex contains government offices, the headquarters of CBC North, a cinema, and a large hotel and multi-use complex. However diminished, the project retains the legacy of earlier ambitions for a building-complex-as-interior-city that is shielded from the elements. **FIG 6**

While the Frobisher Bay proposals offered a futuristic, high-modernist vision of Arctic urbanism in the mold of the International Style, another emergent strand of thinking called for an Arctic and subarctic urban vernacular. Swedish architect Ralph Erskine's work remains an important foray into this vein of large-scale urban design for the North. Erskine (1914–2005) drew international architectural attention in the early 1960s, in part through his cold-climate-responsive urban designs for the Swedish mining towns of Svappavaara and Kiruna. In 1970, the federal government hired him to develop a proposal for Resolute, the country's most northerly community and one of the coldest inhabited places in the world. The design scheme continued ideas initially developed in his siteless 1958 proposal for "An Ecological Arctic Town." The design brief for Resolute sought to integrate and consolidate the 140 Inuit—making up 32 households—who were forcibly relocated to the area in 1953

6 opposite
New Town II, re-drawn axonometric view, Frobisher Bay (now Iqaluit), Nunavut. Peter Dickinson Associates with Rounthwaite & Fairfield, 1960.

7 right
Resolute Bay project, perspective view, Resolute Bay, Nunavut. Ralph Erskine, c. 1976.

from farther south. This group was forced to settle within five miles (eight kilometers) of the fluctuating population of 250 to 600 administrative and military personnel who lived near the air base. The new town was intended to accommodate 1,200 residents in all, with provisions for a future population of 3,000. **FIG 7**

The initial relocation of Inuit families from the south to the desolated high Arctic in the 1950s as well as the town plan later proposed by Erskine are both instances of "social engineering," according to historian Alan Marcus. Indeed, many aspects of Erskine's design revealed the gaps between modernism and culturally-informed design.[17] The horseshoe-shaped perimeter building was to contain apartments for government personnel as well as a communal area with shops, a restaurant, and a library, with a swimming pool and an indoor botanical garden attached at the top.[18] These programs were to encircle a low-density fabric of individual homes for Inuit, a freestanding church, and a school—creating a contentious social organization in which *qallunaat,* or non-Inuit, would surround and look down upon Inuit.

Erskine's overall massing concept employs an urban "windscreen" to create a protected microclimate. However, the location and role of the windscreen perimeter wall conflicted with local practice. The town was sited on a hill—presumably for views to the bay, which

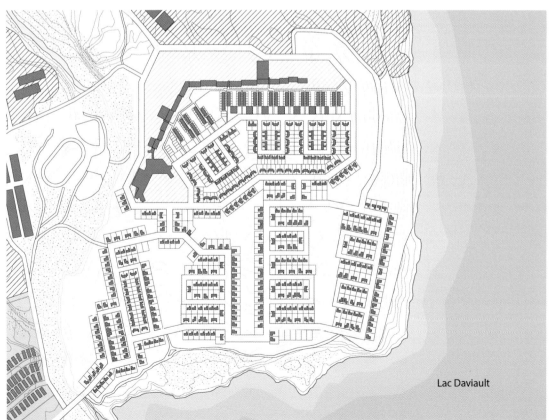

Lac Daviault

8 opposite, top
Fermont, Quebec, view with windscreen wall and civic buildings in foreground. Desnoyers Schoenauer, 1972; with subsequent work by Desnoyers, Mercure, Gagnon, Sheppard architectes in association with Laroche et Derry architectes.

9 opposite, bottom
Fermont, Quebec, re-drawn plan showing original site strategy and the expansion of town since opening.

10 right
Fermont, Quebec, view of windscreen wall with entrances and circulation cores marked by color.

appealed to the *qallunaat* sensibility. Yet Inuit preferred to build their settlements near the shore for access to hunting and fishing sites. Furthermore, Erskine's focus on protection from the wind, which again appealed to a Euro-Canadian sensibility, overlooked the fact that wind plays an essential role in clearing snow, and an enclosure wall would encourage snowdrifts to pile up in the center—exactly where Inuit houses were to be located.[19] Construction began on a fragment of the perimeter building, but the project was abandoned in 1978 for economic reasons and left only partially realized. Despite the initiative's problems Erskine's Resolute experiment is notable for attempting to merge a comprehensive vision of the environment and social life with a direct response to climate. It was a search for an Arctic vernacular.

Subsequent town planning projects inspired by Resolute proved more successful, including the town plan of Fermont in northern Quebec, built as a company town in 1972 for Quebec Cartier Mining with its nearby iron ore mine. **FIGS 8–11** Located 745 miles (1,200 kilometers) northeast of Montreal, the town was to house 5,000 inhabitants, although its population mostly hovered closer to 3,500 and has declined to 2,500 in the past two decades.[20] The project, designed by Montreal-based firm Desnoyers Schoenauer,[21] embraced Erskine's concept of the windscreen wall to protect the area in the "shadow" of the screen from prevailing winter winds. The 0.8-mile-long (1.3-kilometer) windscreen building consolidated all the public functions and organized them along an interior street. According to architect Adrian Sheppard, the aim "was simple and unequivocal: to design a human settlement in the form of a physical setting which is conducive to good family and community life. In so doing, the planners had to address two main concerns: the physical conditions, and the other psychosocial realities."[22]

Norbert Schoenauer (1923–2001), a housing scholar and planner, identified four previous generations of subarctic settlement: temporary and periodic settlements inhabited by Indigenous people; haphazard and informal settlements built by the pioneers; "new towns" built by large mining companies modeled on typical suburban patterns; and towns modeled on the suburbs but with a more compact, commercial town center.[23] He describes Fermont as a fifth-generation subarctic town. It is organized around three climate-responsive design

11 left
Fermont, Quebec, view of interior street in windscreen wall. Desnoyers Schoenauer, 1972; with subsequent work by Desnoyers, Mercure, Gagnon, Sheppard architectes in association with Laroche et Derry architectes.

12 opposite, top
Housing proposal for Frobisher Bay, unit study of prefabricated module, Iqaluit, Nunavut. Moshe Safdie and associates, architects and planners, 1974.

13 opposite, bottom
Housing proposal for Frobisher Bay, site model showing aggregation pattern of prefabricated housing units on the site.

premises: compact land use, the creation of microclimates through building massing, and the provision (through the interior street) of year-round climate-controlled access to communal facilities. These ideas were intimately linked to concerns for energy conservation, limiting the impact on the natural physical environment, and affording the inhabitants the greatest amount of physical comfort in the winter months.[24]

Located on the northwest boundary of Fermont, the windscreen building yields a protective microclimate for the lower-density residential buildings on the leeward side, but it causes more snow to accumulate. The encircling building contains all the necessary community facilities: commercial stores, town hall, fire station (now relocated), school, swimming pool, cinema, sports center, police station, hotel, and even three prison cells. Apartments are located on the upper floors. For reasons of wind flow, the central part of the building is five and a half stories high, while the extremities are three and a half stories. In order to maximize the protective effect of the screen, housing units are distributed with decreasing density the farther they are from the windscreen. A diversity of housing types was offered to accommodate various inhabitants. Townhouses are the closest to the windscreen; farther away are the semidetached units; and detached bungalows are at the outskirts. While the project creates a highly defined community in spatial and planning terms, it falls short of its full potential as a socially dynamic public realm. Nonetheless, it remains one of the most compelling site-specific and purpose-built modern experiments in urban form to be found in the subarctic and Arctic regions.

Experiments II: Prefabrication

As comprehensive new towns were being envisioned, the 1970s also saw a higher degree of technological experimentation at the building scale. Canadian architects, such as Papineau Gérin-Lajoie Le Blanc architectes and Moshe Safdie (1938–), among others, offered new technological responses to building in the Arctic. Due to the extreme climate and difficult access, the challenges—including material performance, material transport, availability of

skilled labor, and, of course, the significant costs of all of these—are unmatched by those in design and construction anywhere else in Canada.

Following the success of the Habitat 67 experimental housing project in Montreal [see pages 46–47 and 162–163], in 1974 Moshe Safdie was invited by the government of the Northwest Territories to develop prototypes to replace government housing. **FIGS 12–13** One scheme he proposed was a series of modular, structurally independent octagonal units, which could be arranged in rows and terraced on a slope facing the bay. The modular strategy meant the units could be extended horizontally, vertically, or diagonally. The repetitive nature of this project raised the question of how many units one might cluster within a given neighborhood or community and still achieve a reasonable population density. They were to be made of stress-skinned panels covered with a fiberglass gelcoat, and they'd be built on piles, with only a cold room and a vestibule at grade. The elevated main level, based on an octagonal layout, had two wedges omitted from the plan to provide light and views. The remaining six wedges contained kitchen, dining area, and bedrooms, with a common living room and stair in the central space.

Safdie had difficulty relating the project to context, because the community was still transitioning from its former identity as a military camp. Reflecting on this dilemma, he

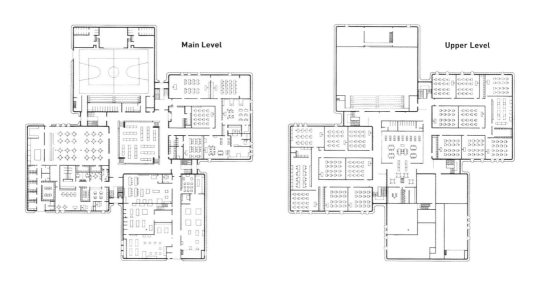

Main Level

Upper Level

17 above
**Nakasuk Elementary
School, Iqaluit, Nunavut.
Papineau Gérin-Lajoie
Le Blanc architectes, 1973.**

18 opposite
**Igloolik Research Centre
under construction,
Igloolik, Nunavut. Papinau
Gérin-Lajoie Le Blanc
architectes, 1975.**

noted that "contextualism was to recognize the extraordinary conditions that are unique to the place, but there wasn't an architectural heritage that one could identify with the region; one had to invent something new."[25] The project was to be built by a Japanese firm that was considering setting up in Canada. When the company withdrew, alternative construction methods rendered the prototype too expensive.[26]

Possibly the most successful experiments of this era were designed by Montreal firm Papineau Gérin-Lajoie Le Blanc architectes (PGL). Montreal had long been a vital connection to the eastern Arctic, because it possessed a strategic port for shipping materials and goods and offered access to prefabrication and resupply businesses. Over three decades, PGL developed designs that were both innovative for the time and acknowledged the specific logistical challenges of modern Arctic architecture.

In 1968, under the leadership of principal Guy Gérin-Lajoie (1928–2015), the firm began work in the Arctic with a small addition to the school in Pangnirtung, on Baffin Island. PGL's first stand-alone building in the North was the Gordon Robertson Educational Centre in Frobisher Bay, Iqaluit, completed in 1973. **FIGS 14–16** Along with six later projects by PGL, it employed what Gérin-Lajoie called a "composite total building" concept, which integrated a system of faceted, prefabricated panels made of glass fiber–reinforced polyester resin with an internal layer of insulating foamed polyurethane. Gérin-Lajoie advocated for this system because of its speed and ease of construction and its potential to make use of local labor and skills. The building enclosures could be erected in thirty-five days by a team of four workers and one supervisor, and the panels were small enough to be lifted without heavy machinery. The quick build time allowed the frame and skin to be constructed during the short summer season and the interior to be finished afterward within a climate-controlled shell.[27] As historian Marie-Josée Therrien notes: "[Gérin-Lajoie] approached the challenges of the region with the enthusiasm of an inventor and the mindset of an industrial designer, at a time when the field of plastic manufacturing was making major strides."[28]

The 1973 Nakasuk Elementary School in Iqaluit is emblematic of many of PGL's buildings, which are notable for their unique shape, geometric cladding, and seemingly hermetic quality due to a scarcity of windows, reflecting a perception of the climate as inhospitable.[29] **FIG 17** In the Nakasuk School, modularity shapes the interior space as well as the exterior cladding, and provisions for an addition are also incorporated into the design. PGL completed five public projects in Iqaluit alone, and their use of prefabricated fiber-reinforced plastic began to define, at the time, a local vernacular suggestive of an Arctic approach to architecture. **FIG 18**

Constructing Consensus

Many of these urban design, architectural, and technological experiments occurred in an era when decision-making in the Arctic was still overseen by federal authorities in Ottawa. In recent decades, communities have grown and the territories have gained political autonomy; in tandem, an increasing number of buildings have been designed that better accommodate culturally integrated programs and practices. This can be seen in firms such as Ferguson Simek Clark Engineers and Architects (now Stantec Architecture), Pin Matthews Architects (later Pin/Taylor Architects, now Taylor Architectural Group), EVOQ (formerly FGMDA, and led by Arctic-specialized principal Alain Fournier) and, more recently, Kobayashi Zedda Architects and Blouin Orzes Architectes. This contemporary Arctic vernacular is primarily seen across the territories in social and cultural projects, such as schools, cultural centers, and government facilities.

The Legislative Assembly of the Northwest Territories in Yellowknife, by Ferguson Simek Clark and Pin Matthews Architects, in association with Matsuzaki Wright Architects, provides a distinct example of a northern vernacular. Completed in 1993, it resulted from lengthy debate and discussions on an architectural identity for the Northwest Territories. **FIGS 19–20** The team chose a location on the southern edge of Frame Lake, where the building would nestle into rock outcroppings with minimal disturbance of the trees and ground. By facing the building to the lake rather than to the urban center of Yellowknife, the design intent was to connect the low-slung legislature to its natural

19 above
Legislative Assembly of the Northwest Territories, Yellowknife, Northwest Territories. Ferguson Simek Clark Engineers and Architects and Pin Matthews Architects in association with Matsuzaki Wright Architects, 1993.

20 right
Legislative Assembly of the Northwest Territories, ground-floor plan.

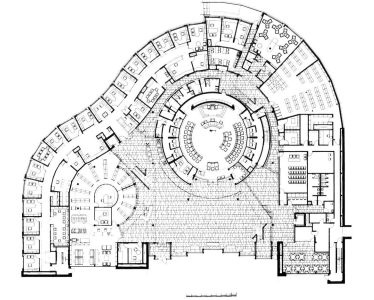

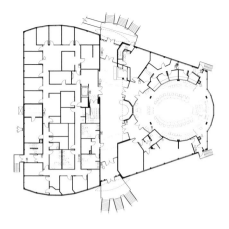

surroundings, encouraging government members to identify themselves within the landscape. A great hall serves as a community gathering space, and the legislature includes a one-story caucus as well as administrative offices that wrap around a drum-shaped chamber. The exterior is clad with a mix of sheet and cast panels made from zinc mined within the territory. The Legislative Assembly includes a comprehensive landscape design developed with landscape architect Cornelia Hahn Oberlander (1921–) of Vancouver. By embracing the principle of minimal intervention, the plan takes advantage of native plant species to conserve biological diversity. A subsequent collaboration between Pin and Oberlander, at the East Three Secondary School in Inuvik (2012), explores similar ambitions of integrating building and landscape.

A few years later, the Legislative Building of Nunavut (1999) in Iqaluit was completed by Montreal-based ARCOP Group with Keith Irving of Full Circle Architecture in Iqaluit, to house the territory's newly formed government. **FIGS 21–22** When Nunavut was established in 1999, government institutions were strategically decentralized and spread throughout the territory. This stemmed from a desire to distribute the wealth of administrative jobs, as well as from an attempt to imagine a less hierarchical political structure that brought government closer to residents.[30] As a result, the designers of the legislature were also asked to construct smaller, community-based government buildings and housing.[31] ARCOP's Norman Glouberman and Bruce Allan, the lead architects on the project, suggested constructing government housing in Iqaluit as a first step; the housing would be used as a training ground for local tradespeople, who would then work on the legislature building. In order to leverage the skills gained from housing construction, the legislature was designed as a heavy timber structure, an unusual move for a public building in Nunavut. The program was effective: 70 percent of the workforce was Inuit.[32] The ark-like profile of the building is shaped in response to wind and snow. The resulting legislature is one of the most striking buildings in Iqaluit, even though it is unceremoniously located in a downtown parking lot. The temporary nature of the facility may explain the perfunctory siting—it was designed to be leased by Nunavut Construction Company to the government for twenty years and then converted to offices once a permanent legislature is built.[33]

21 opposite, left
Nunavut Legislature
Building, Iqaluit, Nunavut.
ARCOP Group with Full
Circle Architecture, 1999.

22 opposite, right
Nunavut Legislature
Building, first-floor plan.

23 above
Keewatin Regional
Education Centre, Rankin
Inlet, Nunavut. Ferguson
Simek Clark Engineers and
Architects, 1986.

The design of schools is perhaps the clearest record of architecture's evolving role in the Arctic region, and represents the political and cultural aspirations embedded within both federal and territorial governments.[34] In many Arctic communities, the school takes on a significant role—serving simultaneously as place of learning, performance space, and meeting and education space for community groups, among other functions. Yet the design of schools remains a difficult issue because of the profoundly troubling legacy of residential schools in Canada; for many Indigenous people forcibly removed from their homes as children, schools were places of physical and emotional abuse, and indeed of cultural genocide.[35]

Since the 1980s, when most residential schools had closed, there have been several significant education buildings designed by architects such as Ferguson Simek Clark, Pin / Taylor, and Stantec. Community consultation is increasingly integrated into the early phases of the design process to better integrate Indigenous values and priorities. The Maani Ulujuk Elementary and Junior High School in Rankin Inlet (1982), by Clive Clark of Boigon and Armstrong Architects, exemplifies early efforts at taking a consultative approach, and dozens of additional schools and community centers followed in similar fashion.[36]

The Keewatin Regional Education Centre (1986), designed to house 108 students in double rooms, with two apartments for supervisors, innovated in its approach to massing and building envelope. **FIG 23** The protruding volumes were designed to enable easy expansion of the building at a future date. The red metal volumes adjacent to each window were adapted, with input from Gino Pin and Harold Strub, to enable a fresh-air vent in each room without permitting snow to enter. These seemingly simple innovations hint at new northern vernaculars.

Pin / Taylor Architects' many school designs include the Kiilinik High School (2002) in Cambridge Bay, Nunavut; the K'Alemi Dene School (2009) in N'Dilo near Yellowknife, Northwest Territories; and the East Three Secondary School (2012) in Inuvik. The Kiilinik High School is a low, saucer-like building with a rounded roof. **FIGS 24–25** The simplicity of the form is both modern and traditional. A cultural heritage center and public library

24 opposite
Kiilinik High School,
Cambridge Bay, Nunavut.
Pin / Taylor Architects,
2002.

25 right
Kiilinik High School,
interior.

are incorporated into the building; in small Arctic communities, modest populations and high construction costs require buildings to serve multiple functions. The rounded building turns its back to the wind: its geometry minimizes snow buildup on and around the building and uses natural wind-flow patterns to scour the perimeter of snow. Clerestory glazing and skylights extend the amount of light entering the school in winter, when daylight is limited, while reducing the amount of solar gain from the long summer sun. Like many of Pin's building, the Kiilinik School is clad in a simple material palette: its exterior is made primarily of relatively inexpensive corrugated steel, which is resistant to cold temperatures, wind, and freeze-thaw impacts.

Like Pin / Taylor Architects, Kobayashi + Zedda Architects (KZA), based out of Whitehorse, Yukon, have developed a body of work responding to the Arctic's unique climate and culture, as well as the logistical realities specific to Yukon. A formative early project for the Yukon firm was the 1998 Dänojà Zho Cultural Centre in Dawson City, Yukon, completed under the predecessor firm Florian Maurer Architect (of which Jack Kobayashi was copartner) [see pages 128–129]. **FIG 26** The building was originally conceived as the Han Cultural Centre—a place for the Han people, the original residents of the area, to tell their story. It is sited with a remarkable view to the Yukon River, activating the town's relationship to the water's edge. The center offers spaces to collect and display artifacts and to host cultural events from dance to storytelling. Inspired in part by the structural logic of Indigenous fish racks and traps, the building evokes this traditional construction both in its materials and building forms and sits in striking contrast to the Klondike-era Edwardian architecture of most of Dawson City. The delicate façade structure represents a significant challenge in the north, where volumes tend to be simple and monolithic in order to achieve stringent building performance.[37]

A more recent cultural centre by KZA, the John Tizya Centre, completed in 2011 in Old Crow, evolves the notions of a northern vernacular. The cultural center is the second building KZA has built in this remote Yukon community, and has no road and, very unusual for the north, no boat access. As a result, all building materials had to be sent by plane and were limited to 3.3 feet (one meter) in width, the dimension of the

plane aperture. **FIG 27** To this end, the building is constructed using Structural Insulated Panels (SIPs) to minimize on-site labor costs and material waste. As with many of their recent projects, building massing, use of color, and expressive use of technology begin to form a highly regionally specific architectural expression.[38]

Piqqusilirivvik is the Inuktitut name for the Inuit Cultural Learning Facility in Clyde River, Nunavut, by the Iqaluit office of Stantec Architecture with Fielding Nair Interna-tional. **FIGS 28–29** The project was opened in 2011 after a six-year process of collabo-rative integrated design. This entailed a two-year-long feasibility study involving workshops with elders and cultural advocates, in addition to research on folk schools and alternative education. Another year of elder consultation by the government of Nunavut included visits to many facilities around the territory to develop a working brief and proto-program. A three-year collaborative integrated design process followed, with workshops at all stages, both on-site in Clyde River and via virtual meetings.

The learning center represents a programmatic shift toward aligning public governance with local organizations and grassroots initiatives that strengthen and foreground cultural practices and learning methods. Rather than a static school or cultural center, it is active and constantly evolving—a laboratory for testing a curriculum that is taught and learned on the land, and which promotes the transfer of knowledge of traditional skills and crafts while reinforcing language skills. The building contains dedicated spaces for a sewing workshop, woodshop, library, skin preparation workshop, and large-capacity kitchen. These are arranged, according to one of the designers, "in a configuration that opens into and overlaps with flexible communal gathering and studio areas."[39] The building is a single story to support elders' needs and maintain a direct connection to the ground. In addition, Clyde River is known for some of the largest snowfalls and strongest winds in Nunavut; the building is therefore shaped and oriented to mitigate snow drift at its entries, clerestories, and mechanical intakes. One striking aspect of the project is its siting: it is somewhat removed from the town itself, since it was conceived as a territorial facility, as opposed to serving a single community.

More recent projects, such as the 2018 Illusuak Cultural Centre completed by Saunders Architecture with Stantec in Nain, Nunatsiavut, represent a new shift in priorities for cultural buildings in the North. **FIG 30** Here, a more global modernist sensibility, with expanded formal and material aspirations, is in evidence. The project is a multigenerational cultural center for the Labrador Inuit, and includes an exhibition space, auditorium, café, and offices for the Nunatsiavut government and Parks Canada. Located about 125 miles

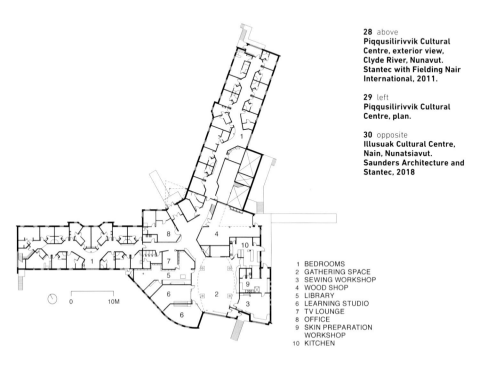

28 above
Piqqusilirivvik Cultural Centre, exterior view, Clyde River, Nunavut. Stantec with Fielding Nair International, 2011.

29 left
Piqqusilirivvik Cultural Centre, plan.

30 opposite
Illusuak Cultural Centre, Nain, Nunatsiavut. Saunders Architecture and Stantec, 2018

1 BEDROOMS
2 GATHERING SPACE
3 SEWING WORKSHOP
4 WOOD SHOP
5 LIBRARY
6 LEARNING STUDIO
7 TV LOUNGE
8 OFFICE
9 SKIN PREPARATION
   WORKSHOP
10 KITCHEN

0   10M

(200 kilometers) south of Torngat Mountains National Park, the Illusuak Cultural Centre is also envisioned as a beacon to promote cultural and ecological tourism in a region where the lack of intercommunity roads makes this challenging. Given the complex nature of building in the Arctic and subarctic, and the tendency toward cost efficiency, the formal ambition of Illusuak is notable.[40] More successfully than most Arctic buildings, it navigates between the existing fabric of the town and the natural geography of the water's edge (its proximity to the water demanded the construction of a raised ground). The project fuses a reinterpretation of fluid traditional forms with modern construction detailing, offering a new understanding of an Arctic vernacular.

Conclusions, Projections

Historically, architecture in the Arctic was a colonialist tool imposed by newcomers, bringing about conformity via modernity. Historian Harold Kalman, in his 1994 *History of Canadian Architecture*, cites a northern architect of the time: "Many Northern designers have adopted an approach to design that is more pragmatic, and consequently less appealing…[producing] 'tight and well constructed buildings [that] strive to work in harmony with the local climate and circumstance.'"[41] Such an argument, while true, might be taken as an excuse for architecture stripped of all quality. While not without failures, the technological and urban experiments of the 1970s were important in their quest for innovation and climatic responsiveness. Toward the end of the twentieth century, however, there emerged a generation of architects working across the Arctic that sought to identify a more culturally appropriate architecture.

In a region where all permanent buildings and settlements are less than seventy years old, what a truly Arctic architecture, landscape, and planning might look like is yet to be fully imagined. With an unfortunate amount of design being supplanted by concerns for expediency and efficiency, and curtailed by a fear of committing more mistakes, there is still not enough design risk-taking in Arctic architecture. New material assemblies, culturally informed programs, climatic-inclusive responses, co-designing methods, and approaches to logistics beckon the contemporary Arctic vernacular. Architecture and planning could potentially be effective tools of cultural empowerment—a means of making unique community patterns and family traditions spatially manifest.

Several new factors are emerging as the next challenges for architecture and planning in the Arctic. One of the limitations of recent work is a continued focus on singular buildings rather than the relationship among buildings and how they produce an urban realm. Another factor is the increasing relevance and role that an Arctic public realm might serve for its inhabitants. As Arctic communities continue to grow in population and in built footprint, how might mobility and seasonality shape urban thinking? A third factor is better responding to how most of the Arctic's Indigenous people (and many *qallunaat*) feel most content out on the land. The relationship of architecture to ground, landscape, and territory is an essential concept. A fourth factor is the increased need for Indigenous architects from the Arctic working in the Arctic—there is an urgent need for a design school in the northern territories. Architects have an enormous responsibility to design the Arctic's communities and the collective realm in a way that reflects its people, their values, their identity, and their sense of place today.

Centers
of Influence

13

The Architecture of Quebec: Competition, Culture, and Conservation

David Theodore

Quebec politicians like to debate whether the province, home to North America's largest French-speaking population, is a *distinct society*. This political term is frustratingly contentious, but its use has broadened to refer to more than just Quebecers' political battle for special constitutional and linguistic rights within Canada. It's now shorthand for the province's unique, identifiable features of education, language, governance, immigration patterns, demographics, and pop culture that animate daily life and public ritual.

But does Quebec have a distinct architecture? If we look at form and style only, perhaps not. Contemporary buildings in Quebec look a lot like buildings anywhere in North America. Mies van der Rohe's Westmount Square (with Greenspoon, Freedlander, Dunne, Platcha & Kryton, 1967) and KPMB Architects' two skyscrapers for Concordia University in Montreal (with Fichten Soiferman et associés architectes, 2011) are remarkable projects in Montreal's skyline that are formally similar to projects by the same architects in Toronto. Saucier + Perrotte's Perimeter Institute for Theoretical Physics (2004) in Waterloo, Ontario, for instance, is a spectacular icon that clearly extends the firm's work in Quebec, which includes the Cinémathèque québécoise (1997) and Collège Gérald-Godin (1999). **FIGS 1–2** The Perimeter Institute boasts a black anodized aluminum facade along with modular glass boxes and *passerelles*, details worked out for Montreal and seemingly

1 opposite
**Perimeter Institute for
Theoretical Physics,
north facade, Waterloo,
Ontario. Saucier + Perrotte
architectes, 2006.**

2 above
**Cinémathèque québécoise,
Montreal, Quebec. Saucier
+ Perrotte architectes,
1997.**

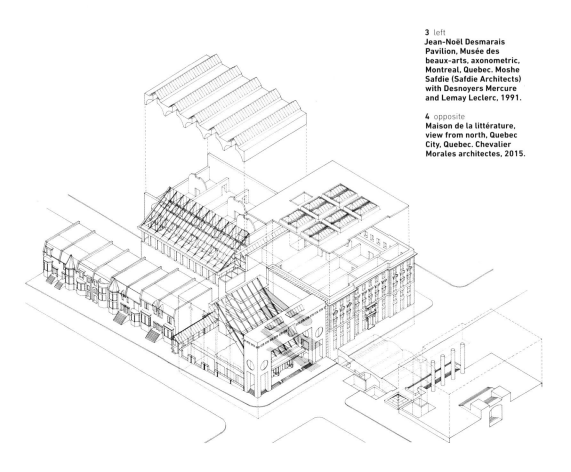

3 left
**Jean-Noël Desmarais
Pavilion, Musée des
beaux-arts, axonometric,
Montreal, Quebec. Moshe
Safdie (Safdie Architects)
with Desnoyers Mercure
and Lemay Leclerc, 1991.**

4 opposite
**Maison de la littérature,
view from north, Quebec
City, Quebec. Chevalier
Morales architectes, 2015.**

transposed to Waterloo. Yet the institute is located near other signature work, from Patkau Architects, Barton Myers, and, once again, KPMB. Indeed, rather than being visually distinct from other Canadian buildings, recent Quebec architecture exemplifies the trends and standards of taste that reign across Canada.

But this visual resemblance does not tell the whole story. Quebec architects have tried to produce distinct architecture, but not by producing buildings that are stylistically or visually Quebecois. The distinction has to do instead with how buildings get commissioned, why they are built, and how they are used to advance social goals and promote economic and artistic values.

Recent design and construction in the province reflects the ever-present tensions between tradition and modernism in Quebec's history.[1] On the side of tradition, historians tie the rise of a heritage conservation and preservation movement directly to the province's nationalist movements, particularly in Montreal.[2] These historians argue that the identification of a distinct historic architecture validates the longstanding struggle for recognition that Quebec comprises a distinct, sovereign nation. The discussion of Quebec as a nation independent from Canada has dominated the political history of the province since the so-called Quiet Revolution began around 1960. This was

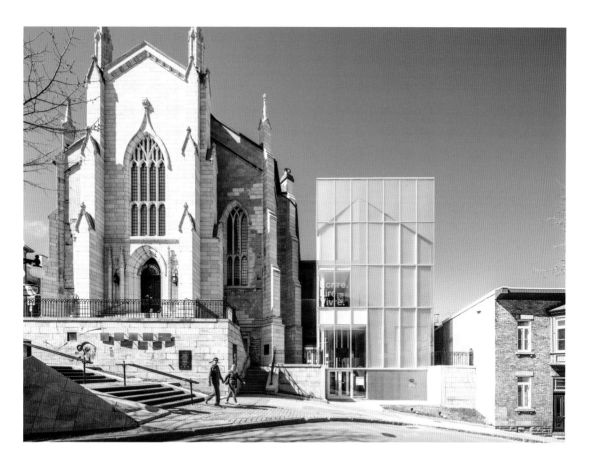

an age of rapid social and political change, marked by the secularization of health care and education, the nationalization of hydroelectric power, and the francization of government and government services. In 1976 Quebecers elected a government that advocated for separating from Canada, but the notion was defeated in referendums in 1980 and 1995.

On the side of modernism, Quebec has an active system of competitions for public and civic architecture. The system's threefold purpose is to democratize and broaden the selection of architects who get commissions, to publicize state-funded projects, and to obtain better architecture. The state government, including both elected politicians and provincial bureaucracy, does not advocate a particular style but instead funds contemporary architecture as part of its support for a panoply of arts and cultural programs.[3]

A distinctly Quebec building is generally defined by these basic elements: competition, culture, conservation. The building is commissioned through a competition process; its purpose is to promote *québécois* culture; and it directly engages an existing, often historic, structure. The list of such projects is long. For the Jean-Noël Desmarais Pavilion (1991) of the Musée des beaux-arts in Montreal designed by Moshe Safdie (1938–), preservationists successfully lobbied to have the architect incorporate the century-old facades of the

**Maison de la littérature,
view of library, Quebec City,
Quebec. Chevalier Morales
architectes, 2015.**

**Maison de la littérature,
cross-section and second-
floor plan.**

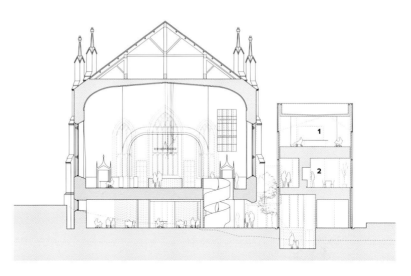

1 COMIC ARTS STUDIO
2 WRITER'S RESIDENCE
3 EXHIBITION ROOM
4 MULTIPURPOSE ROOM
5 PERMANENT EXHIBITION
6 CIRCULATION DESK
7 SCREENING ROOM
8 COLLECTIONS

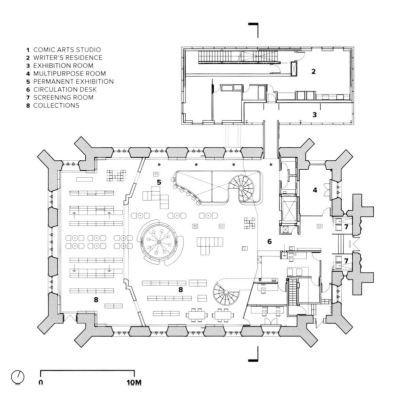

0   10M

7 left
Maison de la littérature, library and balcony, Quebec City, Quebec. Chevalier Morales architectes, 2015.

8 opposite
Musée Pointe-à-Callière, Montreal, Quebec. Dan Hanganu architectes, 1992.

New Sherbrooke Apartments into the design. **FIG 3** The Musée de la civilisation in Quebec City, also a competition-winner designed by Moshe Safdie (with Belzile Brassard Gallienne Lavoi, Sungur Incesulu, and Desnoyers Mercure, 1980), integrated historic office buildings in the Old Port. Nearby, the Maison de la littérature by Chevalier Morales Architectes (2015) perfectly demonstrates the three basic elements: the architects won a competition to remodel an 1848 neo-Gothic church. Originally a touchstone of the English-speaking Methodist community, the building is now dedicated to the propagation of secular French culture. The architects conserved the original structure, renovating the windows and painting the interior white, and added a prismatic glass-walled rectangular annex that holds studios and, behind metallic louvers, an apartment for a writer-in-residence. **FIGS 4–7**

This template—competition, culture, and conservation—is heuristic; other projects of note fulfill only parts of the formula. This is the case with two buildings that have their origins in archaeological digs that were carried out around 1980. The Musée Pointe-à-Callière (Hanganu/Provencher Roy/Lapointe Magne, 1992), a museum of archaeology and history, was not directly commissioned through a competition. **FIGS 8–12** The built project, however, conserves a small collection of seven heritage buildings and displays the

9 above
**Musée Pointe-à-Callière,
entrance hall, Montreal,
Quebec. Dan Hanganu
architectes, 1992.**

10 opposite, top left
**Musée Pointe-à-Callière,
underground gallery.**

11 opposite, top right
**Musée Pointe-à-Callière,
tower.**

12 opposite, bottom
**Musée Pointe-à-Callière,
conceptual sketch.**

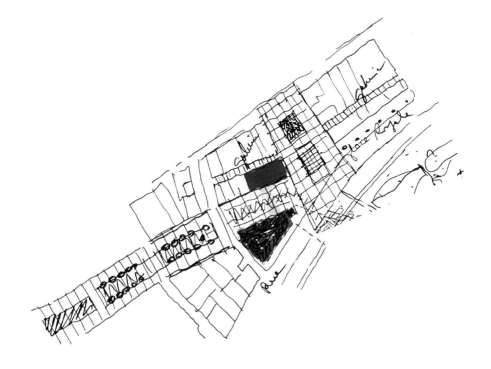

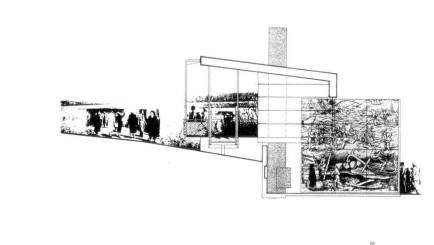

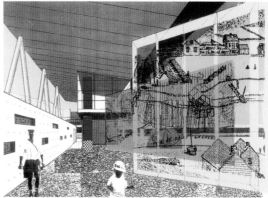

13 opposite, top
Centre d'interprétation du
Bourg de Pabos, view from
east, Pabos Mills, Quebec.
Atelier Big City, 1993.

14 opposite, bottom
Centre d'interprétation
du Bourg de Pabos,
Interpretation Centre,
sections.

15 left
Centre d'interprétation
du Bourg de Pabos,
Interpretation Centre,
interior view.

16 right
Centre d'interprétation
du Bourg de Pabos,
Interpretation Centre,
concept drawing.

foundations of others. The design—a tour-de-force from Romanian émigré Dan S. Hanganu (1939–2017)—directly evokes the contours of the Royal Insurance building, which stood on the site from 1860 until a fire destroyed it in 1947. Hanganu composed facades from Montreal greystone (a type of limestone) historically used for prominent buildings in the city. In contrast, architecture firm Atelier Big City's Centre d'interprétation du Bourg de Pabos (1993) preserves no existing buildings. **FIGS 13–16** Atelier Big City won one of the pilot competitions that the Ministry of Culture ran in order to evaluate the potential of a province-wide competition system. The interpretation center, built in the Gaspésie, helps visitors understand the seventeenth-century fishing industry of the region. The building has large, movable walls that pivot to display exhibitions when the building is open, and close to form a compact box when it's not. The design exults in architectural elements, combining exposed-steel structural supports, ramps, floating boxes, and a vibrant mix of colors used to code program and enliven graphics—and just because the architects love color.

The architectural conservation of significant buildings—along with their adaptive re-use through additions, repurposing, renovations, and amalgamations—has itself generated major new projects. At the Maison Alcan complex (ARCOP, 1983), an atrium links five historic buildings built between 1872 and 1928 with a new tower. **FIG 17** The project was

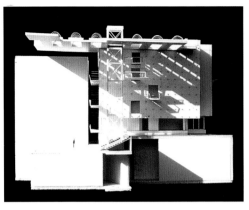

celebrated for the careful attention to historic conservation, overseen by Julia Gersovitz (1952–), and a meticulous aluminum curtain wall designed by Norman Slater (1921–2003). Yet its enduring legacy is the atrium contrived to conjoin the freestanding buildings. ARCOP (with Provencher Roy et associés) repeated the trick for the Centre de commerce mondiale (World Trade Center) in Montreal in 1992. Perhaps the most clever use of this strategy occurred five years later when Dan Hanganu architectes and Provencher Roy et associés used it to win a competition for the relocation of the Montreal Archives Centre to Viger Square (2000, part of the province-wide Bibliothèque et Archives nationales du Québec). **FIG 18** And the most spectacular version is seen in the CDP Capital building (now Édifice Jacques-Parizeau) (2003), designed by the consortium Gauthier Daoust Lestage / Faucher Aubertin Brodeur Gauthier / Lemay et associés. **FIG 19** Here, a thirteen-story horizontal skyscraper spans two city blocks. The atrium connects old and new buildings in a vast galleria at the second level. The atrium is articulated by white-painted steel columns and primarily lit through a wall of fritted glass on the south side.

The Quiet Revolution

Architecture in Quebec is marked by distinct approaches to land use, city making, commissioning, and state support for public and cultural institutions—all of which have been shaped by the province's history. In Quebec, modernization was split in two: the processes of urbanization and of secularization did not happen in parallel. Urbanization transformed Quebec well before World War I (Montreal is sometimes called the cradle of Canadian industry for its concentration of manufacturers established after the Lachine Canal opened in 1825), while secularization did not occur until after World War II. In fact, postwar secularization happened in tandem with deindustrialization as urban areas in Quebec switched from industrial to service economies. In 1960, the election of the Jean Lesage government led to a series of sociopolitical reforms known as the Quiet Revolution; these changes displaced the control that previously was held by the Catholic Church in areas such as education and health care, and by the Protestant elite in business affairs.

Architecture has been an important symbol in this revolution, and an active participant, accommodating the institutions generated by a newly secular state committed to the flourishing of French-language culture.

But just how does a society widely felt to be under the clerical control of the Catholic Church adapt to secular life?[4] As the provincial government took on the responsibilities formerly carried out by religious orders, architects were called on to design buildings for education, health, and transportation that would support the Quebec of the future. The initial network of twenty-five metro stations in Montreal, for instance, opened in 1966, just in time for the World's Fair in 1967 (Expo 67) [see pages 40–49]. Its planners promoted sophisticated architectural planning, incorporating innovative industrial design and a robust graphic program. Each station was given a unique identity, a goal achieved by commissioning a local architect for each, along with artwork from Quebec artists. Among the early stations, one standout is Peel Station, designed by Papineau, Gérin-Lajoie, Le Blanc architectes (PGL, 1966) with art from *automatiste* Jean-Paul Mousseau (1927–1991). **FIG 20** The combination of graphic design, architecture, and art transforms a mundane commute into a voyage inside a *Gesamtkunstwerk*. The élan of the initial proposal, however, has been lost in recent changes to the system. Though three new twenty-first century stations off the

20 opposite
**Peel Metro Station, view of
the concrete colonnade and
structure from the metro
platform, Montreal, Quebec.
Papineau Gérin-Lajoie
Leblanc architectes, 1966.**

21 right
**Anne-Marie Edward
Science Building at John
Abbott College, view
from public courtyard,
Sainte-Anne-de-Bellevue,
Quebec. Saucier + Perrotte
architectes, 2012.**

Island of Montreal in Laval extend the system to the suburbs, the stations have been treated as utilitarian infrastructural investments rather than opportunities to promote culture by commissioning work through the competition system.

Other infrastructure networks first imagined during the Quiet Revolution continue to provoke architectural experimentation. The network of postsecondary general and vocational colleges known as CEGEPs (Collèges d'enseignement général et professionnel du Québec) is a prime example. The state set up CEGEPs as a first step in taking over responsibility for education from the Catholic Church. The goal was to increase the percentage of college-educated citizens in the province and democratize access to higher learning, especially for accredited training. The original twelve CEGEPS in 1967 grew to forty-six by 1972.[5] Many early colleges were established in existing buildings. In 1971, John Abbot College, one of the few English-speaking CEGEPs, opened in a set of early twentieth-century red-brick structures on the West Island of Montreal. Today, the college is organized around Saucier + Perrotte's refined and elegant Anne-Marie Edward Science Building (2012). **FIG 21** The six-story building, kinked to wrap around a one-hundred-year-old gingko tree, features a facade of weathering steel, a sculptural staircase inside a light-filled atrium, and a glass-and-aluminum curtain wall ranging from transparent to translucent.

Quebec politicians promoted two events in particular to galvanize and symbolize the transformed society: Expo 67 and the 1976 Olympic Games. Expo 67 influenced architecture in diverse ways, directly and indirectly resulting in a corpus of buildings in addition to icons, such as Moshe Safdie's Habitat 67 housing complex.[6] [see pages 46–47 and 162–163] The expo's success generated novel institutions that subsequently became architectural clients; for example, in 1968 the government established the Institut de tourisme et d'hôtelerie du Québec (ITHQ) to provide leadership and support for the hotel industry, precisely because Expo 67 brought culinary culture and the economic power of tourism to the province's attention. The ITHQ received its first home in Montreal in 1970. In 2006, Lapointe Magne et associés with Aedifica won a Governor General's Award for readapting it, creating one of the earliest energy-saving double-skin facades in the province. **FIG 22** Expo 67 also

generated structural change in the profession. Scholars argue, for instance, that the high participation rate of women in Quebec architectural culture is a direct result of the cultural openness of Expo 67.[7]

If Expo 67 was the symbol of an unconstrained future, the 1976 Olympic Games—the first in which the host nation did not win an Olympic gold medal—symbolized Quebec's political and economic decline [see pages 80–82]. While the Olympic Games put Quebec on the world stage, they cast a dark shadow, especially over Montreal. The whole event went wildly over budget, creating municipal debt that was not paid off until 2006. The site, a zone of mixed public and private development, now holds a bland cinema complex and the equally banal twenty-thousand-seat Saputo Soccer stadium (2008). More successful are the recent projects—both on the grounds and in the neighboring Botanical Gardens—that were commissioned through competitions. The former Olympic velodrome is now, in its new form, one of Quebec's most visited attractions: a science museum called the Biôdome (Williams Asselin Ackaoui et associés with TPL, 1992). One of the Botanical Garden's showpieces is Saucier + Perrotte's Pavillon du Jardin des Premières-Nations (also with Williams Asselin Ackaoui et associés, 2001). **FIGS 22–25** Set between two themed gardens, the pavilion includes an undulating, prefabricated concrete roof floating over a verdant landscape.

22 opposite
Institut de tourisme et
de d'hôtelerie du Québec
(ITHQ) renovation, main
entrance and double-skin
facade, Montreal, Quebec.
Lapointe Magne & Aedifica,
2006.

23 above
Pavillon du Jardin des
Premières-Nations,
exterior view, Montreal,
Quebec. Saucier + Perrotte
architectes, 2001.

24 right
Pavillon du Jardin des
Premières-Nations, plan.

25
Pavillon du Jardin des
Premières-Nations,
interior view, Montreal,
Quebec. Saucier + Perrotte
architectes, 2001.

26 above
**Grande Bibliothèque,
competition-phase
rendering, Montreal,
Quebec. Patkau Architects
with Croft Pelletier and
Menkès Shooner Dagenais
architectes, 2005.**

27 opposite
**Grande Bibliothèque,
interior.**

Select artifacts are displayed outside in glass cases protected only by the roof. Half of the indoor functions are buried underground, beneath rooms covered in weathering steel.

Ironically, both of these international events promoting Quebec's nationalist identity relied largely on architects from outside Quebec. When it comes time to build, a number of institutions in the province continue to struggle with the conflicting desires for an architect of international renown and for an architecture that promotes Quebec identity, as well as with parsimonious budgets. One prominent example is the 2000 international competition for the Grande Bibliothèque. The building was to be the flagship of the province-wide Quebec library and archives system, modeled on a wave of new central libraries cropping up in cities such as Phoenix, Vancouver, and Seattle. Iraqi-born British architect Zaha Hadid won an honorable mention for her entry. It would have been Hadid's first commission in North America, but the jury judged it technically ambitious—and, therefore, economically risky. Instead, the first prize went to a consortium led by Vancouver-based Patkau Architects (with Croft Pelletier and Menkès Shooner Dagenais, 2005). **FIGS 26–27** It is now the most visited public library in all of the French-speaking world, partly due to the varied interiors provided by a spiraling *promenade architecturale* and a compact, daylight-filled underground connection to the city's central metro station.

One promise of the Quiet Revolution was that important commercial and civic commissions might open up to French-speaking architects. A turning point was when Canadian Pacific Railway executives chose Roger D'Astous (1926–1998), a francophone who had studied for a year at Taliesin West with Frank Lloyd Wright (1867–1959), as the architect of their new railway hotel in Montreal, the 616-room Château Champlain (with John-Paul Pothier, 1967). At thirty-eight stories, it was, for a time, the tallest hotel in Canada. D'Astous (with Luc Durand) also designed the Olympic Village, a pair of pyramidal buildings with 980 apartments to house athletes at the 1976 games. Another young firm identified with the emerging possibilities for French-speaking architects was PGL, which, as mentioned above, won the commission for Peel metro station, as well as for the Quebec Pavilion at Expo 67. They also designed the Mirabel airport, a new international terminal that opened in 1975, just in time for the Olympic Games [see pages 86–89]. PGL's modular design incorporated flexibility for future change based on the projected growth of air traffic. Sadly, the airport closed to passenger traffic in 2004 and is now demolished.

The Competition System

Around 1990, the Quebec Ministry of Culture and Communications began to experiment with architectural competitions. Organizations such as the Ordre des architectes du Québec argued that in supporting cultural and civic facilities through public funding, the state had a duty to ensure the quality of institutional architecture. One key strategy adopted to achieve quality was the architectural competition, a process advocated by two Quebec design journals: *Section a: Revue d'architecture/Architecture Magazine* (1983–1986) and *ARQ: Architecture/Quebec* (1981–present).[8] The use of design competitions in Quebec has allowed for younger Quebec firms to secure public commissions, although it has not opened up commissions to as broad a group as many had hoped. A more complex issue has been the effective lowering of budgets. Quebec has neither a strong tradition of private charitable donations for architecture, as seen in the United States, nor the tradition of public funding found in Europe. In addition, architects building in Quebec with public money are subject to strict government schedules indifferent to the specific costs and timetables needed for museums, concert halls, and libraries.

If the infrastructure projects of the Quiet Revolution addressed Quebec society as a whole, recent competitions have focused on more modest improvements to underserved neighborhoods. Montreal, for instance, has built recreation and sport facilities where few existed before. For the Centre sportif de la Petite-Bourgogne (1997), Saia et Barbarese architectes used a skylit indoor street to separate a swimming pool from basketball courts and training rooms. **FIG 28** The result is a strong example of how architects adapt international trends—the influence of contemporary European architects, such as Rem Koolhaas/OMA, is clear—to the mores of a Montreal community. More recently, Saucier + Perrotte (with HCMA, 2015) designed the Stade de soccer de Montréal, a training facility for soccer

28
Centre sportif de la Petite-
Bourgogne, interior street,
Montreal, Quebec. Saia
Barbarèse Topouzanov
architectes, 1997.

development in the Saint-Michel district. **FIG 29** The building sits on the edge of the Miron Quarry, which the city first used as a waste disposal site but is now turning into a large urban park. The building's forms echo the fissures and layers of stone in the quarry. An immense, twisted black roof made of a visible cross-laminated timber structure makes the building an instant landmark for a neighborhood that has become the landing point for multiple soccer-playing immigrant communities. The southern edge of the quarry is occupied by the Cité des arts du cirque, a complex dedicated to the circus arts featuring outstanding buildings also commissioned through competitions, including the international headquarters of the renowned Cirque du soleil (Dan S. Hanganu, 1997, additions by FABG in 2000 and 2008), the National Circus School (Lapointe Magne et associés, 2003), and a circular performance venue called TOHU (Schème/Jacques Plante/Jodoin Lamarre Pratte et associés, 2004).

Since government funding for cultural buildings has come attached with a mandate to commission architects through competitions, and since competition-winning projects tend to be striking landmarks, one clear effect of competitions has been the production of iconic buildings outside major cities, such as tourism facilities. Many have gone on to win provincial and national design awards. Atelier In Situ's elegant wood pavilion at the Jardins de Métis in Gaspésie (with Vlan paysages, 2004) provides a permanent welcome

29 opposite
Stade de soccer de Montréal, view from soccer field, Montreal, Quebec. Saucier + Perrotte architectes with HCMA, 2015.

30 right
Amphithéâtre Cogeco, Trois-Rivières, Quebec. Atelier Paul Laurendeau with Beauchesne Architecture, 2015.

center for visitors to the gardens and to its annual International Garden Festival. The festival has showcased a cavalcade of talent, with projects chosen through an open competition each year, including works from Catalyse Urbaine, Hal Ingberg, Claude Cormier, NIP Paysage, and Collectif EKIP. The Amphithéâtre Cogeco (2015), designed by Paul Laurendeau and realized with Beauchesne Architecture, has succeeded in attracting tourists to the postindustrial city of Trois-Rivières. **FIG 30** Its thin red roof, which soars overhead on eight slender columns, is now a beloved icon and a sign of the city's economic ambitions.

Competition-winning architecture has also helped religious organizations downsize their buildings for their aging communities. Dan S. Hanganu's Abbey Church for the Benedictine Monastery at Saint-Benoît-du-Lac (1994) and Atelier Pierre Thibault's Abbaye Val Notre-Dame for the Cistercian order (2009), although very different in character, both make the most of magnificent natural settings. **FIGS 31–32** A sign of the times is that these religious buildings, too, include facilities for accommodating tourists.

Architectural competitions have also transformed the public library system. Notoriously, Quebec had few public libraries before the Quiet Revolution.[9] At the beginning of the twentieth century, Canadian communities jostled to build free public libraries with funding from the American industrialist Andrew Carnegie—but of the 125 Carnegie libraries in Canada, none were built in Quebec. Starting with the competition for the Grande Bibliothèque at the end of the twentieth century, new political support for the public library system has galvanized library architecture. Adapting churches as libraries has been one way to retain a social purpose for religious buildings no longer in use.[10] In Quebec City, Dan Hanganu (with CLC architects, 2013) repurposed the Église de Saint-Denys-du-Plateau, originally designed by Jean-Marie Roy (1925–2011) in 1964, to create the Bibliothèque Monique-Corriveau. To provide a foil to the dramatic, modernist concrete of the church, he added a rectangular glass pavilion housing a white-painted steel structure and stair.

Quebec municipalities are investing in libraries just as digital access has exploded; simultaneously, the idea of the library as a third space for community gatherings and study has taken hold. The result, ironically, is that the new libraries give too much room

to books, especially at the expense of social areas. For instance, the Benny Library inside Notre-Dame-de-Grâce Cultural Centre (2016), a competition project won by Atelier Big City, Fichten Soiferman et associés architectes, and L'OEUF, originally featured a street-oriented entrance café that was cut from the final building. It's a disappointing loss because the architects took pains to provide room for multiple user groups, designing generous activity areas that overlap along a sectional zigzag.

Recent libraries in Quebec are also distinct because the program, technical requirements, scale, and budget are similar for all of the competition briefs; thus, there is homogeneity among the winning projects. They are generally two-story affairs with a stair that doubles as an informal reading area or amphitheater, and they usually feature a community room near the front entrance that can be used for exhibitions, meetings, and concerts even when the library is closed. Architects have adapted this model to a surprising variety of sites throughout the province. For example, Atelier TAG's Bibliothèque Raymond-Lévesque (with Jodoin Lamarre Pratt, 2011) takes a linear plan and wraps it around a small courtyard, creating a community focal point in the Longueuil borough of Saint-Hubert. **FIG 33**

Unfortunately, in more recent years, Quebec's competition system has rarely been used to commission major projects. In instances such as the controversial competition

for the expansion of the Palais des congrès, Montreal's downtown convention center, the choice of architect was but a part of an overall developer package.[11] The original Palais, commissioned through a competition in 1984 won by Victor Prus (1917–2017), occupied a brutalist concrete structure straddling the Ville-Marie expressway and an underground subway line. In 2000, Quebec architects boycotted a call for offers to expand the center because the government's real-estate arm (Société immobilière du Québec) included the condition that the architects would be chosen on the basis of the lowest fees. Eventually, architects were selected as part of a developer bidding process. The winning team (a design consortium of Tétreault, Parent, Languedoc et associés, Saia et Barbarese architectes, Dupuis, Dubuc et associés [Aedifica], with Hal Ingberg architecte, independent architectural consultant, 2002) incorporated a series of existing buildings within the shell of the new expansion; for example, they repurposed an old fire station while also building a new one. The architects did their job well. The Palais' multicolored glass facade has become an icon of Montreal's new profile as a City of Festivals and a tourist destination. FIG 34 Yet, ever since, the government has awarded major commissions—including two university superhospitals, a multibillion-dollar investment in architecture—under public-private partnership models (P3s).[12]

These projects, including the long-anticipated home for the Montreal Symphony Orchestra (Diamond Schmitt Architects with Aedifica, 2011), have appeared in the city without emphasizing the lessons urbanism painstakingly learned since the Quiet Revolution. These projects reject the process of creating fine-grained streets through mixed programming; they neither reinforce the traditional Montreal urban grid nor repurpose existing buildings. Moreover, they do not work toward integration and continuity in existing neighborhoods through massing and materials. In particular, they do not address the city's legacy of greystone street facades, as did projects such as the Canadian Centre for Architecture [see pages 202–204], the Musée Pointe-à-Callière, and the CDP Capital Centre. The lack of quality in these P3 projects is implicit evidence that competitions do help achieve quality.

A frequent criticism of the competition system is that with public monies in play, too much value is placed on cost control and delivery. In 2013, the Musée des beaux-arts de Montréal held a competition for a new pavilion, the Michal and Renata Hornstein Pavilion for Peace. Atelier TAG, in consortium with Jodoin Lamarre Pratt, won the commission with evocative perspective renderings that promised a sophisticated limestone facade, recalling the greystone heritage of Montreal's civic buildings. In the course of design development and construction, however, the stone was exchanged for external vertical aluminum

louvers—a measure that visibly altered the competition-winning concept but which the client reported ensured the on-time, on-budget delivery of the project. Indeed, the pavilion opened in 2016, just in time for Montreal's 375th anniversary in 2017.

In contrast, a project with a similar program arrived well over the initial budget and later than originally planned, but to international acclaim: namely, the Pierre Lassonde Pavilion (2016), an addition to the Musée national des beaux-arts du Québec in Quebec City. **FIG 35** In 2010, the museum held an international competition in search of a "starchitect" and subsequently announced OMA's Rem Koolhaas (1944–) as the winner.[13] The design was, in fact, carried out entirely by OMA New York, under the leadership of Shohei Shigematsu. Provencher Roy et associés, OMA's Quebec partner on the design, ensured that the design—whose signature moves include a 60-foot (18.3 meters) cantilever suspended 41 feet (12.5 meters) in the air—could be carried out with local construction teams and budgets. The irony of engaging an international architecture firm for a building that promotes Quebecois culture has mostly passed under the radar.

Planning the City

Urban development in the postwar era was as heroic and aggressive in Quebec as anywhere, with raised expressways ripping through the historic fabric of Trois-Rivières, Montreal, and Quebec City. Demolition was a key aspect of making room for new buildings in cities. One oft-cited example is the City of Montreal's razing of the "Faubourg à m'lasse," a working-class neighborhood, in order to build a tower for the Canadian French-language public broadcasting service (Maison de Radio-Canada, Tore Bjornstad, 1973).[14] Four years later, the La Cité project in Montreal (Eva Vecsei with Longpré Marchand Dobush et Stewart, 1977) called for commercial and residential skyscrapers near McGill University, a proposal defiantly resisted by the local Milton Park community.[15] Although a reduced version of the development was built, the resistance gave rise to an organized preservation movement.

Alongside local demolition, however, has come a recognition that Quebec's historic architecture is of international concern: UNESCO added the Historic District of Old

Quebec City to its World Heritage List in 1985, and, more recently, in 2006, Montreal was officially designated a UNESCO City of Design (the only one in Canada).

Quebec has also seen the creation of new cities in remote regions. Much urban settlement, particularly in the north, has been driven by the exploitation of natural resources. Fermont, for example, incorporated in 1974, is a company town adjacent to iron mines in the northeastern region of the province. The plan by Norbert Schoenauer (Desnoyers Schoenauer) takes inspiration from the environmental design ideas of Anglo-Swedish architect consultant Ralph Erskine [see pages 362–366]. **FIG 36** It is centered on a structure known as "the Wall," a four-to-six story, 0.8 mile-long (1.3 kilometer-long) windscreen building angled to block the prevailing winds.[16] A continuing challenge for architects is to find sensitive and appropriate ways to build in northern Quebec. Contemporary architecture in First Nations communities, for instance, is a growing concern. One project that serves as a model is Douglas Cardinal's design for the Cree town of Oujé-Bougoumou near Chibougamau east of James Bay in 1992, created in consultation with local elders [see pages 128–130].

In southern Quebec, architects have been asked to transform postindustrial sites into districts for the so-called creative class, aping urban theory popularized by Toronto-based professor Richard Florida (1957–). The stakes are clear in a project such as the redevelopment of Saint-Roch in Quebec City. This former working-class neighborhood has received investment from multiple levels of government to develop culture, education, and new technologies. The first investments came from the city and were used for municipal projects. Quebec's mayor asked Toronto urbanist Ken Greenberg to help design an urban park, the Jardin de Saint-Roch (1993, now the Jardin Jean-Paul-L'Allier), which was soon followed by facilities for artists. Émile Gilbert readapted nine connected buildings into Méduse, a city-funded, community-based artists' cooperative, in 1995. Saint-Roch now boasts restaurants, cafés, hotels, and—the sine qua non of revitalization—tech companies.

Funding for such endeavors often comes from provincial tax credit programs tied to the viability of small- and large-scale entrepreneurship.[17] Such a program spurred the creation of the Cité du Multimédia in Montreal in 1998. The development involved the construction

37 left
Discreet Logic (now AutoDesk) Building, edifice zone, Montreal, Quebec. Atelier In Situ, 1997.

38 right
La Promenade Samuel-de Champlain, Quebec City, Quebec. Daoust Lestage with Williams Asselin Ackaoui and Option Aménagement, 2008.

of offices for creative professionals in an industrial district of nineteenth-century warehouses and factories on the east side of Griffintown. In 1933, the Canadian National Railway had split the neighborhood in half with an elevated train line, a division reinforced in 1966 by the construction of the Bonaventure Expressway parallel to the tracks, built to link downtown to the site of Expo 67 (the Expressway was demolished in 2017 and is now a park). The Cité's most acclaimed building is Phase 8 by Dupuis LeTourneux (2003, now known as the Louis-Charland Building). Its eight-story, fritted-glass facade is visible from the expressway and the train tracks, and serves as a visual gateway to the whole district.

Within Griffintown, the entanglement of government programs and entrepreneurship overlaps with cultural initiatives. At the intersection of all these forces is a successful series of buildings by Atelier In Situ, a firm that, as the name suggests, specializes in readapting buildings. They placed a digital software company in a former boat-building factory (Discreet Logic; 1997); they installed Restaurant Da Emma (1998) in the basement of an eighteenth-century warehouse, once a prison for women; and they transformed the Darling Foundry, a disused metalworking factory, into a permanent home for the arts group Quartier Ephémère (2002). **FIG 37** Nearby in Old Montreal, Atelier In Situ collaborated with Shapiro Wolfe on the Phi Centre (2012), housed in an 1861 dry goods warehouse.

Established through private philanthropy, it is a recent example of the ongoing vitality of the arts-center model.

Quebecers' support for institutional initiatives over private ones has led to some innovative urban design processes. A key prototype was the campaign to revitalize the Old Port in Montreal in time for the City's 350th anniversary in 1992. The master plan, designed by Peter Rose / Cardinal Hardy / Jodoin Lamarre Pratt, included a linear park strategically dotted with pavilions [see pages 216–217]. For the restaurant Maison des Éclusiers (1993), architecture firm Cardinal Hardy used concrete and steel to reference the form and materials of existing and demolished industrial buildings. More recently, Daoust Lestage with Williams Asselin Ackaoui and Option Aménagement used a similar strategy at La Promenade Samuel-de Champlain. **FIG 38** Created for Quebec City's 400th anniversary in 2008, it is an exemplary combination of park, sports terrains, and follies that utterly remakes the St. Lawrence River waterfront, formerly given over to a highway.

Two other Daoust Lestage urban design projects involved bringing citizens as well as landowners into participatory planning processes. For the Place des Festivals in the Quartier des Spectacles (2009) the firm transformed underutilized land surrounding Montreal's performing arts center, Place des Arts, into a permanent year-round festival site.[18] **FIG 39** Drawing on strategies from planning and architecture, the design is conceived as an urban promenade that allows for small-scale, seasonal installations. The firm also planned the remarkably harmonious Quartier International de Montréal district (with Clément Demers and Provencher Roy et associés, 2004). Gaining buy-in from the surrounding landowners allowed for a much more thorough overhaul of the district's civic areas, including the refurbishment of Square Victoria, the creation of a new square named Place Jean-Paul Riopelle, and the deployment of bespoke urban furniture by industrial designer Michel Dallaire (1942–). The project has spurred development of tall condominium, hotel, and office buildings in the area, which is nevertheless still dominated by the Montreal icon from 1965, La Tour de la Bourse, designed by Italian architects Luigi Moretti and Pier Luigi Nervi (with Greenspoon Freedlander & Dunne).

Conclusion: Single-Family Homes and the Future of Quebec Architecture

I have structured this account of architectural production in Quebec since 1967, through the triadic rubric of competition, culture, and conservation. That rubric helps show that architecture and architectural practice are a valued part of civic life in Quebec—perhaps more so than in any other region of Canada. The public sector has influenced Quebec architecture through heritage preservation laws and through its support for competitions as a commissioning mechanism. In architecture, the rapid process of postwar secularization meant a change in how, why, and for whom architects worked. The role of the state in the production of architecture, therefore, cannot be underestimated. Recent architecture

is rooted in political decisions, including the birth of the sovereignty movement and the distinct social ethos it created. The use of public funds has also meant relatively low budgets, even for high-profile projects in Quebec, and a concomitant concern for modesty and judiciousness.

One goal of the competitions is to open up commissions for civic buildings to new voices, allowing smaller architectural firms to gain access to larger commissions through a robust competition system. Whether this policy has been successful is up for debate. The list of competition winners over the last half-century is surprisingly short and rarely admits new names. Therefore, in speculating about the future of architecture in Quebec, we might turn to the talented cohort of smaller offices adapting urban single-family homes to address social, geographic, environmental, and political issues. Quebec architects are currently re-examining Montreal's housing stock, readapting and reshaping the ubiquitous (and iconic) triplex, which has flourished in the city since the nineteenth century, to accommodate twenty-first-century life.

Developed to house the workers migrating from the countryside, these three-story brick houses, in which each floor has a self-contained residence, are joined by party walls every 25 feet (7.6 meters) and set back from the sidewalk to leave room for small gardens and steep iron staircases. The most celebrated design within Montreal is Jacques Rousseau's Maison Coloniale (1990). **FIG 40** The design pulls in references to urban history, the morphology of the city, vernacular construction techniques, and the elements of the typical Montreal triplex. The interior evokes a Montreal back lane with rough concrete, spiraling metal staircases, plywood floors, and garage doors. From the outside, its two concrete towers make it appear simultaneously deeply rooted in its site and provocatively out of place. Younger firms such as Pelletier de Fontenay and La Shed have also found their voices experimenting with the triplex's construction details, materials, planning, and beauty. Also worthy of mention are the light-and-brick formalisms of Thomas Balaban, the livability promoted by Nature Humaine, and the wonderfully finicky "inhabitable sculptures" of Jean-Maxime Lebrecque. It remains to be seen if this sensitivity to domestic design scales up if and when this generation of architects has a chance to build civic buildings.

In light of the above examples, it becomes clear that to include the competition system in the rubric of what distinguishes Quebec architecture has one obvious downside: it leaves out architecture commissioned and constructed outside of that system, notably commercial and domestic buildings. However, architects over the past half-century have engaged the other two parts of the triad—issues of heritage conservation and cultural promotion— in house design while also experimenting with a much broader array of issues, especially outside of the major cities. Peter Rose and Erik Marosi's striking Bradley House in North Hatley (1977) points to the ongoing influence of classic design principles [see pages 188– 189]. YH2's Géométrie Bleu (2003) on Les Îles-de-la-Madeleine displays the importance of regional culture and vernacular traditions. Pierre Thibault's sequence of award-winning wood-and-glass houses near Quebec City shows an ongoing fascination with the contrast between stunning rural landscapes and rigorous modern design. The off-reservation dwellings that Architectes de l'urgence du Canada helped build for the Anicinape community of Kitcisakik expose the need for better architecture in First Nations communities [see chapter 4]. And L'OEUF's House in Four Fields near Mont Tremblant (2015) speaks to ways architects are grappling with climate change and food security.

The architecture of the single-family home, then, also conforms to the rubric. We can understand all architecture in Quebec—commercial, civic, and domestic—through the same heuristic. If it is tempting to extrapolate that this three-pronged approach to architectural practice will continue in the future, it is because it has been so successfully implanted in the politics of everyday life. Debates about buildings in Quebec tend not to focus on formal tectonic qualities, but rather on the ways they articulate social values and tensions: the collective will versus individual expression, conservation and memory versus modernization and growth, a distinct Quebec architecture versus a desire to participate in global trends. Civic engagement remains the key forum for meaningful architecture in Quebec, a region where a distinct sense of a collective self is strong, reinforced by language and cultural traditions—and by architecture.

14

Toronto Architecture: Form and Reform

Elsa Lam

The week of September 13, 1965, some seventy thousand visitors entered Viljo Revell (1910–1964) and John B. Parkin Associates' New City Hall and Square in Toronto for the first time. **FIG 1** Guided building tours and a program of orchestral performances and square dances culminated in an evening event called "Toronto-A-Go-Go." The edifice in downtown Toronto, with its two curved towers and oyster-shell-shaped council chamber, was the most visually distinguished modernist building to arrive in the provincial capital city: to this day, the profile of the towers adorns the city logo.

The opening of New City Hall also marked a time of local growth: in the two decades following the Second World War, the combination of the baby boom and immigration doubled the city's population.[1] Toronto and its suburbs went through a period of intense development to accommodate the influx. Much of Toronto's architecture in the 1950s was influenced by the city's conservative Anglo-Saxon culture. Traditionalist firms, such as Marani & Morris and Mathers & Haldenby, produced stripped-down neoclassical buildings for banks and other businesses; they employed modern structural innovations but clad them in familiar brick and stone facades.[2]

But the same era also saw the emergence of a faction of modernist architects, including Peter Dickinson (1925–1961) of Page & Steele, Gordon Adamson (1904–1986) of Adamson

Associates, and Uno Prii (1924–2000). Together, these designers began to add modernist commercial, apartment, and institutional buildings to the built landscape of the city and its suburban outskirts.[3] Some, such as Dickinson, were British expats who brought an English modernist aesthetic, influenced by the 1951 Festival of Britain, to their work in Toronto. The work of these Toronto modernists was showcased in Don Mills, a progressive garden-city-style suburb to the northeast of downtown. Founded in 1953, Don Mills's developers aimed to promote modern architecture: all of the community's initial buildings were designed by company-selected architects, including Henry Fliess (1921–), James Murray (1919–2008), Irving Grossman (1926–), and Michael Bach (1916–1972).[4]

The most prominent among these practices was the partnership of British-born architects John Burnett Parkin (1911–1975) and John Cresswell Parkin (1922–1988, no blood relation). Under the banner of John B. Parkin Associates, the duo's early work included a number of low-slung, clean-lined commercial and industrial buildings in Don Mills. The Don Mills Convenience Centre (1955), erected just as regional shopping centers were emerging in North America, was a set of freestanding pavilions linked by covered walkways and open courtyards, and included canopies made of slender steel columns and metal decking. **FIG 2** The firm's own office was a minimalist steel-and-glass box with an open-plan

1 opposite
New City Hall and Square,
view from south, Toronto,
Ontario. Viljo Revell with
John B. Parkin Associates,
1965.

2 right
Don Mills Convenience
Centre, view of public
walkways and courts,
Toronto, Ontario. John B.
Parkin Associates, 1955.

interior, located nearby at Don Mills and York Mills Roads (1955). At times, the designers' rational, geometric structures used exposed concrete frames or included brick infill panels. The latter was the case in their competition-winning headquarters for the Ontario Association of Architects in the posh downtown residential neighborhood of Rosedale (1954). The plan was inspired by the designs of Walter Gropius (1883–1969), with whom John C. Parkin had studied. A decade later, the firm would design Toronto's new Aeroquay One terminal, a glass-walled ring encircling a square-plan parking garage that intricately wove together car and air traffic flows (1964; demolished 2004). The plan was seen as a major design innovation that influenced many other airports. By that time, John B. Parkin Associates had become the largest architectural firm in Canada.

By the early 1960s, modernist firms had more or less won out against traditionalist firms, and their victory was marked by a series of large-scale downtown developments.[5] The most prominent were New City Hall and the Toronto Dominion Centre (1967–1969). The latter, by Mies van der Rohe (1886–1969) with John B. Parkin Associates and Bregman & Hamann, was among the largest building projects in Mies's career. The finely detailed complex of two towers and a one-story banking hall was clad in dark glass with verticals resembling structural I-beams; it was set atop a podium with a shopping concourse sunk underground. The complex's sleek profiles dominated the skyline. On the southeast corner of the same intersection of King and Bay Streets, the center of Canada's financial sector, the glass and stainless steel that formed the main tower of Commerce Court by I. M. Pei & Partners with Page & Steele (1972) boasted 56-foot-long (17-meter-long) structural spans, creating an expansive, transparent lobby while retaining the historic bank building as one of its wings. FIG 3 Modernist forms were paired with opulent materials at the nearby First Canadian Place by Edward Durell Stone Associates with Bregman & Hamann (1975), a skyscraper clad with Carrera marble panels, and at Webb Zerafa Menkès Housden Partnership (now WZMH)'s Royal Bank Plaza towers (1976–1979), whose faceted facade uses mirrored, gold-coated glass.

Following the style of the times, and in the wake of New City Hall and the Centennial projects' success, the use of structural concrete also took firm hold, as seen in the

1.5-million-square-foot (457,000-square-meter) Sheraton Centre (John B. Parkin and Associates with Searle, Wilbee, and Rowland, and Seppo Valjus, 1972) erected opposite New City Hall. The Sheraton Centre incorporated elevated outdoor gardens—another trope of the era—as did the brutalist-style Hilton Toronto hotel, on the nearby corner of University Avenue (Searle, Wilbee, and Rowland with Reno C. Negrin Architects, 1975). On Bloor Street, the Manulife Centre (Clifford & Lawrie) included Toronto's tallest apartment building at the time of its construction in 1974, towering fifty-one stories high and fronted by a muscular office block that cantilevered over store facades at its base.

Toronto City Hall Legacy Firms

New City Hall was commissioned through an open design competition, a process that attracted international attention and talent to Toronto going beyond Viljo Revell's winning project. The yearlong global design competition, launched in September 1956, attracted some 520 entries from 42 countries. The eight finalists ranged from the Danish firm of Haldo Gunnløgsson & Jørn Nielson to a number of American entrants, including the well known Perkins+Will and the recently established I. M. Pei & Associates. An outlier among

3 opposite
View of Toronto skyline
from the south circa 1973,
showing Toronto Dominion
Centre and Commerce
Court towers.

4 above
New College (Wetmore and
Wilson Halls), aerial view,
Toronto, Ontario. Fairfield &
Dubois, 1964 and 1969.

the finalist entries was a truncated ziggurat of a building topped by a weave-patterned concrete roof, designed by a group of four students from Harvard's Graduate School of Design
in Boston. The quartet included American Macy DuBois (1929–2007) and Australian John
Andrews (1933–), both of whom moved to Toronto in 1958.

After several years with John B. Parkin and Associates, DuBois left to join architect
Robert Fairfield, forming Fairfield and DuBois in 1962. In his new firm, DuBois championed the sculptural use of masonry and exposed concrete in Toronto, with buildings
such as the heroic yet climate-sensitive Central Technical School Art Centre (1962) and
the Saarinen-influenced New College at the University of Toronto (1964–69). **FIG 4** The
latter is notable for its well-proportioned courtyard surrounded by residences and spaces
for learning.

John Andrews, for his part, also worked with John B. Parkin and Associates until 1962,
after which he established his own firm and taught at the University of Toronto, soon becoming chairman of the department of architecture. Andrews's firm came to prominence
with the design of Scarborough College (1966, with Page & Steele architects), a megastructure that laid the foundation for the University of Toronto's satellite campus east of
downtown [see pages 108–113 and 157–160].

John Andrews Architects was a key designer of Metro Centre, an ambitious 1960s masterplan for redeveloping the city's downtown railway lands with a series of megastructures. Only one component of the plan was ultimately realized: the iconic CN Tower (Webb Zerafa Menkès Housden Partnership with John Andrews and Quinn Dressel, 1976), which allowed for broadcast signals to travel over the increasingly tall buildings being constructed in Toronto's downtown. **FIG 5** The world's tallest freestanding structure for over thirty years, the tower is architecturally notable for its tapering form that extends from a Y-shaped base, and for making innovative use of concrete slip-forming for its construction. Andrews also began winning commissions in the United States, including for Gund Hall, which houses the architecture school at his alma mater, Harvard University (1972). In 1973, he expanded his practice to his native Australia, to which his offices were eventually relocated.

Infill Architecture and the Municipal Reform Movement

Just as the University of Toronto was a launch pad for John Andrews, it also proved an attractor for foreign-born architect Jack Diamond (1932–). Diamond left apartheid South Africa for the United States and was working for Louis Kahn (1901–1974) when he was recruited to become the founding director of the University of Toronto's architecture masters program in 1964, which he did while working as a partner with John Andrews. Diamond also edited the *Journal of the Royal Architectural Institute of Canada*, which allowed him extensive travel and a means for establishing a national network of contacts.[6]

In 1969, Diamond formed a partnership with American architect Barton Myers (1934–), another student of Louis Kahn's, who had moved to Toronto the year earlier. Informed by Diamond's grounding in urban design, the firm's projects exhibited a particular sensitivity to working within the city's Victorian fabric. York Square, one of Diamond and Myers's early projects (1968), wrapped a postmodernist brick ribbon around a series of preserved townhomes, creating a new courtyard in the process [see page 187–188]. **FIG 6**

This community-based approach contrasted with the modernist planning of large-scale plaza and tower-in-the-park projects exemplified by the downtown banking towers, new

city hall, and apartment towers that replaced Victorian houses in the St. James Town neighborhood. Context-driven architecture and urbanism received high-level political support after a series of related issues—opposition to car-oriented high-rises, concerns about urban renewal projects, advocacy for the protection of heritage buildings, and struggles against planned downtown expressways—led to the formation of a coalition of activists and aldermen, including American expat Jane Jacobs (1916–2006), who had moved to Toronto in 1968. The group championed politicians sympathetic to their interests to run in the 1972 December municipal election. These so-called reform politicians won a slim majority on city council under new mayor David Crombie (1936–), who was also recruited to the cause.[7] Former alderman John Sewell (1940–), who was mayor from 1978 to 1980, continued the efforts of the faction. As a young law student, Sewell had been involved in the protests to protect Trefann Court, a small Victorian neighborhood east of downtown, from demolition and replacement by high-rises.[8]

One of the reform council's first initiatives was to freeze downtown development to a height of 45 feet (13.7 meters), while a Core Area Task Force reexamined planning approaches to the area. The task force sponsored the 1974 report *On Building Downtown*, coauthored by architect, theorist, and teacher George Baird (1939–), urbanist-architect Roger du Toit (1939–2015), and planner Stephen McLaughlin.[9] Rather than functioning as a prescriptive plan, the comprehensive document presented principles and examples of how to sensitively build upon the character and quality of the urban fabric, with particular attention to environmental design and the public realm. In later writings, Baird continued arguing for conserving and building on the existing urban fabric.[10]

Some of the recommendations of *On Building Downtown* made their way into the Central Area Plan passed by the council in 1976. The new plan encouraged mixed-use development of the core, requiring retail at grade and increasing permissible residential densities to allow for housing to become viable on downtown sites. It prohibited large, open plazas, and preserved historic buildings through density bonuses.[11]

At the time that the Central Area Plan was being implemented, several of its ideas were tested in the Sherbourne Lanes project (Diamond and Myers, 1976, completed by Myers

after his partnership with Diamond ended in 1975). A developer had planned to replace a series of Victorian houses at Dundas and Sherbourne with a high-rise. The Diamond and Myers scheme instead rehabilitated the rowhouses and tucked a set of midsize apartment buildings behind them. Beverley Place, also started by the partnership but in this case completed by Diamond (1978), combines restored Victorian homes with new buildings that add density to a downtown residential block in a similarly sensitive manner. **FIG 7**

The centerpiece of the reform council's efforts to protect inner-city buildings and introduce affordable housing was the development of the mixed-use, mid-rise St. Lawrence neighborhood [see pages 229–230], which extends the city's grid in a fine-grained development structured around a central green. The development—including the bottom-up, consultative city-planning approach behind it—was a pointed rebuke to urban renewal initiatives that involved extensive demolition and the disruption of the existing street grid, particularly at Regent Park (John E. Hoare Jr. and Page & Steele Architects, 1947–1957) and Alexandra Park (Jerome Markson Architect with Webb Zerafa Menkès Housden Partnership and Klein & Sears Architects, 1967–1969).

Other large projects of the era were influenced by the new planning strictures. The initial plan for the Eaton Centre from the mid-1960s involved demolishing most of Old City

Hall. The realized version by Bregman & Hamann with Zeidler Partnership, completed in 1979, is still a megastructure [see pages 169–173], yet one that remains sensitive to the larger neighborhood: it preserves Old City Hall, wraps around an existing church, ties into the street grid and subway system, and introduces a long galleria that aspires to function as an indoor street.

The Toronto Reference Library (Raymond Moriyama Architects, now MTA, 1977) is likewise a large building, and the hub of one of the world's busiest urban library systems. **FIG 8** But the five-story brick building is terraced back along the diagonal, reducing the building's exterior mass as seen from Yonge and Bloor Streets, among the city's most important intersections. The reform council pushed for the building to be surrounded by a brick envelope that related to surrounding construction, rather than by the originally proposed glass skin. The library's drama is unveiled inside, with a soaring, skylight-topped atrium surrounded by terraces for reading and research. An indoor pond greets visitors, and a pair of futuristic transparent elevator tubes rises out of a pool of water.

The YMCA of Greater Toronto by A. J. Diamond & Partners (now DSAI, 1984) continues the firm's bold yet sensitive approach to infill by deftly inserting a large athletic center downtown. Deferring to an existing fire station and making room for a park, the through-block building uses the tools of postmodernism to offer a clear and cogent expression of the facility's various components. **FIGS 9–12** The ongoing ability of Diamond's firm to work with complex infill situations is shown in the very large Bahen Centre for Information Technology for the University of Toronto (2002), which makes the most of an irregular site by stitching together a series of smaller buildings and adding three landscaped courtyards.[12]

A fantastical take on infill is evidenced by Cloud Gardens Conservatory, by Baird Sampson with WZMH (1993). **FIG 13** Constructed atop a parking garage, the narrow park includes a series of ascending terraces that incorporate a garden, waterfall, and tropical conservatory—a verdant counterpoint to the surrounding skyscrapers.

Montgomery Sisam Architects has excelled in creating quality buildings that integrate quietly with their urban surroundings. Particularly active in the healthcare sector, the firm's use of contextually driven form is evident in the brick-clad Ronald McDonald

12 opposite
YMCA of Greater Toronto, main stair, Toronto, Ontario. A. J. Diamond & Partners, 1984.

13 right
Cloud Gardens and Cloud Gardens Conservatory, view from south, Toronto, Ontario. Baird Sampson with WZMH, Milus Bollenberghe Topps Watchorn (landscape architects), Margaret Priest and Tony Scherman (artists), 1993.

House Toronto (2011). With KPMB and Kearns Mancini Architects, they also created a masterplan for the Centre for Addiction and Mental Health in 2001. With the aim of destigmatizing mental health issues, the plan knits the isolated facility back into the city fabric by extending the street grid into the site. Nearby, Montgomery Sisam's Humber River Bicycle and Pedestrian Bridge (1996) is an elegant piece of infrastructure whose steel webbing forms an abstracted version of the "Thunderbird," a local First Nations icon.

Engaging with Toronto's Landscapes

The desire to create buildings that function as part of a harmonious urban fabric derives in part from Toronto's geography, which led to a city with a relatively compact street layout throughout its downtown core and adjacent residential neighborhoods. The central part of the city developed between the shoreline of Lake Ontario to the south and the two rivers that run perpendicular to it—the Don River to the east and the Humber River to the west. The Don Valley Parkway, a major expressway, was completed in 1967, its route following the Don River Valley. Leading into these river valleys is a large network of ravines, many of which contain small waterways and recreational trails.

The waterfront of Toronto was long an industrial zone characterized by warehouses and other facilities related to the then-active harbor, which is sheltered by the curving line of several outlying islands. As warehousing and manufacturing industries sought less expensive land in the suburbs in the 1950s, they left behind a swath of industrial facilities and brownfields.

One of the first moves toward reclaiming the waterfront for civic use was the construction of Ontario Place, designed by German-born Eberhard Zeidler (1926–) of Craig, Zeidler and Strong (now Zeidler Partnership Architects) and completed in 1971 [see page 169]. Inspired by Zeidler's never-realized 1968 Harbour City plan for a Venice-like residential district on Lake Ontario, the exhibition and performance complex was built over the lake by way of a system of mast-hung pavilions and included a 115-foot-diameter (35-meter-diameter) dome for large-format film projection.

A year after the completion of Ontario Place, the federally initiated Harbourfront Project began the process of converting the central waterfront to cultural, recreational, and residential uses. Queen's Quay Terminal (Zeidler Partnership Architects, 1983) is one legacy of that effort. FIG 14 Originally the art deco Terminal Warehouse (1926), it housed goods that arrived in the busy Toronto port for distribution by rail. The original building's mushroom-capped poured-concrete columns, which were pioneering for their time, are retained in the repurposed structure's mix of galleries, commercial spaces, and condo units, and are handsomely showcased in a multistory atrium.[13] Until 1980, ice to serve the warehouse was manufactured in the adjacent freezer plant, which has been converted into The Power Plant Contemporary Art Gallery (Lett/Smith Architects, 1987). Next door, the low-slung York Quay Centre (renovations and addition by Natale and Scott, 1995), part of what is now the arts-focused Harbourfront Centre, was once a garage for a trucking company and retains its steel-truss structure.

The adaptive reuse of industrial infrastructure on Toronto's waterways has continued since the 1980s to produce numerous office and condominium buildings. On a larger scale, it has resulted in the rehabilitation of the Gooderham & Worts facility—one of the largest Victorian industrial complexes remaining in North America—as the Distillery District arts

and residential precinct (masterplan by architectsAlliance, coordinating architects ERA and James Goad, Cityscape, 2003). Close by, the Don Valley Brick Works factory and quarry, once one of the main sources of building material for the city, has been transformed into an environmentally focused community and cultural center called Evergreen Brick Works (Joe Lobko and du Toit Architects, 2010) [see pages 219–221].

Of the residential structures created on the waterfront in the mid-1980s, the most noteworthy include Daniel Li's Harbour Terrace (1987) and Arthur Erickson's King's Landing (1982). Both are mid-rise, lake-facing structures. In the latter, sunrooms and common areas with curved glass ceilings cascade down the facade, allowing for a generous sharing of light and waterfront views among residents while presenting a modest profile to the street.

Since the turn of the millennium, the central waterfront's development has been headed by Waterfront Toronto, a corporation jointly created by the municipal, provincial, and federal governments in 2001. It has remediated brownfields in the area, stewarded the creation of a series of high-quality parks along the lakeshore, as well as overseen institutional, commercial, and residential developments. Some of the landscapes that Waterfront Toronto has commissioned have a practical role. For instance, a flood protection landform underlies Michael Van Valkenburgh Associates' Corktown Common park (2014), allowing for the development of adjacent lands. To the east, the planned renaturalization of the Don River's mouth will unlock for development the currently flood-prone port lands—a massive, largely empty tract next to downtown (2017–ongoing).

To the west of downtown, the Fort York Visitor Centre, by Vancouver's Patkau Architects with Toronto's Kearns Mancini Architects (2014), addresses the pre-1850s lakefront, before infilling extended the shoreline to its present location. **FIG 15** To recall the site's geographic and political history, the centre's front facade is built of a series of vertical and hinged-open Corten panels, tracing the line of the former ramparts from the 1790s. Native grass plantings evoke the watery landscape that would have abutted the site two centuries ago.

Other buildings engage with Toronto's ravine landscapes. The form of John Andrews's Scarborough College [see pages 108–113 and 157–160] is conceived as an extension of the adjoining ravine's slope. Raymond Moriyama's (1929–) Centennial Centre for Science and

Technology (1964, now Ontario Science Centre) terraces down into the Don Valley [see pages 36–40]. Moriyama & Teshima (now MTA) would later design Science North (1984), a kind of counterpart to the Ontario Science Centre. Located in Sudbury, Ontario, it includes a hexagonal exhibition building perched atop a rock crater and linked to an administrative building by an underground rock tunnel, engaging with the area's rich mining landscape.

Exemplary approaches to engaging with the ravine can also be found in a pair of projects by Shim-Sutcliffe, the firm founded by Brigitte Shim (1958–) and Howard Sutcliffe (1958–). Integral House (2009), built for mathematician James Stewart, appears as a two-story structure from the street but descends a further three stories along the curvilinear rear elevation of its ravine site, with oak fins dematerializing the facade.[14] Located on the opposite side of the Don Valley, the Residence for the Sisters of Saint Joseph (2013) takes on a sinuous form that echoes the curve of its narrow, ravine-side site. **FIGS 16–19** Facing the city, the four-story building is clad with green aluminum and Corten steel fins that nod to the treed landscape beyond; facing the valley, the building is clad with brick and punctuated by a glass bubble containing the chapel.[15]

Two Kings

The idea of the downtown core as a vibrant, high-density, mixed-use precinct was expanded in a regeneration initiative implemented in 1996. The policy, known as the "Two Kings," targeted the areas of King-Spadina (in west downtown) and King-Parliament (in east downtown), which historically served as manufacturing districts but declined in the 1970s as industrial activity migrated to the suburbs. The industrial zoning was replaced by a progressive regulatory system: new structures were to be compatible with the established pattern and scale of local buildings, but their use was free to respond to market demand.

Six years following the policy's implementation, eighty-six development projects were either built, under construction, or being planned in the two areas.[16] This included new structures as well as adaptive reuses of warehouses into commercial and residential spaces.

19 opposite
Residence for the Sisters of Saint Joseph, chapel interior, Toronto, Ontario. Shim-Sutcliffe Architects, 2013.

20 right
Twenty Niagara Condos, parkside view, Toronto, Ontario. Wallman Clewes Bergman Architects, 1998.

ArchitectsAlliance has been responsible for many of the condominium projects in these zones and elsewhere in Toronto. Two projects by the firm served as test cases for the new policy. Twenty Niagara (by the firm's predecessor, Wallman Clewes Bergman Architects, 1998) is a six-story park-facing block laid out around two elevator cores, allowing individual access to each of the condominiums. **FIG 20** Each unit has east and west exposures, mimicking the privacy and spaciousness of single-family homes.[17] Tucked behind a row of warehouses, the nearby District Lofts (2001) is divided into two narrow bars, creating a range of units, some with north and south exposures. **FIG 21** The building includes a semipublic exterior courtyard on the sixth floor and a retail base that extends the urban fabric of the neighboring warehouse street.[18]

Steps away, Queen Richmond Centre West (Sweeny & Co, 2015) takes a structurally innovative approach to the adaptive reuse of the King-Spadina district's warehouses. **FIG 22** Two existing brick buildings are preserved and a new commercial building perched between and atop them, supported by asterisk-shaped steel columns that punctuate the center's public atrium.

In the King-Parliament district, the Two Kings policy has most noticeably resulted in developments in and around the historic Distillery District. The most ambitious concentration of these is in the midrise Canary District, an ensemble constructed by a joint venture of architectsAlliance and KPMB Architects in association with Daoust Lestage and MJMA. In its first phase, the area served as the athlete's village for the 2015 Pan / ParaPan American Games; the same buildings have since been converted to a mix of private, subsidized, and student residences, with further structures to follow.

Educational Campuses

Due to its location in the center of the city, the University of Toronto has had an important impact on the city's architecture. Founded in the mid-1800s, its earliest buildings were constructed in a range of styles that reflected the choices of its various denominational colleges; the central University College gradually added its own teaching and research facilities,

often in a Gothic-inspired mode. A century later, the anticipated influx of students from the baby boom spurred the westward expansion of the downtown campus, the establishment of satellite campuses in Scarborough and Mississauga, and a wave of new construction in all three locations [see chapter 3]. New buildings on the original campus included the brutalist John P. Robarts Research Library (Warner Burns Toan & Lunde with Mathers & Haldenby, 1973), whose massive concrete tower of book stacks has its counterpart in a delicate adjoining wing atrium, which puts rare books on display in a jewel box–like setting.[19]

Since then, the university has added a number of notable works of contemporary architecture to its campus. The postmodern Earth Sciences Centre (Bregman & Hamann Architects with A. J. Diamond, Schmitt and Company, 1989) occupies half of a large urban block, transforming a former vehicular route into an open indoor space that functions as a central gathering area. Woodsworth College (1992), which weaves around two historic houses, integrates an old drill hall, and links well-detailed interior spaces with a new quadrangle, was started by Barton Myers Associates and completed by Kuwabara Payne McKenna Blumberg (now KPMB Architects). **FIG 23** The latter firm was founded by Bruce Kuwabara (1949–), Thomas Payne (1949–), Marianne McKenna (1950–), and Shirley Blumberg (1952–), who had worked together in Myers' office before establishing their own firm in 1987.

21 opposite, left
District Lofts, view from west, Toronto, Ontario. ArchitectsAlliance, 2001.

22 opposite, right
Queen Richmond Centre West, view from east, Toronto, Ontario. Sweeny & Co, 2015.

23 right
Woodsworth College, view of interior, Toronto, Ontario. Barton Myers Associates and Kuwabara Payne McKenna Blumberg, 1992.

In 1997, the university established a design review committee to participate in the architect selection for future projects. A number of bold buildings were added to the campus under this new process. The deconstructivist Graduate House residence by American firm Morphosis with Teeple Architects (2000) is intended as a gateway to the campus, sporting industrial-like precast concrete, perforated aluminum facades, and a scaffold-like cantilever that projects a "University of Toronto" sign over Harbord Street. A more understated building, the Donnolly Centre for Cellular and Biomolecular Research, by architectsAlliance and Behnisch Architekten (2005), occupies a slender site with an atrium that incorporates the east brick facade of the adjacent Rosebrugh Building (Darling & Pearson, 1920) and includes a verdant bamboo forest courtyard. Victoria College's Isabel Bader Theatre (Lett/Smith Architects, 2001) is a dignified addition towards the northeast corner of the downtown campus. The university's interstitial spaces have also been designed with care, as shown in architecture and landscape firm gh3's cross-emblazoned Trinity College Quadrangle (2008).

More recently, the Goldring Centre for High-Performance Sport by Patkau Architects and MJMA (2014) squeezes a large program—a competition-sized basketball and volleyball court—on a tight site by sinking the court underground and encircling it with a glass ground floor that invites daylight and spectators to the perimeter. **FIG 24** Oversized steel

24
Goldring Centre for High-
Performance Sport, view
from east, Toronto, Ontario.
Patkau Architects and
MJMA, 2014.

trusses span the 180-foot-long (55-meter-long) site, supporting the suspended upper-floor exercise areas and athletic clinics.

Within the university precinct, the Toronto headquarters of management consulting firm McKinsey & Company (1999) by Taylor Hariri Pontarini Architects displays an elegant architectural language that highlights the tactile qualities of local wood and Algonquin limestone. **FIG 25** The stone-clad building frames a private courtyard and centers on a naturally lit atrium furnished with fireplaces and cherry wood furniture, fostering a warm, collaborative work environment.[20] As Hariri Pontarini Architects, the firm has developed a number of other institutional buildings, including the management-focused Schulich School of Business at York University (2003) and Richard Ivey Building at Western University, in London, Ontario (2013).

Toronto's postsecondary institutions also include OCAD University, which has made its presence known with a colorful building on stilts: the Sharp Centre for Design, by Alsop Architects with Robbie/Young + Wright (2005). Ryerson University's campus has long been hidden in the downtown core, but it has also recently come to architectural prominence with a pair of projects: the sensitive rehabilitation of the Maple Leaf Gardens hockey arena into an athletics center (Turner Fleischer and BBB, 2012), and the construction of

25 left
**McKinsey & Company, main
entry as seen from street,
Toronto, Ontario. Taylor
Hariri Pontarini Architects,
1999.**

26 right
**Erindale Hall student
residence, view from north,
Mississauga, Ontario. Baird
Sampson Neuert Architects,
2005.**

27 opposite
**Terrence Donnelly Health
Sciences Complex, view
from north, Mississauga,
Ontario. Kongats Architects,
2011.**

its crystal-like Student Learning Centre (Snøhetta with Zeidler Partnership, 2015) facing bustling Yonge Street.

Centennial College has several small campuses inside and outside of downtown. Its Athletic and Wellness Centre, which sports a silo-like facade rendered in curved glass (Kongats Architects, 2012), gives a highway-facing presence to the Progress campus, located northeast of downtown. The Ashtonbee campus of the same college is undergoing a series of renewals led by MJMA; the first of these is a building housing the library and student centre (2014) that bridges the main road into campus, acting as a billboard from the nearby thoroughfare.

While the John Andrews building remains the architectural highlight of the University of Toronto's Scarborough campus, the university's Mississauga campus has in recent decades commissioned several contemporary architectural additions. Among the most successful of these is the Erindale Hall student residence (Baird Sampson Neuert, 2005), a narrow building whose glazed ground floor retains visual continuity with its forested setting, and whose outdoor colonnades provide an inviting path toward the main campus. **FIG 26** The Hazel McCallion Academic Learning Centre by Shore Tilbe Irwin & Partners (now Perkins+Will, 2006) was an early adopter of the idea of putting study

spaces, rather than books, at the heart of a university library. The outstanding Terrence Donnelly Health Sciences Complex (Kongats, 2011) is a stack of box volumes wrapped in a visually compelling skin of stainless-steel ribs, which subtly reflect and refract daylight. **FIG 27**

The public school system also has a long history of constructing buildings of note throughout the city. Early exemplars, built to accommodate the postwar surge in enrollment, include the modernist Sunnylea School (John B. Parkin Associates, 1943) and the George Harvey Vocational School in York (John B. Parkin Associates, 1950).[21] The Toronto Board of Education's in-house architects continued creating progressive designs, including the jauntily canopied Lord Lansdowne Public School (Frederick Etherington and Peter Pennington, 1961).

In recent decades, the quality of school architecture has benefited from a design-related submission and shortlisting process first implemented by the North York Board of Education in the 1990s.[22] The results, which were built on standard budgets, include the Claude Watson School for the Arts (Kohn Shnier Architects, 2007), with its boldly cantilevered library sheltering an outdoor amphitheater. **FIG 28** Teeple Architects with Shore Tilbe completed site-responsive designs for Gateway Public School (1998) and Eglinton Spectrum

28 opposite, top
Claude Watson School of the Arts, view from east, Toronto, Ontario. Kohn Shnier Architects, 2007.

29 opposite, bottom
Bata Shoe Museum, view from north, Toronto, Ontario. Moriyama & Teshima Architects, 1995.

30 right
BCE Place Galleria, Toronto, Ontario. Santiago Calatrava with Bregman + Hamann and Spencer Higgins, 1992.

Public School (1999); the former hugs a ravine while the latter provides a strong urban edge at a major Toronto intersection.

Cultural Renaissance

A recession in the early 1990s slowed the development of Toronto architecture, but two private projects of the time stand out for their contributions to the public realm. Moriyama & Teshima's Bata Shoe Museum (1995), funded by the footwear manufacturer Tomas Bata Jr. (1914–2008) and his wife Sonja (1926–2018), is a shoebox-like container for showcasing an international footwear collection and housing research facilities; its shard-shaped entrance is angled to capture Toronto's late-day sun. **FIG 29** In the financial district, BCE Place (now Brookfield Place, Bregman & Hamann with Skidmore, Owings and Merrill, 1990) incorporates the facades of a series of buildings from the mid-1800s, tying them together with a soaring galleria by Santiago Calatrava (with Bregman + Hamann and Spencer Higgins, 1992). **FIG 30** Built to follow the city's recommendation to spend at least 1 percent of a project's construction budget on public art, the white steel canopy contributes a space of quality and grace to downtown Toronto.

31 above
Art Gallery of Ontario
expansion, view of galleria,
Toronto, Ontario. Gehry
International and ERA
Architects, 2008.

32 opposite
Four Seasons Centre for
the Performing Arts, view
of atrium from street,
Toronto, Ontario. Diamond
and Schmitt Architects,
2006.

In 2003, the architectural fortunes of Toronto were renewed with what the City called its "cultural renaissance"—a $257-million federal and provincial investment into eight major construction projects, intended to attract cultural tourism to the city and mark it as an international economic capital.

The designers for the projects included several international firms. A spiky addition to the Royal Ontario Museum was completed by Studio Daniel Libeskind with B+H in 2007, though the result has been widely criticized. A more successful project was the renovation of the Art Gallery of Ontario (2008), led by Gehry International with ERA Architects. **FIG 31** The design adds a glass-and-timber galleria along the main facade, as well as a corkscrew stair that wends from the central courtyard up the back of the building, facing a park. The renovation builds on earlier expansions to the gallery's original home in the Georgian-styled Grange mansion. These included additions by the Parkin Partnership (1974 and 1977), among them a skylight-topped sculpture court dedicated to sculptor Henry Moore (1898–1986), whose abstract piece *The Archer* is placed in New City Hall's plaza. A further expansion, which increased gallery space and added a brick-and-sandstone facade along Dundas Street (now demolished), was started by Barton Myers and completed in 1993 by Myers in joint venture with KPMB Architects.

Major local firms were involved in the other cultural renaissance projects. A downtown opera house, the Four Seasons Centre for the Performing Arts, was designed by Diamond Schmitt (2006) and would lead the firm to theater commissions in cities including Montreal, Ottawa, New York City, and Saint Petersburg. A glowing, glass-fronted lobby facing University Avenue makes the Four Seasons the place to see and be seen on performance nights; the lobby also includes a grand, oversized stair that doubles as seating during noon-hour concerts. **FIG 32**

KPMB Architects led several of the other projects in this wave, including the renovation of the 1982 Roy Thomson Hall, originally designed by Arthur Erickson (1924–2009) with Mathers & Haldenby. A rare case of a stand-alone downtown building set in its own plaza, the building is a sculpted glass drum fronted by a sunken courtyard; KPMB's renovation focused on improving the acoustics in the concert hall. The firm undertook a more comprehensive renovation for the Gardiner Museum of Ceramic Art, transforming a 1983 building by Keith Wagland into a much larger institution that handsomely displays the firm's characteristic stately massing and fine detailing (2006).

Two additional projects by KPMB showcase the firm's deft ability to elegantly weave contemporary form with heritage buildings. The National Ballet School, completed in joint

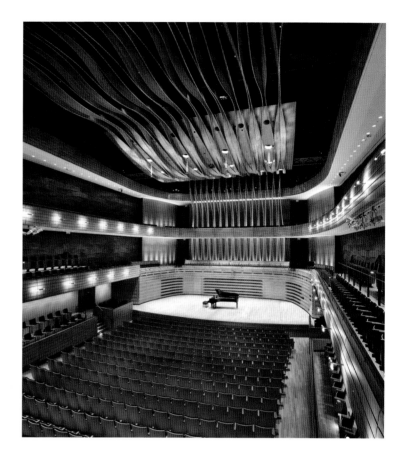

venture with Goldsmith Borgal (2005), integrates a 1850s house into the school's lobby and cafeteria area. **FIG 33** Glass-faced rehearsal studios are prominent on the front facade, acclimating dancers to being "on display" as they train for performance. The Royal Conservatory of Music's TELUS Centre for Performance and Learning (2009), for its part, wraps in an L-shape around the High Victorian university building that served as the conservatory's headquarters since 1963. **FIGS 34–38** A new atrium runs beside and behind the heritage structure, giving access to a 1,135-seat concert hall with an undulating wood ceiling canopy that provides warm acoustics.

Residential Developments and Suburban Growth

Toronto's residential fabric is a study in contrasts. The downtown core includes many tightly knit residential neighborhoods built up from the 1870s through the 1930s, which are primarily composed of wood-framed, brick-clad, semidetached and detached homes on relatively narrow lots. Surrounding the downtown core, a post-WWII immigration boom spurred a wave of car-oriented suburban residential development. Metropolitan Toronto's

planning policy insisted on high densities, resulting in a slew of concrete slab apartment buildings in the so-called "inner suburbs" close to the downtown core. In 2017, there are nearly twelve hundred high-rises in the city housing a million residents; overall, Toronto has the second-highest number of high-rise buildings in North America.[23]

To accommodate Toronto's continually growing population, density is being added to all of these areas. Some architects are experimenting with laneway housing in downtown neighborhoods, although current planning policy makes the needed approvals and infrastructural upgrades for such developments challenging. The city's first architect-designed laneway home, 5 Leonard Place, was created by Jeffrey Stinson (1933–2008) as his own house, built in 1989 with the help of his sons.[24] Shim-Sutcliffe's Laneway House (1993) is a modest 1,350-square-foot (125-square-meter) building at the end of an alley in Toronto's east end. The main level of the house is sunk 2 feet (0.6 meters) below grade, creating greater privacy for the two-story home and its small courtyard garden.[25] Superkül's 40R_Laneway House (2008) converts a former blacksmith's shop into a compact residence, introducing a light shaft and tiny courtyard to naturally illuminate and ventilate the residence. **FIG 39**

Firms such as Batay-Csorba are experimenting with new configurations that bring added density to standard Toronto lots; their Double Duplex (2016) boasts a section with a

35 opposite, left
TELUS Centre for Performance and Learning, atrium, Toronto, Ontario. KPMB Architects, 2009.

36 opposite, right
TELUS Centre for Performance and Learning, view of secondary entrance from Philosopher's Walk.

37 above
TELUS Centre for Performance and Learning, view from northeast.

38 right
TELUS Centre for Performance and Learning, second-floor plan.

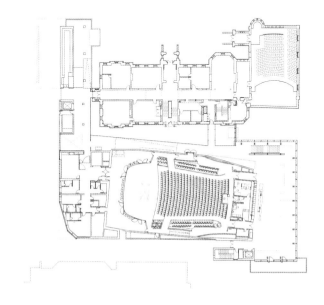

39 left
**40R_Laneway House,
aerial view, Toronto,
Ontario. Superkül, 2008.**

40 opposite, top
**River City, view from west,
Toronto, Ontario. Saucier
+ Perrotte architectes
with ZAS Architects, 2013
(phase 1); 2015 (phase 2);
ongoing.**

41 opposite, bottom
**Whitby Public Library and
Civic Square, view from
library atrium, Whitby,
Ontario. Shore Tilbe Irwin
and Partners, 2005.**

partially sunken ground floor and two-story-high openings, resulting in a pair of spacious, open-plan, two-unit homes on a lot that would normally host half that density. The Grange Triple Double by Williamson Chong (now Williamson Williamson, 2015) is nestled near to Toronto's Spadina Chinatown. It stacks three units on a double-wide lot; discreet, flexible connections between the units allow for various scenarios of multigenerational living in future years.

The growth in Toronto's population has included a significant contingent of millennials interested in living downtown, which in turn has spurred residential and commercial development. Recently, downtown high-rises have been strongly shaped by the city's Tall Building Design Guidelines, first implemented in 2006, which have resulted in a uniformity of character and construction methods that leaves little room for architectural innovation. An exception is the million-square-foot River City, by Montreal-based Saucier + Perrotte architectes with Toronto's ZAS Architects (Phase 1, 2013; Phase 2, 2015; Phases 3 & 4, ongoing). **FIG 40** This condominium development's design quality distinguishes it from many of the quickly proliferating towers downtown. Sculpted with a high degree of formal individuality, the black-and-white tapered volumes frame a series of raised courtyards and offer views of the downtown skyline.

42 above
Regent Park Aquatic Centre, interior view, Toronto, Ontario. MJMA, 2012.

43 opposite
Brampton Soccer Centre, view of skylit circulation, Brampton, Ontario. MJMA, 2007.

Designs of interest are also happening in the interstices: Underpass Park (The Planning Partnership and PFS Studio, 2015) and the Bentway (Public Work in collaboration with Greenberg Consultants, 2018–ongoing) are public spaces tucked under the Gardiner Expressway, providing outdoor amenity for the rapidly densifying residential areas alongside.

While residential housing in the suburbs remains conventional on the whole, Toronto architects have contributed a variety of civic amenity spaces of note. North of the city, KPMB's Vaughan City Hall (2011) frames one side of a future civic precinct. On a smaller scale, the Whitby Public Library and Civic Square (2005) by Shore Tilbe Irwin and Partners pairs a grand interior space with a new urban square. **FIG 41** As Perkins+Will, the same office has developed a specialty in community spaces, with recreation centers in Brooklin (2012) and Oak Ridges (2012) that make references to the surrounding rural landscapes—the former with a series of barn-form structures and the latter with an oversized outdoor porch looking out onto Lake Wilcox, once a weekend pleasure ground for early-twentieth-century city dwellers.

MJMA's recreation centers are also standouts in the Toronto area, including their Governor General's–award winning Rotary Park Pool in Etobicoke (1997) and Regent

Park Aquatic Centre downtown (2012), both of which are elegant, modest structures that enclose a carefully controlled sequence of spaces. **FIG 42** Skylit, glazing-lined corridors as well as gymnasium-side clerestories are frequently used in their buildings, including the Brampton Soccer Centre (2007), bringing natural light deep into a type of building that often lacks connection to the outdoors. **FIG 43**

Other suburban civic spaces make use of existing cues from the recent past. RDH Architects' Mississauga Library Project (2011) adaptively reuses three mid-century modern libraries in the west Toronto suburb, adding glazing, canopy-frame systems, and exterior terraces to revitalize the pavilions while retaining their original aesthetic sensibility.

Half of Toronto's population self-identifies as being of a visible minority, and the city's architecture at times reflects this ethnic diversity. Some parts of Scarborough, for instance, include heavy concentrations of Chinese residents and businesses; Teeple Architects' soaring Scarborough Chinese Baptist Church (2007) is tailored to this thriving community and features a sanctuary for sixteen hundred worshippers as well as a gymnasium and a suite of teaching spaces. **FIGS 44-45** Closer to downtown, the high profile Aga Khan Museum (Moriyama & Teshima with Maki & Associates, 2014), along with the adjacent Ismaili Centre (Moriyama & Teshima with Charles Correa Associates, 2014), rose up in Toronto in part thanks to the country's strong Ismaili community: thousands of Ugandan Ismailis were welcomed in Canada after being expulsed from their home country by dictator Idi Amin in the 1970s. MJMA's aforementioned Regent Park Pool includes the city's first universal change rooms as well as screens that can be lowered to block the large poolside windows, allowing for use by diverse populations; the programming includes women-only swims for local Muslims.

Redesigning Modern Toronto

In the mid-1960s, many of the projects that were most remarkable in Toronto were of a classic modernist cast: often with single-purpose zoning, they included towers in parks and elevated urban plazas. Today, these same structures and areas are being remade in line with

the values of Toronto urbanism that have emerged in the intervening decades—in particular, restoring the city's Victorian urban fabric and introducing a mix of uses.

Emblematic efforts in this regard include the revisiting of Alexandra Park and Regent Park [see pages 230–236], large-scale urban renewal projects to the west and east of downtown, respectively. In both cases, former through-streets are being restored, knitting the previously sequestered communities back into the larger city. Previously, the areas primarily comprised low-rise subsidized housing; now they include a mix of market housing, subsidized housing, and additional community facilities.

Affecting an even greater area is the Tower Renewal Project [see page 261], which targets some twelve hundred residential high-rises built between 1945 and 1984. Initiated by ERA Architects in 2011, it sets out a template for retrofitting these behemoths to make them more energy efficient. It has also successfully advocated for the rezoning of towers to allow commercial activity in and around their bases—activities that were absent or operating illegally under the previous single-use zoning. While the project is still young, the hope is that entrepreneurial opportunities will bring new life at the pedestrian scale to these towers, whose original design was predicated on extensive car use.

Nathan Phillips Square
alterations and green
roof, view of performance
pavilion, Toronto, Ontario.
PLANT Architect in joint
venture with Perkins+Will,
ongoing.

Perhaps the most iconic effort to revisit Toronto's modernist legacy started in 2007, when the City launched an international competition to redesign Nathan Phillips Square—the plaza designed by Viljo Revell in front of New City Hall. The winning entry, as constructed by PLANT Architect in joint venture with Perkins+Will, opens up the square by removing the clutter that had accumulated at its center.[26] **FIG 46** New pavilions, including an open stage and a café, echo the modernist language of Revell's 1965 design. The hard edges of the existing block are softened with an accessible green roof on the city hall's podium, as well as gardens and seating along the plaza's perimeter.

These projects are subtle rather than flashy in their architectural and urban design, aspiring to integrate into the city rather than stand out from it. In this sense, they contribute toward Toronto as the quintessential Canadian city: a place whose built fabric and well-mannered civic structures reflect the population's values of modesty and the accommodation of differences. But Toronto's remarkably diverse population is an asset that has yet to be fully explored in its architecture. In the mid-twentieth century, British émigré architects, including Peter Dickinson, brought ideas from England to Canada, and later architects, such as Raymond Moriyama, brought sensibilities from Japan and elsewhere to designs in Toronto. What ideas might the current generation of young architects—hailing from Ireland to Iran—bring to the city? Architecturally, Toronto's challenge is to build on its Victorian scaffolding in a way that creates a rich, heterogeneous tapestry, open to future change and a bounty of ever-renewing architectural ideas.

15

The New West Coast

Adele Weder

On May 2, 1986, the gates swung open for Vancouver's World Exposition on Transportation and Communication—or, as it is more simply known, Expo 86. Filled with pavilions themed by nation and, in many cases, by corporation, the five-month-long fair attracted over 22 million visitors from across the country and around the world. The unprecedented attention would impact the city's architectural trajectory for the next three decades.

From the early 1950s to the 1970s, the wider conversation around new Vancouver architecture had been mostly qualitative, focusing on the deft use of regional materials, the careful integration into the site, and the poetic gravitas of distinctive forms, whether in North Shore post-and-beam houses or the monumental high-rises along Georgia Street.[1] By the early 1980s, the design culture of the city entered the throes of postmodernism before becoming limited by a severe recession. After Expo 86 concluded in the fall of 1986, Vancouver architects grappled with a mandate that was more quantitative: how to design great swaths of housing units for a fast-growing but geographically circumscribed city while responding to the natural setting that had helped distinguish its architecture in the first place.

A key event that shaped Vancouver's development was the decontamination and rezoning of the former Expo lands in the False Creek area after the provincial government sold the lands to a private-sector developer in 1988. Six years earlier, the City of Vancouver

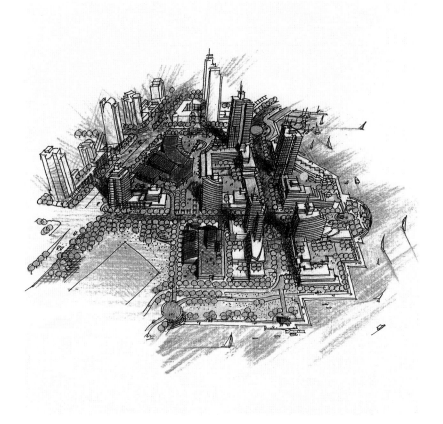

had commissioned a series of benchmark studies for the broader downtown area's future growth. Those reports helped inform the city's View Protection Guidelines, adopted in 1989. These guidelines ensured slot views of the nearby mountains and provided garden areas in the middle of blocks, creating a kind of vertical garden city and reformatting the contemporary downtown core. The studies also generated the city's basic planning paradigm: each city block would have four narrow towers, each sprouting out of a podium base of townhouses or retail outlets intended to animate the immediate vicinity.[2] The guidelines required that the towers be set back and included ground-floor stipulations, which allowed daylight to reach the sidewalks and ensured a consistent, human-scaled "streetwall" for pedestrians.[3]

False Creek became one of the earliest sites to showcase slender, finely detailed glass-and-steel condo towers that were shaped by the View Protection Guidelines. The developer, Concord Pacific, appointed Downs Archambault with architect Graham McGarva and landscape architect Don Vaughan to help produce the conceptual scheme: a strand of residential towers surrounding the city's century-old Roundhouse railway switching station. The station's restoration and repurposing would be bankrolled by the development itself, culled from the additional profits that would be gained from the relaxed density and

height restrictions in a new kind of deal now known as density bonusing. The ambitious scheme, successfully completed over the following decade, marked the beginning of a new era of West Coast Modernism: vertical architecture. From here on, the sky above Vancouver would be the new frontier.

The new high-rises—many designed by James K. M. Cheng (1947–), with the firm's characteristic white mullions, narrow verticality, and sleek, modern materiality—contrast sharply with the adjacent low-rise red-brick Roundhouse Community Arts & Recreation Centre, the result of the newly repurposed building. **FIG 1** The Roundhouse was first restored by Hotson Bakker Architects to serve as one of the Expo 86 pavilions. In 1993, under public pressure, the developer struck a density-bonus deal, which helped finance its restoration and programmatic conversion in exchange for the City granting extra height allowances for adjacent high-rises. Transformed by Graham McGarva of VIA Architecture in the mid-1990s, the building now stands at the foot of the towers above, acting as a crucial resource for the families that have filled the neighborhood, and an architectural reminder of the city's century-old industrial vernacular. Throughout the city, highly selective heritage preservation projects, public parks, and cultural facilities have similarly resulted from the sale of the airspace above them.

3 left
One Wall Centre, Vancouver, British Columbia. Busby & Associates, 2001.

4 opposite, left
Living Shangri-La Hotel and Residences, view of plaza and podium levels, Vancouver, British Columbia. James K. M. Cheng Architects, 2009.

5 opposite, right
Living Shangri-La Hotel and Residences, plaza.

The construction of condo towers in downtown Vancouver accelerated throughout the 1990s. The design guidelines guaranteed a decent amount of public space and amenities but limited the design options for the developers and their architects.[4] One of the more literally iconic homages to Vancouver's industrial and natural past is Richard Henriquez's seventeen-story Eugenia Place Tower, completed in 1987, at the foot of Denman Street near the edge of Stanley Park [see pages 205–208]. **FIG 2** An oak tree was planted on its penthouse deck; the height above street level is intended to convey the approximate height of the original towering first-growth trees that once stood on the site—which would have stood roughly twenty stories high.

Into the Airspace

Vancouver's city center is now filled with towers that are the product of complex negotiations. One of the most complicated examples of this process is One Wall Centre, completed in 2001 by Busby & Associates (now part of Perkins+Will Canada). **FIG 3** Its notched curvilinear form is a visually striking counterpart to the rectilinear buildings surrounding it, although its originally mandated light-glass facade was built instead with dark glass—the

controversial result of what many perceived as a defiant move by the developer, who had preferred the dark-glass option. The landscape architecture, by Phillips Farevaag Smallenberg, is equally elegant but similarly constrained by commercial concerns beyond the designers' control. Its rise above the sidewalk and its backless benches discourage loitering, making it more of a picturesque base for the tower—a life-size diorama for sidewalk-strollers—than an inviting, interactive park.

Of the many architects who have proposed or built towers on podiums, one firm has emerged as the most prolific and dominant: the aforementioned James K. M. Cheng Architects. Cheng's version of the tower-and-podium format does not merely punctuate the urban landscape; it defines it. His slender, elegant, and—for better and worse—similar-looking towers of glass and steel cover large sections of the city's downtown core and beyond.

One Wall Centre was the highest building in the city until it was superseded by Cheng's Living Shangri-La (2009), a hotel and condo tower with high-end retail stores and an open plaza at street level. This is Cheng's most visually distinctive tower. FIGS 4–6 Its unique "button mullions"—small, square copper plates affixed over the window-wall junctions—imbue the tower with a sense of stability and formality. The mullions' hue appears to shift from bronze to gold-green to violet depending on the time of day, the weather, and the

6 above
Living Shangri-La Hotel and Residences, skyline view, Vancouver, British Columbia. James K. M. Cheng Architects, 2009.

7 opposite
Watermark Restaurant and Lifeguard Facilities, Vancouver, British Columbia. AA Robins Architect, 2005.

vantage point of the viewer. The color of its facade glass is not the monotonous standard silicone-green, but an elegant blue-gray. The Shangri-La's design shows an attempt to incorporate public space that is accessible to passers-by, though the street-level public plaza suffers from the downtown's wind-tunnel syndrome. The plaza is now partly filled by a series of offsite temporary Vancouver Art Gallery installations.

While its sporadic attempts at creating inner-city plazas have met with limited success, Vancouver excels at linear public spaces along almost all of its waterfront, directing gazes outward to the boats, barges, and adventurers in the distance. Though zoning laws have severely limited any development on these seaside spaces for most of the city's history, the turn of the millennium brought with it a new, selective openness. After much fractious public input, in 2005 the Watermark Restaurant and Lifeguard Facilities by AA Robins Architect reframed the city's popular Kitsilano Beach as a sand-filled public plaza anchored by the emphatically modernist building. **FIG 7** In 2012, the generously glazed Cactus Club restaurant by Acton Ostry Architects replaced a dilapidated concession stand to become the architectural coda at the south end of Denman Street.[5]

The largest-scale and most ambitious of these waterfront design transformations has been the multiphase overhaul of Coal Harbour—an epic project that will take many more

8 left
Coal Harbour, Phase I,
Vancouver, British
Columbia. Phillips
Farevaag Smallenberg,
1997.

9 opposite
Belkin Art Gallery,
Vancouver, British
Columbia. Peter Cardew
Architects, 1995.

years yet to complete. **FIG 8** At this rehabilitated industrial port facing the Burrard Inlet, Phillips Farevaag Smallenberg (Phase I) and PWL Partnership (Phase II) went beyond simply capturing ocean and mountain views; the design harnesses the instrinsic amenities of an idyllic coastal setting. The balustrade along the ocean walkway draws inspiration from the city's design history—evoking the deco-like abutments of the historic Burrard Bridge—while using steel, glass, and concrete to create a highly contemporary form of linear park. Instead of creating the typical focus on urban life, the design draws the spectator to the activities transpiring on the water. The waterfront had almost certainly been the focus for First Nations peoples who had first inhabited the area, the design team noted. Colonists, however, had found it hard to fathom the breadth of human engagement with the waterfront: "What was not clear to these European explorers was the fact that for native West Coasters, the sea was many things at once: front door to the community, market, fishing grounds, battleground, communication hub and civic plaza."[6] Like most of Greater Vancouver, Coal Harbour had been highly animated prior to colonization. As the twenty-first century approached, a renewed appreciation for the inherent desirability of the northern waterfront would reanimate it, this time through and by design.

Architectural Plasticity

While the sleek tower-on-podium formula has given Vancouver a polished, urban, and largely unified appearance, a countervailing design approach has provided healthy architectural variety. Peter Cardew (1939–), designer of the distinctively sculptural 1978 Crown Life Building while at Rhone & Iredale [see pages 281–283], went on to establish his own eponymous firm and designed buildings whose angles and rounded contours offered a new plasticity that distinguished them from the rectilinear vernacular. On a First Nations reserve in the Chilcotin countryside in central British Columbia, Cardew's Stone Band School (1992) features a circular sunken pit and a conical skylight above it, abstracted signifiers of the region's traditional pit houses [see pages 126–127].[7] Back in Vancouver, Cardew's 1995 Morris and Helen Belkin Art Gallery on the University of British

Columbia (UBC) campus fuses sharply angled projections with a curved central peak; the latter's gentle arc offers a soft counterpoint to the blade of the main gallery's clerestory window. **FIG 9** Against the backdrop of Thompson Berwick & Pratt's orthogonal campus architecture from the mid-twentieth century, Cardew's gallery reads as a humanist manifesto.

Cardew has also designed strikingly beautiful smaller projects that are very subtly inflected by canted lines, such as the Sturdy-Wardle Residence in West Vancouver (1998) in downtown Vancouver. **FIG 10** His 1995 Odlum Drive Live/Work Studios four-plex features highly visible diagonal seismic bracing—which serves an important function in a regional earthquake zone, but also aesthetically distinguishes the residential building from the city's formulaic modern and neotraditional multiunit developments. **FIG 11**

Another champion of plasticity has been Bing Thom Architects (BTA), whose founding principal designed the popular iceberg-shaped Northwest Territories Pavilion at Expo 86. After a series of respectable local projects, Bing Thom (1940–2016) made his national reputation with the 1997 Chan Centre for the Performing Arts at UBC, designed as two integrated ovoid volumes nestled in a copse of trees. **FIGS 12–13** In collaboration with landscape architects Elizabeth Watts and Cornelia Hahn Oberlander (1921–), Thom conceived

10 left
**Sturdy-Wardle Residence,
West Vancouver, British
Columbia. Peter Cardew
Architects, 1998.**

11 right
**Odlum Drive Live/
Work Studios four-
plex, Vancouver, British
Columbia. Peter Cardew
Architects, 1995.**

12 opposite
**Chan Centre for the
Performing Arts, interior,
Vancouver, British
Columbia. Bing Thom
Architects, 1997.**

13
Chan Centre for the
Performing Arts, exterior,
Vancouver, British
Columbia. Bing Thom
Architects, 1997.

14 left
Arena Stage, Washington, DC. Bing Thom Architects, 2010.

15 opposite
BC Cancer Research Centre, Vancouver, British Columbia. Henriquez Partners Architects, 2004.

the Chan Centre massing as deferential to its natural setting, which he interpreted as the vegetation on the site rather than the ocean in the distance. Although the university initially mandated the trees be cleared from the lot, Thom convinced his client otherwise, embracing instead the fundamental criterion of early West Coast Modernism: sensitivity to the existing site.

The Chan Centre would eventually serve as the model for BTA's 2010 Arena Stage theater in Washington, DC. **FIG 14** The internationally acclaimed American project was conceived as a renovation and expansion of the theater company's 1960 building, encasing its two original stages within a curvilinear glass curtain-wall and adding a new, third theater space for experimental productions.

The distinctive fenestration of the 2004 BC Cancer Research Centre, by Henriquez Partners, is another example of a new inventiveness. **FIG 15** Its circular windows show Richard Henriquez's (1941–) penchant for compressing representative symbols into lively urban punctuation. Although its inspiration stems from a distinctly nonorganic form—the glass petri dishes used by researchers—it remains a welcome counterpoint to the rectilinear forest of buildings around it.

The Vancouver design team that is arguably the most successful champion of site-specific individuality is Patkau Architects, which relocated from Edmonton to Vancouver in 1984. Rather than deferring to any historic paradigm—either classical or early modernist—founders John (1947–) and Patricia (1950–) Patkau favor unique spatial and constructional solutions, and an intimate engagement with each individual site. Architectural historian Andrew Gruft has referred to the defining characteristic of the Patkaus' work as "its specificity." He writes:

> The way each project is tailored to its particular set of circumstances does not allow the simple transfer of solutions from one project to the next. In a world of rapid change this may seem misguided, but the so-called flexibility of most generic solutions now seems a simplistic and unworkable strategy.[8]

Following a series of thoughtful and successful house designs on Vancouver Island in the late 1980s [see pages 292-294], Patkau Architects exemplified this approach masterfully in

their 1992 Barnes House on a forested 5-acre (2-hectare) property just outside of Nanaimo, BC. **FIG 16** The house is compact but highly complex, with an irregular floor plan that follows the variegated topography of the land. A wood-framed structure clad in stucco with a vaulted timber ceiling, the house seems to grow directly out of its rocky outcrop. The deference of the floor plan to the contours of the site generates a spatial dynamism inside; its walls seem to expand and contract as you walk through it. A similar experience is generated inside the firm's 2012 Shaw House in Vancouver, whose spatial compression and expansion also defers strategically to the site. In contrast to the Barnes House, the Shaw Residence is built not on verdant acreage but on a narrow urban waterfront lot crowded by adjacent structures; it brilliantly conceals its surroundings—save for the surreal frontal view of ocean and mountains.

In 1993, the Patkaus received wider attention with the opening of the Canadian Clay & Glass Gallery in Waterloo, Ontario, its organic palette of wood and brick in visual defiance of the conventionally abstracted white-cube theme of most museums. It exemplifies the generous glazing of West Coast Modernism, and its broad awnings evoke the warehouse overhangs in Vancouver's formerly industrial Yaletown district. The gallery was the first of several important cultural commissions across the country, including the 2005 Grande

Bibliothèque in Montreal [see pages 406–407] and the 2014 Fort York Visitor Centre in Toronto [see page 437].

Much of the Patkaus' residential work has served as conceptual prototypes for their larger commissions. The non-orthogonal grid underlying the Barnes House and its careful deference to the foliage outside makes it a conceptual predecessor of Strawberry Vale Elementary School in Victoria (1996), which is composed of a series of pod-like classrooms that harness views and offer access to outdoor spaces, which become a series of adjunct "living classrooms."

Most notably, the firm's 2009 Linear House on Salt Spring Island—a long, dark, and narrow form that seems to course through the site like a submarine—has informed one of the firm's most comprehensively successful projects: the Audain Art Museum in the ski resort town of Whistler, BC (2016). **FIGS 17–20** For this museum, the firm was offered a challenging site crowded with trees and centered on a floodplain that compelled the architects to situate the bulk of the building over the ground, like a bridge. The museum boasts many of what can now be recognized as signature Patkau qualities: bold massing outside, a complex spatial interplay inside, and a diligent attention to the unique qualities of the site.

19 opposite, top
**Audain Art Museum,
entrance, Whistler,
British Columbia. Patkau
Architects, 2016.**

20 opposite, bottom
**Audain Art Museum, view
of entry bridge.**

21 above
**Beaty Biodiversity Centre,
University of British
Columbia, Vancouver,
British Columbia. Patkau
Architects, 2009.**

22 left
**Buchanan Courtyard
renewal, University
of British Columbia,
Vancouver, British
Columbia. PUBLIC:
Architecture +
Communication, 2011.**

23 opposite
**Sauder School of Business,
University of British
Columbia, Vancouver,
British Columbia. Acton
Ostry Architects, 2010.**

Patkau Architects' Aquatic Ecosystems Research Laboratory and Beaty Biodiversity Centre (2009) figure among the structures that have transformed the University of British Columbia campus in recent years. **FIG 21** The university's architectural ambitions accelerated with the arrival of Gerry McGeough as planning and design director in 2007. Under McGeough's guidance, the campus has added more than a dozen varied and significant buildings to its stock: in addition to the Biodiversity Centre, it has renewed its image with the Pharmaceutical Science Building by Montreal's Saucier + Perrotte with Vancouver's HCMA (2012), the Bioenergy Research & Demonstration Facility by McFarland Marceau Architects (2012), the new Student Union Building by DIALOG with B+H Architects (2015), and the Engineering Student Centre by Urban Arts Architecture (2016). One of the most prolific animators of the campus's public space has been its smaller infill projects, many of them designed by Public: Architecture + Communication, including highly contemporary wayfinding, transit shelters, built-in exterior seating, and the origami-like 2011 Buchanan Courtyard Pavilion—all of which have helped make the sprawling suburban campus a more urbane and pedestrian-friendly community. **FIG 22**

Along with the new buildings, the university has selectively commissioned some transformations of original buildings, most notably the 2010 Sauder School of Business

transformation by Acton Ostry Architects. **FIG 23** The project entailed the construction of a five-story wraparound addition with an entirely new facade, and an interior reconfiguration of the original 1965 Thompson Berwick & Pratt building. The heart of the transformation is the building's full-height atrium with its glazed walls and skylights, which draw light into classrooms and corridors. The plan defers to the more interactive, student-centered mode of learning now embraced by university faculties in general and business schools in particular. Thus the Sauder School is packed with breakout rooms, lounges, and extra-wide stairways flanked with oversized risers that transform the circulation areas into communal gathering spaces.

New Housing Paradigms

With the city's residential fabric largely bifurcated into two architectural extremes— compact two-bedroom condos and large, expensive single-family houses—it's the typical middle-class family that has been architecturally shortchanged. A handful of smaller firms have addressed this dearth in imaginative ways. An alternative housing paradigm borne of industrial conversion was created in 2002 by architect Bruce Haden, who transformed an

autobody shop and parking area in the city's gritty Strathcona neighborhood into a six-unit townhouse complex still known as Koo's Garage, after its original incarnation. **FIG 24** More family-oriented than Cardew's Odlum Drive, Koo's units are strategically laid out to foster interactive sightlines between neighbors, both in the street-front balconies and the rear common garden areas. It actively defies the sprawling dimensions and preciousness of the conventional single-family home.

With living space increasingly at a premium in Vancouver, architects have been experimenting with new modes of densification that harness the concept of design flexibility. In 2005, Lang Wilson Practice in Architecture Culture (LWPAC), in collaboration with Hotson Bakker Boniface Haden Architects (now part of DIALOG), created the ROAR multifamily residence in Vancouver's Point Grey neighborhood. **FIG 25** Its raw concrete structure and the spatial openness within its ten living units required an adventurous spirit of the first residents. Beyond its design bravura, ROAR offers an intermediate scale for housing: it is vastly denser than the single-family house, but much more house-like than a condo tower.

ROAR primed LWPAC for its next major urban housing project, MONAD. **FIGS 26–29** Completed five years later, this four-plex offers a similar tableau of glass planes framed

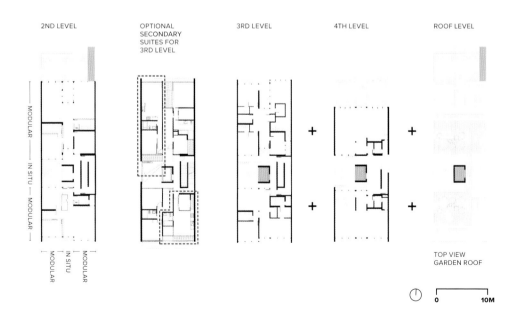

2ND LEVEL

MODULAR — IN SITU — MODULAR

MODULAR — IN SITU — MODULAR

OPTIONAL
SECONDARY
SUITES FOR
3RD LEVEL

3RD LEVEL

4TH LEVEL

+

+

ROOF LEVEL

+

+

TOP VIEW
GARDEN ROOF

0   10M

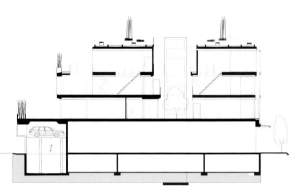

by concrete. The living units, plus subgrade storage and parking, are configured within one 33-by-120-foot (10-by-36.6-meter) single-family lot, quadrupling the number of households on the property.[9] MONAD additionally offers the ability to adapt spontaneously to changing household circumstances and needs: empty nesters can instantly downsize a three-bedroom condo by closing off part of the unit with a pocket wall, creating a self-contained guest room or rental unit. The concept brings dwelling into the realm of the sharing economy, as has already happened for taxi service, as with Uber, and short-term rental services, as with Airbnb. Both ROAR and MONAD have been conceived as potentially replicable prefabricated modular units—though that reality has yet to come to fruition.

Creating compact interiors is another strategy for designing within inevitably shrinking areas. This was heroically demonstrated in 2011 in the century-old Burns Block building at 18 West Hastings Street, in which Carscadden Stokes McDonald Architects created a series of thirty tiny "micro-loft" rental suites. Just as the midcentury modernists had done in earlier times, architect Bruce Carscadden looked to Japan for inspiration—this time for contemporary ideas on how to configure 291-square-foot (27-square-meter) suites into efficient, well-lit, and highly liveable units.[10] The solution is to think of both furniture and rooms as

convertible and ephemeral: beds transform into desks, tables spring out of walls and vanish back into them, bathroom doors double as shower-stall doors, living rooms transmogrify into dining rooms or kitchens or bedrooms. The microliving concept, though contentious for a municipality whose single-family neighborhoods are filled with 6,000-square-foot (557-square-meter) "monster houses," will no doubt grow not only in popular acceptance, but in necessity in the years to come. Perhaps the micro ethos will even evolve to subdivide or replace the under-occupied monster houses.

As part of the city's toolkit for densifying and creating new housing options, the laneway home has become another Vancouver paradigm. Built as infill at the rear of the city's standard 33-by-120-foot (10-by-36.6-meter) lots, laneway homes can be similar in size to mid-century bungalows: up to 1,600 square feet (148.7 square meters). Several firms have specialized in custom and formulaic laneway houses, the latter most often modelled on neotraditional houses, sometimes taking on a loosely modernist style.

For midsize single-family homes—between 1,800 and 3,600 square feet (167.3 and 334.6 square meters)—much of the best work is now being built outside of Vancouver, where sites are more generous and visually dramatic. D'Arcy Jones Architecture, who has won respect for his transformations of existing Vancouver houses, is now garnering a strong reputation for new builds in other regions, including the Okada Marshall House (2016) in East Sooke on Vancouver Island, and the Friesen Wong House (2014) in Coldstream, British Columbia.[11] **FIGS 30–31**

Another small firm, BattersbyHowat, has designed a number of homes that carry forward the West Coast Modern aesthetic and approach to site. **FIG 32** The firm's exceptional skills in proportion, material selection, and view composition have been applied to the underserved multiplex market—a type that is fast becoming the archetypal family home by default because of the growing cost of single-family homes. BattersbyHowat's four-unit townhouse building at 2386 Cornwall Avenue is a complex stack of units interlocked with one other, Rubik's Cube–style, to generate roughly the same area per home as standard bungalows. On a smaller scale, the dual-unit residence of founding partners David Battersby and Heather Howat showcases an alternative approach to the conventional duplex plan.

32 opposite
Helmut Eppich House renovation, Vancouver, British Columbia. BattersbyHowat Architects, 2015 (Original architect Arthur Erickson, 1972).

33 right
Waterfall Building, Vancouver, British Columbia. Arthur Erickson with Nick Milkovich Architects, 2001.

Instead of configuring each unit as an identical plan that is a mirror image of its neighbor, the units are customized to each inhabitant's lifestyle, with a much larger and more elaborate kitchen for Battersby, a conveniently compact kitchen for Howat, and several common outdoor spaces.

Arthur Erickson (1924–2009), whose design brilliance transformed Greater Vancouver in the 1960s and 1970s [see chapter 9], was more uneven in his output after returning to Vancouver from Toronto and Los Angeles in the 1990s, not least because tower developers would occasionally value the marketing cachet of his name over the inherent design values of his work. But in working closely with Nick Milkovich Architects, Erickson achieved a higher design caliber in smaller-scale projects: the elegant Waterfall Building (2001) condominium complex near Granville Island, whose name bespeaks the vertical fountain that defines its threshold; and, for an entirely different demographic, the Portland Hotel (1999) on the city's downtown eastside, which accommodates the city's most marginalized and hard-to-house people. **FIG 33** A three-hour drive south of Vancouver, Erickson and Milkovich's Museum of Glass in Tacoma, Washington (2002), is defined by a large, steel-paneled, angular cone known as the "Hot Shop" where visitors can watch artists blow molten glass into its final sculptural form. **FIG 34**

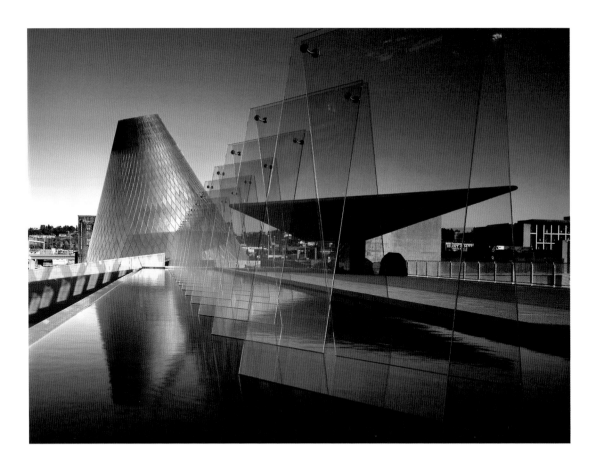

34 above
Museum of Glass, Tacoma,
Washington. Arthur
Erickson with Nick
Milkovich Architects, 2002.

35 opposite
City Centre Library, Surrey,
British Columbia. Bing
Thom Architects, 2011.

On the Periphery

As the core became financially straitjacketed by real-estate values that severely limited what kinds of sites architects had to work with, the notion of downtown being the nexus of creativity, as it was for fashion, art, and innovation, was no longer the case for architecture. Architects who once made masterpieces in the central city have had to build farther afield. The West Coast's most respected design-focused firms—Patkau Architects, Bing Thom Architects (now known as Revery Architecture), and Hughes Condon Marler Architects (HCMA)—now do much of their best work in the less-expensive suburbs, or out of town entirely.

Surrey, a sprawling municipality southeast of Vancouver, has nurtured some of the region's strongest architecture in the past decade, precisely because it has the available land and is not yet taken up wholesale by developers. Surrey has been literally transformed by the work of BTA, particularly its urbanizing 2003 Central City project, which configured a university atop a shopping mall; the City Centre Library, which evokes the prow of a ship (2011); and the Guildford Aquatic Centre, with SHAPE Architecture, a community center addition that transformed the walkability of the adjacent thoroughfare (2016). **FIGS 35–36** HCMA's Grandview Heights Aquatic Centre, enabled by the residential development planned for its surroundings, will provide a stunning anchor to the

37 opposite
Grandview Heights Aquatic Centre, Surrey, British Columbia. HCMA, 2016.

38 right
Gleneagles Community Centre, West Vancouver, British Columbia. Patkau Architects, 2003.

new sprawl of neotraditional townhouses (2016). **FIG 37** Patkau Architects has also designed a landmark in Surrey, the 1992 Newton Library, as well as in West Vancouver, the 2003 Gleneagles Community Centre. **FIG 38**

Suburban densification and the construction of cultural hubs have both compelled and helped bankroll an expansion of the region's mass-transit infrastructure. The SkyTrain rail system now delivers passengers from the far-flung suburbs of Richmond, Burnaby, New Westminster, and Surrey right into downtown Vancouver and back. While many of the SkyTrain stations are generic concrete shells, a few are architectural standouts, notably the 2002 Brentwood Town Centre Station in Burnaby, by Busby + Associates / Perkins + Will. **FIG 39–40** A sleek, glass-sheathed ovoid of wood and steel that glows at night, the station provides a beacon-like gateway to the city.

Mass Timber: The Next Vancouver Paradigm

Just as West Coast postwar architects made much of their reputations on their devotion to wood, a newer generation is reharnessing wood for a postmillennial ethos focused on the use of renewable, low-carbon construction methods and materials. Plywood was the innovative "engineered wood" of the midcentury; now architects are turning to the systemic use of mass-timber structural components, including glulam, cross-laminated timber (CLT), and laminated veneer lumber (LVL) [see page 261].

Though Europe has been the main proponent of mass-timber framing systems, British Columbia is their main beachhead within North America.[12] A small number of Vancouver firms, including Mcfarlane Green Biggar, McFarland Marceau, and Perkins+Will, began exploring new ways to harness the potential of wood as a structural material. The mass-timber movement gained further traction after 2007, when architects Michael Green and Steve McFarlane, along with engineers Eric Karsh and Robert Malczyk, visited Austria for a Passivhaus conference and looked closely at the works of Hermann Kaufmann and other architects. The designers returned to Vancouver, motivated to use mass timber in

39 above
Brentwood Town Centre
Station, interior, Vancouver,
British Columbia. Busby +
Associates / Perkins+Will,
2002.

40 left
Brentwood Town Centre
Station, exterior.

41 opposite
Ronald McDonald House BC
& Yukon, Vancouver, British
Columbia. MGA | Michael
Green Architecture (project
commenced by McFarlane
Green Biggar Architecture
+ Design), 2014.

more of their work. Since then, a dedicated manufacturing facility has been established in Penticton, in central British Columbia, to supply locally sourced CLT. More firms are using mass timber in an expanding range and scale of architectural projects—not just for building higher, but also as an alternative structural material for supporting walls and cantilevered planes, such as in DGBK Architects' 2013 Dowling Residence in West Vancouver and Patkau Architects' 2017 Trail's End House in Whistler.

Michael Green Architecture's 2014 Wood Innovation and Design Centre (WIDC) in Prince George, in northern British Columbia, has become a showcase of sorts for mass timber, which serves as the structural framework as well as the ceiling and walls of the six-story, 97-foot-high (29.5-metre-high) structure. But WIDC is more useful as advertisement than architecture. Although widely covered in the press, the building lacks the standard of detailing and logical spatial organization that its architects usually attain in their projects. Ten months later, a much finer building by the same firm opened: Ronald McDonald House BC (2014), a temporary accommodation for young hospital patients and their parents. **FIG 41** The seventy-three-family building in Vancouver boasts a CLT structure, although in this case it is hidden behind masonry outside and drywall inside, a decision made to achieve economy of space and to limit costs. The building is organized

into zones with gradations of privacy, while generously wide corridors accommodate wheel-chairs, strollers, and exhausted parents traversing the hallways in the middle of the night. This is a building intended to quell human anxiety, and it works wonderfully. The deft abstraction of a traditional pitched roofline into a modernist language projects both the semiotics of home and the reassurances of state-of-the-art health care. WIDC is a better-known building because, for a fleeting moment, it could assume bragging rights connected to its then-remarkable height as an all-wood structure. But Ronald McDonald House is more effectively designed and the better mass-timber paradigm to celebrate.

Establishing new standards of height or span is a good thing, if it is done for logical design purposes rather than as an end in itself. A case in point is the roof of Fort McMurray International Airport (2014) in northern Alberta, by the Vancouver-based Office of McFarlane Biggar, which boasts the longest horizontal expanse of CLT panels in the world. **FIG 42** That feature is more than a quantifiable superlative: it allows for a dramatically open expanse of floor space and a sense of visual warmth on an otherwise cold, stark site.

Meanwhile, mass timber continues to rise to new heights with the construction of Brock Commons, an eighteen-story student residence at the University of British Columbia, which upon its completion in 2017 became the tallest contemporary mass-timber building

in the world. **FIG 43** Designed by Acton Ostry Architects, with Austria-based Hermann Kaufmann as a consultant, this 190-foot-high (57.9 meter high) structure is built with a hybrid framework of wood, steel, and concrete. Unlike WIDC, it doesn't attempt to look like a wood building. On an aesthetic level, it approaches banality, especially compared to the fineness of the firm's nearby Sauder School of Business. But its significance lies in the precedent it sets for the successful use of mass timber in high-rise development: the eighteen-story project was completed on budget and, with its prefabricated components assembled quickly on-site, ahead of schedule. Its height is logical for a campus desperately in need of housing and densification, though we should now hope that Vancouver's next wood-framed high-rise will offer beauty as well as function. Its facade is mostly clad in Trespa panels, and its glulam supporting columns are sheathed in drywall, while the CLT floorplates are topped with concrete. This marks a privileging of function and logic over the need to "showcase" wood to the public. As Bruce Haden wrote in his 2017 review of the project:

> Ultimately, the question "why didn't you expose the wood?" speaks to architects' strong bias toward the visual—but it avoids the central question of how to best make tall wood buildings commonplace. No one ever asks why you can't see the 2×4s in conventional wood frame construction.[13]

Conclusion

Brock Commons, like so many of the projects shown on these pages, signifies a continued regional commitment to architectural innovation. Sometimes that innovation centers on sustainability, at other times on aesthetics or affordability or flexibility; the best buildings embrace all four qualities. Vancouver continues to be celebrated for its urbanism—measured largely by the ability of architects, developers, and planners to configure enough living units within its geographically restricted boundaries. But as it moves forward into the next century, the city's architects, planners, politicians, and citizens are fiercely debating how to respond to successive waves of people and capital streaming into the region: tall towers or gentle density, light transit or heavy-handed subway interventions.

As the second decade of the millennium draws to a close, a number of new towers are sprouting up in Vancouver, including several exotic-looking architectural gyrations designed by architects from other continents. At the same time, the city's housing crisis is reaching epic proportions as working families find themselves shunted aside in favor of clients lured to the predictable investment of formulaic two-bedroom, glass-walled condominiums—nicknamed "safety deposit boxes in the sky"—or to the glamor of the fanciful new shapes.

The Canadian poet Earle Birney (1904–1995) wrote his ode "the shapers: Vancouver" in 1958, near the crest of the postwar building boom. Even then, he perceived a city under threat of being overpowered by its own architectural novelties, of losing its identity in the wash of new forms:

> in the grandiloquent glitter
> we are lost for a way
> for a line
> bent for a mere eye's pleasure
> a form beyond need
>
> is there a rhythm drumming from vision?
> shall we tower into art   or ashes?[14]

Sixty years later, Birney's question resonates. The global economic forces that were so helpful in kick-starting the city's building sector over three decades ago are now threatening to homogenize its architecture and displace a good share of its inhabitants, leading—ironically—to the social anarchy that postwar modernism was intended to prevent. It will be up to a new generation of architects to ensure that tomorrow's architecture towers into art, or at least a viable place to live.

Notes

INTRODUCTION

1 See Harold Kalman, *A History of Canadian Architecture*, 2 vols (Toronto: Oxford University Press, 1994). Other key books on modern Canadian architecture include: Carol Moore Ede, *Canadian Architecture, 1960–70* (Toronto: Burns and MacEachern Ltd., 1971); William Bernstein and Ruth Cawker, *Contemporary Canadian Architecture: The Mainstream and Beyond* (Don Mills: Fitzhenry and Whiteside, 1982); Leon Whiteson, *Modern Canadian Architecture* (Edmonton: Hurtig Publishers Ltd., 1983); Lisa Rochon, *Up North* (Toronto: Key Porter Books Ltd., 2005); Rhodri Windsor Liscombe and Michelangelo Sabatino, *Canada: Modern Architectures in History* (London: Reaktion Books, 2016).

2 See Greg Bellersby, ed., *The West Coast Modern House: Vancouver Residential Architecture* (Vancouver: Figure 1, 2015).

3 See Rhodri Windsor Liscombe, *The New Spirit: Modern Architecture in Vancouver, 1938–1963* (Vancouver: Douglas & McIntyre, 1997).

4 See Henry-Russell Hitchcock and Philip Johnson, *The International Style* (New York: W. W. Norton & Company, Inc., 1932).

5 See Christopher Armstrong, *Making Toronto Modern: Architecture and Design 1895–1975* (Montreal & Kingston: MQUP, 2014).

6 See André Lortie, ed., *The 60s: Montreal Thinks Big* (Montreal: Canadian Centre for Architecture/Douglas & McIntyre Inc., 2004).

7 See Serena Keshavjee, ed., *Winnipeg Modern: Architecture 1945–1975* (Winnipeg: University of Manitoba Press, 2006).

8 See Kenneth Frampton, "Towards a Critical Regionalism: Six Points Towards an Architecture of Resistance," in Hal Foster, ed., *Anti-Aesthetic: Essays on Postmodern Culture* (Seattle: Bay Press, 1983).

9 Liscombe and Sabatino, *Canada*, 335.

1. THE CENTENNIAL PROJECTS

1 James Harley, *Iannis Xenakis: Kraanerg* (Farnham, Surrey: Ashgate, 2015), 46.

2 Canada, and Vincent Massey, *Report: Royal Commission on National Development in the Arts, Letters and Sciences, 1949–1951* (Ottawa: King's Printer, 1951), 220.

3 Ibid., 221.

4 Ibid., 381.

5 Michelangelo Sabatino, "A Wigwam in Venice: The National Gallery of Canada Builds a Pavilion, 1954–1958," *Journal of the Society for the Study of Architecture in Canada* 32, no. 1 (2007): 3–14.

6 John Diefenbaker, "A Task for the Profession," *RAIC Journal* 37, no. 2 (1960): 287.

7 Walter B. Bowker, ed., "The 57th Assembly," *Journal RAIC/L'IRAC* 41, no. 7 (1964): 34. Author of article not credited.

8 Peter H. Aykroyd, *The Anniversary Compulsion: Canada's Centennial Celebrations, a Model Mega-Anniversary* (Toronto: Dundurn Press, 1992), 197.

9 Ibid., 181.

10 Frank MacKinnon, *Honour the Founders! Enjoy the Arts!: Canada's Confederation Memorial in Charlottetown* (Charlottetown, P.E.I.: Fathers of Confederation Buildings Trust, 1990), p. 3.

11 Ibid., 3–6.

12 Ibid., 82–83.

13 Edward MacDonald, *Cradling Confederation: The Founding of Confederation Centre of the Arts Charlottetown* (Charlottetown, PEI: Confederation Centre of the Arts, 2013), 24.

14 Interview with Jack Long, "Cornerstones," *The Calgary Herald*, February 28, 1999, accessed January 18, 2017, http://search.canadiana.ca/view/ac.pc_1476.

15 Peter Buchanan, "Back to the Future," *The Canadian Architect* 39, no. 3 (March 1994): 22.

16 Ibid., 24.

17 "Expo 67 Quick References," accessed January 16, 2017, http://expo67.morenciel.com/an /references2.php.

18 Peter C. Newman, "It could change the whole direction of Canada's history," *The Toronto Star* (April 28, 1967), 1.

19 "Expo 67," Library and Archives Canada, accessed November 28, 2016, http://www .collectionscanada.ca/expo/0533020101_e.html.

20 André Lortie, *The 60s: Montreal Thinks Big* (Montreal: Canadian Centre for Architecture / Douglas & McIntyre Ltd., 2004), 190.

21 Reyner Banham, *Megastructure: Urban Futures of the Recent Past* (New York: Harper and Row, 1967), 114–116.

22 Ibid., 115–116.

23 Ibid., 91.

24 Lortie, *The 60s*, 70.

25 Marshall McLuhan, "Inside the Five-Sense Sensorium," *The Canadian Architect* 6, no. 6 (June 1961): 49–54; Marshall McLuhan, "The Invisible Environment," *The Canadian Architect* 11, no. 5 (May 1966): 71–74; and *The Canadian Architect* 11, no. 6 (June 1966): 73–75.

26 "International Business Machines Corporation," *The Canadian Encyclopedia*, accessed January 18, 2017, http://www.thecanadianencyclopedia .ca/en/article/international-business-machines -corporation-ibm/.

27 McLuhan, "The Invisible Environment," 71.

28 Sarah Jennings, *Art and Politics: The History of the National Arts Centre* (Toronto: Dundurn Press, 2009), 211–219.

29 Louis Applebaum et al, *Report of the Federal Cultural Policy Review Committee* (Ottawa: Minister of Supply and Services, 1982), 6.

30 Ibid., 6.

31 Ibid., 6.

2. THE ARCHITECTURE OF PUBLIC INSTITUTIONS

1 Vincent Massey et al, *Report of the Royal Commission on National Development in the Arts, Letters and Sciences* (Ottawa: King's Printer, 1951), 221.

2 Ibid.

3 Editorial, "Competitions," *RAIC Journal* 38, no. 08 (August 1961): 35; Massey et al, *Report of the Royal Commission*, 220.

4 "Plan for the National Capital," accessed November 12, 2016, https://qshare.queensu.ca /Users01/gordond/planningcanadascapital /greber1950/Full_text_Greber1950.pdf.

5 The process resumed in 1977 when a limited competition was won by Parkin Associates. The National Gallery was not completed, however, until 1983–88 when a scheme for designs by Parkin/ Safdie, a joint venture of Parkin Associates and Moshe Safdie, was built on another site. Harold Kalman, *A History of Canadian Architecture*, vol. 2 (Toronto: Oxford University Press, 1994), 825–826.

6 "Stop Press! National Gallery Competition Results," *The Canadian Architect* 22, no. 4 (April 1977): 54.

7 See *The Canadian Architect* 28, no. 4 (April 1983): 4; "Preview: National Gallery and Museum of Man," *The Canadian Architect* 29, no. 2 (February 1984): 22.

8 The other architects whose names were put forward were Douglas Cardinal, Arthur Erickson, Raymond Moriyama, Barton Myers, Ron Thom, and Eberhard Zeidler.

9 "The Canadian Architectural Competition: A Partisan Historical Reflection" in Detlef Mertins and Virginia Wright, eds., *Competing Visions: the Kitchener City Hall Competition* (Toronto: The Melting Press, 1990), 22.

10 "Canadian Museum of History," *The Canadian Encyclopedia*, accessed November 14, 2016, http://www.thecanadianencyclopedia.ca/en /article/canadian-museum-of-history/.

11 "Interview with Moshe Safdie," *The Canadian Architect* 29, no. 2 (February 1984): 31.

12 "The National Museum of Man, Hull, Quebec," *The Canadian Architect* 29 no. 2 (February 1984): 32.

13 Russell Bingham, "Canadian War Museum," accessed November 18, 2016, http://www .thecanadianencyclopedia.ca/en/article /canadian-war-museum/.

14 See Paul duBellet Kariouk, "The Canadian War Museum," *Canadian Architect* 50, no. 9 (September 2005).

15 See Janine Debanné, "Glass Menagerie," *Canadian Architect* 56, no. 9 (September 2011).

16 Ibid., 32.

17 Bingham, "Canadian Museum for Human Rights," http://www.thecanadianencyclopedia .ca/en/article/canadian-museum-for-human -rights/, accessed 18 November 2016.

18 Lisa Landrum, "Difficult Harmonies / Canadian Museum for Human Rights," *Canadian Architect* 59, no. 11 (November 2014): 22 ff.

19 Ibid.

20 Ibid.

21 Statistics Canada, accessed December 24, 2016, http://www12.statcan.ca/census-recensement /2006/as-sa/97-550/figures/c5-eng.cfm.

22 "Kitchener City Hall Competition," *The Canadian Architect* 34, no.11 (November 1989): 34.

23 *The Canadian Architect* 39, no. 7 (July 1994): 24.

24 Kenneth Frampton, "Intimate Monumentality, Kitchener City Hall," *The Canadian Architect* 39, no. 7 (July 1994): 16.

25 See Trevor Boddy, "Peter Cardew's Interior," *Canadian Architect* 45, no. 2 (February 2000).

26 Jim Taggart, "Connect the Sprawl," *Canadian Architect* 49, no. 3 (March 2004): 20.

27 See "Revitalization of Nathan Phillips Square Competition," *Canadian Architect* 51, no. 10 (October 2006); and "Finalists named in Nathan Phillips Square Revitalization Design Competition," *Canadian Architect* 51, no. 12 (December 2006).

28 "Shore Tilbe Irwin & Partners and PLANT Architect win Nathan Phillips Square Revitalization Competition," *Canadian Architect* 52, no. 3 (March 2007).

29 Marie-Josée Therrien, "Canada's Embassies: a Brief History," *Canadian Architect* 44, no. 6 (June 1999): 18.

30 A complete discussion of the evolving role can be found in Marie-Josée Therrien, *Au-delà des frontières: l'architecture des ambassades canadiennes, 1930–2005* (Québec: Presses de l'Université Laval, 2005).

31 Jim Strasman, "New Canadian Chancery," *The Canadian Architect* 29, no. 6 (December 1984): 39.

32 "Shade Laws, Security and Symbolism/Canadian Chancery, Tokyo," *The Canadian Architect* 36, no. 11 (November 1991): 22.

33 Adele Weder, "Report: A Berlin Chronicle," *Canadian Architect* 44, no. 6 (June 1999): 20.

34 John Bentley Mays, "Diplomatically Speaking," *Canadian Architect* 51, no. 2 (February 2006): 33.

35 Marie-Josée Therrien, "Canada's New Face in Korea," *Canadian Architect* 53, no. 7 (July 2008): 26.

36 Douglas MacLeod, "Killing this and that," *The Canadian Architect* 37, no. 7 (July 1992): 29.

37 "Odds & Ends," *The Canadian Architect* 12, no. 7 (July 1967): 5; "Expo '70 Competition, Winning Design: Erickson/Massey," *The Canadian Architect* 12, no. 8 (July 1967): 29.

38 Ibid.

39 "Review: Canadian Pavilion Expo 70, Architects: Erickson/Massey," *The Canadian Architect* 15, no. 7 (July 1970): 48.

40 Ibid.

41 Macy DuBois, "Going to the Fair" *The Canadian Architect* 35, no. 10 (October 1990): 37.

42 "Projects," *The Canadian Architect* 28, no. 3 (March 1983): 6.

43 Peter Pragnell, "Expo 86/A misconceived midway," *The Canadian Architect* 31, no. 07 (July 1986): 34.

44 See Stanley Matthews, "The Fun Palace: Cedric Price's experiment in architecture and technology," *Technoetic Arts* 3, no. 2 (2005).

45 "CN Pavilion, Expo 86, Vancouver, Peter Cardew, Architect: *The Canadian Architect* Awards of Excellence," *The Canadian Architect* 30, no. 12 (December 1985): 34.

46 Montreal's Olympic Stadium—the centrepiece of the 1976 Olympics—has not had a main tenant since 2004 and the building is falling into disrepair, while other facilities have been repurposed.

47 "The Montreal Olympics," *The Canadian Architect* 21, no. 9 (September 1976): 32.

48 See John Hix, "2: The Velodrome," *The Canadian Architect* 21, no. 9 (September 1976): 47–51.

49 Jack Todd, "The 40-Year Hangover: How the 1976 Olympics Nearly Broke Montreal," *The Guardian*, July 6, 2016, accessed December 28, 2016, https://www.theguardian.com/cities /2016/jul/06/40-year-hangover-1976-olympic -games-broke-montreal-canada.

50 See https://www.thecanadianencyclopedia.ca /en/article/1967-centennial-celebrations-emc, accessed 12 October 2018.

51 See David Graham and Laura New, "All Aboard the Confederation Train," *Quebec Heritage* 4, no. 4 (July–August 2007): 18.

52 See Charles Waldheim, "Terminal Optimism," *Canadian Architect* 49, no. 10 (October 2004).

53 In air navigation, the letters designating a Canadian airport always begin with a "Y," allegedly a holdover from the days when airports were weather stations and the US National Weather Service established airport codes, allotting Canada a "Y."

54 Lisa Rochon, "Trillium Terminal Three/Toronto International Airport," *The Canadian Architect* 36, no. 6 (June/July 1991): 23.

55 See Waldheim, "Terminal Optimism."

56 Jim Taggart, "Interior Passages," *Canadian Architect* 50, no. 10 (October 2005): 24.

3. CAMPUS ARCHITECTURE

1 Marshall McLuhan, "Classrooms Without Walls," *Explorations* 7 (May 1957): 19–23. McLuhan expanded this theme in *Understanding Media* (New York: McGraw-Hill Book Co., 1964), and *The City as Classroom: Understanding Language*

and Media (Agincourt, Ont.: The Book Society of Canada, 1977).

2   Marshall McLuhan and G. B. Leonard, "The Future of Education: The Class of 1989," *LOOK* magazine (Feb. 21, 1967): 23–25.

3   Stefan Muthesius, *The Postwar University: Utopianist Campus and College* (New Haven and London: Yale University Press, 2000).

4   Thomas Howarth, "Banff Session 64," *RAIC Journal* (July 1964): 48.

5   Michael Sorkin, *Other Plans. Pamphlet Architecture 22* (New York: Princeton Architectural Press, 2001), 27.

6   Northrup Frye, "The Definition of a University" (Nov. 4, 1970), in Jean O'Grady and Goldwin French, eds., *Northrup Frye's Writings on Education* (Toronto: University of Toronto Press, 2001), 421.

7   Vincent Massey memorandum dated Feb. 4, 1960, quoted in Ron Thom, "Massey College," *RAIC Journal* (Oct. 1963): 38.

8   Ron Thom, "Massey College," *The Canadian Architect* 5, no. 12 (Dec. 1960): 41, in full 38–46.

9   Robertson Davies, "Massey College," *The Canadian Architect* 8, no. 10 (Oct. 1963): 47.

10 Thom, "Massey College," 41.

11 Douglas Shadbolt, *Ron Thom: The Shaping of an Architect* (Vancouver: Douglas & McIntyre, 1995), 19.

12 Brigitte Shim, "Reflections on Massey College," in Adele Weder, ed., *Ron Thom and the Allied Arts* (Vancouver: West Vancouver Art Gallery, 2014), 44.

13 Tom Symons, "Opening Address," (Oct. 17, 1964), Trent Archives.

14 Quoted in "Trent University," *Canadian Interiors* (June 1969): 30–31.

15 "Champlain College, Trent University," *The Canadian Architect* 12, no. 12 (Dec. 1967): 34, in full 28–36.

16 Thom, "Master Plan, Trent University," (23 April 1964), Trent Archives.

17 Arthur Erickson, "Trent University," *Canadian Interiors* (June 1969): 29–30.

18 Lisa Rochon, "The mugging of Thom's Trent," *Globe and Mail* (Dec. 1, 2004), accessed September 16, 2017, https://beta.theglobeandmail.com/arts/the-mugging-of-thoms-trent/article747426/.

19 Witold Rybczynski, "A Tale of Two Colleges," *Architect* (July 2015), accessed September 16, 2017, http://www.architectmagazine.com/design/a-tale-of-two-colleges_o.

20 David Jackel, "Out of My Head," *The Varsity,* 85.1 (Sept. 20, 1965): 5.

21 John Andrews and Jennifer Taylor, *Architecture, A Performing Art* (Guildford: Lutterworth Press, 1982), 47.

22 John Andrews, "Design Philosophy," *RAIC Journal* 41, no. 7 (July 1964): 65. This journal reports on the 1964 Banff sessions, with sections on Scarborough, Simon Fraser, and York, pp. 51–66.

23 Kenneth Frampton, "Scarborough College," *Architectural Design,* vol. 37 (Apr. 1967): 185, in full 178–87.

24 Oscar Newman, "Scarborough: The program, people and principles that shape it," *Architectural Forum* (May 1966): 54, in full 32–41, 52–55.

25 "Architecture—What Is the Question" (address to the AIA Pacific Chapter, Jan. 14, 1963), in *Speeches by Arthur Erickson.* Manuscript. (Vancouver: UBC Library, 1978).

26 Arthur Erickson, "The Architectural Concept," *The Canadian Architect* 11, no. 2 (Feb. 1966): 40, in full 35–69.

27 Ibid, 41.

28 Arthur Erickson, "The Weight of Heaven," *The Canadian Architect* 9, no. 3 (Mar. 1964), 50, in full 48–53.

29 Erickson, "Architectural Concept," 41.

30 Arthur Erickson, *The Architecture of Arthur Erickson* (Montreal: Tundra Books, 1975), 134.

31 Hugh Johnston, *Radical Campus: Making Simon Fraser University* (Vancouver and Toronto: Douglas & McIntyre, 2005), 127–35.

32 Erickson, "Architectural Concept," 40–41.

33 In a 1977 interview about *The City as Classroom*, Marshall McLuhan acknowledges Ivan Illich's 1970 Deschooling Society as a key inspiration. However, McLuhan emphasizes the correlation of classroom and city: "Illich, I thought, was quite right in suggesting that we live in a new environment in which all the answers are now outside the school room. And, therefore, he suggests, 'why don't we close the schools?' And I say, why not put the questions in the classroom: if the answers are now outside, let's get the questions inside and set up a dialogue between the outside and the inside." Marshall McLuhan, "City as Classroom," interview by Carl Scharfe (1977), accessed April 1, 2017, https://www.youtube.com/watch?v=aX9j_3bxZU0.

4. FIRST NATIONS ARCHITECTURE

1   See Joy Monice Malnar and Frank Vodvarka, *New Architecture on Indigenous Lands* (Minneapolis: University of Minnesota Press, 2013).

2 Note sent to Odile Hénault, December 2016.

3 Verna J. Kirkness and Jo-ann Archibald, *The First Nations Longhouse* (Vancouver: The University of British Columbia Press, 2001), 52-53. The authors, who were there from the very beginning, documented the entire journey that led from dream to construction.

4 "Featured Projects: Hesquiaht Community School," McFarland Marceau Architects Ltd, accessed April 3, 2018, http://www.mmal.ca /hesquiaht/description.html.

5 The construction of these centers was prompted after the airing of a BBC documentary showing Davis Inlet (Labrador) children sniffing glue.

6 From an in-house publication produced by EVOQ Architecture, 2017.

7 Alfred Waugh is from the Fond Du Lac (Denesuline) First Nation of northern Saskatchewan. He also has English and Swedish heritage.

8 Kirkness and Archibald, *The First Nations Longhouse*, 19.

9 "President's message," Nicola Valley Institute of Technology website, accessed January 15, 2018, http://nvit.ca/messagefromthepresident.htm.

10 Jim Taggart, "Modern Vernacular," *Canadian Architect* 47, no. 8 (August 2002), accessed January 15, 2018, https://www.canadianarchitect. com/features/modern-vernacular/.

11 "NVIT Multipurpose Gathering Space," Formline Architecture, accessed April 3, 2018, https://formline.ca/.

12 "Nicola Valley Institute of Architecture," Formline Architecture, accessed April 15, 2016, https://formline.ca/.

13 Blackfoot Crossing, accessed January 15, 2018, http://www.blackfootcrossing.ca/about-us.html.

14 "Nk'Mip Desert Cultural Centre" Media Kit, DIALOG, accessed April 11, 2017, https://www .dialogdesign.ca/.

15 Interview with Roberto Pacheco, May 2017.

16 Lubor Trubka Associates Architects, accessed February 1, 2018, https://www.lubortrubka.com /project?id=15.

17 Jim Taggart, *Toward a Culture of Wood Architecture* (Vancouver: Abacus Editions, 2011), 83.

18 "News Release," Trent University, accessed February 1, 2018, http://www.trentu.ca/news /pressreleases/architect02.html.

19 This has been amply written about by Professor David Newhouse, from Trent University's Chanie Wenjack School for Indigenous Studies.

20 "Project Architect: Christie Pearson with Danny Bartman," LGA Architectural Partners, accessed February 1, 2018, http://www.christiepearson.ca /native-child/.

21 From a conversation between Dean Goodman and Odile Hénault, June 24, 2017.

22 Vancouver architect Joe Wai sadly passed away while this chapter was being written. See one of his articles in *The Tyee*, which alludes to the Skwachàys Lodge and Residence, accessed January 15, 2018, https://thetyee.ca/Opinion /2011/07/06/HealingLodge/.

23 "Winnipeg's Indigenous Population," CBC, accessed February 1, 2018, http://www.cbc.ca /news/canada/manitoba/aboriginal-population -statistics-canada-1.4371222.

24 "First Nations," Prairie Architects Inc., accessed January 15, 2018, http://www.prairiearchitects .ca/first-nations.

25 Interview with Odile Hénault, April 15, 2018.

26 Firm Profile, McFarland Marceau Architects Ltd., accessed February 1, 2018, http://www.mmal.ca /unya/description.html.

27 Excerpt from Brook McIlroy website, accessed February 15, 2018, http://brookmcilroy.com /thunder-bay-indigenous-spirit-garden-pavilion.

28 Quoted from Brook McIlroy website, accessed February 15, 2018, http://brookmcilroy.com /news_news.php?year=2013.

29 Quoted from Kendra Jackson, "A Corten-Clad Monument in the Prairies Reflects on Métis Life," *Azure Magazine* (January 2017), accessed January 15, 2018, http://www.azuremagazine.com/article /batoche-installation-metis-saskatchewan/.

30 "Projects: John Tizya Visitor Reception Centre," Kobayashi + Zedda architects, accessed April 3, 2018, http://kza.yk.ca/projects/john-tizya-visitor -reception-centre/.

31 Quote from James K. Bird, speaker, First Indigenous Architecture and Design Symposium, organized by the RAIC, Ottawa, May 27, 2017.

32 Conversation with Odile Hénault, April 18, 2018.

33 David Fortin, "Bauhaus of the North," *Canadian Architect* 62, no. 10 (October 2017), 34–35.

5. MEGASTRUCTURES AND HIGH-TECH

1 The Bakema discovery of Split is discussed in Tom Avermaete, "Team 10's Reinvention of the Critical Capacity of the Urban Tissue," in Max Risselada and Dirk van den Heuvel, eds: *Team 10, 1953–81: In Search of a Utopia of the Present* (Rotterdam: NAi, 2005). The Avermaete essay starts on page 306. The reference to Bakema and Split is on page 310.

2 Tange and the Metabolists are discussed in Rem Koolhaas and Hans Ulrich Obrist, *Project Japan: Metabolism Talks...* (Cologne: Taschen, 2011).

3 A description of the design and construction of Scarborough College can be found in Jennifer Taylor and John Andrews, *John Andrews: Architecture a Performing Art* (Melbourne: Oxford University Press, 1982), 30–47.

4 A description of the design and construction of Simon Fraser University can be found in Nicholas Olsberg and Ricardo Castro, eds., *Arthur Erickson: Critical Works* (Vancouver: Douglas and McIntyre, 2006), 85–91.

5 In his essay "Western Monoliths: Arthur Erickson's Design for Two Universities," in Olsberg and Castro, eds., *Arthur Erickson: Critical Works*, Georges Teyssot also makes reference to the obvious parallel between the Hollein image and Erickson's concept for Lethbridge. See page 85.

6 A description of the design and construction of the University of Lethbridge can be found in ibid., 93–97.

7 A description of the design and construction of Habitat 67 can be found in Moshe Safdie, Judith Wolin, ed., *For Everyone a Garden* (London: MIT Press, 1974), 62–80.

8 The team of associates included the following individuals: A. Banelis, I. Grinnel, N. Hancock, R. H. Jacobs, F. Kulsar, A. Roberts, J. Rohn, and P. Wakayama. I am grateful to Peter Wakayama, as well as to Martin Fiset and Thomas Strickland, for assisting me in the preparation of my discussion of the McMaster project.

9 In describing the design and construction of the project in a booklet produced by the firm, Zeidler suggests that the building "probably functions more like a city than a single building." Eberhard Zeidler, *Healing the Hospital* (Toronto: Zeidler Partnership, 1974).

10 A description of the design and construction of the McMaster Health Sciences Centre can be found in Eberhard Zeidler and Stefano Pavarini, *Zeidler Roberts Partnership: Ethics and Architecture* (Milan: L'Arca Edizioni, 1999), 113–129.

11 Ibid., 143–157.

12 Ibid., 167–187.

13 Interestingly enough, in the same August 1975 issue of the *The Canadian Architect* in which the +15 system is discussed, there is included a diagram showing a conceptual layout of such a system for downtown Calgary from 1967, credited to Affleck, Debarats, Dimakopoulos, Lebensold, and Sise. It would seem that outside consultants had made propositions along these lines prior to the formal adoption of the idea by the city itself.

14 A description of the design and construction of Robson Square can be found in Olsberg and Castro, eds., *Arthur Erickson: Critical Works*, 153–159.

15 See Reyner Banham, *Megastructure: Urban Futures of the Recent Past* (London: Thames and Hudson, 1976).

16 See James A. Murray, "Habitat 67: The Critical Eye," *The Canadian Architect* 12, no. 10 (October 1967).

17 I discuss these criticisms of Berlin Free University in my essay "Review of Free University Berlin: AA Publication/Exhibition in the Members' Room, May 21–June 18, 1999" in George Baird, *Writings on Architecture and the City* (London: Artifice Books, 2015).

6. POSTMODERNISM

1 Influential postmodern philosophers include Jean Baudrillard, Jacques Derrida, Michel Foucault, Jean-François Lyotard, and Gianni Vattimo. Literary critic and political theorist Fredric Jameson (1934–) and architectural historian Charles Jencks (1939–) have also been key figures in discussions on postmodernism.

2 Concepts of time-space simultaneity and fluidity in architecture and city planning were set out by Siegfried Gideon in his 1941 book *Space, Time and Architecture: The Growth of a New Tradition* (Cambridge, MA: Harvard University Press). Gideon asserted that early-twentieth-century architecture and urbanism were radically impacted by notions of simultaneity derived from cubism. This sense of a fluid spatial continuum, along with the reduced significance of distance, is integral to postmodernist thought.

3 The Philadelphia School was an ideological and pedagogical school of thought centered at the University of Pennsylvania Graduate School of Fine Arts from around 1955 to 1965. It evolved as a response to the limitations of the modern movement in architecture and planning. The leaders were Louis Kahn and Robert Venturi. Other participants included Edward Bacon, Denise Scott Brown, Robert Geddes, Romaldo Giurgola, Ian McHarg, and George Qualls. Robert Venturi's *Complexity and Contradiction in Architecture* (New York: The Museum of

Modern Art Papers on Architecture, 1966), was followed by field research with students at the Yale University School of Architecture in 1968, leading to the publication of *A Significance for A&P Parking Lots, or Learning from Las Vegas*, by Robert Venturi, Denise Scott Brown, and Steven Izenour (Cambridge, MA: MIT Press, 1972).

4   Charles Moore designed Sea Ranch with Donlyn Lyndon, William Turnbull, Jr., and Richard Whittaker, in collaboration with landscape architect Lawrence Halprin. *The Place of Houses* by Charles Moore, Gerald Allen, and Donlyn Lyndon (New York: Holt, Reinhart and Winston, 1974) is a postmodern treatise on place as both physical location and the fulfillment of humankind's spiritual needs.

5   Oliver Wainwright, "James Gowan Obituary," *The Guardian*, June 21, 2015. During 1956–63, Gowan (1923–2015) was in partnership with James Stirling (1926–1992), a fellow Scotsman. Their 1963 Engineering Building at Leicester University sent shock waves through the international architectural community and was hailed as Britain's first postmodernist work of architecture.

6   Moshe Safdie, "Private Jokes in Public Places," *The Atlantic Monthly* (December 1981): 62–68.

7   See Larry Richards, "Ottawa's Crystal Palace," *Canadian Art* (Summer 1988): 50–59; and Trevor Boddy, "A Critique: Architecture on the Fast Track," *The Canadian Architect* 33, no. 6 (June 1988): 44–49.

8   See Paul Goldberger, "A New Embassy Mixes the Appropriate and Awkward," *New York Times*, July 9, 1989.

9   Charles Jencks and George Baird, eds., *Meaning in Architecture* (New York: George Braziller, 1970).

10 See "Seven Essays in Ontario Vernacular: Selected Projects 1973–76 by the Office of George Baird Architect," in Ching-Yu Chang, ed., *Process Architecture No. 6: A Perspective of Modern Canadian Architecture* (Tokyo: Process Architecture Publishing, 1978), 146.

11 Ibid., 142–149.

12 Telephone interview with Peter Rose, September 1, 2016.

13 In my September 1, 2016, interview with Rose, he referred to his approach in the 1970s as "organic postmodernism," which meant focusing on topography and situating the building in the landscape. Rose noted that, while a student at Yale, he was inspired by Vincent Scully's lectures on the sophisticated siting of Greek temples.

14 Melvin Charney, *Parables and Other Allegories: The Work of Melvin Charney, 1975–1990* (Montreal: Canadian Centre for Architecture, 1991), 69.

15 See Larry Richards and Ian Wakefield, "The Edmonton City Hall Competition," *Trace* 1, no. 3 (1981): 27–41.

16 Eric Fiss, Brian Lyons, and Larry Richards established Networks Limited in Halifax in 1978, and artist Frederic Urban joined the studio in 1979. After completing more than twenty-five projects in the Maritime region, Networks was disbanded in 1980. See "Lyons Tower" in *Larry Richards: Works 1977–80* (Halifax: Tech-Press, 1980), 30; and "Lyons Tower" in *Domus*, no. 620 (September 1981): 34.

17 Kenneth Frampton, "Towards a Critical Regionalism: Six Points for an Architecture of Resistance," in Hal Foster, ed., *Postmodern Culture* (London: Pluto Press, 1983), 16–30.

18 Stephen Dobney, ed., *Barton Myers: Selected and Current Works* (Melbourne: The Images Publishing Group, 1994), 56.

19 Peter Arnell and Ted Bickford, eds., *Mississauga City Hall, A Canadian Competition* (New York: Rizzoli International Publications, 1984), 30.

20 Ibid., 134.

21 Ibid.

22 Phyllis Lambert, "Introduction," in Larry Richards, ed., *Canadian Centre for Architecture: Building and Gardens* (Montreal: Canadian Centre for Architecture and MIT Press, 1989), 11.

23 Ibid., 13.

24 Phyllis Lambert, "Design Imperatives," in ibid., 58.

25 Melvin Charney, "A Garden for the Canadian Centre for Architecture," in ibid., 90.

26 Larry Richards, "Critical Classicism and the Restoration of Architectural Consciousness," in ibid., 135.

27 Richard Henriquez, *Richard Henriquez: Selected Works, 1964–2005* (Vancouver: Douglas & McIntyre, 2006), 86–91 and 110–123.

28 Henriquez's surrealistic visions are discussed in Howard Schubert's insightful exhibition catalog, *Richard Henriquez: Narrative Fragments* (Windsor: Windsor Gallery, 2012).

29 The Museum of Modern Art in New York presented "Deconstructivist Architecture," organized by Philip Johnson in association with Mark Wigley, from June 23 to August 30, 1988. The exhibition featured seven international architects whose work emphasized fracturing and disharmony. The same year, Heinrich Klotz's *The*

History of Postmodern Architecture (Cambridge, MA: MIT Press, 1988) was published.

30 In *The Story of Post-Modernism: Five Decades of the Ironic, Iconic and Critical in Architecture* (New York: Wiley, 2011), Charles Jencks extends the scope of postmodernism into the twenty-first century. Also see the proceedings of the conference, "Postmodern Procedures," organized by Sylvia Lavin at Princeton University, December 4–5, 2016; and note the exhibition, *Architecture Itself and Other Postmodernist Myths*, curated by Lavin and presented at the Canadian Centre for Architecture, Montreal, November 11, 2018, to April 11, 2019.

31 Colin Fournier, "Reassessing Postmodernism," *The Architectural Review*, October 30, 2011, accessed February 5, 2018, https://www.architectural-review.com/rethink/viewpoints/reassessing-postmodernism/8621635.article.

7. URBAN REVITALIZATION

1 M. Seelig and J. Seelig, "Recycling Vancouver's Granville Island," *Architectural Record* (September 1990): 79–80.

2 See Roger Kemble, "Granville Island: A Critique," *The Canadian Architect* 25, no. 8 (August 1980).

3 See Peter Rose, "Master Plan for the Old Port of Montreal," in Louise Pelletier, ed., *Architecture, Ethics, and Technology* (Montreal: McGill-Queen's Press-MQUP, 1994), 83–97.

4 Robert Fulford, *Accidental City: The Transformation of Toronto* (Toronto: MacFarlane, Walter & Ross, 1995), 37.

5 Seana Irvine and Erin Elliott, *Transformation: The Story of Creating Evergreen Brick Works* (Toronto: Evergreen) accessed October 3, 2018, https://www.evergreen.ca/downloads/pdfs/Transformation-EBW.pdf.

6 Alex Bozikovic, "Non-profit's Renovation Project in Toronto Is a Lesson in Building a Green Future," *Globe and Mail*, February 28, 2017, accessed March 2, 2017, http://www.theglobeandmail.com/life/home-and-garden/architecture/non-profits-toronto-renovation-project-a-lesson-in-how-to-build-a-green-future.

7 See Alberto Pérez-Gómez and David Weir, *Towards an Ethical Architecture: Issues within the Work of Gregory Henriquez (*Vancouver: Blueimprint, 2006).

8 John Bentley Mays, "An Ethical Plan," *Canadian Architect* 53, no. 1 (February 2007), accessed December 31, 2016, https://www.

canadianarchitect.com/features/an-ethical-plan/.

9 Urban Land Institute, ed., *ULI Case Studies: Woodward's.* Issue brief (April 1, 2014).

10 R. W. Liscombe and M. Sabatino, *Canada: Modern Architectures in History* (London: Reaktion Books, 2006), 149.

11 Ibid., 150.

12 John Bentley Mays, "A Clean Slate?" *Canadian Architect* 50, no. 8 (August 2005).

8. ENVIRONMENTAL ARCHITECTURE

1 E. F. Schumacher, *Small is Beautiful: Economics as if People Mattered* (New York: Harper & Row, 1973).

2 Steven Mannell, *Living Lightly on the Earth: Building an Ark for Prince Edward Island 1974–76* (Halifax: Dalhousie Architectural Press, 2018).

3 The design team included researchers from the University of Saskatchewan and the Saskatchewan and National Research Councils. The Saskatchewan Conservation House is said to have inspired the German PassivHaus concept. PassivHaus adopts the super-insulated and airtight envelope approach, but dispenses with the active solar-heating system. Instead, heat generated by household activities—people and appliances—meets the modest needs resulting from the radically reduced heat losses. Solsearch Architects independently developed a version of this concept in their Conserver Houses, with several examples built in Charlottetown between 1978 and 1980. A small greenhouse off the living room on the south side enabled passive solar gains while offering the light, humidity, and aromas of year-round plant growth; the main volume was a super-insulated airtight box with high-performance windows. A Conserver House had no furnace, but drew on the domestic water heater as backup for extreme conditions. As Ole Hammarlund noted, "With body heat who needs solar?"

4 The R-2000 house standard (1982) followed a similar environment-excluding approach, with increased insulation and airtight walls, windows, and doors; though windows could still be opened, central heat-recovery ventilation systems providing controlled fresh air were preferred. Each of ten thousand R-2000–certified houses typically saved 50 percent on energy and 41 percent on emissions, and tens of thousands more houses used R-2000

approaches outside the certification scheme, leading to significant improvement in the overall energy performance of new houses in Canada by the 1990s.

5 This formulation is adapted from Kenneth Frampton, who uses the term "prophylactic" to contrast Richard Neutra's sealed, exterior-excluding approach to enclosure with that of R. M. Schindler, whose layered enclosures invited tempered exchanges of exterior air, heat, and humidity. See Kenneth Frampton with Yukio Futagawa (photographer), *Modern Architecture 1851–1945* (New York: Rizzoli, 1983), 373.

6 The paradox of an economy premised on infinite growth on a planet of limited biological capacity was identified in The Club of Rome's bestselling *Limits to Growth* (1972). The challenge of reconciling economy and environment was identified but not addressed by the 1972 UN Conference on the Environment in Stockholm; the conflict remains a common theme in media and politics today.

7 Gro Harlem Brundtland et al., and World Commission on Environment and Development, *Our Common Future: The Report of the World Commission on Environment and Development* (Oxford: Oxford University Press, 1987).

8 The Boyne River school was closed in 2003 due to provincial funding cuts.

9 The "living machine" was developed in the 1980s by John Todd and New Alchemy Institute, based on the solar aquaculture system used at the Ark for PEI.

10 Paul Kernan, Richard Kadulski, and Michel Labrie, *Old to New: Design Guide, Salvaged Building Materials in New Construction* (Vancouver: Greater Vancouver Regional District, Policy & Planning Department, 2001).

11 The grid-tied unit used a smart meter to connect to the Toronto grid for electrical storage rather than the battery bank of the off-grid unit, and it had a connection to city mains for potable water needs.

12 GBC developed the comprehensive and detailed GBTool to conduct the case study assessments. GBTool is a useful research and academic tool, but it was judged far too cumbersome for use in a professional design setting and so did not fit the bill as a possible universal assessment standard.

13 Ecomodernism proposes an accelerated rate of modernization through technological improvement, "decoupled" from its historical negative environmental consequences, as a solution to global environmental and development challenges. See "An Ecomodernist

Manifesto" (2015), accessed March 15, 2018, http://www.ecomodernism.org.

14 It is worth noting that LEED is a successful example of self-reform by the building industry, with projects voluntarily exceeding the requirements of government regulation. That said, the establishment of LEED in Canada relied upon significant government and academic effort.

15 "Living Building Challenge," accessed March 15, 2018, https://living-future.org/lbc/.

16 The 2030 Challenge is the vision of US architect and educator Edward Mazria, a longtime passive solar and renewable energy advocate, who in 2002 founded Architecture 2030, a nonprofit organization devoted to transforming the built environment from a major contributor to the carbon emissions problem to a major part of the solution.

17 CMHC's "Equilibrium" Net Zero Housing program (2007) extends the R-2000 energy efficiency standard of the 1980s to provide a cross-country catalogue of exemplary sustainable houses. Projects include urban and inner-suburban infill and retrofit examples, recognizing the embodied system energy and sustainability benefits of urban settings, but also include examples set in exurban sprawl of dubious overall sustainability.

18 Centre for Interactive Research on Sustainability, "CIRS Building Manual," accessed August 29, 2018, http://cirs.ubc.ca/building/building-manual/.

19 While growth in "green buildings" presently exceeds construction sector growth as a whole, in 2017 just 1.1 percent of global building stock by area was LEED certified. US Green Building Council, "Benefits of Green Building," accessed March 15, 2018, https://www.usgbc.org/articles/green-building-facts; Navigant Research, "Global Building Stock Database," accessed March 15, 2018, https://www.navigantresearch.com/research/global-building-stock-database.

20 Benny Farm was the Gold Award winner for North America in the regional phase and the Bronze Award winner in the subsequent global phase, chosen from over 1,500 projects from 118 countries.

9. WEST COAST LAND CLAIMS

I would like to thank Jana Tyner and Rachel Farquharson for their invaluable research assistance.

1 Prime Minister Pierre Elliott Trudeau had been forced to reposition his Indigenous policy after the defeat of his government's 1969 white paper, which sought to fold First Nations into the new "just society" and thus annul their special status and land claims.

2 Composed of lumber framing and plywood panels, units could be configured on a 33-by-100-foot (10-by-30.5-meter) lot and replicated across whole blocks. "This Is a Factory-Built House?" *Plywood World*, Vancouver (January-April 1968): 6.

3 Ibid.

4 Similar preoccupations can be seen in Jones and Emmons's 1961 Case Study House #24, which proposed a housing model that could be replicated for suburban development, and Richard Neutra's Plywood House for the California House and Garden Exhibition in 1936, which used a light metal frame and plywood panels to construct a single-story house that could be disassembled, transported, and reassembled. Moshe Safdie's Habitat 67 for Montreal's Expo 67 explored prefabricated units but was constructed of reinforced concrete and stacked vertically.

5 Barry Downs, quoted in "Mobility in Three Stages," *Western Homes and Living* (April 1969): 32–34.

6 Donald MacKay, *Empire of Wood: The MacMillan Bloedel Story* (Toronto: Douglas & McIntyre, 1983), 244.

7 See Matthew Soules, "Deconstructing Liveability: Perspectives from Central Vancouver," in Gaia Carmellino and Federico Zanfi, eds., *Post War Middle-Class Housing: Models, Construction and Change* (Bern: Peter Lang, 2015), 332–335.

8 Christopher Alexander's "Cells for Subcultures" was an influential text at this time. See John Punter, *The Vancouver Achievement: Urban Planning and Design* (Vancouver: UBC Press, 2003), 37.

9 Designed in 1977–78, the project was stalled and not realized until much later. Kathryn Iredale with Sheila Marineau, *Finding a Good Fit: The Life and Work of Architect Rand Iredale* (Vancouver: Blueimprint, 2008), 215.

10 Bob Quintrell, interview with Arthur Erickson, "The Seven O'Clock Show," CBC, June 24, 1966.

11 On the changes to city planning initiated by the 1953 Vancouver City Charter, see Punter, *The Vancouver Achievement,* 8, 13–14.

12 Victor Gruen, *The Heart of Our Cities: The Urban Crisis: Diagnosis and Cure* (London: Thames and Hudson, 1965).

13 For discussion of this development, see Punter, *The Vancouver Achievement*, 21–23; Donald Gutstein, *Vancouver Ltd.* (Toronto: James Lorimer and Co, 1975); and Donald Gutstein, "Neighbourhood Improvements: What It Means in Calgary, Vancouver and Toronto," *City Magazine* I, no. 5–6 (August/September 1975): 15–28.

14 The writing on Erickson is extensive. Significant and more comprehensive texts are: Nicholas Olsberg and Richard L. Castro, eds. *Arthur Erickson Critical Works* (Vancouver and Seattle: Vancouver Art Gallery, Douglas & McIntyre and University of Washington Press, 2006); Nicholas Olsberg "Canada's Greatest Architect," in Rhodri Windsor Liscombe, ed., *The Canadian Fabric* (Vancouver and Toronto: UBC Press, 2011), 429–445; David Stouck, *Arthur Erickson: An Architect's Life* (Madeira Park: Douglas & McIntyre, 2013); Michelangelo Sabbatino, "Arthur Erickson and essential tectonics," *The Journal of Architecture* 13, no. 4 (2008): 493–514. Key works by Arthur Erickson are documented in *The Architecture of Arthur Erickson* (Vancouver: Douglas and McIntyre, 1988) and *Habitation, Space, Dilemma and Design* (Ottawa: Canadian Housing Design Council, 1966).

15 Interview with Rainer Fassler, in Iredale, *Finding a Good Fit*, 132.

16 Donald Luxton and Associates, *1500 West Georgia Street: Statement of Significance.* July 2015, accessed November 10, 2016, http://www.rezoning.vancouver.ca /applications/1500wgeorgia/documents /13-heritage.pdf.

17 Barry Downs, "Building as Landform," unpublished manuscript, Downs's private collection. Accessed June 2016.

18 Discretionary planning was introduced between 1972 and 1975, allowing planners to negotiate design aspects such as height, setback, and site coverage ratios.

19 Joan Lowndes, "Architecture in an Indigenous Manner," *Vancouver Sun* (1975).

20 North Vancouver Civic Centre, Opening Ceremony Brochure, March 8, 1975.

21 Arthur Erickson, quoted in John Arnett, "Architect Reaches into B.C.'s Past for Design," *UBC Reports* (Jan. 18, 1972): 3.

22 Ibid.

23 Mildred F. Schmertz, "Spaces for Anthropological Art," *Architectural Record* (May 1977): 103.

24 Although Erickson insisted they face north toward the artificial lake envisioned between

the museum and cliff's edge, they are displayed facing east and west. This is seen both in archival photographs and in the present-day museum. See David Stouck, *Arthur Erickson*, 385.

25 The photograph is mentioned by Dr. Harry Hawthorn, first director of the Museum of Anthropology. The photograph also perpetuated the misconception that the indigenous peoples were disappearing, which justified land confiscation and other prejudices.

26 Arthur Erickson, quoted in Arnett, "Architect Reaches into B.C.'s Past for Design," 2.

27 Henry Hawthorn, Conversation with Ted Lindbergh, *Vanguard* (August 1976): np.

28 *The Canadian Architect* 22, no. 9 (September 1977): 34–35.

29 Pierre Elliot Trudeau, quoted in "A Proud Day for the Haida," *Vanguard* (August 1976): 9.

30 Haida Gwaii Heritage Centre, accessed October 20, 2016, www.haidaheritagecentre.com.

31 Julian Jacobs, "Modern, Post Modern or What?" *The Canadian Architect* 28, no. 9 (September 1983): 21, 38.

32 Marco Polo, Bronwen Ledger, and Beth Kapusta, "Conversations with Patkau Architects" (1991 and 1993) in Brian Carter, ed., *Patkau Architects: Selected Topics, 1983–93* (Halifax: TUNS, 1994), 18.

10. PRAIRIE FORMATIONS

The author would like to thank David Murray (Edmonton), Bernie Flaman (Regina), Andrew Wallace (Saskatoon), Neil Minuk (Winnipeg), and Lisa Landrum (Winnipeg) for sharing their knowledge and passion for architecture in the Prairie Provinces.

1 See Harold Kalman, *A History of Canadian Architecture,* vol. 2 (Toronto: Oxford University Press, 1994).

2 See Serena Keshavjee, ed., *Winnipeg Modern: Architecture 1945–1975* (Winnipeg: University of Manitoba Press, 2006).

3 See Bernard Flaman, *Architecture of Saskatchewan: A Visual Journey, 1930–2011* (Regina: CPRC Press, 2013).

4 See Trevor Boddy, *Modern Architecture in Alberta* (Regina: University of Regina Press, 1987); and Catherine Crowston, ed., *Capital Modern: A Guide to Edmonton Architecture and Urban Design, 1940–1969* (Edmonton: Art Gallery of Alberta, 2007).

5 See "Prairie Architecture Examined," *The Canadian Architect* 24, no. 10 (October 1979): 21–30.

6 See Faye Helner, "Étienne Gaboury: Manitoba Modernist," in Keshavjee, *Winnipeg Modern*, 228–243.

7 Étienne Gaboury, "Precious Blood Church," *The Canadian Architect* 14, no. 10 (October, 1969): 44.

8 Étienne Gaboury, "Metaphors and Metamorphosis," in Faye Hellner, ed., *Étienne Gaboury* (Saint-Boniface: Editions du Blé, 2005), 32–33.

9 See the film "Architect Clifford Wiens Industrial Chic," on YouTube, accessed Feb. 4, 2018, https://www.youtube.com/watch?v=wtveUhqGdtQ.

10 See Trevor Boddy, *The Architecture of Douglas Cardinal* (Edmonton: NeWest Press, 1989), 66.

11 See Barry Johns, "Critique: Head-Smashed-In Buffalo Jump Interpretive Centre," *The Canadian Architect* 33, no. 11 (November 1988): 24–28.

12 Brian Allsopp, "Post-Modern–the Image and the Challenge," *The Canadian Architect* 24, no. 10 (October 1979): 34–36.

13 See Essy Baniassad, "Architecture and the Prairies: Observations on the Works of Barry Johns," in Brian Carter and Essy Baniassad, eds., *Barry Johns Architects* (Halifax: Tuns Press, 2000).

14 Brian Allsopp, "Building Appraisal: Edmonton Advanced Technology Centre," *The Canadian Architect* (April 1989): 26.

15 Barry Johns, "Making Places," in Carter and Baniassad, *Barry Johns Architects*, 15.

16 See Kenneth Frampton, "Towards a Critical Regionalism: Six Points Towards an Architecture of Resistance," in Hal Foster, ed., *Anti-Aesthetic: Essays on Postmodern Culture* (Seattle: Bay Press, 1983).

11. EASTERN EDGE

1 Christine Macy, *Free Lab* (Halifax: TUNS Press, 2008).

2 The Ghost Architectural Laboratory program was offered annually between 1994 and 2012. It is documented in *Ghost: Building an Architectural Vision* by Brian MacKay-Lyons (New York: Princeton Architectural Press, 2008).

3 Robert Mellin, *Tilting* (New York: Princeton Architectural Press, 2003).

12. ARCTIC ARCHITECTURE

1 Internal colonialism, in a Canadian context, refers to uneven development and exploitation

motivated by government policies and practices on Indigenous Canadians. John D. O'Neil cites "internal colonialism rather than 'acculturation' as an analytical framework for understanding change related stress." John D. O'Neil, "Colonial Stress in the Canadian Arctic: An Ethnography of Young Adults Changing," in Craig R. Janes, ed., et al., *Anthropology and Epidemiology* (Netherlands: Springer, 1986), 250.

2 David Damas, *Arctic Migrants/Arctic Villagers: The Transformation of Inuit Settlement in the Central Arctic* (Montreal: McGill-Queen's University Press, 2002), 19.

3 Statistics Canada 1971, 2016. The territory of Nunavut has the fastest rate of growth in Canada, at 12.7 percent. Statistics Canada 2016. Population size and growth rate, Canada, provinces and territories, 2006 to 2011 and 2011 to 2016. Accessed Sept 1, 2017, http://www.statcan.gc.ca/daily-quotidien/170208/t002a-eng.htm.

4 Frank Tester, "Iglutaasaavut (Our New Homes): Neither 'New' nor 'Ours': Housing Challenges of the Nunavut Territorial Government," *Journal of Canadian Studies* 43, no. 2 (Spring 2009): 138.

5 "Housing By and For Inuit," *Inuit Today* 5, no. 10 (November 1976), 25.

6 Harold Strub, *Bare Poles: Building Design for High Latitudes* (Ottawa: Carleton University Press, 1996), 14.

7 Canada Mortgage and Housing Corporation, "A Preliminary Evaluation of the Performance of Super-Insulated Demonstration Houses Built in Keewatin, NWT" (1982), accessed November 20, 2014, ftp://ftp.cmhc-schl.gc.ca/cmhc/94_202.html.

8 Gabriella Goliger, "Arctic Housing Update," in William C. Wonders, ed., *Canada's Changing North*, (Montreal and Kingston: McGill-Queen's University Press, 2003), 321.

9 The larger multiunit housing structures compound the challenges found in single-family units because they elevate occupants even farther off the ground than the conventional single-story dwelling with pile foundations. Ten-unit structures and larger are on hold in Nunavut for a number of reasons—land availability, community density, maintainability, accessibility, equipment needs, and insufficient parking. However, according to Nunavut Housing Corporation, they may be built again, depending on need and land availability. Based on an interview with Gary Wong, Director of Infrastructure at Nunavut Housing Corporation, Nov. 8, 2017.

10 Montreal architect Alain Fournier of EVOQ, has pursued similar work in northern Quebec. He has developed housing that employs pile foundations, which are common in Nunavut but less so in the Nunavik region, and embraces some of the energy efficiency logics of the Passivhaus, including water heat exchangers. Fournier's Nunavik housing prototype integrates both a cold and warm porch, storage in the attic space of the pitched roof, kitchens composed of large mobile storage units suited to the preparation of country food, and secure, separated storage for hunting gear.

11 See interview on the impact of sprawl in northern cities with Jack Kobayashi in Lola Sheppard and Mason White, eds., *Many Norths: Spatial Practice in a Polar Territory* (New York: Actar, 2017), 66.

12 See Frank Tester, "Iglutaasaavut (Our New Homes): Neither 'New' nor 'Ours,'" 153.

13 Ibid., 141.

14 The Distant Early Warning (DEW) Line was a joint Canadian-US set of radar installations across the Arctic employed to detect Soviet bombers during the Cold War. For more on the DEW Line see Frances Jewel Dickson, *The DEW Line Years: Voices from the Coldest Cold War* (Lawrencetown Beach, NS: Pottersfield Press, 2007).

15 Andrew Waldron, "Frobisher Bay Future: Megastructure in a Meta-Land," *Architecture and Ideas*, vol. VIII (2009): 26.

16 Ibid., 29.

17 Both Jérémie Michael McGowan and Alan Marcus have been critical of Erskine's proposal for Resolute. Marcus notes that although the scheme "relaxes its form into the contours of the landscape" and embraces an "egalitarian environment," "systemic flaws appear to have been overlooked." Alan Marcus, "Place with No Dawn," in Rhodri Windsor Liscombe, ed., *Architecture and the Canadian Fabric* (Vancouver: University of British Columbia Press, 2011), 304.

18 Ibid., 288.

19 Ibid., 289.

20 "Census Profile, Fermont, Quebec," Statistics Canada, accessed February 15, 2018, http://www12.statcan.gc.ca/census-recensement/2016/dp-pd/prof/details/page.cfm?Lang=E&Geo1=POPC&Code1=1061&Geo2=PR&Code2=24&Data=Count&SearchText=Fermont&SearchType=Begins&SearchPR=01&B1=All&GeoLevel=PR&GeoCode=1061&TABID=1.

21 Desnoyers Schoenauer planners worked with Desnoyers Mercure Leziy Gagnon Sheppard Architects.

22 Adrian Sheppard, "Fermont: The Making of a New Town in the Canadian Sub-Arctic." Lecture delivered on July 11, 2007, at the Ion Mincu School of Architecture and Urbanism, Bucharest, Romania. From the lecture notes revised in March 2012.

23 Norbert Schoenauer, "A New Version of the Company Town," *Journal of Architectural Education* 29, no. 3 (Feb., 1976): 10–11. Accessed October 2017, https://www.jstor.org/stable /pdf/1424490.pdf?refreqid=excelsior% 3Aa6bce8876a598b565e69bf70e7d91e75.

24 See Adrian Sheppard, "Fermont." See also William O'Mahony's description of Fermont in William C. Wonders, ed., *Canada's Changing North* (Montreal: McGill-Queen's University Press, 2003), 310–313.

25 From an unpublished interview by the authors with Moshe Safdie on September 27, 2013.

26 See interview with Gino Pin, head of the GNWT Public Works at the time, in Sheppard and White, eds., *Many Norths*, 178.

27 See interview with Guy Gérin-Lajoie, in Sheppard and White, eds., *Many Norths*, 158.

28 Marie-Josée Therrien, "Built to Educate: The Architecture of Schools in the Arctic from 1950 to 2007," in *JSSAC* 40, no. 2 (2015): 25–42.

29 The lack of windows in PGL's work, while striking, is paralleled by similar design strategies elsewhere in Canada at the time, when windows in school design were seen as a distraction to students.

30 See Jack Hicks and Graham White, *Made in Nunavut: An Experiment in Decentralized Government* (Vancouver: UBC Press, 2015).

31 Based on an interview conducted with Norman Glouberman and Bruce Allan, February 14, 2017. See also Nunavut Construction Corporation (NCC) News Release, "Nunavut Construction Corporation Dedicates New Legislative Assembly Facility to Past and Future Generations," Iqaluit, NU, March 30, 1999. The infrastructure projects consist of 250 housing units and 10 office buildings, including the Legislative Assembly facility. NCC arranged 100 percent of the financing through financial institutions in the private sector. They constructed office buildings and staff housing units in each of the eleven communities designated by the decentralization model for the government of Nunavut (Cape Dorset, Pangnirtung, Pond Inlet, Iqaluit, Igloolik, Arviat Rankin Inlet, Baker Lake, Kugluktuk, Cambridge Bay, and Gjoa Haven).

32 Ibid.

33 Ibid. See Annette Bourgeois, "NCC's Architect Unveils the House of Nunavut," *Nunatsiaq News* (December 19, 1997).

34 See Marie-Josée Therrien's fine analysis of the evolution of school design in the Canadian Arctic, "Built to Educate."

35 See the report of the Truth and Reconciliation Commission of Canada, "Honouring the Truth, Reconciling for the Future" (May 31, 2015).

36 See Therrien's analysis of the Maani Ulujuk School in "Built to Educate," 37.

37 In a further expression of Indigenous capacity and self-expression, the building was constructed by the First Nations–owned construction firm Han Construction.

38 As in KZA's Old Crow Research Centre, photovoltaic panels are an important material that also enhance building performance. The solar panels perform primarily in the arctic summer months and generate excess power to help offset diesel-generated electricity. The Vuntut Gwitch'in First Nation will sell power back to the utility— the John Tizya Centre is the first grid-tied building in the Yukon to have this capacity.

39 From a conversation by the authors with Joshua Armstrong in 2013.

40 Building in Nunatsiavut—just as in Nunavut— can be expensive, with short windows of construction, a frequent lack of local skilled labor, and a climate that pushes building envelopes to their limits.

41 Harold D. Kalman, *A History of Canadian Architecture*, vol. 2. (Toronto: Oxford University Press: 1994), 704.

13. THE ARCHITECTURE OF QUEBEC

The author wishes to acknowledge the generous help of David Covo, Morgan Matheson, Violetta Molokopy, and Adrian Sheppard.

1 See Brian Young and John A. Dickson, *A Short History of Quebec*, 4th ed. (Montreal: McGill-Queen's University Press, 2008); Peter Gossage, and J. I. Little, *An Illustrated History of Quebec: Tradition and Modernity* (Don Mills, Ont.: Oxford University Press Canada, 2012); Paul-André Linteau, René Durocher, and Jean-Claude Robert, *Quebec: A History 1867–1929*, trans. Robert Chodos (Toronto: James Lorimer 1983, original 1979), 125–7; André Pratte and Jonathan Kay, eds., *Legacy: How French Canadians Shaped North* America (Toronto: Signal, 2016); Dimitry Anastakis, *The Sixties: Passion, Politics, and Style*

(Montreal: McGill-Queen's University Press, 2008); France Vanlaethem, "The Ambivalence of Architectural Culture in Quebec and Canada, 1955–1975," in Dimitry Anastakis, ed., *The Sixties* (Montreal: McGill-Queen's University Press, 2008), 127–44.

2 See Martin Drouin, *Le combat du patrimoine à Montréal, 1973–2003* (Sainte-Foy: Presses de l'Université du Québec, 2005); and Claude Marsan, *Montréal en évolution: quatre siècles d'architecture et d'aménagemen,* 4th ed. (Québec: Presses de l'Université du Québec, 2016).

3 See Georges Adamczyk, "Concours et qualité architecturale," *ARQ/Architecture Québec* (February 2004): 4–5, 24. For a comprehensive review and database of competitions, see the Canadian Competitions Catalogue (ccc.umontreal.ca).

4 See Michael Gauvreau, *The Catholic Origins of Quebec's Quiet Revolution, 1931–1970* (Montreal: McGill-Queen's University Press, 2005).

5 See Gary Caldwell and Simon Langlois, "Les cégeps vingt ans après," *Recherches sociographiques* 27, no. 3 (1986).

6 See Johanne Sloan and Rhona Richmann Kenneally, eds., *Expo 67: Not Just a Souvenir* (Toronto: University of Toronto Press, 2010); and Chantal Quintric, "Conséquences de l'Exposition internationale de 1967 sur la morphologie urbaine de Montréal," *Annales de Géographie* 80, no. 437 (1971): 45–64.

7 See Annmarie Adams and Peta Tancred, *Designing Women: Gender and the Architectural Profession* (Toronto: University of Toronto Press, 2000), 117–19.

8 For more on French-language architecture publishing, see Renata Guttman, "Architecture in Canada: French-language publishing, 1981–1995," *Art Libraries Journal* 21, no. 3 (1996): 4–28.

9 This lack is usually attributed to the Catholic Church's control over education. See "Bibliothèques et architecture," thematic issue of *Documentation et bibliothèques* 60, nos. 2–3, (April–September 2014); and Jacques Plante, ed., *Architectures de la connaissance au Québec* (Québec: Les Publications du Québec, 2013).

10 See Luc Noppen and Lucie K. Morisset, *Les Églises du Québec: Un Patrimoine à Réinventer* (Quebec: Presses de l'Université du Québec, 2006).

11 See David Theodore, "Bright Lights, Big Price Tag: The New Palais des congrès Is Worth Every Cent," *Maisonneuve* no. 3 (Spring 2003), 68–70.

12 See McGill University Health Centre Glen (MUHC; 2015), IBI Group Architects/

Beinhaker Architect; Centre Hospitalier de l'Université de Montréal, Cannon Design and NEUF Architectes (CHUM; 2017). See André Picard, "In Pursuit of 'Superhospitals,' the Public Interest Came Last," *Globe and Mail* (June 22, 2015).

13 See, for example, Paul Wells, "Architecture: Buildings That Will Be and Might Have Been: Paul Wells on Rem Koolhaas' Winning Design and Which Buildings Got the Shaft," *Macleans,* May 24, 2010, accessed February 15, 2018, http://www.macleans.ca/politics/ottawa/architecture-buildings-that-will-be-and-might-have-been/.

14 For an expansive photographic archive of the Faubourg, see Archives de Montréal, accessed February 15, 2018, http://archivesdemontreal.com/2013/10/15/les-quartiers-disparus-de-montreal-le-secteur-de-la-societe-radio-canada-faubourg-a-mlasse-9-juillet-1963/.

15 See Drouin, *Combat du patrimoine à Montréal, 1973–2003.*

16 See Norbert Schoenauer, "Fermont and Windscreens," *The Canadian Architect* 16, no. 10 (October 1971): 45–7.

17 See Diane-Gabrielle Tremblay and Serge Rousseau, "The Montreal Multimedia Sector: A Cluster, a New Mode of Governance or a Simple Co-Location?" *Canadian Journal of Regional Science* 28, no. 2 (2005): 299–328.

18 For a multiperspectival view on the project, see Simon Harel, Laurent Lussier, and Joël Thibert, *Le Quartier des spectacles et le chantier de l'imaginaire montréalais* (Quebec: Les Presses de l'Université Laval, 2013). Place des Arts was designed by ARCOP and opened in 1963; see Laurent Duval, *L'étonnant dossier de la Place des Arts: 1956–1967* (Montréal: L. Courteau, 1988).

14. TORONTO ARCHITECTURE

Many thanks to Alex Bozikovic and George Baird for their comments on a draft of this chapter, as well as to Raymond Moriyama, Jack Diamond, Bruce Kuwabara, and Peter Clewes for interviews that contributed to the content and direction of the text. Patricia McHugh and Alex Bozikovic's book *Toronto Architecture: A City Guide* (USA: McClelland & Stewart, 2017) was an invaluable resource in confirming building dates and names of firms at the time of construction.

1 The population of Toronto grew from 951,549 in 1941 to 1,824,481 in 1961, according to Statistics Canada census data.

2 See Detlef Mertins, "Mountain of Lights," in Bureau of Architecture and Urbanism (ed.), *Toronto Modern Architecture: 1945–1965* (Toronto: Coach House Books, 2002), 10–19.

3 See Christopher Armstrong, *Making Toronto Modern: Architecture and Design, 1895–1975* (Montreal: MQUP, 2014), 173–214.

4 Brigitte Shim, "Don Mills, New Town," in Bureau of Architecture and Urbanism (ed.), *Toronto Modern Architecture: 1945–1965*, 33.

5 Mertins, "Mountains of Lights," 18.

6 Several members of the Toronto design community had their offices in a row of four-story brick-and-timber warehouses on downtown Colborne Street, near the Saint Lawrence market, from the mid-1960s onward. John Andrews had his offices in one loft, working with partners Roger du Toit and Jack Diamond. Ron Thom, who was then at work finishing Massey College and beginning the development of the Trent University master plan [see chapter 3], occupied a floor of another one of the Colborne Street buildings. See Douglas Shadbolt, *Ron Thom: The Shaping of an Architect* (Vancouver: Douglas and McIntyre, 2013).

7 See John Sewell, *The Shape of the City* (Toronto: University of Toronto Press, 1993), 174–198.

8 "Trefann Court," Wikipedia article, accessed February 26, 2018, https://en.wikipedia.org/wiki/Trefann_Court.

9 Other contributors included Robert Hill, Bruce Kuwabara, Allan Littlewood, Donald McKay, Belinda Sugarman, and John van Nostrand. Born in Toronto, George Baird trained in England with Joseph Rykwert. In 1967, John Andrews recruited him to the University of Toronto, where he became chair of the architecture program from 1983 to 1985, and faculty dean from 2004 to 2009.

10 *On Building Downtown* was followed by a City commission to write *Built-Form Analysis: A Working Paper on the Implications for Built Form of Land-Use Policies Relating to Housing, Mixed Uses, and Recreation Space in the Inner Core Area* (Toronto, 1975), a landmark study which yielded insights into the unintended consequences of the city's planning practices and zoning regimes. Baird also co-edited issue 108 of *Design Quarterly* magazine (titled "Vacant Lottery") with Barton Myers, addressing many of these issues (1978). When established in 1972, Baird's firm included four graduating students from the University of Toronto—Joost Bakker, Bruce Kuwabara, John van Nostrand, and Barry Sampson—who would later become prominent in their own right (Sampson became a partner in the firm).

11 See City of Toronto, *Official Plan Amendments. Central Area Plan Review: Minutes and Report* (Toronto: Planning Board, 1976).

12 See Marco Polo, "Green Giant," *Canadian Architect* 48, no. 1 (January 2003): 20–25.

13 See "Waterfront Renovation," *The Canadian Architect* 28, no. 10 (October 1983): 14–21.

14 See John Bentley Mays, "High Notes," *Canadian Architect* 55, no. 2 (February 2010): 12–17.

15 See Kenneth Frampton, "Nun's Sense," *Canadian Architect* 59, no. 8 (August 2014): 20–25.

16 See Canadian Mortgage and Housing Corporation, *Residential Intensification Case Studies: The "Kings Regeneration" Initiative* (Ottawa: CMHC, 2003).

17 See Kenneth Hayes, "Updating the Walk-up," *Canadian Architect* 43, no. 10 (October 1998): 24–27.

18 See Marco Polo, "Contextual Modernism," *Canadian Architect* 48, no. 4 (April 2003): 16–19.

19 See Martin L. Friedland, introduction to Larry Wayne Richards, *University of Toronto: The Campus Guide* (New York: Princeton Architectural Press, 2009).

20 See George Kapelos, "Collegial Think Tank," *Canadian Architect* 46, no. 2 (February 2001): 20–25.

21 See Rhodri Windsor Liscombe and Michelangelo Sabatino, *Canada: Modern Architectures in History* (London: Reaktion Books, 2016), 185–186.

22 See Nyla Matuk, "Schools of Thought," *Canadian Architect* 46, no. 8 (August 2001): 14–17.

23 McHugh and Bozikovic, *Toronto Architecture*, 270–272.

24 See Brigitte Shim and Donald Chong, eds., *Site Unseen: Laneway Architecture and Urbanism in Toronto* (Toronto: University of Toronto Faculty of Architecture, 2004).

25 Annette W. LeCuyer, ed., *Shim Sutcliffe: The Passage of Time* (Halifax: Dalhousie Architectural Press, 2014), 16–17, 40–61.

26 The competition design team consisted of PLANT Architect, Shore Tilbe Irwin & Partners (now Perkins+Will), Hoerr Schaudt Landscape Architecture, and Adrian Blackwell Urban Projects.

15. THE NEW WEST COAST

The author would like to thank many individuals who have given extra time to share their thoughts and information for this essay, including Joost Bakker, Barry Downs, Ray Spaxman, and Michael

Geller; though it should be noted that not all will necessarily agree with its contents.

1 See chapter 9. Emblematic of this are three buildings on Georgia Street: the MacMillan Bloedel Building, designed by Erickson Massey Architects; and the Westcoast Transmission and Crown Life Buildings by Rhone & Iredale, with Peter Cardew as principal designer on the latter.

2 Two of the key reports were headed by George Baird (1939–) and Roger Du Toit (1939–2015) respectively. Jane Jacobs' *Death and Life of Great North American Cities* (New York: Random House, 1961) was an influential text for their report, confirmed *Greening Downtown* co-author Joost Bakker in an interview on Oct. 14, 2016.

3 Jonathan Barnett, and Larry Beasley, *Ecodesign for Cities and Suburbs* (Washington: Island Press, 2015), 173.

4 John Punter, *The Vancouver Achievement* (Vancouver: UBC Press, 2003), 204.

5 See Adele Weder, "Beach Banquet," *Canadian Architect* 57, no. 10 (October 2012): 20–25.

6 Kelty McKinnon, "SuperNatural," in Kelty McKinnon, ed., *Grounded: The Work of Phillips Farevaag Smallenberg* (Vancouver: Blueimprint, 2010), 251.

7 Adele Weder, "Architecture of Hope Revisited," *The Tyee*, Feb. 27, 2009, accessed February 15, 2018, https://thetyee.ca/Photo/2009/02/27/ArchHope/.

8 Andrew Gruft, *Patkau Architects* (Barcelona: Editorial Gustavo Gili, S.A., 1997), 11.

9 See Adele Weder "Rarified Prefab," *Canadian Architect* 58, no.1 (January 2013).

10 See Adele Weder, "Living in 226 Square Feet on Vancouver's East Side," *The Globe and Mail* (Feb. 9, 2012).

11 D'Arcy Jones Architecture's Emerging Architectural Practice Award is covered in the May 2017 edition of *Canadian Architect*.

12 In Joseph Mayo's book of international case studies, *Solid Wood: Case Studies in Mass Timber Architecture, Technology and Design* (Adington: Routledge, 2015), Vancouver architects are responsible for four of the five North American case studies documented.

13 Bruce Haden, "Reaching New Heights," *Canadian Architect* 62, no. 2 (February 2017): 36.

14 Excerpted from "the shapers: Vancouver," by Earle Birney, 1958, with permission of Wailan Low, executor of the estate of Earle Birney.

Acknowledgments

Writing a book has much in common with creating a building. Both start with a pure concept—the napkin sketch, the kernel of an idea, the perilous words "someone should write a book about that." Things quickly get much more labor-intensive and complex. But through it all, we remained convinced that someone *really* ought to write a book about the past fifty years of architectural production in Canada. And so we did.

Both buildings and books are collaborative efforts. Graham Livesey would like to acknowledge the enduring support of his sons, Aidan and Ellis, and the inspiration from Allison and her family. Elsa Lam edited much of this book at a treadmill desk carrying a baby in a fabric sling. She would like to thank that infant, Aiden, for taking some long naps in the past year—as well as her husband, James, and parents, Rosalie and Andrew, for their help and encouragement.

Near the beginning of this project, we drew up a wish list of authors. We were thrilled when all of them accepted the invitation to participate. Thanks to George Baird, Brian Carter, Ian Chodikoff, Odile Hénault, George Kapelos, Lisa Landrum, Steve Mannell, Sherry McKay, Marco Polo, Larry Richards, Colin Ripley, Lola Sheppard, David Theodore, Adele Weder, and Mason White for the invaluable insight they have brought to each chapter. Many thanks as well to Kenneth Frampton, who has long been an inspiration to all of us, for adding his foreword to this volume. The book is truly richer for the many voices contained in it.

Thank you to Kevin and Jennifer Lippert at Princeton Architectural Press for their vote of confidence in this project, and to Abby Bussel for shepherding it through to the manuscript stage. The production skills of Kristen Hewitt, the eagle eyes of Hannah Fries, and the design talent of Ben English have contributed enormously to the book.

Canadian Architect magazine has been a backbone for this endeavor, especially Alex Papanou. The book was jolted into reality by a major grant from the Canada Council for the Arts. In particular, thanks to Brigitte Desrochers for championing contemporary and critical practice in architecture, including through this book. The book also received financial support from the Royal Architectural Institute of Canada, PCL, and architectsAlliance. We are grateful for their support of this endeavor, as well as for the many contributions they have made to Canada's built environment over the past decades.

Several firms come up again and again in the chronicle of modern and contemporary Canadian architecture, and they have generously made many images of their work available to us and covered the cost of rights to publish those images. Our gratitude for this significant in-kind support goes to Barry Downs Architect, Diamond Schmitt Architects, Henriquez Partners Architects, KPMB Architects, MacKay-Lyons Sweetapple Architects, Patkau Architects, Peter Cardew Architects, Moriyama & Teshima Architects, Perkins+Will Canada, Revery Architecture (formerly Bing Thom Architects), Safdie Architects, Saucier + Perrotte architectes, and Zeidler Partnership Architects.

Of the many architectural photographers whose work appears in these pages, we would like to extend a special thanks to Tom Arban, Robert Burley, James Dow, Steven Evans, Shai Gil, Nic Lehoux, Ema Peter, and Simon Scott for offering us a large number of their photos for publication.

Archivists Maggie Hunter at the University of Calgary's Canadian Architectural Archives and Alison Skyrme at Ryerson University's Library and Archives Special Collections were unstinting in their efforts to locate many of the images in this book.

We also thank the following institutions and archives that supplied photos for the book: Aanischaaukamikw Cree Cultural Institute, Bibliothèque et archives nationales du Québec, Canadian Centre for Architecture (Montreal), Canadian Museum of History, Canadian War Museum, Confederation Centre of the Arts, Dixon Slide Collection–McGill University Library, Edmonton Public Library, Erickson Estate Collection, Fonds de la Commission de transport de Montréal–Archives de la STM, Institute of Art History (Zagreb, Croatia), Ministère de la Culture et des Communications (Québec), Museum of Anthropology–University of British Columbia, Museum of Modern Art (New York), Museum of Northern British Columbia (Prince Rupert), Museum of Vancouver, Library and Archives Canada, the National Ballet of Canada Archives, Provincial Archives of Alberta, Royal British Columbia Museum and Archives, Saskatchewan Archives Board, Saskatoon Public Library Local History Room, the Vancouver Art Gallery, Trappist Monks of the Abbey of Our Lady of the Prairies, University of California Santa Cruz Special Collections, University of Manitoba Archives and Special Collections, University of Toronto Scarborough Library–Archives & Special Collections, West Vancouver Museum, and Winnipeg Architecture Foundation.

We are grateful to the following firms for providing images for the book and discussing details of their work with the editors and authors: AA Robins Architect, Acton Ostry Architects, aodbt architecture + interior design, Atelier Big City, Atelier In Situ, Atelier Paul Laurendeau, Atelier Pierre Thibault, Baird Sampson Neuert Architects, Barry Johns Architecture, Barton Myers Associates, BattersbyHowat Architects, Beck Vale Architects & Planners, BGHJ Architects, B+H Architects, Blouin Orzes architectes, Breathe Architecture, Brook McIlroy, Bruce Haden Architect, CCM2, Chevalier Morales architectes, Cibinel Architecture, Claude Cormier + Associés, Clifford Wiens, Daoust Lestage, D'Arcy Jones Architecture, David Penner Architect, Davignon Martin Architecture + Interior Design, DIALOG, DMA architectes, Douglas Cardinal Architect, DPA+PSA+DIN Collective, Architects and Designers, DTAH, ERA Architects, EVOQ Architecture, Faucher Aubertin Brodeur Gauthier, FormLine Architecture, Fowler Bauld & Mitchell,

Form:Media and Ekistics Plan + Design, Gehry International Architects, Giannone Petricone Associates, GPP Architecture, HCMA, Helga Plumb Architect, Henry Hawthorn, James K. M. Cheng Architects, Jodoin Lamarre Pratte, John Hix Architect, JYW Architecture, Kirkland Partnership, Kobayashi + Zedda Architects, Kohn Shnier Architects, Kongats Architects, Lapointe Magne, Lemay, LEMAYMICHAUD Architecture Design, LGA Architectural Partners, L'OEUF, Lubor Trubka Associates Architects, LWPAC, McFarland Marceau Architects, Michael Graves Architecture and Design, MJMA, Michael Green Architecture, Morris Adjmi Architects, Niall Savage, Nick Milkovich Architects, Office of McFarlane Biggar Architects + Designers, OMA, Omar Gandhi Architect, Peter Rose + Partners, PFS Studio, Prairie Architects, Public: Architecture + Communication, Richard Kroeker Design, Rubin & Rotman Architects, Saia Barbarèse Topouzanov, Saunders Architecture, Shim-Sutcliffe Architects, Smoke Architecture, Stantec Iqaluit, Sturgess Architecture, Susan Fitzgerald Architecture, Taylor Architecture Group, Teeple Architects, the Marc Boutin Architectural Collaborative, and Venturi Scott Brown and Associates.

Thanks to the photographers who have been generous in allowing their work to be reprinted in these pages, including: Nigel Baldwin, Richard Barry, Alexis Birkill, James Brittain, Michel Brunelle, Sama Jim Canzian, Mario Carrieri, Ricardo Castro, David Covo, Marc Cramer, Doublespace Photography, John Fulker, Timothy Hursley, Pat Kane, Gerry Kopelow, Martin Kramer, Michael Sherman Photography, Lisa Landrum, Carol Moore Ede, Morley Baer Photographs, Rina Pitucci, Marco Polo, Rocco's Photography, Pureblink (Jose Uribe), Guillaume Rosier, Eugen Sakhnenko, Lola Sheppard, and Frederic Urban. Thanks as well to the estates of Guy Gérin-Lajoie, Jordi Bonet, Melvin Charney, Graham Warrington, Shadrach Woods, and H. Roger Jowett.

Additional images were supplied by the Canadian Press, Ed Mirvish Enterprises, Esto, Getty Images, Projectcore, and West Edmonton Mall. Permissions for several images were obtained through SODRAC. Thank you to the staff of *Canadian Architect* and the Royal Architectural Institute of Canada for making work from their publications available for this book.

Many individuals contributed to the realization of this book, and we would like to extend special thanks to Clive Clark, Gabriel Feld, Roy Gaiot, Terrance Galvin, Ryan Gorrie, Anca Hanganu, Sascha Hastings, John Howarth, Dennis Jarvis, Larry Jones, Garth Norbraten, Robert Pacheo, John Quirke, Gilles Saucier, Jim Taggart, L. Frederick Valentine, Neil Whaley, and Ansgar Walk.

Finally, thank you to all of those Canadian architects and designers whose work appears in these pages, as well as those whose work could not be included without making a book ten times the size. This book's *raison d'être* is the work that you have done in creating Canada's architecture and its architectural culture over the past fifty years.

Contributors

George Baird, OAA, FRAIC, is an architect, educator, and writer. He is a partner in Baird Sampson Neuert Architects, a former professor at Harvard's Graduate School of Design, and a former dean of the Daniels Faculty of Architecture, Landscape, and Design at the University of Toronto. Baird received the Royal Architectural Institute of Canada Gold Medal in 2010, and is recipient of the 2012 AIA/ACSA Topaz Medallion for Excellence in Architectural Education. He was appointed a Member of the Order of Canada in 2015 for his contributions to architecture.

Brian Carter, Hon. FRAIC., is a graduate of Nottingham School of Architecture and the University of Toronto. A registered architect in the UK, he worked in practice with Arup in London prior to his appointment as Chair of Architecture at the University of Michigan. Subsequently he served as dean of the School of Architecture and Planning at the University at Buffalo, the State University of New York, where he is currently a professor of architecture. He is the designer of several award-winning buildings and author of numerous articles and books.

Ian Chodikoff, OAA, FRAIC, is an architect and advocate for inclusive, healthy, and vibrant built environments. He holds degrees in architecture and urban design and was awarded the 2003 Druker Travelling Fellowship from Harvard University's Graduate School of Design to study the effects of transnational migration on patterns of urbanization. Since then, Ian has taught and published extensively and continues to investigate various urban-related phenomena. He is a former executive director of the Royal Architectural Institute of Canada and a former editor of *Canadian Architect* magazine.

Odile Hénault is a multilingual architectural critic and writer, trained as an architect at the Technical University of Nova Scotia. In 1983, she founded the award-winning Canadian architectural magazine *Section a*. She moved to Barcelona, Spain, in 1986 where she edited and published a book on Mies van der Rohe's Barcelona Pavilion and contributed to international publications such as *Architecture* (US) and *L'Architecture d'Aujourd'hui* (France). She became president of the Ordre des architectes du Québec in 1994 and was instrumental in establishing the institutional framework for the province's architectural competitions program. A former director of the Association of Collegiate Schools of Architecture

(ACSA), she has been living in Quebec since 2004 and is a regular contributor to *Canadian Architect* magazine.

George Thomas Kapelos, OAA, FRAIC, is an architect and planner and is a professor in the department of architectural science at Ryerson University. He has authored articles and books, and curated exhibitions on aspects of postwar Canadian architecture, including *Competing Modernisms: Toronto's New City Hall and Square* (Dalhousie Architectural Press, 2015) and *Interpretations of Nature* (McMichael Canadian Art Collection, 1994), for which he received an Award of Excellence from the Canadian Museums Association. Kapelos studied architecture at Princeton and Yale, and planning at the Harvard University Graduate School of Design. He is past president of the Society for the Study of Architecture in Canada, and a continuing senior fellow at Massey College in Toronto.

Elsa Lam, FRAIC, is editor of *Canadian Architect* magazine. She was the 2012 winner of the Phyllis Lambert Prize for writing in architecture, awarded for her doctoral dissertation "Wilderness Nation: Building Canada's Railway Landscapes, 1885–1929," completed at Columbia University with advisors Kenneth Frampton and Vittoria di Palma. Lam studied architectural history at McGill University and architectural design at the University of Waterloo. She has written extensively for architecture periodicals, as well as collaborated on the editing and writing of several books on design history.

Lisa Landrum, MAA, AIA, MRAIC, is an associate professor and associate dean (research) in the faculty of architecture at the University of Manitoba. She is a registered architect in the United States and Canada. Landrum earned her professional degree at Carleton University and a master's and doctorate in architectural history and theory from McGill University. Her many publications examine architectural agency and representation, especially dramatic modes of representation implicit in the works and words of architects.

Graham Livesey, FRAIC, is a professor in the Master of Architecture Program at the University of Calgary, where he teaches design, history, and urban design; he was the administrative head of the program for nine years. He studied architecture at McGill University and holds a doctorate from Technical University of Delft. He was a principal of Down + Livesey Architects from 1995 to 2004. Livesey has served with a wide range of organizations and is currently a regional correspondent to *Canadian Architect*. He undertakes research in contemporary urbanism and modern architecture and recently coedited, with Dr. Antony Moulis, a four-volume anthology on Le Corbusier (Routledge, 2018).

Steven Mannell, NSAA, FRAIC, is founding director of Dalhousie University's College of Sustainability. He is a practicing architect and professor of architecture. His research includes twentieth-century waterworks architecture, the conservation of modern built heritage, and the late-twentieth-century emergence of "ecological" architecture. He is the author of *Atlantic Modern: The Architecture of the Atlantic Provinces 1950–2000* (Dalhousie Architectural Press, 2004) and *Living Lightly on the Earth: Building an Ark for Prince Edward Island 1974–76* (Dalhousie Architectural Press, 2018).

Sherry McKay is an associate professor in the School of Architecture and Landscape Architecture at the University of British Columbia (UBC), where she teaches architectural history and theory. Her present research focuses on postwar "urban housekeeping" and the class dimensions of modern apartment life. Two current book projects are a history of the UBC School of Architecture with Raymond Cole and a study of the design value of infrastructure with AnnaLisa Meyboom. She was the book review editor for *Building Research & Information* (UK) from 2010 to 2017, and editor, with Leslie Van Duzer and Chris Macdonald, of the series *West Coast Modern House* (ORO Editions with SALA, UBC).

Marco Polo, FRAIC, is a professor in Ryerson University's department of architectural science. He publishes extensively on architecture and design, and was editor of *Canadian Architect* from 1997 to 2003. His exhibition *41° to 66°—Architecture in Canada: Region, Culture, Tectonics*, co-curated with John McMinn of the University of Waterloo, was selected to represent Canada at the 2008 Venice Biennale of Architecture. With Colin Ripley, Polo curated and wrote *Architecture and National Identity: The Centennial Projects 50 Years On*, an exhibition and publication examining the role of Canada's 1967 Centennial Projects in the articulation of a national identity.

Larry Wayne Richards, FRAIC, AIA/IA, is a Toronto-based educator and writer and recipient of the Royal Architectural Institute of Canada's national Advocate for Architecture Award. A graduate of Yale University, he taught at Dalhousie University and Nova Scotia Technical College, then served as director of the University of Waterloo School of Architecture from 1982 to 1987. He was dean of the Daniels Faculty of Architecture, Landscape, and Design at the University of Toronto from 1997 to 2004, where he continues as Professor Emeritus. Books by Richards include *CCA: Building and Gardens* (MIT Press, 1989) and *University of Toronto: The Campus Guide* (Princeton Architectural Press, 2018).

Colin Ripley, OAA, MRAIC, is a professor in Ryerson University's department of architectural science and was chair of the department from 2012 to 2015. He is a partner and director of the critical practice RVTR. Since 2007, RVTR has been published widely and has received awards including the 2009 Canada Council Professional Prix de Rome in Architecture. In 2014, Ripley published, with Marco Polo, *Architecture and National Identity: The Centennial Projects 50 Years On* (Dalhousie Architectural Press), which accompanied an exhibition displayed at venues across Canada.

Lola Sheppard, OAA, OAQ, is an associate professor at the School of Architecture at the University of Waterloo. She is a founding partner of Toronto-based firm Lateral Office. Her work and research have focused on architecture's relationship to geography, territory, and emergent urbanisms, with a particular focus on arctic regions. She is the coauthor, with Mason White, of *Many Norths: Spatial Practice in a Polar Territory* (Actar, 2017). She was awarded the 2012 RAIC Young Architect Award, and her firm has received the 2011 Emerging Voices Prize from the Architectural League of New York and the 2010 Professional Prix de Rome from the Canada Council for the Arts.

David Theodore, MRAIC, is an assistant professor in the Peter Guo-hua Fu School of Architecture at McGill University, where he holds the Canada Research Chair in Architecture, Health, and Computation. He received a doctorate in the history of architecture, medicine, and science from Harvard University. An active design journalist and critic, he is currently a regional correspondent for *Canadian Architect* and a contributing editor at *Azure*. His recent scholarship explores the history and theory of computers in the organization, construction, and management of hospitals and prisons.

Adele Weder, Hon. MRAIC, is an architectural writer, editor, and curator. She holds a Master of Advanced Studies in Architecture from the University of British Columbia, as well as degrees in journalism and the humanities. A correspondent for numerous journals in Canada and abroad, she is also the coauthor of books on B. C. Binning, Selwyn Pullan, Ron Thom, and Dan Hanganu. Her curatorial projects include the exhibition *Ron Thom and the Allied Arts*, which toured venues across Canada from 2013 to 2015. She lives in Vancouver and Haida Gwaii, British Columbia.

Mason White, MRAIC, is an associate professor in the Daniels Faculty of Architecture, Landscape, and Design at the University of Toronto. He is a founding partner of Toronto-based firm Lateral Office and editor of the journal *Bracket*. White received the 2012–13 Friedman Visiting Professorship at UC Berkeley and the 2008–09 Arthur Wheelwright Fellowship from Harvard's Graduate School of Design. He is the coauthor, with Lola Sheppard, of *Many Norths: Spatial Practice in a Polar Territory*. Lateral Office has exhibited its research at venues including the Seoul and Chicago Architecture Biennials and the Venice Biennial of Architecture, where the firm was selected to prepare the exhibition *Arctic Adaptations: Nunavut at 15*.

Index

Italic page numbers refer to illustrations

Credits

CHAPTER 1. **1** ANTHONY CRICKMAY, THE NATIONAL BALLET OF CANADA ARCHIVES. **2** PHOTOGRAPHER UNKNOWN, *CANADIAN ARCHITECT* MAGAZINE FONDS, RYERSON UNIVERSITY LIBRARY AND ARCHIVES. **3** HUGH ROBERTSON, COURTESY PANDA ASSOCIATES FONDS, CANADIAN ARCHITECTURAL ARCHIVES, UNIVERSITY OF CALGARY. **4** GRAHAM WARRINGTON, COURTESY OF THE ESTATE OF GRAHAM WARRINGTON AND *CANADIAN ARCHITECT* MAGAZINE FONDS, RYERSON UNIVERSITY LIBRARY AND ARCHIVES. **5** PHOTOGRAPHER UNKNOWN, ROYAL ARCHITECTURAL INSITUTE OF CANADA, *JOURNAL RAIC*. **6** PHOTOGRAPHER UNKNOWN, CONFEDERATION CENTRE OF THE ARTS. **7** ART JAMES, *CANADIAN ARCHITECT* MAGAZINE FONDS, RYERSON UNIVERSITY LIBRARY AND ARCHIVES. **8** ART JAMES, *CANADIAN ARCHITECT* MAGAZINE. **9–10** H. ROGER JOWETT, COURTESY ALEXANDER JOWETT AND *CANADIAN ARCHITECT* MAGAZINE FONDS, RYERSON UNIVERSITY LIBRARY AND ARCHIVES. **11** PHOTOGRAPHER UNKNOWN, JORDI BONET COMMITTEE, © ESTATE OF JORDI BONET / SODRAC 2018. **12** H. ROGER JOWETT, COURTESY ALEXANDER JOWETT AND *CANADIAN ARCHITECT* MAGAZINE FONDS, RYERSON UNIVERSITY LIBRARY AND ARCHIVES. **13** ART JAMES, *CANADIAN ARCHITECT* MAGAZINE. **14** H. ROGER JOWETT, COURTESY ALEXANDER JOWETT AND *CANADIAN ARCHITECT* MAGAZINE FONDS, RYERSON UNIVERSITY LIBRARY AND ARCHIVES. **15** PHOTOGRAPHER UNKNOWN, PROVINCIAL ARCHIVES OF ALBERTA. **16** PHOTOGRAPHER UNKNOWN, EDMONTON PUBLIC LIBRARY. **17** ROCCO'S PHOTOGRAPHY, PRIVATE COLLECTION. **18** PHOTOGRAPHER UNKNOWN, PROVINCIAL ARCHIVES OF ALBERTA. **19** PHOTOGRAPHER UNKNOWN, MUSEUM OF VANCOUVER. **20** HENRY KALEN, HENRY KALEN FONDS, UNIVERSITY OF MANITOBA ARCHIVES AND SPECIAL COLLECTIONS. **21** PHOTOGRAPHER UNKNOWN, MUSEUM OF VANCOUVER. **22** COURTESY JACK LONG FONDS, CANADIAN ARCHITECTURAL ARCHIVES, UNIVERSITY OF CALGARY. **23** CAROL MOORE EDE. **24** REG IGNNELL/TORONTO STAR/GETTY IMAGES. **25–26** COURTESY RAYMOND MORIYAMA FONDS, CANADIAN ARCHITECTURAL ARCHIVES, UNIVERSITY OF CALGARY. **27** PHOTOGRAPHER UNKNOWN, LIBRARY AND ARCHIVES CANADA. **28** PHOTOGRAPHER UNKNOWN, DIXON SLIDE COLLECTION, MCGILL UNIVERSITY LIBRARY. **29** PHOTOGRAPHER UNKNOWN, *CANADIAN ARCHITECT* MAGAZINE FONDS, RYERSON UNIVERSITY LIBRARY AND ARCHIVES. **30–31** PHOTOGRAPHER UNKNOWN, LIBRARY AND ARCHIVES CANADA. **32** GABOR SZILASI, BIBLIOTHÈQUE NATIONALE DE QUÉBEC. **33** PHOTOGRAPHER UNKNOWN, LIBRARY AND ARCHIVES CANADA. **34** *CANADIAN ARCHITECT* MAGAZINE. **35** PHOTOGRAPHER UNKNOWN, CANADIAN CENTRE FOR ARCHITECTURE; GIFT OF MAY CUTLER. **36** PHOTOGRAPHER UNKNOWN, LIBRARY AND ARCHIVES CANADA.

CHAPTER 2. **1** ART JAMES, *CANADIAN ARCHITECT* MAGAZINE FONDS, RYERSON UNIVERSITY LIBRARY AND ARCHIVES. **2** HARRY FOSTER, CANADIAN MUSEUM OF HISTORY PHOTO ARCHIVES S97-18026. **3** TOM ARBAN. **4** COURTESY CANADIAN WAR MUSEUM, CWM2012-0013-0054-DM. **5–9** TOM ARBAN. **10** HOWARD SUTCLIFFE, DELINEATOR, *CANADIAN ARCHITECT* MAGAZINE FONDS, RYERSON UNIVERSITY LIBRARY AND ARCHIVES, COURTESY KPMB. **11** EDUARD HUEBER, COURTESY KPMB **12** STEVEN EVANS PHOTOGRAPHY, COURTESY KPMB. **13** COURTESY PETER CARDEW ARCHITECTS. **14** MARTIN KRAMER. **15–16** COURTESY MORIYAMA & TESHIMA ARCHITECTS. **17** THOMAS WEINHOLD/FOTO DESIGN, COURTESY KPMB. **18** FOTO DESIGN, COURTESY KPMB. **19** KIM YONG KWAN, COURTESY ZEIDLER ARCHITECTURE. **20** ERNEST SATO, COURTESY

ARTHUR ERICKSON FONDS, CANADIAN ARCHITECTURAL ARCHIVES, UNIVERSITY OF CALGARY. **21–23** ARTHUR ERICKSON, COURTESY ARTHUR ERICKSON FONDS, CANADIAN ARCHITECTURAL ARCHIVES, UNIVERSITY OF CALGARY. **24** PHOTOGRAPHER UNKNOWN, COURTESY ARTHUR ERICKSON FONDS, CANADIAN ARCHITECTURAL ARCHIVES, UNIVERSITY OF CALGARY. **25** HORST THANHÄUSER, COURTESY REVERY ARCHITECTURE. **26** COURTESY ZEIDLER PARTNERSHIP. **27** COURTESY PETER CARDEW AND *CANADIAN ARCHITECT* MAGAZINE FONDS, RYERSON UNIVERSITY LIBRARY AND ARCHIVES. **28** COURTESY CANADIAN NATIONAL RAILWAYS AND *CANADIAN ARCHITECT* MAGAZINE FONDS, RYERSON UNIVERSITY LIBRARY AND ARCHIVES. **29** THE CANADIAN PRESS / OLYMPIC ORGANIZING COMMITTEE. **30** PHOTOGRAPHER UNKNOWN, *CANADIAN ARCHITECT* MAGAZINE FONDS, RYERSON UNIVERSITY LIBRARY AND ARCHIVES. **31** RICHARD LAM / THE CANADIAN PRESS. **32** COURTESY PANDA ASSOCIATES FONDS, CANADIAN ARCHITECTURAL ARCHIVES, UNIVERSITY OF CALGARY. **33** COURTESY JOHN B. PARKIN FONDS, CANADIAN ARCHITECTURAL ARCHIVES, UNIVERSITY OF CALGARY. **34** COURTESY PANDA ASSOCIATES FONDS, CANADIAN ARCHITECTURAL ARCHIVES, UNIVERSITY OF CALGARY. **35** COURTESY ROBERT BURLEY AND *CANADIAN ARCHITECT* MAGAZINE FONDS, RYERSON UNIVERSITY LIBRARY AND ARCHIVES. **36** GÉRIN-LAJOIE LE BLANC FONDS, CANADIAN CENTRE FOR ARCHITECTURE, GIFT OF GUY GÉRIN-LAJOIE. **37** DAVID BURDENY, COURTESY OMB.

CHAPTER 3. **1** LISA LANDRUM. **2** COURTESY RON THOM FONDS, CANADIAN ARCHITECTURAL ARCHIVES, UNIVERSITY OF CALGARY. **3** LISA LANDRUM. **4** H. ROGER JOWETT, COURTESY ALEXANDER JOWETT AND *CANADIAN ARCHITECT* MAGAZINE FONDS, RYERSON UNIVERSITY LIBRARY AND ARCHIVES. **5–6** TOM ARBAN. **7** COURTESY RON THOM FONDS, CANADIAN ARCHITECTURAL ARCHIVES, UNIVERSITY OF CALGARY. **8** JOHN FLANDERS, COURTESY JOHN FLANDERS PHOTOGRAPHY COLLECTION, CANADIAN ARCHITECTURAL ARCHIVES, UNIVERSITY OF CALGARY. **9** LISA LANDRUM. **10** COURTESY RON THOM FONDS, CANADIAN ARCHITECTURAL ARCHIVES, UNIVERSITY OF CALGARY. **11** LISA LANDRUM. **12** STEVEN EVANS PHOTOGRAPHY. **13** TOM ARBAN, COURTESY TEEPLE ARCHITECTS. **14** DOUBLESPACE PHOTOGRAPHY. **15** © RYERSON IMAGE CENTRE, COURTESY DSAI. **16** STEVEN EVANS PHOTOGRAPHY. **17** MARC CRAMER, COURTESY SAUCIER + PERROTTE. **18** MICHEL BRUNELLE, COURTESY ANCA HANGANU. **19** UNIVERSITY OF TORONTO SCARBOROUGH LIBRARY, ARCHIVES & SPECIAL COLLECTIONS, UTSC ARCHIVES LEGACY COLLECTION, F113. **20** COURTESY JOHN ANDREWS FONDS, CANADIAN ARCHITECTURAL ARCHIVES, UNIVERSITY OF CALGARY. **21** COURTESY ARTHUR ERICKSON FONDS, CANADIAN ARCHITECTURAL ARCHIVES, UNIVERSITY OF CALGARY. **22** COURTESY RICARDO CASTRO. **23** COURTESY ARTHUR ERICKSON FONDS, CANADIAN ARCHITECTURAL ARCHIVES, UNIVERSITY OF CALGARY. **24** COURTESY NIC LEHOUX.

CHAPTER 4. **1** COURTESY MUSEUM OF NORTHERN BRITISH COLUMBIA. **2** STEVEN EVANS PHOTOGRAPHY, COURTESY MCFARLAND MARCEAU ARCHITECTS. **3** JAMES DOW, COURTESY PATKAU ARCHITECTS. **4** COURTESY GREGORY HENRIQUEZ. **5** COURTESY PETER CARDEW ARCHITECTS. **6** MARTIN TESSLER, COURTESY ACTON OSTRY ARCHITECTS. **7** COURTESY NIGEL BALDWIN. **8** COURTESY CCM2. **9** COURTESY MCFARLAND MARCEAU ARCHITECTS. **10** RICHARD HARTMIER, COURTESY KOBAYASHI + ZEDDA ARCHITECTS. **11–13** GASTON COOPER, COURTESY EVOQ ARCHITECTURE. **14–15** NIC LEHOUX,

COURTESY FORMLINE ARCHITECTURE. **16** NIC LEHOUX, COURTESY DIALOG. **17** STÉPHANE GROLEAU, COURTESY LEMAYMICHAUD ARCHITECTURE DESIGN. **18** DAVID WHITTAKER, COURTESY BROOK MCILROY. **19** PETER POWLES PHOTOGRAPHY, COURTESY LUBOR TRUBKA ASSOCIATES ARCHITECTS. **20–21** MITCH LENET PHOTOGRAPHY & DIGITAL ARTS, PUBLISHED WITH THE PERMISSION OF AANISCHAAUKAMIKW CREE CULTURAL INSTITUTE. **22** TOM ARBAN, COURTESY DSAI. **23–24** BEN RAHN/A-FRAME, COURTESY LGA ARCHITECTURAL PARTNERS. **25** RACHEL MAI, COURTESY JYW ARCHITECTURE. **26–28** NIC LEHOUX, COURTESY FORMLINE ARCHITECTURE. **29** © 2016 LINDSAY REID, COURTESY SMOKE ARCHITECTURE. **30** COURTESY MCFARLAND MARCEAU ARCHITECTS. **31** DAVID WHITTAKER, COURTESY BROOK MCILROY. **32** PETE LAWRENCE, COURTESY FORM:MEDIA AND EKISTICS PLAN + DESIGN. **33** COURTESY BLOUIN ORZES ARCHITECTES. **34** COURTESY KOBAYASHI + ZEDDA ARCHITECTS. **35** UBC/PAUL JOSEPH PHOTOGRAPHY, COURTESY FORMLINE ARCHITECTURE. **36** COURTESY TERRANCE GALVIN

CHAPTER 5. **1** NENAD GATTIN, COURTESY PHOTOARCHIVES NENAD GATTIN, INSTITUTE OF ART HISTORY, ZAGREB, ID. NO. 2680A. **2** COURTESY GABRIEL FELD AND ESTATE OF SHADRACH WOODS. **3** RICHARD BARRY. **4** UNIVERSITY OF TORONTO SCARBOROUGH LIBRARY, ARCHIVES & SPECIAL COLLECTIONS, UTSC ARCHIVES LEGACY COLLECTION, F113. **5** SIMON SCOTT, ERICKSON ESTATE COLLECTION. **6** DIGITAL IMAGE © THE MUSEUM OF MODERN ART/LICENSED BY SCALE/ART RESOURCE, NY. PHILIP JOHNSON FUND (434. 1967). **7** SIMON SCOTT PHOTOGRAPHY, CANADIAN ARCHITECT MAGAZINE FONDS, RYERSON UNIVERSITY LIBRARY AND ARCHIVES. **8** COURTESY OF THE COLLECTION OF SAFDIE ARCHITECTS. **9** ART JAMES, *CANADIAN ARCHITECT* MAGAZINE FONDS, RYERSON UNIVERSITY LIBRARY AND ARCHIVES. **10** H. ROGER JOWETT, COURTESY ALEXANDER JOWETT AND *CANADIAN ARCHITECT* MAGAZINE FONDS, RYERSON UNIVERSITY LIBRARY AND ARCHIVES. **11** ART JAMES, *CANADIAN ARCHITECT* MAGAZINE FONDS, RYERSON UNIVERSITY LIBRARY AND ARCHIVES. **12** COURTESY ZEIDLER ARCHITECTURE. **13** HIRO NAKASHIMA, *CANADIAN ARCHITECT* MAGAZINE FONDS, RYERSON UNIVERSITY LIBRARY AND ARCHIVES. **14** ART JAMES, *CANADIAN ARCHITECT* MAGAZINE FONDS, RYERSON UNIVERSITY LIBRARY AND ARCHIVES. **15** COURTESY ZEIDLER ARCHITECTURE. **16** PHOTOGRAPHER UNKNOWN, *CANADIAN ARCHITECT* MAGAZINE FONDS, RYERSON UNIVERSITY LIBRARY AND ARCHIVES. **17** ART JAMES, COURTESY ZEIDLER ARCHITECTURE. **18** JOHN FULKER, GIFT OF JOHN FULKER, COURTESY WEST VANCOUVER MUSEUM. **19** HARRY KALEN, COURTESY UNIVERSITY OF MANITOBA ARCHIVES & SPECIAL COLLECTIONS AND *CANADIAN ARCHITECT* MAGAZINE FONDS, RYERSON UNIVERSITY LIBRARY AND ARCHIVES. **20** COURTESY GERRY KOPELOW. **21** SIMON SCOTT PHOTOGRAPHY, *CANADIAN ARCHITECT* MAGAZINE FONDS, RYERSON UNIVERSITY LIBRARY AND ARCHIVES. **22–23** © EZRA STOLLER/ESTO.

CHAPTER 6. **1** ROBERT BURLEY, COURTESY ROBERT BURLEY AND *CANADIAN ARCHITECT* MAGAZINE FONDS, RYERSON UNIVERSITY LIBRARY AND ARCHIVES. **2** ROLLIN LA FRANCE, COURTESY VENTURI, SCOTT BROWN AND ASSOCIATES. **3** MORLEY BAER, COURTESY SPECIAL COLLECTIONS, UNIVERSITY LIBRARY, UNIVERSITY OF CALIFORNIA SANTA CRUZ, MORLEY BAER PHOTOGRAPHS, 1951–1989. **4** COURTESY MICHAEL GRAVES ARCHITECTURE AND DESIGN. **5** ART JAMES, *CANADIAN ARCHITECT* MAGAZINE FONDS, RYERSON UNIVERSITY LIBRARY AND ARCHIVES. **6** COURTESY BAIRD SAMPSON NEUERT ARCHITECTS. **7** ALAN MAPLES, COURTESY PETER ROSE + PARTNERS. **8** COURTESY PETER ROSE + PARTNERS. **9** MELVIN CHARNEY, COURTESY CANADIAN CENTRE FOR ARCHITECTURE AND THE ESTATE OF MELVIN CHARNEY/SODRAC, GIFT OF MELVIN CHARNEY, DR1994:0017. **10** MELVIN CHARNEY. COURTESY CANADIAN CENTRE FOR ARCHITECTURE AND THE ESTATE OF MELVIN CHARNEY/SODRAC. MELVIN CHARNEY FONDS, GIFT OF DARA CHARNEY, DR2012:0012:080:003:001. **11** COURTESY HENRIQUEZ PARTNERS ARCHITECTS. **12** DICK BUSHER, *CANADIAN ARCHITECT* MAGAZINE FONDS, RYERSON UNIVERSITY LIBRARY AND ARCHIVES. **13** PETER BEECH, COURTESY WINNIPEG ARCHITECTURE FOUNDATION. **14** COURTESY MICHAEL KIRKLAND. REPRINTED FROM *TRACE*, VOLUME 1, NO. 3, P. 35. **15** COURTESY PHILIP J. CARTER. **16** FREDERIC URBAN. **17** DRAWING BY STEPHEN BLOOD, COURTESY MACKAY-LYONS SWEETAPPLE ARCHITECTS LIMITED. **18** PAT KANE. **19–20** PATRICIA LAYMAN BAZELON, COURTESY LAUREN TENT AND *CANADIAN ARCHITECT* MAGAZINE FONDS, RYERSON UNIVERSITY LIBRARY AND ARCHIVES. **21** COURTESY KPMB ARCHITECTS. **22–23** COURTESY ROBERT BURLEY AND *CANADIAN ARCHITECT* MAGAZINE FONDS, RYERSON UNIVERSITY LIBRARY AND ARCHIVES. **24** CANADIAN CENTRE FOR ARCHITECTURE © CCA. **25** RICHARD PARE, COURTESY CANADIAN CENTRE FOR ARCHITECTURE, PH1990:0067. **26** COURTESY ROBERT BURLEY AND CANADIAN CENTRE FOR ARCHITECTURE, PH1990:0159. **27–31** COURTESY HENRIQUEZ PARTNERS ARCHITECTS. **32** COURTESY WEST EDMONTON MALL. **33** NED NATURA, COURTESY MORRIS ADJMI ARCHITECTS. **34** EUGEN SAKHNENKO. **35** DAVID COVO. **36** EUGEN SAKHNENKO. **37** COURTESY GEHRY INTERNATIONAL, ARCHITECTS, PROJECTCORE, AND ED MIRVISH ENTERPRISES.

CHAPTER 7. **1–2** SIMON SCOTT, *CANADIAN ARCHITECT* MAGAZINE FONDS, RYERSON UNIVERSITY LIBRARY AND ARCHIVES. **3** COURTESY ARTHUR ERICKSON FONDS, CANADIAN ARCHITECTURAL ARCHIVES, UNIVERSITY OF CALGARY. **4** COURTESY PETER ROSE + PARTNERS. **5** TOM ARBAN, COURTESY DSAI. **6** COURTESY DSAI. **7** COURTESY DTAH. **8** NIKKOL ROT, COURTESY L'OEUF. **9** COURTESY L'OEUF. **10–11** DEREK LEPPER, COURTESY HENRIQUEZ PARTNERS ARCHITECTS. **12–13** BOB MATHESON, COURTESY HENRIQUEZ PARTNERS ARCHITECTS. **14** DARRYL HUMPHREY, COURTESY HENRIQUEZ PARTNERS ARCHITECTS. **15–16** PHOTOGRAPHER UNKNOWN, *CANADIAN ARCHITECT* MAGAZINE FONDS, RYERSON UNIVERSITY LIBRARY AND ARCHIVES. **17** ART JAMES, *CANADIAN ARCHITECT* MAGAZINE FONDS, RYERSON UNIVERSITY LIBRARY AND ARCHIVES. **18** SHAI GIL, COURTESY GIANNONE PETRICONE ASSOCIATES. **19** LISA LOGAN, COURTESY DSAI. **20** SCOTT NORSWORTHY, COURTESY MJMA.

CHAPTER 8. **1–2** SOLSEARCH ARCHITECTS, COURTESY BGHJ ARCHITECTS. **3** FISHERIES AND ENVIRONMENT CANADA. **4** SASKATCHEWAN ARCHIVES BOARD, HENDRICK GROLLE FONDS, R-99-153-1. **5** SASKATCHEWAN ARCHIVES BOARD, HENDRICK GROLLE FONDS, R-1314 FILE I.106. **6** DUDLEY THOMPSON, COURTESY PRAIRIE ARCHITECTS. **7** HENRY KALEN, KALEN FONDS, UNIVERSITY OF MANITOBA ARCHIVES AND SPECIAL COLLECTIONS. **8** COURTESY JOHN HIX. **9–10** ELIZABETH JONES / APPLIED PHOTOGRAPHY, COURTESY HELGA PLUMB ARCHITECT. **11–12** © JEFF GOLDBERG/ESTO. **13** COURTESY MICHAEL SHERMAN PHOTOGRAPHY - MICHAELSHERMAN.CA. **14–15** COURTESY BREATHE ARCHITECTS. **16** LINDSAY REID, COURTESY PRAIRIE ARCHITECTS. **17** HENRY KALEN, COURTESY PRAIRIE ARCHITECTS. **18** STEVEN EVANS PHOTOGRAPHY, COURTESY PERKINS+WILL. **19** BUSBY + ASSOCIATES / ARCHITECTSALLIANCE, COURTESY PERKINS+WILL. **20** GERRY KOPELOW, COURTESY KPMB ARCHITECTS. **21** COURTESY KPMB ARCHITECTS. **22** SCOTT NORSWORTHY, COURTESY TEEPLE ARCHITECTS. **23** COURTESY TEEPLE ARCHITECTS. **24** MARTIN TESSLER, COURTESY PERKINS+WILL. **25** COURTESY PERKINS+WILL. **26** NIC LEHOUX, COURTESY PERKINS+WILL. **27** EMA PETER, COURTESY MGA | MICHAEL GREEN ARCHITECTURE. **28** GRAEME STEWART, COURTESY ERA ARCHITECTS.

CHAPTER 9. **1** COURTESY BARRY DOWNS. **2** © EZRA STOLLER/ ESTO. **3** JOHN FULKER, COURTESY WEST VANCOUVER MUSEUM. **4–5** COURTESY BARRY DOWNS. **6** PHOTOGRAPHER UNKNOWN, COURTESY OF ROYAL BC MUSEUM AND ARCHIVES, 1-27967. **7** © EZRA STOLLER/ESTO. **8** ERICKSON ESTATE COLLECTION. **9** COURTESY COLLECTION OF NEIL WHALEY. **10** SIMON SCOTT, COURTESY HENRIQUEZ PARTNERS ARCHITECTS. **11** SIMON SCOTT. **12** CHRISTOPHER ERICKSON, ERICKSON ESTATE COLLECTION. **13** COURTESY THE VANCOUVER ART GALLERY. **14** ALEXIS BIRKILL. **15** COURTESY PETER CARDEW ARCHITECTS. **16–17** COURTESY BARRY DOWNS. **18–19** COURTESY MUSEUM OF ANTHROPOLOGY. **20** ERICKSON ESTATE COLLECTION. **21** COURTESY MUSEUM OF ANTHROPOLOGY. **22–24** COURTESY HENRY HAWTHORN. **25–28** COURTESY PATKAU ARCHITECTS. **29** COURTESY JAMES K. M. CHENG. **30–31** COURTESY PERKINS+WILL. **32** JAMES DOW, COURTESY PATKAU ARCHITECTS

CHAPTER 10. **1** HENRY KALEN, HENRY KALEN FONDS, UNIVERSITY OF MANITOBA ARCHIVES AND SPECIAL COLLECTIONS. **2** CREATIVE PROFESSIONAL PHOTOGRAPHERS, COURTESY SASKATOON PUBLIC LIBRARY, LOCAL HISTORY

ROOM, CP-5925-A-5. **3–5** HENRY KALEN, HENRY KALEN FONDS, UNIVERSITY OF MANITOBA ARCHIVES AND SPECIAL COLLECTIONS. **6–7** COURTESY GPP ARCHITECTURE INC. **8** HENRY KALEN, HENRY KALEN FONDS, UNIVERSITY OF MANITOBA ARCHIVES AND SPECIAL COLLECTIONS. **9** HENRY KALEN, HENRY KALEN FONDS, UNIVERSITY OF MANITOBA ARCHIVES AND SPECIAL COLLECTIONS, WITH PERMISSION FROM CLIFFORD WIENS. **10** KARL HINRICHS, WITH PERMISSION FROM CLIFFORD WIENS. **11–15** COURTESY DOUGLAS CARDINAL ARCHITECT. **16** HENRY KALEN, HENRY KALEN FONDS, UNIVERSITY OF MANITOBA ARCHIVES AND SPECIAL COLLECTIONS. **17** PRAIRIE AGRI PHOTO, CARMEN, MANITOBA. COURTESY OF THE TRAPPIST MONKS OF THE MONASTERY OF NÔTRE-DAME-DES-PRAIRIES. IMAGE PREPARED FOR PUBLICATION BY GARTH NORBRATEN AND JOHN HOWARTH. **18–19** COURTESY JAMES DOW. **20** COURTESY GORDON ATKINS FONDS, CANADIAN ARCHITECTURAL ARCHIVES, UNIVERSITY OF CALGARY. **21** COURTESY BECK VALE ARCHITECTS & PLANNERS. **22** COURTESY JAMES DOW. **23–25** COURTESY BARRY JOHNS. **26** ROY OOMS, LIGHTWORKS, COURTESY L. FREDERICK VALENTINE. **27** ROGER BROOKS, COURTESY DAVID PENNER ARCHITECT. **28–29** ROBERT LEMERMEYER, COURTESY STURGESS ARCHITECTURE. **30** GERRY KOPELOW, COURTESY CIBINEL ARCHITECTURE. **31** COURTESY DPA+PSA+DIN COLLECTIVE, ARCHITECTS AND DESIGNERS. **32** JAMES BRITTAIN. **33** COURTESY AODBT ARCHITECTURE + INTERIOR DESIGN. **34** YELLOWCAMERA, COURTESY MBAC. **35** RIC KOKOTOVICH, COURTESY DAVIGNON MARTIN ARCHITECTURE + INTERIOR DESIGN.

CHAPTER 11. **1** DENNIS JARVIS. **2** JAMES STEEVES, COURTESY MACKAY-LYONS SWEETAPPLE ARCHITECTS. **3** UNDINE PROUL, COURTESY MACKAY-LYONS SWEETAPPLE ARCHITECTS. **4–5** JAMES STEEVES, COURTESY MACKAY-LYONS SWEETAPPLE ARCHITECTS. **6** NICOLE DELMAGE, COURTESY MACKAY-LYONS SWEETAPPLE ARCHITECTS. **7–8** JAMES BRITTAIN. **9–10** COURTESY RICHARD KROEKER. **11** GREG RICHARDSON, COURTESY OMAR GANDHI ARCHITECT. **12** DOUBLESPACE PHOTOGRAPHY. **13–14** GREG RICHARDSON, COURTESY SUSAN FITZGERALD ARCHITECTURE. **15–16** JAMES STEEVES, COURTESY NIALL SAVAGE. **17–18** BENT RENÉ SYNNEVÅG, COURTESY SAUNDERS ARCHITECTURE. **19–20** ALEX FRADKIN, COURTESY SAUNDERS ARCHITECTURE. **21** ADAM MØRK, COURTESY FOWLER BAULD & MITCHELL.

CHAPTER 12. **1–2** RICHARD S. BUSHELL, COURTESY LARRY JONES. **3** IHOR PONA, COURTESY TAYLOR ARCHITECTURE GROUP. **4–5** COURTESY *CANADIAN ARCHITECT*. **6** DRAWING BY CINDY CAO AND TRISTAN SITO, COURTESY LOLA SHEPPARD. **7** COURTESY MATS EGELIUS. **8** COURTESY GUILLAUME ROSIER. **9** DRAWING BY MONICA PATEL, COURTESY LOLA SHEPPARD. **10–11** COURTESY GUILLAUME ROSIER. **12–13** COURTESY SAFDIE ARCHITECTS. **14–16** COURTESY ESTATE OF GUY GÉRIN-LAJOIE. **17** COURTESY LOLA SHEPPARD, 2017. **18** COURTESY ESTATE OF GUY GÉRIN-LAJOIE. **19–20** COURTESY TAYLOR ARCHITECTURE GROUP. **21** ANSGAR WALK. **22** COURTESY JOHN QUIRKE. **23** COURTESY CLIVE CLARK. **24–25** COURTESY TAYLOR ARCHITECTURE GROUP. **26** RICHARD HARTMIER, COURTESY KOBAYASHI + ZEDDA ARCHITECTS. **27** COURTESY KOBAYASHI + ZEDDA ARCHITECTS. **28** DAVE BROSHA, COURTESY STANTEC IQALUIT. **29** COURTESY STANTEC IQALUIT. **30** BENT RENÉ SYNNEVÅG, COURTESY SAUNDERS ARCHITECTURE.

CHAPTER 13. **1** MARC CRAMER, COURTESY SAUCIER + PERROTTE ARCHITECTES. **2** ÉRIC PICHÉ, COURTESY SAUCIER + PERROTTE ARCHITECTES. **3** COURTESY SAFDIE ARCHITECTS. **4–5** DOUBLESPACE PHOTOGRAPHY. **6** COURTESY CHEVALIER MORALES ARCHITECTES. **7** DOUBLESPACE PHOTOGRAPHY. **8** STÉPHAN POULIN, COURTESY ANCA HANGANU. **9–11** MICHEL BRUNELLE, COURTESY ANCA HANGANU. **12** DAN S. HANGANU, COURTESY ANCA HANGANU. **13–16** COURTESY ATELIER BIG CITY. **17** MARK RAMSAY ELSWORTHY 2016, © MINISTÈRE DE LA CULTURE ET DES COMMUNICATIONS. **18** MICHEL BRUNELLE, COURTESY ANCA HANGANU). **19** STEVE MONTPETIT, COURTESY FAUCHER AUBERTIN BRODEUR GAUTHIER. **20** FONDS DE LA COMMISSION DE TRANSPORT DE MONTRÉAL, ARCHIVES DE LA STM, 4-966-440. **21** MARC CRAMER, COURTESY SAUCIER + PERROTTE ARCHITECTES. **22** © MICHEL BRUNELLE, COURTESY LAPOINTE MAGNE. **23** MARC CRAMER, COURTESY SAUCIER + PERROTTE ARCHITECTES. **24** COURTESY SAUCIER+PERROTTE

ARCHITECTES. **25** MARC CRAMER, COURTESY SAUCIER + PERROTTE ARCHITECTES. **26** COURTESY LEMAY. **27** BERNARD FOUGÈRES, COURTESY PATKAU ARCHITECTS. **28** MICHEL BRUNELLE, COURTESY SAIA BARBARÈSE TOPOUZANOV. **29** OLIVIER BLOUIN, COURTESY SAUCIER + PERROTTE ARCHITECTES. **30** ADRIEN WILLIAMS, COURTESY ATELIER PAUL LAURENDEAU. **31** RICHARD-MAX TREMBLAY, COURTESY ANCA HANGANU. **32** COURTESY ATELIER PIERRE THIBAULT. **33** MARC CRAMER, COURTESY JODOIN LAMARRE PRATTE ARCHITECTES. **34** MARC CRAMER, COURTESY SAIA BARBARÈSE TOPOUZANOV. **35** BRUCE DAMONTE, COURTESY OMA. **36** COURTESY DMA ARCHITECTES. **37** ALAIN LAFOREST, COURTESY ATELIER IN SITU. **38–39** MARC CRAMER, COURTESY DAOUST LESTAGE. **40** © PAUL LABELLE. JACQUES ROUSSEAU FONDS, CANADIAN CENTRE FOR ARCHITECTURE.

CHAPTER 14. **1** ART JAMES, *CANADIAN ARCHITECT* MAGAZINE FONDS, RYERSON UNIVERSITY LIBRARY AND ARCHIVES. **2** COURTESY PANDA ASSOCIATES FONDS, CANADIAN ARCHITECTURAL ARCHIVES, UNIVERSITY OF CALGARY. **3** ART JAMES, *CANADIAN ARCHITECT* MAGAZINE FONDS, RYERSON UNIVERSITY LIBRARY AND ARCHIVES. **4** H. ROGER JOWETT, COURTESY ALEXANDER JOWETT AND *CANADIAN ARCHITECT* MAGAZINE FONDS, RYERSON UNIVERSITY LIBRARY AND ARCHIVES. **5** COURTESY CN AND *CANADIAN ARCHITECT* MAGAZINE FONDS, RYERSON UNIVERSITY LIBRARY AND ARCHIVES. **6** IAN SAMPSON, COURTESY DSAI. **7** KARL SILVA, COURTESY DSAI. **8** COURTESY MORIYAMA & TESHIMA ARCHITECTS. **9** LENSCAPE, COURTESY DSAI. **10** STEVEN EVANS PHOTOGRAPHY, COURTESY DSAI. **11** COURTESY FIONA SPALDING-SMITH AND DSAI. **12** STEVEN EVANS PHOTOGRAPHY, COURTESY DSAI. **13** COURTESY ROBERT BURLEY AND BAIRD SAMPSON NEUERT ARCHITECTS. **14** COURTESY FIONA SPALDING-SMITH AND ZEIDLER PARTNERSHIP ARCHITECTS. **15** PATKAU ARCHITECTS WITH KEARNS MANCINI ARCHITECTS, COURTESY PATKAU ARCHITECTS. **16** POSITIVE IMAGING PHOTOGRAPHY, COURTESY SHIM-SUTCLIFFE ARCHITECTS. **17–18** BOB GUNDU, COURTESY SHIM-SUTCLIFFE ARCHITECTS. **19** JAMES DOW, COURTESY SHIM-SUTCLIFFE ARCHITECTS. **20** SID TABAK, COURTESY ARCHITECTSALLIANCE. **21** TOM ARBAN, COURTESY ARCHITECTSALLIANCE. **22** DOUBLESPACE PHOTOGRAPHY. **23** STEVEN EVANS PHOTOGRAPHY, COURTESY KPMB ARCHITECTS. **24** TOM ARBAN. **25** COURTESY MARIO CARRIERI. **26** TOM ARBAN, COURTESY BAIRD SAMPSON NEUERT ARCHITECTS. **27** SHAI GIL. **28** TOM ARBAN, COURTESY KOHN SHNIER ARCHITECTS. **29** COURTESY MORIYAMA & TESHIMA ARCHITECTS. **30** EMA PETER, COURTESY B+H ARCHITECTS. **31** RINA PITUCCI. **32** TOM ARBAN, COURTESY DSAI. **33–35** TOM ARBAN, COURTESY KPMB ARCHITECTS. **36–37** EDUARD HUEBER, COURTESY KPMB ARCHITECTS. **38** COURTESY KPMB ARCHITECTS. **39** TOM ARBAN. **40** COURTESY JOSE URIBE/PUREBLINK. **41** BEN RAHN/A-FRAME, COURTESY PERKINS+WILL. **42** SHAI GIL, COURTESY MJMA. **43** TOM ARBAN, COURTESY MJMA. **44–45** COURTESY SHAI GIL. **46** STEVEN EVANS PHOTOGRAPHY, COURTESY PERKINS+WILL

CHAPTER 15. **1** COURTESY BARRY DOWNS. **2** COURTESY HENRIQUEZ PARTNERS ARCHITECTS. **3** COURTESY NIC LEHOUX. **4–5** PAUL WARCHOL, COURTESY JAMES K. M. CHENG ARCHITECTS. **6** COURTESY JAMES K. M. CHENG ARCHITECTS. **7** ALAN KAPLANAS, COURTESY TONY ROBINS. **8** BRETT HITCHINS, COURTESY PFS. **9** COURTESY TIMOTHY HURSLEY. **10** MARTIN TESSLER, COURTESY PETER CARDEW ARCHITECTS. **11** COURTESY PETER CARDEW ARCHITECTS. **12–14** NIC LEHOUX, COURTESY REVERY ARCHITECTURE. **15** NIC LEHOUX, COURTESY HENRIQUEZ PARTNERS. **16–21** JAMES DOW, COURTESY PATKAU ARCHITECTS. **22** NIC LEHOUX, COURTESY PUBLIC: ARCHITECTURE + COMMUNICATION. **23** COURTESY NIC LEHOUX. **24** MARTIN KNOWLES, COURTESY BRUCE HADEN ARCHITECT. **25–26** NIC LEHOUX, COURTESY LWPAC. **27** COURTESY LWPAC. **28** NIC LEHOUX, COURTESY LWPAC. **29** COURTESY LWPAC. **30–31** UNDINE PRÖHL, COURTESY D'ARCY JONES ARCHITECTURE. **32** SAMA JIM CANZIAN, COURTESY BATTERSBYHOWAT ARCHITECTS. **33** GERRY KOPELOW, COURTESY NICK MILKOVICH. **34** COURTESY NIC LEHOUX. **35–36** EMA PETER, COURTESY REVERY ARCHITECTURE. **37** COURTESY EMA PETER. **38** JAMES DOW, COURTESY PATKAU ARCHITECTS. **39–40** COURTESY NIC LEHOUX. **41** EMA PETER, COURTESY MGA | MICHAEL GREEN ARCHITECTURE. **42** EMA PETER, COURTESY OMB. **43** MICHAEL ELKAN, COURTESY ACTON OSTRY ARCHITECTS.

Published by Princeton Architectural Press
202 Warren Street, Hudson, NY 12534
www.papress.com

Co-published by Canadian Architect
101 Duncan Mill Road, Suite 302, Toronto, ON M3B 1Z3
www.canadianarchitect.com

Canada Council   Conseil des arts
for the Arts   du Canada

We acknowledge the support of the Canada Council for the Arts.
Nous remercions le Conseil des arts du Canada de son soutien.

Editor: Kristen Hewitt
Designer: Benjamin English

Special thanks to: Paula Baver, Janet Behning, Abby Bussel,
Jan Cigliano Hartman, Susan Hershberg, Stephanie Holstein,
Lia Hunt, Valerie Kamen, Jennifer Lippert, Sara McKay,
Parker Menzimer, Wes Seeley, Rob Shaeffer, Sara Stemen,
Jessica Tackett, Marisa Tesoro, Paul Wagner, and Joseph Weston
of Princeton Architectural Press —Kevin C. Lippert, publisher

Front cover: Museum of Anthropology, Vancouver, British Columbia.
Erickson / Massey, 1976. (Photograph by Christopher Erickson,
Erickson Estate Collection)

Back cover: Habitat 67, Montreal, Quebec. Moshe Safdie, 1967.
(Photographer unknown, Libraries and Archives Canada)

Library of Congress Cataloging-in-Publication Data
NAMES: Lam, Elsa, editor. | Livesey, Graham, 1960– editor.
TITLE: Canadian modern architecture, 1967–2017 / Elsa Lam and
   Graham Livesey, editors.
DESCRIPTION: First edition. | New York : Princeton Architectural,
   [2019] | Includes bibliographical references and index.
IDENTIFIERS: LCCN 2019001594 | ISBN 9781616896454
   (hardcover : alk. paper)
SUBJECTS: LCSH: Architecture–Canada–History–20th century.
   | Architecture–Canada–History–21st century. | Architecture,
   Modern–20th century. | Architecture, Modern–21st century.
CLASSIFICATION: LCC NA745 .C27 2019
   | DDC 720.971/0904–dc23
LC record available at https://lccn.loc.gov/2019001594